ENCYCLOPEDIA OF
CRYPTOLOGY

ENCYCLOPEDIA OF
CRYPTOLOGY

DAVID E. NEWTON

ABC-CLIO

Santa Barbara, California
Denver, Colorado
Oxford, England

Library of Congress Cataloging-in-Publication Data

Newton, David E.
    Encyclopedia of cryptology / David E. Newton
      p. cm.
    Includes bibliographical references and index.
    1. Cryptography—Encyclopedias. I. Title.
  Z103.N344 1997   652'.8'03—dc21 97-28018

ISBN 0-87436-772-7 (alk. paper)

03 02 01 00 99 98   10 9 8 7 6 5 4 3 2   (cloth)

ABC-CLIO, Inc.
130 Cremona Drive, P.O. Box 1911
Santa Barbara, California 93116-1911

This book is printed on acid-free paper ∞.

*For Wendy and Deb
and in memory of Pam*

Contents

Introduction

Secret writing for the transmission of messages has been practiced for nearly 4,000 years. According to David Kahn, the great historian of cryptology, the first example of an intentionally altered message can be traced to a tomb in ancient Egypt dated about 1900 B.C. In the 40 centuries since that event, secret messages have been used by politicians and diplomats, military officers and infantrymen, smugglers and thieves, retail merchants and bankers, officials and scholars of the highest rank, and the simplest citizens of nations around the world.

In some respects, the history of cryptology is a record of some of the most brilliant and arcane intellectual accomplishments known to the human race. A series of contests has developed between, on the one hand, men and women committed to the development of secret systems that no one but the intended recipients can solve and, on the other hand, equally committed workers searching out the flaws in such systems, endeavoring to ensure that no such system is produced.

In recent years, the struggles between those who produce systems of secret writing—the cryptographers—and those who try to break those systems—the cryptanalysts—have made use of mathematical systems of dizzying complexity. Indeed, in the late twentieth century mathematics has taken cryptology far beyond the comprehension of all but the most sophisticated students. In addition, the most advanced computer technology available has been enlisted in the produc-

tion of ever more complex and elegant methods of writing and breaking systems of secret writing.

Yet throughout the history of cryptology, secret writing has been totally immersed in social, political, economic, military, and personal issues of immense intrigue and interest. Some of the greatest decisions of history have been made as the result of secret messages successfully sent or intercepted and deciphered. Presidential elections have been lost, great battles won, and the innocent wrongly convicted of crimes and the guilty released.

This book attempts to provide an introduction to the grand panorama that is cryptology. First, some of the basic fundamental concepts of cryptography and cryptanalysis are introduced. In some respects, these concepts are simplicity itself. Secret writing involves essentially one of two approaches: the rearranging of words and/or letters or the substitution of one word or letter for another. These techniques—transposition and substitution—and their many variations are described in the text.

Modern variations of these two systems are enormously complex, involving advanced forms of mathematics generally unfamiliar to readers at the introductory level. No general introduction can hope to describe in much detail the computer systems that are now being used to protect secret information that passes over public channels (for example, the Internet) every moment of every day. Rather, this book serves as an introduction to give the reader understanding of the general meaning of most terms now in use in cryptology, and provides additional sources for those who wish to pursue a topic in more detail.

Effort has also been made to place the technical aspects of cryptology into a more general context. Stories about how cryptanalysis helped the U.S. Navy win the Battle of Midway or how cryptography was used in the effort to construct the first nuclear weapons are examples of the profound effects of the work of cryptographers and cryptanalysts on the great events of history. Many of these examples are included in this book.

The temptation to detail every event in which cryptology plays some role has been resisted. Many of these stories have already been told, most notably in Kahn's *Codebreakers;* furthermore, an interest in spies and espionage agents may lead into a whole field of fascinating tales of intrigue with only a minimal connection to cryptology. Where appropriate, introductions to these stories are included along with suggestions for further reading.

This work is thus neither fully comprehensive nor totally detailed. Rather, it directs interested readers toward some of the most important topics and issues related to cryptology and offers extensive recommendations for additional reading on those topics of special interest.

Some Basic Terminology in Cryptology

Like most academic disciplines, cryptology is a field in which many concepts are interconnected in a complex fashion. Readers of this book may find it difficult to pick an individual topic that can be read totally in isolation from other relevant topics; therefore, fundamental concepts are presented in greater detail. The beginning student of cryptology should have a command of the basic terminology in cryptology that follows (boldface terms are defined in more detail in the body of the text).

Cryptology itself is the science that deals with secret writing—messages that are manipulated in some manner to make them difficult or impossible for some other person to read. The science of writing secret messages is known as **cryptography,** and the science/art of learning the contents of secret messages not meant for the receiver is known as **cryptanalysis.** Those involved in these two fields are known respectively as **cryptographers** and **cryptanalysts.**

Most secret messages are classified either as **codes** or as **ciphers.** A code is a form of cryptography in which a letter, number, symbol, or word stands for another letter, word, or phrase. In the most common form of codes, a set of numbers or a set of letters stands for a word or phrase. For example, the **codenumber** 82941 might be chosen to represent the phrase LINCOLN MEMORIAL, and the **codeword** qorwz to represent the name BORIS YELTSIN.

Many messages are encoded for secrecy, but messages are encoded for other reasons as well. When business was conducted by telegraph, companies found it helpful to use codewords or codenumbers to stand for longer phrases. For example, the codeword njlze might be used for the phrase BUY SHARES OF GOLD BULLION. Transmitting the codeword would cost less than transmitting the complete phrase for which it stands.

A cipher is a form of cryptography in which each letter or number in a message is represented by one or more other letters, numbers, or symbols. The original message, written in English or some other language, is known as the **plaintext.** The secret message into which it is converted is known as the **ciphertext.** In the simplest form of encipherment, each letter in the plaintext is replaced by some other letter in the ciphertext. For example, suppose that plaintext letter A is represented by ciphertext letter z; plaintext letter B, by ciphertext letter y; plaintext letter C, by ciphertext letter x;

plaintext letter D, by ciphertext letter *w;* and so on, as shown in the chart below.

```
PLAIN:  A  B  C  D
cipher:  z  y  x  w
```

Then the plaintext word BAD is represented by the ciphertext word yzw.

Cipher systems are of two general types. First, the letters or words of which the message is made can be switched around according to some previously-agreed-on system, known as **transposition.** For example, two individuals might agree to write to each other in a cipher system that reverses the letters in every word. The plaintext sentence GO TO BATTLE, then, would be enciphered as og ot elttab. Many kinds of transposition cipher systems have been invented, including **columnar transposition, geometrical transposition, rail fence transposition,** and **route transposition.**

The second approach to cipher systems is to replace each letter in the plaintext messages by one or more letters, numbers, or symbols. The system described above by which the word BAD is enciphered as yzw is an example of **substitution.**

As with transposition, many forms of substitution are possible. In the simplest form, each letter of plaintext is replaced by one and only one letter, number, or symbol of ciphertext, a form known as **monoalphabetic substitution.** In another form, each letter of plaintext is replaced by two or more letters, numbers, or symbols of ciphertext, a system known as **polyalphabetic substitution.**

The terms *code* and *cipher* are often used interchangeably, even by those who know the difference between the two. For example, David Kahn's *Codebreakers,* probably the most famous book ever written about cryptology, deals with both codes and ciphers.

When used in cryptology, the prefix *en-* means to change from plaintext into code

or ciphertext. Therefore, to **encode** means to change from plaintext to code, and to **encipher** means to change from plaintext to ciphertext. The more general term **encrypt** means to change from plaintext into either code or ciphertext, or some combination of the two.

Similarly, the prefix *de-* means to convert from code or ciphertext to plaintext. A message that has been **decode**d has been changed from code form to plaintext, and one that has been **decipher**ed has been converted from ciphertext to plaintext. In general, to **decrypt** means to change from some hidden form of writing (code or ciphertext or a combination of the two) into plaintext.

As would be expected, the suffix *-er* refers to a person who performs one of the above operations. A decoder is the person who discovers the meaning of a code, a decipherer changes ciphertext into plaintext, and a **decrypter** performs either or both of these operations.

The critical piece of information used to convert plaintext to ciphertext is known as the **key** to the cipher system. The key can consist of a single word, a number, or a phrase of any length. The key to the BAD = yzw cipher system used above could be expressed in words as "To encipher a message, replace each letter of plaintext by the corresponding letter from the alphabet reversed."

Messages are often sent without first being enciphered or encoded. They are said to be sent "in clear" or as **cleartext.**

Messages can also be transmitted in a hidden, but not secret, form. That is, the plaintext itself is transmitted, but in some form that makes it very difficult to read. For example, a photograph of the message could be taken and reduced to a very small size known as a **microdot.** Such messages are known as steganograms and the technique for producing them as **steganography.**

A-1

The name given to a code developed for use by the U.S. Navy in World War I. The code was developed by Lt. (jg) W. W. (Poco) Smith, recently assigned to the newly created Office of Naval Operations, and was intended to replace three older naval codes: the Secret Code of 1887, SIGCODE, and a radio code.

Smith's approach to his assignment provides a view of how cryptology was handled during the period. He wrote a long set of five-letter codegroups with plaintext corresponding to each codeword. He cut the lists apart with a pair of scissors and threw the individual slips of paper into a large bucket. Finally, Smith drew out individual slips of paper one at a time and arranged columns of codewords and definitions next to each other. The resulting list formed the new code, later given the name A-1. The process was so time-consuming that Smith's new code was not ready for use until after the United States entered World War I.

A-1 was also the name given to a superenciphered code developed by the State Department for use in international communications in the 1920s.

For further reading: David Kahn, *The Codebreakers: The Story of Secret Writing*, New York: Macmillan, 1967, pp. 386–387.

A-3

A voice-scrambling device invented at the Bell Telephone Laboratories in the 1930s and later used to scramble voice commu-nications across the Atlantic and Pacific Oceans. The scrambler operated on the principle of band-splitting, in which the original sound wave was broken down into five subdivisions. The tones in each subdivision were then inverted to produce a scrambled message. By 1937, the A-3 was in operation on both coasts, scrambling high-level oral communications among New York, Washington, and the European capitals, and among San Francisco, Honolulu, and Tokyo. News of the outbreak of World War II was delivered to President Franklin D. Roosevelt in a scrambled telephone message from U.S. Ambassador to France William C. Bullitt on 1 September 1939.

See also: ciphony.

THE ABC CODE

One of the earliest and most successful codebooks designed for use by businesses as a means of reducing the cost of sending information by telegraph. *The ABC Code* was published in 1874 by William Clausen-Thue, manager of a shipping company and later a Fellow of the Royal Geographic Society. One feature that made the book popular with businesses was the very large list of words it contained.

See also: codebook.

ABEL, RUDOLPH IVANOVICH

The highest-ranking Soviet spy ever cap-tured, tried, and convicted of espionage

KGB agent Rudolph Ivanovich Abel (left) was arrested in 1957 after his partner turned him in.

in the United States. Abel was a colonel in the KGB, the notorious intelligence service of the Soviet Union. He was originally posted to Canada in 1948 to initiate high-level espionage activities, but soon moved his activities to New York City. He assumed the role of a retired photofinisher and artist. With a radio receiver in his room at the Latham Hotel, he was able to receive and decipher messages from Moscow. He sent his responses to KGB headquarters from another location in Brooklyn.

Abel's associate in espionage activities was Reino Hayhanen, a lieutenant colonel in the KGB. Hayhanen arrived in the United States in 1952 and settled in the Hudson Valley, where he set up his own transmitting and receiving equipment for communication with Moscow in his home. He also corresponded with Abel by means of secret "drops" in the New York City area.

One of those drops led to one of the most famous episodes in modern spy stories. In the summer of 1953, a young newsboy in Brooklyn dropped a nickel he had been given in payment for his deliveries. The nickel broke open when it hit the pavement, revealing a tiny piece of microfilm. The boy, James Bozart, took the nickel and the microfilm to the police, who passed it on to the FBI.

The best cryptanalysts available to the U.S. government were totally baffled by the cryptogram, and it might never have been solved but for an unexpected turn of events in the relationship between Abel and Hayhanen. The former began to feel uncomfortable with the latter's work, and suggested that Hayhanen return to Moscow for a "vacation." Understanding the likely conclusion to such a "vacation," Hayhanen interrupted his return trip to Moscow in Paris, where he surrendered himself at the American embassy on 4 May 1957.

As a result of Hayhanen's information, the U.S. government arrested Abel and brought him to trial. Details of the VIC cipher used by Abel and Hayhanen were brought out in court testimony. By then, Hayhanen had passed on information about the cipher to government cryptanalysts, and they were finally able to solve the mysterious "broken nickel" cryptogram of 1953. Abel was convicted and, on 25 October 1957, sentenced to 30 years (Wrixom says 45 years) in prison for espionage. He served less than 5 years, however. On 10 February 1962, Abel was exchanged for Francis Gary Powers, the American pilot of a U-2 spy plane shot down over Russia two years earlier.

The direction of Hayhanen's life after the trial has not yet been documented. He apparently assumed a low-profile lifestyle, and is believed to have died in 1961, as the result of either alcoholism or an automobile accident.

For further reading: Louise Bernikow, *Abel*, New York: Trident Press, 1970; James B. Donovan, *Strangers on a Bridge: The Case of Colonel Abel*, New York: Atheneum, 1964.

ABWEHR

The German agency responsible for counterespionage and other forms of intelligence activities. The agency was created with a staff of six officers following the 1919 signing of the Treaty of Versailles. Its original function was strictly counterintelligence, the German word for which is *abwehr*. In the two decades following its creation, however, the agency grew in size and significantly expanded its range of operations. By the early 1930s, the Abwehr was assigned responsibility for all military intelligence activities. The nonmilitary counterparts of the Abwehr were the Sicherheitsdienst (Security Service, or SD) and the Reichssicherheitshauptamt (Reich Central Security Office, or RSHA).

The activities of the Abwehr were separated into three divisions. Section I was responsible for secret intelligence activities, such as the development of invisible inks and the maintenance of contact with secret agents. Abwehr II was assigned responsibility for sabotage and other special projects, and Abwehr III, for counterespionage activities.

The Abwehr lost its independence in 1944 when Hitler merged it with the RSHA, making it a special division of that organization.

For further reading: Paul Leverkuehn, *German Military Intelligence,* London: Weidenfeld & Nicolson, 1954.

ACCESS CONTROL

Any system for limiting the use of some resource to authorized users only. For example, I might be interested in reading a computer file stored in your computer that contains the opening chapter of a book you are writing. The question for security experts is how, if at all, I should be prevented from having access to that information.

In general, access can be described as discretionary or nondiscretionary. Decisions about discretionary access are made by the owner of the data or information. For example, you might feel that I should be able (or not be able) to look at the file containing your new chapter, that is, have discretionary access to that information.

Nondiscretionary access means that some person or agency has decided that only certain individuals should be allowed to see information or data. Another way of describing nondiscretionary access is to say that the information is under mandatory access control. This form of control is often exerted in terms of various levels of secrecy. The U.S. Department of Defense established the following levels of control: unclassified, confidential, secret, and top secret.

Computer programs are now written to include certain levels of access control. A program might be designed, for example, to be available only to an individual with a secret clearance. Anyone with a lower-level security clearance would be unable to access the information contained in the program.

For further reading: D. W. Davies and W. L. Price, *Security for Computer Networks: An Introduction to Data Security in Teleprocessing and Electronic Funds Transfer,* Chichester: John Wiley & Sons, 1984, pp. 336–340; Charlie Kaufman, Radia Perlman, and Mike Speciner, *Network Security: Private Communication in a Public World,* Englewood Cliffs, NJ: Prentice-Hall, 1995, pp. 26–28; Jerome Lobel, *Foiling the System Breakers: Computer Security and Access Control,* New York: McGraw-Hill, 1986; Rolf T. Moulton, *Computer Security Handbook,* Englewood Cliffs, NJ: Prentice-Hall, 1986; U.S. Congress, Office of Technology Assessment, *Information Security and Privacy in Network Environments,* OTA-TCT-606, Washington, DC: GPO, September 1994, pp. 28, 48.

ACCIDENTAL REPETITION

The presence in ciphertext of two-, three- or more-letter combinations that suggest the presence of a digraph, trigraph, or polygraph in the message. For example, the repeated presence of the sequence JWN might suggest to a decipherer that the letter *J* stands for t, *W* for h, and *N* for e. The repeated occurrence of *JWN* in the message, then, could be interpreted as standing for the word *the.*

However, some letter combinations will occur within the ciphertext by chance alone, and such combinations are of no value in deciphering the message. Chance combinations of this type are known as accidental repetitions.

ACCREDITED STANDARDS COMMITTEE (ASC X9)

A committee that sets data security standards for U.S. banking and other financial services industries.

> For further reading: http://www.itd.nrl.navy.mil/ITD/5540/ieee/cipher/cipher-archive.html (Electronic Issue No. 4).

ACME CODE

One of the many commercial codebooks that became popular in the 1930s as a means of saving money on telegrams by condensing messages into codewords. Although not inherently better than many of its competitors, the *Acme Code* was a substantial commercial success.

> See also: codebook.
> For further reading: *Acme Commodity and Phrase Code*, San Francisco: Acme Code Co., 1923.

ACROSTIC

A composition in which some combination of letters form a hidden message. For example, if one reads the first letter in each line of the following poem, a secret message is revealed.

> As any wise man will know,
> Women have charms of unending bliss,
> And can bring to all who would care to know,
> Knowledge, joy, happiness, and delight,
> E'en though the price is sometimes much great!

ACTIVE CARD

See smart card.

ACTIVE INTRUSION-DETECTION SYSTEM

A system that attempts to detect efforts by some enemy to break into an information-transmission system. Such systems look for clues that unusual or abnormal events are taking place to gain access to information, for example, an extended log-on period in which someone may be guessing at a valid password. The U.S. Department of Defense designed a variety of active intrusion-detection systems as part of its Information Warfare initiative.

> See also: firewall.
> For further reading: Warwick Ford, *Computer Communications Security*, Englewood Cliffs, NJ: Prentice-Hall, 1994; Jeffrey I. Schiller, "Secure Distributed Computing," *Scientific American* (November 1994): 72–76.

ADDITIVE

A string of digits that can be added to a codenumber during the process of superencipherment. For example, suppose that the codenumber 51038 is used for the phrase THE S.S. DORIAN SAILS AT MIDNIGHT. A person wanting to save money on a telegraph transmission could simply substitute the codenumber for the longer phrase. However, if an additional element of secrecy were desired, the codenumber could be superenciphered with an additive known to both encoder and decoder. Suppose the previously-agreed-on additive is 32714. Then the encicode (enciphered code) for the phrase THE S.S. DORIAN SAILS AT MIDNIGHT would be

CODENUMBER:	51038
ADDITIVE:	32714
ENCICODE:	83752

> See also: encicode; superencipherment.
> For further reading: Wayne G. Barker, *Cryptanalysis of an Enciphered Code Problem Where an "Additive" Method of Encipherment Has Been Used*, Laguna Hills, CA: Aegean Park Press, n.d.

ADDITIVE CIPHER

A substitution system in which the ciphertext is obtained by adding some integral number to the plaintext. Mathematically, an additive cipher can be expressed as $C = P + n$, where n may be any number from 1 to 25. The original cipher developed by Julius Caesar, for example, is an additive cipher with $n = 3$.

See also: Caesar, Gaius Julius.
For further reading: Henry Beker and Fred Piper, *Cipher Systems: The Protection of Communications*, New York: John Wiley & Sons, 1982, pp. 16–19; Albrecht Beutelspacher, *Cryptology: An Introduction to the Art and Science of Enciphering, Encrypting, Concealing, Hiding and Safeguarding Described without Any Arcane Skullduggery but Not without Cunning Waggery for the Delectation and Instruction of the General Public*, Washington, DC: Mathematical Association of America, 1994, pp. 4–11.

ADDITIVE INVERSE

A subtraction operation. Algebraically, the same result is obtained by subtracting some number, n, from some other number, x, or by adding the negative of n, $-n$, to x. In other words: $x - n = x + (-n)$.

In such a case, the negative number added to the base is said to be the additive inverse of the number itself.

ADFGVX CIPHER

A cryptosystem devised and used by the Germans toward the end of World War I.

David Kahn has called the cipher "probably the most famous field cipher in all cryptology." One reason for its fame is its difficulty. The best cryptanalysts among Allied intelligence agencies were nearly frustrated by the cipher. The second reason for its fame is that on one of the occasions when the cipher was broken, its solution provided the French army with key information that allowed them to repulse the German attack along the Somme front.

The ADFGVX cipher gets its name from the fact that these six letters, and only these six, are used in the encipherment of a message. The first step in using the cipher involves a form of checkerboard substitution, in which each letter of plaintext is represented by a pair of cipher letters. The system is similar to that proposed by Polybius more than 2,000 years earlier.

Consider the checkerboard format shown below in Figure 1, and suppose the plaintext message to be transmitted is THREE BATTALIONS LEAVE TODAY. The first step in using the ADFGVX cipher is to locate each plaintext letter in the matrix and write the two coordinates of that letter. For example, the letter *T* in the plaintext (indicated in italics in the matrix below) can be represented by the bigram *af*. The letter *H* (also indicated in italics) is

	a	d	f	g	v	x
a	I	L	*T*	0	M	E
d	F	V	Z	D	R	N
f	8	J	4	Y	9	A
g	W	Q	2	3	X	P
v	U	K	1	*H*	B	7
x	6	C	Y	5	0	S

Figure 1

T	H	R	E	E	B	A	T	T	A	L	I	O	N	S	L	E	A	V	E	T	O	D	A	Y
af	vg	dv	ax	ax	vv	fx	af	af	fx	ad	aa	xv	dx	xx	ad	ax	fx	dd	ax	af	xv	dg	fx	fg

Figure 2

represented by the bigram *vg*. When this process is repeated for each letter in the message, the substitution cipher shown in Figure 2 results.

A checkerboard substitution of this kind is not very difficult to solve. However, in the next step, the cipher message obtained from the first step is superenciphered by using a system of columnar transposition. Specifically, the ciphertext is laid out into a second matrix, as shown in Figure 3 (notice that nulls are added to complete the matrix).

```
B  E  R  L  I  N
a  f  v  g  d  v
a  x  a  x  v  v
f  x  a  f  a  f
f  x  a  d  a  a
x  v  d  x  x  x
a  d  a  x  f  x
d  d  a  x  a  f
x  v  d  g  f  x
f  g  d  x  g  v
```

Figure 3

The keyword used to encipher and decipher the message, BERLIN in this case, is placed at the end of the table. The alphabetic sequence of the letters in the keyword determines the order in which columns are to be taken off from the table. That is, the column headed by the letter B is to be taken off first, followed by the columns headed by the letters E, I, L, N, and R.

In following that pattern, the transposed cipher becomes:

```
aaffx  adxff  xxxvd  dvgdv  aaxfa  fggxf
dxxxg  xvvfa  xxfxv  vaaad  aaddx
```

(A null is added to complete the last set of five cipher letters.)

The most famous decipherment of the ADFGVX cipher was accomplished by the brilliant French cryptologist George Painvin. Painvin was able to break the cipher in early June 1918, just as the German army was ready to begin one of its most aggressive assaults of the war. The French army had no idea where the Germans would strike next, and faced the danger of having to spread their forces too thinly to hold their lines in any one place.

One 3 June, however, Painvin decrypted a German message indicating that the army would attack at a point between Montdidier and Compiègne, about 50 miles north of Paris. He sent this information to the French general staff, which was able to move and mobilize troops in the area in preparation for the German attack. When the attack came on the morning of 10 June, the French were ready. They held and then repulsed the German army, preventing any further breakthrough in the French lines and providing the morale boost the French troops needed to continue their battle.

> **See also:** checkerboard; columnar transposition; Polybius; substitution; superencipherment.
>
> **For further reading:** Brian Beckett, *Introduction to Cryptology,* Oxford: Blackwell Scientific Publications, 1988, pp. 309–312; David Kahn, *The Codebreakers: The Story of Secret Writing,* New York: Macmillan, 1967, ch. 11; Peter Way, *Codes and Ciphers,* n.p.: Crescent Books, 1977, pp. 54–61; Fred B. Wrixon, *Codes and Ciphers,* New York: Prentice-Hall, 1992, pp. 3–4, 154–155.

ADLEMAN, LEONARD M.

A pioneer in public-key cryptography. Adleman, an assistant professor at the Massachusetts Institute of Technology (MIT), collaborated with Ronald L. Rivest and Adi Shamir in 1978 to develop perhaps the most powerful public-key cryptographic system currently available. The system is known as the RSA algorithm in honor of its creators.

Leonard Adleman was born on 31 December 1945 in San Francisco. He received his bachelor's degree in mathematics in 1968 and his Ph.D. in computer science in 1976, both from the University of California at Berkeley. After a two-year teaching assignment at MIT from 1977 to 1979, he accepted an appointment as professor in the department of computer science at the University of Southern California (USC). In 1985 he was appointed Henry Salvatori Professor in that department.

In addition to his work in cryptology, Adleman's research interests include computational complexity, number theory, and immunology and computer viruses. He has written over 40 papers and was awarded the Senior Research Award by the USC School of Engineering in 1991.

See also: RSA algorithm.

AENEAS TACTICUS (AENEAS THE TACTICIAN)

A Greek writer (fl. fourth century B.C.) credited with the first complete guide on means of securing military communications. In his book *On the Defense of Fortified Places*, Aeneas devotes one chapter to this topic. He repeats a number of stories originally told by Herodotus, and explains systems of cryptography and steganography. One of the cipher systems he includes involves replacing the vowels in a communication by dots: one dot for α, two dots for ε, three for ι, and so on. In another system, a message is woven into a card by passing a strand of wool through holes in the card in a predetermined pattern. The person receiving the card would then read the message by removing the wool from the holes according to the agreed-on system.

Interestingly enough, another of the cryptosystems described by Aeneas remained in use as late as World War II. In this system, the cryptographer pricks tiny holes in a book or some other document, indicating the letters to be read in the secret message. For example, the hidden text in the following sentence would be *retreat*.

And the number of men in the room amounted to more than forty.

German spies in both world wars employed this method, as well as a similar one in which invisible ink was used to make dots.

See also: invisible writing; puncture cipher; steganography.
For further reading: *Aeneas Tacticus, Asclepiodotus, Osander* (Loeb Classical Library), London: W. Heinemann, 1923.

AERIAL TELEGRAPH
See optical telegraph.

AFFINE CIPHER
A cipher obtained by operating on a plaintext message first by addition and then by multiplication. To convert the plaintext letter C by this method, 5 might be added to the numerical value of the letter ($C = 3$; $3 + 5 = 8$) and then that sum multiplied by some other constant, such as 5 ($5 \times 8 = 40$). The resulting cipher letter is n (40 modulo 26 = 14 = n).

For further reading: Brian Beckett, *Introduction to Cryptology*, Oxford: Blackwell Scientific Publications, 1988, pp. 84–87; Henry Beker and Fred Piper, *Cipher Systems: The Protection of Communications*, New York: John Wiley & Sons, 1982, pp. 19–24, 257–260; Albrecht Beutelspacher, *Cryptology: An Introduction to the Art and Science of Enciphering, Encrypting, Concealing, Hiding and Safeguarding Described without Any Arcane Skullduggery but Not without Cunning Waggery for the Delectation and Instruction of the General Public*, Washington, DC: Mathematical Association of America, 1994, pp. 12–14.

AGONY COLUMNS
Personal advertisements placed in newspapers during the last half of the nineteenth century. The name appears to derive from the "agony" felt by many of the writers—often young lovers unable to correspond by other means—in being kept from communicating with each other. During the late Victorian era, two people in love were likely to have considerable difficulty in expressing their feelings because personal meetings and expressions of affection were not generally allowed. But such expressions were possible if two lovers could develop a

secret cipher or code with which to write to each other in the newspapers. The ciphers and codes were generally quite simple, and those interested in cryptanalysis made it a game to break the secret messages they found in the agony columns, often responding with a message of their own in the lovers' secret system.

For further reading: David Kahn, *The Codebreakers: The Story of Secret Writing*, New York: Macmillan, 1967, pp. 775–776; Fred B. Wrixon, *Codes and Ciphers*, New York: Prentice-Hall, 1992, pp. 4–5.

ALBERTI, LEON BATTISTA ━━━━

A Florentine cryptographer, often credited with being the Father of Western Cryptology. Alberti was born in Genoa on 18 February 1404, the illegitimate son of a wealthy exile from Florence. He was raised with many of the privileges that would normally be due only a legitimate

The father of Western cryptology, Leon Battista Alberti was one of the first recognized cryptanalysts.

son. Although he was trained in the law at the University of Bologna, for health reasons he turned his attention to the arts and sciences. Alberti was a true Renaissance man, skilled in many areas: architect, painter, poet, dramatist, philosopher, and essayist. He designed a number of important buildings and structures, including the first Trevi Fountain in Rome and the church of Sant'Andrea in Mantua. His work, *De Re Aedificatoria*, is the first book on architecture to appear in print. Alberti died in Rome on 25 April 1472.

Alberti made a number of contributions to the field of cryptology, including the first text on cryptanalysis, a 25-page manuscript he wrote about 1466. In this book he described the use of letter frequencies and letter patterns in the cryptanalysis of messages in both Italian and Latin. Alberti also laid out the principles of polyalphabetic substitution for the first time. These principles were illustrated in a cipher machine he constructed, which consisted of two circular copper plates, one of larger diameter than the other, joined to each other at the center. The circumference of each plate was divided into 24 parts containing 20 letters and 4 numbers, 1–4. (Only 20 letters were needed because *J, U,* and *W* were not then in use, and Alberti regarded *H, K,* and *Y* as redundant.) The letters and numbers on the outer plate were in correct alphabetical and numerical sequence (A, B, C, D, E, . . ., Z, 1, 2, 3, 4), while those on the inner plate were arranged randomly (g, t, c, a, . . . , 3, 1, 4, 2).

The plates were constructed so that the smaller plate could be turned against the larger plate, bringing each letter or number on the outer plate into contact with another letter or number on the inner plate. Each letter or number in a plaintext message on the outer plate was replaced by its comparable letter or number on the inner plate, producing the ciphertext. Using the disk in Figure 4, for example, the message W(V)AIT FOR ME would be enciphered as xdbi ecy sz. To use this system, both sender and receiver of a secret message must have the same device. The

algorithm | 9

Figure 4

receiver would set the disks at the positions previously agreed on, read the cipher letters on the inner wheel, find the comparable letters on the outer wheel, and write out the original plaintext message.

See also: cipher machine; frequency distribution; polyalphabetic substitution.
For further reading: Franco Borsi, *Leon Battista Alberti*, trans. by Rudolf G. Carpanini, New York: Harper & Row, 1977; Augusto Buonafalce, "The Alberti Exhibition," *Crytologia* (April 1996): 132–134; David Kahn, *The Codebreakers: The Story of Secret Writing*, New York: Macmillan, 1967, pp. 125–130; Joan Kelly, *Leon Battista Alberti: Universal Man of the Early Renaissance*, Chicago: University of Chicago Press, 1969; Peter Way, *Codes and Ciphers*, n.p.: Crescent Books, 1977, pp. 18–20.

ALCHEMY

A protoscience, predecessor to modern chemistry. The primary goals of alchemists were to find a way to change base metals (such as lead) into gold and to find the elixir of life, a substance that would provide eternal life to anyone who ingested it. Alchemists employed a great deal of secrecy in their work and often recorded their experiments and discoveries in secret writings consisting of non-alphabetic symbols.

For further reading: E. J. Holmyard, *Alchemy*, Harmondsworth, Middlesex: Penguin Books, 1957; John Read, *Through Alchemy to Chemistry*, London: Bell, 1957; F. Sherwood Taylor, *The Alchemists*, New York: Schuman, 1949.

ALGORITHM

A formal procedure for solving a mathematical problem. Before the advent of the handheld calculator, students generally had to learn a number of algorithms in simple arithmetic, such as dividing one number into another or finding the square root of a number. An algorithm is characterized by the fact that certain discrete steps must be taken ("find the largest number that can be divided into the first two numbers of the dividend") and that those steps may need to be repeated a number of times before a discrete answer is obtained.

In modern cryptology, encipherment and decipherment are both mathematical operations that follow specific algorithms, differing from one cryptosystem to another.

Algorithms can range from the very simple to the very complex. An example of a simple algorithm is the following:

> Begin with any number N and add 5 to that number. If the sum has no more than one digit, add 5 to it. If the sum has two digits, drop the first digit and add 5 to the remaining digit. Repeat.

The algorithms used in cryptography are much more complex (see **Data Encryption Standard** for an example). One might say in cryptography:

> Begin with the number N and add 5 to that number. Then reverse the digits and multiply the digits by each other. Add the product to the reversed digits of the original number. Convert the sum thus obtained to a binary number and rearrange the sequence of the binary digits in random sequence . . . and so on.

An algorithm of this kind may seem quite complex and difficult to follow, which, of course, is its purpose. The idea is to take some original plaintext message, encipher it as a series of numbers, and operate on that message to scramble it beyond all comprehension by any potential cryptographer. The important point, however, is that the algorithm can be written down in clear language, so that the intended receiver can know and use it to decipher the message.

One important way of classifying algorithms in cryptology is as *polynomial time algorithms* or *exponential time functions*. The former term refers to any algorithm that can be solved by some existing computer (known as a *deterministic computer*) within some given period of time, such as one day, one month, or one year. An algorithm of this kind must be regarded as an unsatisfactory cryptosystem because an aggressive and dedicated attack by a cryptanalyst will be able to break the system.

The latter term refers to algorithms that cannot be solved by any existing computer within a given period of time. For example, it might be known that an algorithm can be solved by the best available existing computer in 10^{31} years. The time span is so great that a cryptanalyst could not realistically be expected to break the system.

> See also: class P problem; Data Encryption Standard; strong algorithm; Turing machine.
> For further reading: J. D. Aho, J. E. Hopcroft, and J. D. Ullman, *The Design and Analysis of Computer Algorithms*, Reading, MA: Addison-Wesley, 1974; Brian Beckett, *Introduction to Cryptology*, Oxford: Blackwell Scientific Publications, 1988, pp. 126–130; Henry Beker and Fred Piper, *Cipher Systems: The Protection of Communications*, New York: John Wiley & Sons, 1982, ch. 6; Carl H. Meyer and Stephen M. Matyas, *Cryptography: A New Dimension in Computer Data Security*, New York: John Wiley & Sons, 1982, p. 6, passim (*see* index).

ALICE AND BOB

Names frequently used in cryptology to refer to two individuals involved in the exchange of a message. Mathematicians have traditionally referred to imaginary people involved in word problems as A and B, Mr. X and Miss Y, and so on. At some point in the development of modern cryptology, mathematicians began using first names to describe such characters. When Alice and Bob are joined by third and fourth parties, they are often referred to as Carol and Ted.

ALPHABET

The combination of letters, numbers, or symbols used to construct either a plaintext or ciphertext message. Some examples of alphabets follow:

Uppercase letters:
ABCDEFGHIJKLMNOPQRSTUVWXYZ

Lowercase letters plus numerals:
abcdefghijklmnopqrstuvwxyz 1234567890

Binary numbers containing 8 bytes:
00000000, 00000001, 00000010, 00000100,
…, 11111110, 11111111

Alphabets containing only letters are called *literal* alphabets, and those containing only numbers are *numerical* alphabets. Alphabets can be categorized according to the kinds of symbols they use and the sequence in which those symbols are taken. For example:

> A *normal* alphabet is one that is written in the usual sequence and direction in the custom of the language. In English, it would be the sequence a, b, c, d, etc. written from left to right.
> A *standard* alphabet is one written in sequence from the first letter to the last. If written in a forward direction, the alphabet is called *direct standard*, and in reverse direction, *reversed standard*.
> In a *mixed* alphabet, the letters are irregularly arranged. If they are arranged according to some key, the alphabet is said to be *systematically* mixed, but if they are arranged according to no plan, the alphabet is said to be *randomly* mixed.

Until the middle of the twentieth century, literal and symbolic alphabets were more widely used in the writing of cryptograms. The situation has changed dramatically; most cryptography now involves the conversion of letters (such as a, b, c, d, and so on) to numerical equivalents in the decimal system (a = 111, b = 112, c = 113, d = 121, and so on) and the binary system (a = 00000000, b = 00000001, c = 00000010, d = 00000100, and so on).

See also: ASCII; cipher alphabet; plaintext alphabet.
For further reading: Brian Beckett, *Introduction to Cryptology*, Oxford: Blackwell Scientific Publications, 1988, ch. 1–2; William F. Friedman, *Elements of Cryptanalysis*, Laguna Hills, CA: Aegean Park Press, 1976, sec. 2, 3; Donald D. Millikin, *Elementary Cryptography and Cryptanalysis*, Laguna Hills, CA: Aegean Park Press, n.d., ch. 2.

ALPHABETICAL TYPEWRITER 97 ━━━
See PURPLE.

AMERICAN BLACK CHAMBER ━━━
A cryptanalytic organization created by Herbert O. Yardley, largely from the remnants of the MI8 section of the Military Intelligence Division of which he had been in charge during World War I. The organization took its name from the black chambers created in a number of European states during the Renaissance for the purpose of intercepting and reading the correspondence of other states.

After MI8 was disbanded at the end of the war, Yardley convinced Franklin L. Polk, acting secretary of state, of the value of maintaining a code and cipher operation in the postwar world. After Polk approved the project, Yardley's group of about 20 individuals was located in the former townhouse of T. Suffern Tailer, a New York politician and society leader, and later moved to a three-story brownstone at 141 East 37th Street.

In his own story of the organization, Yardley wrote that his team had "solved over forty-five thousand cryptograms from 1917 to 1929, and at one time or another we broke the codes of Argentina, Brazil, Chile, China, Costa Rica, Cuba, England, France, Germany, Japan, Liberia, Mexico, Nicaragua, Panama, Peru, Russia, San Salvador, Santo Domingo, Soviet Union and Spain. We also made preliminary analyses of the codes of many other governments."

The first assignment given to Yardley's group was probably its most challenging: breaking the Japanese codes. The task was a daunting one because the codes involved the Japanese form of writing known as *katakana*, involving symbols strikingly different from those used in English. Yardley and his colleagues were very successful, however, developing within two years the ability to read essentially everything the Japanese wrote in code.

This breakthrough was particularly important because it allowed U.S. officials to read Japanese coded correspondence involving the Naval Disarmament Conference held in Washington in November 1921. Those officials were thereby able to learn in advance the Japanese "bottom line" on disputed issues before negotiations were held.

The American Black Chamber was dissolved in 1929. The election of Herbert Hoover as president a year earlier portended a stronger moral climate in the federal government, and Yardley was uncertain as to how his "spy operation" would survive in that atmosphere. Indeed, when the new secretary of state, Henry Stimson, heard about the Black Chamber operation, he was outraged. In one of the classic statements in the history of cryptology, Stimson informed Yardley that "Gentlemen do not read each other's mail." He discontinued further funding for Yardley's group and—because this constituted the great majority of its funds—the Black Chamber closed its doors forever on 31 October 1929.

See also: *The American Black Chamber*; black chamber; MI8; Military Intelligence Division; Yardley, Herbert O.
For further reading: David Kahn, *The Codebreakers: The Story of Secret Writing*, New York: Macmillan, 1967, ch. 12; Harold C.

Relyea, *Evolution and Organization of Intelligence Activities in the United States*, Laguna Hills, CA: Aegean Park Press, n.d., pp. 115–119; Herbert O. Yardley, *The American Black Chamber*, Indianapolis: Bobbs-Merrill, 1931; for a list of Yardley's popular writings, *see* Joseph S. Galland, *Bibliography of the Literature of Cryptology*, Laguna Hills, CA: Aegean Park Press, n.d., pp. 206–207.

THE AMERICAN BLACK CHAMBER

A classic book written by Herbert O. Yardley in 1931. The book tells the story of the work of the American cryptanalytic office by the same name. Yardley wrote it partly out of desperation after he lost his job with the U.S. State Department (which financed the American Black Chamber) and was unable to find other work in the dark days of the Great Depression.

The book has been highly praised by historians of cryptology. Reviewer W. A. Roberts called the book "the most sensational contribution to the secret history of the [First World] war, as well as the immediate post-war period." David Kahn, the great historian of cryptology, called the book "the most famous book on cryptology ever published," although his own work has probably made that accolade out-of-date.

A number of critics, however, viewed the book in a different light. One expressed the view that *The American Black Chamber* was "obviously intended for wide, popular perusal, [which] coupled with Yardley's own egotism, resulted in a large number of inaccuracies in the text, rendering it as a very untrustworthy record of the events it pretended to describe. Its failure, too, to speak of many important phases of the work of the Cipher Bureau (MI-8) throws the whole account out of balance."

This reviewer was especially horrified that a civilian would release so much information about a subject as politically delicate as cryptology. He went on to hypothesize that the Japanese government was "particularly bitter because of the revelations concerning the interception of messages to and from their representatives at the Washington Disarmament Conference. . . ." As a result, the Japanese devoted enormous effort to developing more secure cryptographic systems, which made them a much more powerful enemy during World War II. One fruit of the publication of the *American Black Chamber*, according to this reviewer, was that the book "has cost the United States millions of dollars in expense and probably the loss of many thousands of lives."

See also: American Black Chamber; Yardley, Herbert O.
For further reading: Wayne G. Barker, ed., *The History of Codes and Ciphers in the United States during the Period between the World Wars, Part I: 1919–1929*, Laguna Hills, CA: Aegean Park Press, 1979, passim (includes critique mentioned above).

AMERICAN CRYPTOGRAM ASSOCIATION (ACA)

An organization of individuals interested in the construction and solving of cryptograms. The ACA was formed on 1 September 1929 by Dr. C. B. Warner and some of his friends who were interested in the technical aspects of cryptology primarily as a hobby rather than a profession. The organizers hoped "to place the 'cryptogram' on an equivalent basis with chess, thus contributing to the happiness of mankind."

In its earliest years, ACA members were interested in only the simplest of cryptograms—those involving monoalphabetic substitution, to which they gave the name Aristocrat. Today, more complex cryptograms, called Patristocrats, Cryptarithms, Xenocrypts, Cipher Exchange, and special puzzles, are included regularly in the association's journal.

By the mid-1990s, the organization consisted of about 650 members in 47 states and 20 foreign countries. It publishes a bimonthly journal, *The Cryptogram*, which contains information about the organization and its members, various kinds of cryptograms, books related to cryptology, and other items of interest to members. Since 1982 the journal has also included a computer column for members who wish to use computers in the construction and/or solution of cryptograms.

In 1936 the association sponsored the publication of a textbook on cryptography, *Elementary Cryptanalysis*, written by members and edited by Helen Fouché Gaines. The book was republished by Dover Press in 1956 as *Cryptanalysis* and remains today as one of the standard introductory references to the subject. The association has also published a number of other pamphlets and books on the subject of cryptography.

Members of the organization usually take noms de plume (noms), or codenames, under which they submit cryptograms and/or their solutions. Some of the officers and editors of the organization include the pseudonyms G-MAN, LANAI, MICROPOD, ARACHNE, HAVI, PHOENIX, FAT CAT, MEROKE, SCRYER, and PHOENIX. A convention is held annually at different locations.

Information about the association can be obtained from ACA, One Pidgeon Drive, Wilbraham, MA 01095-2603; telephone: (413) 596-6635. Dues are $15 annually.

AMERICAN RADIO SERVICE CODE NO. 1
See Code Compilation Section.

AMERICAN SIGN LANGUAGE
See sign language.

AMERICAN STANDARD CODE FOR INFORMATION INTERCHANGE
See ASCII.

AMERICAN TRENCH CODE
See Code Compilation Section.

ANAGRAM
A word or phrase constructed by transposing the letters of another word or phrase. For example, the word *prod* is an anagram of the word *drop*, the only difference being the sequence of letters. Anagrams are commonly found in the puzzle section of a daily newspaper for the entertainment and amusement of readers. However, anagramming also plays an important role in the decipherment of cryptograms. In attempting to uncover the cipher alphabet from which a particular message is constructed, a cryptanalyst may notice certain sets of letters that suggest the presence of other letters as yet unidentified. In the partially solved example below, the sequence *o r g n* in the ciphertext suggests the presence of the word *oregon* as a key or part of the cipher alphabet used in the message.

```
A B C D E F G H I J K L M N O P Q R S T U V W X Y Z
w        t      o r g n        b   u
```

For further reading: Helen Fouché Gaines, *Cryptanalysis: A Study of Ciphers and Their Solution*, New York: Dover Publications, 1956, ch. 6, 7.

ANONYMITY
Lacking in identification. Anonymity might be a desirable feature in the electronic transmission of a message. For example, Bob might wish to send a message to Alice without Alice knowing that the message comes from him. Unfortunately for Bob, most systems contain automatic instructions for indicating the source of a message. In fact, a message that has been sent through a series of stations usually carries indications to that effect, including the specific pathway taken. Thus, Bob needs some mechanism for overriding the automatic message transmission function that carries his name. One solution is to send the message through some third party, who then transmits the communication to Alice.

For further reading: Albrecht Beutelspacher, *Cryptology: An Introduction to the Art and*

Science of Enciphering, Encrypting, Concealing, Hiding and Safeguarding Described without Any Arcane Skullduggery but Not without Cunning Waggery for the Delectation and Instruction of the General Public, Washington, DC: Mathematical Association of America, 1994, ch. 6; Charlie Kaufman, Radia Perlman, and Mike Speciner, *Network Security: Private Communication in a Public World,* Englewood Cliffs, NJ: Prentice-Hall, 1995, pp. 346–347.

AREA CODE

A set of three digits used for long-distance telephone calls in the United States and Canada. Calling from one region of the two nations to another (and sometimes within a single region) requires dialing the area code before dialing an individual telephone number. Area code 505, for example, is reserved for the state of New Mexico, and area codes 212, 718, and 917 for New York City.

Originally, all area codes contained the digits 0 or 1 as the middle digit, as shown in the examples above. With increased use of telephones for fax machines, cellular telephones, and other communication systems, however, that practice was abandoned because of insufficient X0X and X1X combinations. When area code 503 (once reserved for the state of Oregon) was divided into two parts in November 1995, for example, the new area code was 541.

ARGENTI FAMILY

An Italian family of which at least three members served the papacy as cryptologists between 1585 and 1605. The first member of the family to hold this position was Giovanni Batista, who began service at St. Peter's as clerk to Antonio Elio, a nobleman, who taught him the principles of cryptology. At an age when he was nearly eligible for retirement, Giovanni was selected by Sixtus V as his secretary of ciphers. He held that post until he died in 1591.

Prior to his death, Giovanni passed his knowledge of cryptology to his nephew Matteo, who succeeded his uncle as papal cryptologist, a post he held under five more popes. Matteo was finally removed from office in 1605, apparently because of internal political struggles. Matteo's younger brother, Marcello, who marked time as a cryptologist to one of the cardinals until he could replace his brother, never had that opportunity.

The Argentis' fame rests on a number of important contributions to the development of modern cryptology. For example, they were apparently the first cryptologists to use a mnemonic key (a word or phrase that can be easily remembered). The letters in the key form the first part of the cipher alphabet, with the remaining letters of the normal alphabet following in order, as shown below (where SIXTUS FIVE is the mnemonic key):

s	i	x	t	f	v	e	a	b	c	d	g	h
01	02	03	04	05	06	07	08	09	10	11	12	13

j	k	l	m	n	o	p	qu	r	w	y	z
14	15	16	17	18	19	20	21	22	23	24	25

(Notice that *qu* is taken as a single letter because of the inevitable association of the two in the Italian language.)

The Argentis also developed the practice of running ciphertext together, without breaks between words. This convention, which eventually became an established practice in writing cryptograms, makes it difficult to decrypt messages based on probable words, such as *the* and *and*, and probable digrams and trigrams, such as *th* and *ion*.

After losing his job with the papacy, Matteo found time to write a text on cryptology, which David Kahn said "summarizes the best in Renaissance cryptology."

See also: bigram; mnemonic key; trigram.

ARGOT

A type of code used by individuals who work together or otherwise associate with one another. In many cases, the code is not used to hide messages from anyone but to express social cohesiveness. One of the best-known forms of argot is that used by criminals, who often develop complex and extensive systems of communicating. Some examples of criminal argot includes:

dodge:	a racket
dolly sisters:	two uniformed police officers in a car
dose:	a venereal infection
do time:	a prison sentence
double-insider:	a pocket inside a vest or shirt
double-saw:	a $20 bill
downtown:	police headquarters
drag, to cop a:	smoke a cigarette

See also: hobo codes; jargon code.
For further reading: Hyman E. Goldin, ed., *Dictionary of American Underworld Lingo,* New York: Twayne, 1950; Waldemar Kaempffert, "Criminal Communications," *Century Magazine* (January 1923): 337–346; Don L. Kooken, "Cryptography in Criminal Investigations," *Journal of Criminal Law and Criminology* (March 1936): 903–919; Jacqueline Taschner, "Criminal Codes and Ciphers: What Do They Mean?" *FBI Law Enforcement Bulletin* (January 1985): 18–22.

ARMED FORCES SECURITY AGENCY (AFSA)

A cryptologic organization created in 1949 by the U.S. Defense Department. The decade following World War II clearly illustrated the value of coordinating the efforts of the three major military units, the army, navy, and air force. These units were all brought under the control of the newly created Department of Defense through the National Security Act Amendments of 1949. A similar realization of the value of coordinated efforts in the field of cryptology resulted in the merger of cryptologic agencies of the three services in the formation of the AFSA. AFSA was assigned responsibility for strategic aspects of cryptology, leaving tactical functions to the individual services. It was also made responsible for coordinating cryptologic functions within the individual services.

Coordinating services and operations extended one step further in 1952 when President Harry S. Truman created the National Security Agency (NSA). NSA took over the responsibilities of the AFSA, as well as the cryptologic functions of the State Department and certain other government agencies.

See also: Army Security Agency; National Security Agency/Central Security Service.
For further reading: Harold C. Relyea, *Evolution and Organization of Intelligence Activities in the United States,* Laguna Hills, CA: Aegean Park Press, n.d., pp. 240–273.

ARMS EXPORT CONTROL ACT

See export controls.

ARMY SECURITY AGENCY (ASA)

A cryptologic organization created on 15 September 1945 by action of the U.S. War Department. During World War II, the various cryptologic functions carried out within the U.S. Army were disbursed throughout the service and operated under the command of a variety of officers and units. This inefficient system was eliminated with the creation of the ASA, whose responsibilities included production of communication intelligence; research on techniques for clandestine communications, such as invisible inks, microphotographs, and open codes; technical supervision of communication security activities for the Department of the Army; and preparation, production, storage, distribution, and accounting of all materials used in army cryptosystems. ASA was a short-lived organization, merged only four years later with the cryptologic agencies of the other military services to form the Armed Forces Security Agency.

See also: Armed Forces Security Agency.
For further reading: David Kahn, *The Codebreakers: The Story of Secret Writing,* New York: Macmillan, 1967, pp. 678–681; *The Origin and Development of the Army Security Agency,* Laguna Hills, CA: Aegean Park Press, n.d.; *United States Government Organization Manual, 1964–1965,* p. 159.

ARNOLD-ANDRÉ CODES

Cryptosystems used in communications between Benedict Arnold, commander of the U.S. Army garrison at West Point, and John André, a major in the British army. Arnold planned to betray his country by surrendering West Point and other fortifications to the British. His correspondence on this subject was encoded using various book codes. At first the plotters made use of a code based on volume I of the fifth Oxford edition of the famous English legal work, Blackstone's *Commentaries on the Laws of England*. According to the system agreed on, each word in the code would be represented by three numbers, such as 9.33.14. The first number represented the page on which the word was found; the second number, the line in which the word was found; the third number, the word within the line. Thus the code 9.33.14 referred to the fourteenth word in the thirty-third line on page nine of the book.

In addition, Arnold and André agreed on a small set of codewords to use in referring to particular places and individuals. Some examples were:

Philadelphia: Jerusalem
Detroit: Alexandria
Pittsburgh: Gomorrah
Susquehanna: Jordan
General Washington: St. James
General Sullivan: St. Matthew
General Gates: St. Andrew
General Bird: Judas Iscariot
Indians: Pharisees
Congress: Synagogue

After using this system only once, Arnold found that Blackstone was a poor choice of books because some words could be located only with great difficulty. He decided to substitute Nathan Bailey's *Universal Etymological English Dictionary* in the twenty-first, twenty-third, or twenty-fifth edition. Bailey had the advantage, of course, of including all the words they could possibly want to use, arranged in alphabetical order.

Arnold and André also used invisible inks in some of their communications. These communications carried the letter F at the top to indicate that fire or heat was needed to bring out the hidden message.

As it turned out, the Arnold-André codes were relatively unimportant in resolving the plot by the two officers because André was caught, convicted of espionage, and hanged. Arnold escaped and joined the British army and became a general.

See also: book code; codegroup; invisible writing.
For further reading: Carl Van Doren, *The Secret History of the American Revolution*, New York: Viking Press, 1941.

ARTHA-SASTRA

A classic work on statecraft written by the Indian Kauilya prior to 300 B.C. The book mentions the use of "paintings and secret writings" as methods for transmitting secret messages and is, according to David Kahn, "the first reference in history to cryptanalysis for political purposes."

ASCHE

See Schmidt, Hans-Thilo.

ASCII

An acronym, pronounced "ask-key," for *American Standard Code for Information Interchange*. The ASCII system was developed by the American National Standards Institute and introduced in 1964 as a way of achieving compatibility among various data processing systems. The system represents letters, numbers, and symbols by means of either a binary or octal conversion table. The equivalents are shown below for the first few letters of the alphabet, some numbers, and some symbols used in communications.

Symbol	Octal	Binary
A	101	1 0 0 0 0 0 1
B	102	1 0 0 0 0 1 0
C	103	1 0 0 0 0 1 1
D	104	1 0 0 0 1 0 0
E	105	1 0 0 0 1 0 1
F	106	1 0 0 0 1 1 0
1	061	0 1 1 0 0 0 1
2	062	0 1 1 0 0 1 0
3	063	0 1 1 0 0 1 1
4	064	0 1 1 0 1 0 0
&	046	0 1 0 0 1 1 0
.	056	0 1 0 1 1 1 0
#	043	0 1 0 0 0 1 1
,	054	0 1 0 1 1 0 0

The binary designations used in ASCII consist of seven binary digits, to which an eighth bit is added as a means of checking the other seven bits during transmission. ASCII is now one of the most widely used of all computer cipher systems.

See also: binary number system; octal notation.
For further reading: Jack Belzer, Albert G. Holzman, and Allen Kent, eds., *Encyclopedia of Computer Science and Technology,* New York: Marcel Dekker, 1975, vol. 2, pp. 272–278; R. W. Bemer, "The American Standard Code for Information Interchange: Part Two," *Datamation* (September 1963): 39–44.

ASSOCIATION FOR COMPUTING MACHINERY

An organization founded in 1947 with the following objectives:

1. To advance the sciences and arts of information processing, including, but not restricted to, the study, design, development, construction, and application of modern machinery, computing techniques, and appropriate languages for general information processing; scientific computation; recognition, storage, retrieval, and processing of data of all kinds; and the automatic control and stimulation of processes.
2. To promote the free interchange of information about the sciences and arts of information processing among both specialists and the public in the best scientific and professional tradition.
3. To develop and maintain the integrity and competence of individuals engaged in the practice of the science and art of information processing.

ACM annually sponsors a number of conferences and meetings, and it publishes numerous books and reports on the subject of computer security. ACM headquarters are at 1515 Broadway, 17th floor, New York, NY, 10036; (212) 869-7440; fax: (212) 869-0481; telex: 42-1686; e-mail: acmhelp@acm.org.

ASYMMETRIC CRYPTOGRAPHY

A form of encryption in which one key is used to encrypt a message and a second, different but related key is used to decrypt the message. Asymmetric encryption is also known as **public-key crpytology.**

For further reading: G. J. Simmons, "Symmetric and Asymmetric Encryption," *ACM Computing Surveys* 11:4 (December 1979): 305–330.

ATM MACHINE

See automatic teller machine.

ATTACK

An attempt by a person for whom a message is not intended to listen in on and perhaps modify that message. This definition suggests two general kinds of attack: passive and active. An example of a passive attack is an eavesdropper who is simply interested in finding out what is being sent from one person to another. In this respect, a passive attack is the kind of decryption historically typical of cryptanalysis. Until fairly recently, agent

A listened in to the communications between Mrs. X and Mr. Y to find out what they were saying to each other.

In an active attack, the eavesdropper is interested in going one step further by altering the message being sent. The eavesdropper is interested not only in gathering information but in arranging it so that the correspondents receive false information from each other. The modern-day computer hacker, as an example, breaks into supposedly secure systems not just to find out what a bank, corporation, military organization, individual, or some other entity is saying but to modify the data contained in the uncovered message.

Attack systems are usually subdivided into three general types: ciphertext only, known plaintext, and selected plaintext. Ciphertext-only attacks would seem to be the most obvious forms of attack to the layperson. In this approach, an eavesdropper obtains from some source ciphertext that he or she wishes to read. The task is to find out what plaintext corresponds to this ciphertext.

The key to this process is, of course, the key—that is, the key used by the encipherer to convert plaintext to ciphertext. Many techniques are available to achieve this objective. For example, the first step is likely to be the calculation of frequencies of letters in the ciphertext to see if they correspond with known frequencies of letters in the English language. In a monoalphabetic substitution cipher, the solution for the ciphertext may fall out rather easily. If not, other techniques for decryption are available. A general rule that applies to ciphertext-only attacks is that sufficient text must be available to permit the use of most analytic techniques.

A second method of attack is called known plaintext because it assumes that the eavesdropper has gained access to certain sets of plaintext and ciphertext that allow the key to be determined from these combinations. This method of attack is easier for the cryptanalyst, because some very useful clues are provided that

are not available with ciphertext-only attacks. History is replete with examples of this kind of attack. For example, more than once a careless radio operator has broadcast a message in cipher and then, for one reason or another, rebroadcast a portion of the message in clear. Such a circumstance does not give the cryptanalyst the solution to the cipher system free and clear, but it provides a very useful beginning for the decryption process.

Finally, in a selected plaintext attack, by some means the sender of a message is persuaded to specify a particular plaintext and ciphertext for the eavesdropper. Of course, the sender would not do this favor for the eavesdropper intentionally, but it is possible to obtain this kind of information, particularly with messages that go through third parties (such as a telegraphic office).

See also: cryptanalysis; eavesdropper; frequency distribution; hacker; probable word.

For further reading: D. W. Davies and W. L. Price, *Security for Computer Networks: An Introduction to Data Security in Teleprocessing and Electronic Funds Transfer,* Chichester: John Wiley & Sons, 1984, pp. 35–38; Charlie Kaufman, Radia Perlman, and Mike Speciner, *Network Security: Private Communication in a Public World,* Englewood Cliffs, NJ: Prentice-Hall, 1995, pp. 43–45, passim; Carl H. Meyer and Stephen M. Matyas, *Cryptography: A New Dimension in Computer Data Security,* New York: John Wiley & Sons, 1982, ch. 2; Dominic Welsh, *Codes and Cryptography,* Oxford: Clarendon Press, 1988, pp. 209–212.

AUTHENTICATION ━━━━━━

Any process by which two parties involved in a communication verify the identity of each other and/or the message being conveyed. The former event is known as user authentication, and the latter as message authentication. In everyday life, one of the most common forms of user authentication is a person's signature. In legal transactions, for example, a person's signature is often taken as a guarantee that the person is whom he or she says he or she is. The process of authentication involves an aspect of cryptography because it is assumed that one and only one person can provide the precisely enciphered message—in this case, the exact signature. In messages sent electronically from one computer to another, some form of authentication is required because more traditional forms (such as a signature of a picture identification card) cannot easily be transmitted. Instead, the participants in such a transaction exchange an enciphered message that can be verified as belonging to the parties involved in the transaction. Message authentication is the process by which one party in a transaction confirms that the message received is indeed the message sent. Message authentication is also known as *proof of data origin*.

See also: biometric device; digital signature; Digital Signature Standard; integrity.

For further reading: Henry Beker and Fred Piper, *Cipher Systems: The Protection of Communications*, New York: John Wiley & Sons, 1982, pp. 320–325, 390–393; Albrecht Beutelspacher, *Cryptology: An Introduction to the Art and Science of Enciphering, Encrypting, Concealing, Hiding and Safeguarding Described without Any Arcane Skullduggery but Not without Cunning Waggery for the Delectation and Instruction of the General Public*, Washington, DC: Mathematical Association of America, 1994, ch. 4; D. W. Davies and W. L. Price, *Security for Computer Networks: An Introduction to Data Security in Teleprocessing and Electronic Funds Transfer*, Chichester: John Wiley & Sons, 1984, ch. 5; Charlie Kaufman, Radia Perlman, and Mike Speciner, *Network Security: Private Communication in a Public World*, Englewood Cliffs, NJ: Prentice-Hall, 1995, pt. 2; R. C. Merkel, *Secrecy, Authentication and Public Key Systems*, Epping: Bowker, 1979; Carl H. Meyer and Stephen M. Matyas, *Cryptography: A New Dimension in Computer Data Security*, New York: John Wiley & Sons, 1982, ch. 8; William Stallings, *Network and Internetwork Security: Principles and Practices*, Englewood Cliffs, NJ: Prentice-Hall, 1995, ch. 4, 7; U.S. Congress, Office of Technology Assessment, *Information Security and Privacy in Network Environments*, OTA-TCT-606, Washington, DC: GPO, September 1994, ch. 2; Dominic Welsh, *Codes and Cryptography*, Oxford: Clarendon Press, 1988, ch. 12.

AUTOKEY

A type of key in which the plaintext message itself provides the key to the ciphertext. The autokey was originally developed by Girolamo Cardano in about 1550. Its principle is illustrated in the message below.

KEY: t e n t e n t e n m e n t e n m e n t e n t e n
PLAIN: T E N M E N A R R I V E M O N D A Y W I T H S I X
CIPHER: m i a f i a t v e t z r f s a p e l p m g a l m k

Used in this way, the autokey was also known as a repeating key. A repeating key is not very secure, and the autokey system was considerably improved by Blaise de Vigenère's invention of the priming key in 1586. A priming key begins with a single letter that tells the decipherer with which cipher alphabet the ciphertext begins, and this information provides the first letter of the plaintext message. From that point on, the plaintext itself acts as the key (the autokey) for the remainder of the message.

See also: Cardano, Girolamo; priming key; Vigenère, Blaise de.

For further reading: Brian Beckett, *Introduction to Cryptology*, Oxford: Blackwell Scientific Publications, 1988, ch. 10; Helen Fouché Gaines, *Cryptanalysis: A Study of Ciphers and Their Solution*, New York: Dover Publications, 1956, ch. 16; http://rschp2.anu.edu.au:8080/autokey.html.

AUTOMATIC TELLER MACHINE (ATM)

A device that allows bank customers to make deposits, withdrawals, and transfers of money without benefit of a human bank representative. To make use of an ATM, a customer needs an ATM card containing two things—an account number and a personal identification number (PIN), which provide two separate security checks for any ATM transaction. The account number is read the instant the card is inserted into the machine and thus can be used by anyone, either by the proper owner or by someone who has found or stolen it. The central processing unit within the bank reads the account number and then matches it against the PIN typed in by the customer or the pseudocustomer. The PIN provides a secondary key against which the central processing unit can compare its records to make sure that the account number has been entered by the proper person.

See also: personal identification number.
For further reading: D. W. Davies and W. L. Price, *Security for Computer Networks: An Introduction to Data Security in Teleprocessing and Electronic Funds Transfer*, Chichester: John Wiley & Sons, 1984, pp. 306–321; James J. McAndrews and Robert J. Kauffman, *Network Externalities and Shared Electronic Banking Network Adoption*, Philadelphia: Federal Reserve Bank of Philadelphia, 1993.

B

B-1

A code that included the potential for superencipherment used by the U.S. State Department from the 1920s to the 1930s. The code was so primitive that cryptologist Herbert Yardley once said that it belonged in the sixteenth century, not the twentieth. Although this assessment was accurate, the B-1 code remained in use even after it had become clear that it was easily broken by enemy cryptanalysts.

BABBAGE, CHARLES

English mathematician, probably best known today for his research on automating mathematical operations by means of Difference and Analytical Engines. Babbage was born in Teignmouth, Devonshire, on 26 December 1792. He taught himself mathematics before entering Cambridge University at the age of 18. At the university he formed a club with other students of mathematics designed to reinvigorate the state of English mathematics. He received his degree in 1814, and two years later was elected a member of the Royal Society. During a visit to France, he observed the laborious processes by which essential mathematical calculations (such as those needed for navigation) were made through the combined efforts of hundreds of clerks, and he returned to England committed to the task of building a machine to do them more efficiently. He obtained a small grant from the British government and, by 1835, became so involved in the project that he resigned his post as Lucasian Pro-

fessor of Mathematics at Cambridge, a position he had held since 1826.

Babbage wrote very little about cryptology, but the few notes that remain suggest he was fascinated by the subject and spent extensive amounts of time solving cryptograms. Evidence shows, for example, that he and his friend Charles Wheatstone spent time solving notices in agony columns of the London newspapers. In one essay, Babbage wrote that deciphering was a "fascinating art," but one on which he had "wasted more time than it deserves."

As might be expected, Babbage applied mathematical principles to the solution of cryptograms, with extraordinary success. He is said to be the first to suggest a method for the solution of a Vigenère cipher, a cryptosystem that had been regarded as the "chiffre indéchiffrable" (undecipherable cipher) for nearly three centuries. Unfortunately, because of his reluctance to publish his thoughts and works on cryptology, Babbage's impact on the field was modest. He died in 1871.

See also: agony columns; Vigenère square.
For further reading: Albrecht Beutelspacher, *Cryptology: An Introduction to the Art and Science of Enciphering, Encrypting, Concealing, Hiding and Safeguarding Described without Any Arcane Skullduggery but Not without Cunning Waggery for the Delectation and Instruction of the General Public*, Washington, DC: Mathematical Association of America, 1994, p. 30; Ole I. Franksen, "Babbage and Cryptography, Or, the Mystery of Admiral Beaufort's Cipher," *Mathematics and Computers in Simulation* 35 (1993): 327–367.

BABINGTON PLOT

A plan to assassinate Queen Elizabeth I in 1586 and replace her with Mary Stuart, Queen of Scots. The plan included an extensive exchange among the conspirators of enciphered correspondence, which was read by Thomas Phelippes, an aide to the queen's secretary of state, Sir Francis Walsingham. According to David Kahn, Phelippes was "England's first great cryptanalyst."

The Babington plot evolved during an extended period of intrigue; Mary's Catholic supporters wanted to replace Elizabeth and restore England to the Roman Catholic religion. Mary had been forced to abdicate the Scottish throne in favor of her son, James VI. She fled to England, where she was kept under increasingly tight restraint in a series of castles.

In 1586, Antony Babington, an aide to Mary, seemingly found a safe way of communicating with her while she was being held at an estate in Chartley. He convinced one Gilbert Gifford to smuggle enciphered messages to Mary in a beer keg. The traffic of such messages in and out of Chartley rapidly grew in volume. Among them was a large collection of enciphered messages from the French government outlining its intentions in the plot against Elizabeth. Unbeknownst to Babington, however, Gifford was a double agent, delivering the enciphered messages to Walsingham and Phelippes at almost the same time he passed them to and from Mary. Finally, on 17 July, Mary wrote to Babington indicating her support for "this enterprise" (the assassination of Elizabeth), a letter Phelippes deciphered almost immediately. Mary's letter sealed her fate. She was convicted of high treason by the Star Chamber and, on 8 February 1587, was beheaded.

For further reading: Alan Gordon-Smith, *The Babington Plot*, New York: Macmillan, 1936; David Kahn, *The Codebreakers: The Story of Secret Writing*, New York: Macmillan, 1967, pp. 121–123; Thomas (Penn) Leary, "Cryptology in the 15th and 16th Century," *Cryptologia* (July 1996): 223–241; Peter Way, *Codes and Ciphers*, n.p.: Crescent Books, 1977, pp. 23–26; Fred B. Wrixon, *Codes and Ciphers*, New York: Prentice-Hall, 1992, pp. 126–127.

Political intrigue and cryptography often go hand in hand. Mary, Queen of Scots was charged with treachery and beheaded when she and her followers were discovered exchanging cryptograms.

BACON, FRANCIS ▰▰▰▰▰▰▰▰▰▰

A famous English statesman and natural philosopher who was also interested in the subject of cryptography. Bacon was born in London on 22 January 1561 and died there on 9 April 1626. He studied law at Cambridge, entered practice in 1576, and soon became active in politics. He served in the Parliament and became an adviser to Queen Elizabeth I, and later to her successor, James I. In the field of science, Bacon is perhaps best known for his advocacy of a deductive approach to the study of nature, an approach that relies heavily on experimental collection of data.

Bacon is perhaps best remembered today for a substitution cipher that he developed for enciphering messages. The cipher consists of two levels, the first of which makes use of the following substitution alphabet:

A:	aaaaa	N:	abbaa
B:	aaaab	O:	abbab
C:	aaaba	P:	abbba
D:	aaabb	Q:	abbbb
E:	aabaa	R:	baaaa
F:	aabab	S:	baaab
G:	aabba	T:	baaba
H:	aabbb	U/V:	baabb
I/J:	abaaa	W:	babaa
K:	abaab	X:	babab
L:	ababa	Y:	babba
M:	ababb	Z:	babbb

Notice that in two cases, a pair of letters (I /J and U /V) is represented by a single cipher letter, there being little risk of misunderstanding in either case.

To illustrate how the Baconian cipher is used, suppose that the word ATTACK is to be enciphered. In the first step, each letter is enciphered as follows:

A	T	T	A	C	K
aaaaa	baaba	baaba	aaaaa	aaaba	abaab

The second level of the Baconian code makes use of steganography. The ciphertext is further encoded by introducing some key that will disguise the presence of a's and b's. For example, all of the a's in the ciphertext might be represented by roman script, and all the b's by italics. The ciphertext above could be rewritten by means of the following message:

Retreat as quickly as possible to prevent discovery by the enemy.

To aid in seeing the connection between the ciphertext and its new version, called the covertext, the covertext will be separated into five-letter segments corresponding to each of the letters in the word ATTACK, as follows:

A	T	T	A	C	K
Retre / at as q / uickl / y as po / ssibl / e to prevent

(The rest of the message is irrelevant in this case.)

Notice that one advantage of this system is that the covertext carries a message exactly the opposite of the plaintext, or real message.

Bacon is also remembered for the "virtues of perfect ciphers," which he proposed in his original version of *Advancement of Learning* (1605). He wrote this about ciphers:

> But the vertues of them, whereby they are to bee preferred, are three: that they bee not laborious to write and reade; that they bee impossible to discypher; and, in some cases, that they bee without suspition.

See also: steganography; substitution.

For further reading: Brian Beckett, *Introduction to Cryptology*, Oxford: Blackwell Scientific Publications, 1988, pp. 303–305; E. T. Williams and Helen M. Palmer, *Dictionary of National Biography,* Oxford: Oxford University Press, 1971, vol. 2, pp. 328–360.

BACON, ROGER ▰▰▰▰▰▰▰▰▰▰

English alchemist, astronomer, philosopher, and futurist. Born in Ilchester, Somerset, Bacon (1220–1292) studied at Oxford and obtained his degree from the Faculty of Arts in Paris in 1241. He returned to Oxford to teach about 1247, and a decade later joined the Franciscan order. Bacon was given permission to continue his scientific research, and

Thirteenth-century philosopher and Franciscan monk Roger Bacon, author of *Epistle on the Secret Works of Art and the Nullity of Magic*

eventually he became one of the most creative and imaginative thinkers of that or any other period, outlining plans for such devices as the telescope, automobile, airplane, and steamship.

Bacon's contribution to the field of cryptology came in the form of a book he published in the mid-thirteenth century, *Epistle on the Secret Works of Art and the Nullity of Magic*. The book outlines seven methods by which secret messages can be written, including techniques such as exotic alphabets, characters created by the writer, and shorthand. Bacon is also thought by some authorities to be the author of the Voynich manuscript.

See also: Voynich manuscript.
For further reading: John Henry Bridges, *The Life and Work of Roger Bacon*, London: Williams & Norgate, 1914; William R. Newbold, *The Cipher of Roger Bacon*, Philadelphia: University of Pennsylvania Press, 1928; Markku Peltonen, *The Cambridge Companion to Bacon*, Cambridge: Cambridge University Press, 1996; E. Westacott, *Roger Bacon in Life and Legend*, New York: Philosophical Library, 1953.

BACTERIUM

See malicious software.

BAD GUY

Anyone who makes an attempt to decrypt a message that is not intended for him or her, or who otherwise attempts to defeat a security device. Kaufman, Perlman, and Speciner said, "No moral implications here; some of our best friends are bad guys," the inference being that someone working for the U.S. National Security Agency as a cryptanalyst is, of course, defined as a bad guy because he or she attempts to break into the cryptograms sent by representatives of other nations.

See also: cryptanalysis.

BAMS CODE

An acronym for the Broadcasting for Allied Merchant Ships code developed for use by the British Admiralty during World War II. BAMS was a two-part code to which superencipherment was added. To send the message SUBMARINE SUBMERGED AT CAT ISLAND, for example, the operator would look up the appropriate words and phrases in the BAMS codebook and find that SUBMARINE SUBMERGED = QWAO and AT CAT ISLAND = QVKF. The superencipherment for each codeword was also given in the codebook, with QWAO = 63320 and QVKF = 63211. The message sent, then, was 6 3 3 2 0 6 3 2 1 1. The operator receiving such a message simply referred to his or her own codebook to find the letter and word equivalents of 63320 and 63211.

The BAMS code was never a very sophisticated cryptosystem and, in fact, was compromised early in the war when copies of the codebook were taken from the British merchant ship *City of Baghdad* by the German raider *Atlantis*.

See also: codebook; two-part code.
For further reading: David Kahn, *The Codebreakers: The Story of Secret Writing*, New York: Macmillan, 1967, pp. 465–468.

BAND-SHIFTING

See ciphony.

BAND-SPLITTING

See ciphony.

BANKING AND OTHER FINANCIAL SERVICES

Corporations and other entities involved in the holding, lending, and transfer of funds among individuals, businesses, corporations, and/or entities. Cryptography has become essential for banking and financial services such as automatic teller machine services, electronic transfer of funds, international transactions, and many other routine financial operations.

At one time, the vast majority of financial transactions in the United States and around the world was handled by some form of a paper document (checks are one of the most familiar remaining examples). The advent of computer technology dramatically changed the situation, however. Today, millions of dollars are deposited, withdrawn, and transferred among banks, individuals, and/or corporations hundreds or thousands of miles from one another. In many instances, no paper document is generated for such transactions, and protecting the security, integrity, authenticity, and privacy of transactions is critical to the financial institution(s) involved. Some form of cryptographic encryption is now routinely used in such transactions.

For more than a decade, the U.S. government's Data Encryption Standard (DES) has been used to protect bank and other financial transactions. The specific standards by which such institutions operate are set by the Accredited Standards Committee (ASC X9), which announced in 1995 that it would develop new standards based on triple-DES technology.

Because of the very substantial investment by financial institutions in DES-based cryptographic systems, ASC X9 has been reluctant to consider adopting the Clinton administration's Escrowed Encryption Standard (EES), a decision that has further stalled widespread adoption of EES by nongovernment bodies. Instead, a number of individual financial institutions and related corporations are developing their own key escrow cryptosystems, which make use of either private- or public-key systems.

The Bankers Trust International Corporate Key Escrow system, as one example, uses a hardware device to encrypt information stored in and transmitted through voice, fax, store-and-forward messaging, and data-storage-and-retrieval systems. Bankers Trust developed the system to protect data transmitted worldwide through public-access channels as well as in anticipation of the development and extensive use of "smart cards" for a variety of international transactions.

The Bankers Trust system is similar to the Clinton administration's EES in that it calls for companies to deposit keys (or fragments of keys) with an escrow agent. Those keys would be available to owners at any time in order to decrypt encrypted information. They would also be available to law enforcement agencies that had been given court approval to gain access to otherwise private information. The Bankers Trust system would also allow key owners to change algorithms and keys whenever and as often as necessary as a normal operating security procedure.

See also: authentication; automatic teller machine; digital signature; electronic funds transfer; smart card.

For further reading: D. W. Davies and W. L. Price, *Security for Computer Networks: An Introduction to Data Security in Teleprocessing and Electronic Funds Transfer,* Chichester: John Wiley & Sons, 1984, passim; Charlie Kaufman, Radia Perlman, and Mike Speciner, *Network Security: Private Communication in a Public World,* Englewood Cliffs, NJ: Prentice-Hall, 1995, passim; Carl H. Meyer and Stephen M. Matyas, *Cryptography: A New Dimension in Computer Data Security,* New York: John Wiley & Sons, 1982, passim; U.S. Congress, Office of Technology Assessment, *Information Security and Privacy in Network Environments,* OTA-TCT-606, Washington, DC: GPO, September 1994, passim (*see* index).

BAR CODE

See Universal Product Code.

BAUDOT CODE

A Morse code–like system for use with a teletypewriter. The system was developed by the French inventor J. M. E. Baudot, from whom it received its name. The code consists of the presence or absence of five consecutive electrical pulses. If the number 1 is used to represent the presence of a pulse and 0 to represent the absence of a pulse, a single character in the Baudot code would have the form: 0 0 1 1 0, that is, no-pulse no-pulse pulse

pulse no-pulse. The number of possible permutations of this system is two options (on or off) taken five at a time, or $2^5 = 32$.

Baudot used the 32 possible combinations to represent the 26 letters of the alphabet plus six "stunts," mechanical movements to be made by the machine. The Baudot code is as follows:

A:	11000	Q:	11101
B:	10011	R:	01010
C:	01110	S:	10100
D:	10010	T:	00001
E:	10000	U:	11100
F:	10110	V:	01111
G:	01011	W:	11001
H:	00101	X:	10111
I:	01100	Y:	10101
J:	11010	Z:	10001
K:	11110	α:	01000
L:	01001	β:	00010
M:	00111	γ:	11111
N:	00110	Δ:	11011
O:	00011	ε:	00100
P:	01101	η:	00000

α	=	paragraph break
β	=	carriage return
γ	=	number → letter shift
Δ	=	letter → number shift
ε	=	idle
η	=	blank space

To inscribe a message using this system, holes are punched into a paper tape with the above code patterns. A hole in the tape permits a thin metal pin to pass through, making contact with a metal plate on the opposite side of the tape and allowing a flow of current through an electrical circuit. In places where no hole exists, the pin cannot make contact with the plate, and no current flows.

See also: Morse code; Vernam, Gilbert.

BAZERIES, ÉTIENNE

French army officer and cryptanalyst, widely known for his outstanding skills in breaking ciphers and codes. Bazeries (1846–1931) served in the French army from 1863 to 1899, although he was also assigned to the Bureau du Chiffre (Cipher Bureau) in the Ministry of Foreign Affairs

during the latter part of this period. After his retirement from the military, he was hired again by the ministry, where he was employed in breaking ciphers and codes until 1924.

Bazeries has been called by David Kahn "the great pragmatist of cryptology" because of his incredible skills of cryptanalysis. During his military career, he was able to break every cryptosystem developed by the army. For his own amusement, he also decrypted a number of historical nomenclators dating to Francis I, Francis II, Henry IV, Mirabeau, and Napoléon. He is best known today for two accomplishments, the first being a book written in 1901, *Les Chiffres Secrets Dévoilés* (Secret Ciphers Unveiled). The book was written at least in part to demonstrate the weakness of the French army's cipher system as well as to take revenge on some of his professional colleagues, with whom he had an ongoing debate over cryptologic ideas. Kahn has called Bazeries's book "the most readable book in the whole of the science."

The second accomplishment is a cipher machine he developed, a "cylindrical cryptograph." The device was similar to one invented some time earlier by Thomas Jefferson, and consisted of a series of 20 disks mounted on an iron cylindrical core around which they could be rotated. Each disk contained 25 letters printed around its circumference. The key for the device was the sequence in which the disks were arranged on the cylinder, a sequence that both encipherer and decipherer knew.

To encipher a message, the disks on the cylinder were rotated so that the plaintext letters appeared aligned with each other on one line of the disks. The ciphertext was then read off any other row of letters below that of the plaintext. A portion of the cylinder in two dimensions arranged for enciphering the message THE GENERAL ARRIVES AT NOON is shown in Figure 5. Notice that one possible ciphertext of the message would be: zmxnc bvals kdkdj fhgqp.

```
THEGENERALARRIVESATN (end of cylinder)
eswaqrdxthmyjkuliopc
zmxncbvalskdkdjfhgqp
iopjklnmbvcrewqdsayt
huvjibkonlpmdrzseafq
```

Figure 5

A message consisting of 20 letters or less could be enciphered in a single step, but those containing more than 20 letters (like the one above) had to be broken down into 20-letter units before enciphering.

The French army declined to accept Bazeries's cylindrical cryptograph for its own use, a snub that was probably at least partially responsible for his decision to write *Les Chiffres Secrets Dévoilés*. His hopes for the device were justified, however, when the U.S. Army adopted a version of the Bazeries device, the M-94, for its own cryptologic needs in 1922.

See also: cipher machine; cryptanalysis; cryptosystem; Jefferson, Thomas; M-94; nomenclator.

For further reading: Rosario Candela, *The Military Cipher of Commandant Bazeries; An Essay in Decrypting*, New York: Cardanus Press, 1938; W. F. Friedman, *Signal Corps Training Pamphlet No. 2*, 1921; David Kahn, *The Codebreakers: The Story of Secret Writing*, New York: Macmillan, 1967, pp. 244–250.

BEALE CIPHERS

A set of three ciphers left by Thomas Jefferson Beale in 1819 describing the discovery and hiding place of huge amounts of gold and silver. Beale and 30 companions discovered the precious metals north of Santa Fe while hunting for buffalo. After mining more than a half ton of gold and two tons of silver, Beale and ten other men returned to their homes in Virginia, where they buried their treasure. When Beale left for the West again in 1821, he left a lockbox with local tavern owner Robert Morris, with instructions to open the box only if he (Beale) had not returned in ten years.

Morris waited until 1831 and then broke open the box. Inside he found the story of Beale's adventure along with three coded messages telling where the treasure had been hidden. Morris was instructed to break the codes, dig up the gold and silver, keep one part for himself, and divide the remainder into 30 parts to be distributed to the families of the 30 discoverers of the treasure.

Unfortunately, the messages were extremely difficult to decode. In fact, the first message was decoded only some years later by Morris's friend James B. Ward. This message gave the amount of treasure that had been buried and indicated that the first message provided instructions for locating the burial site.

To this date, no one has been able to decode the remaining two messages found in Beale's strongbox. In 1978 the Beale Cypher Association was organized by Robert E. Caldwell in Beaver Falls, Pennsylvania, to study the ciphers, support research on their decoding, and maintain books and files that might lead to their eventual solution.

For further reading: Brian Beckett, *Introduction to Cryptology*, Oxford: Blackwell Scientific Publications, 1988, pp. 292–294; Paul Horrman, "Ciphernauts: Search for Treasure Buried by T. J. Beale in the 1820s in Virginia," *Omni* (May 1987): 26+; P. B. Innis, "The Beale Fortune," *Argosy* (August 1964): 70–71+; Louis Kruh, "The Beale Cipher as a Bamboozlement," *Cryptologia* (October 1988): 241–246; Stephen M. Matyas, Jr., *The Beale Ciphers, Containing Research Findings, and Documents and Data, as Well as Several Predictions about How the Ciphers Were Constructed*, Hyde Park, NY: privately published, 1996; http://www.cs.ruu.nl/wais/html/na-dir/puzzles/archive/cryptology.html.

BEAUFORT, ADM. SIR FRANCIS

Creator of the system by which wind speeds are designated and also of a popular cryptosystem. Beaufort (1774–1857) first developed the scale of wind speeds in 1806 to provide a quantitative measure that would replace what he called the "uncertain idea of wind and weather [conveyed] by the old expressions of moderate and cloud, etc., etc." The scale consists of 13 levels, numbered from 0 to 12, representing winds ranging from calm (Beaufort number 0) to moderate gale (Beaufort number 7) to hurricane (Beaufort number 12).

In the field of cryptology, Beaufort was one of the first to publish a cipher that could be used by the general public in the transmission of telegrams and the writing of postcards. The Beaufort cipher, first published in 1857, was not intended to be used for secret transmissions, only to reduce the amount of space taken by a message and, thus, its cost of transmission or mailing.

The Beaufort cipher is essentially a Vigenère square with an extra alphabet at the bottom and along the right-hand side. The additional row and column simply made the square easier to read; each corner of the square contained an A.

The instructions for using the Beaufort cipher were printed on the envelope in which the cipher was kept. The user was advised to select for the key "a line of poetry or the name of some memorable person or place, which cannot easily be forgotten." The first step in using the cipher was to read down the first column until the first letter of the plaintext was encountered. The user then read across the row for this letter until the column under the first letter of the key was found. The letter at the intersection of this row and column constituted the first cipher letter of the message. Clearly, the Beaufort cipher is nearly identical to the Vigenère square except that the key and plaintext alphabets are reversed.

See also: mnemonic key; Vigenère square.
For further reading: Brian Beckett, *Introduction to Cryptology*, Oxford: Blackwell Scientific Publications, 1988, pp. 149–150; Harriet Martineau, *Biographical Sketches*, New York: Hurst, 1868, pp. 207–224.

BELASO, GIOVAN BATISTA

Also Bellaso; a sixteenth-century Italian scholar who proposed a simple method for selecting a key to be used in polyalphabetic substitution ciphers. Almost nothing is known about Belaso's life except for a short book he wrote on cryptography, *La cifra del. Sig. Giovan Batista Belaso*. In it Belaso describes a method for selecting a key to be used in determining the specific alphabet for enciphering a message by means of polyalphabetic substitution. He called the key a "countersign" and suggested that it consist of some phrase in Italian, Latin, or any other language. For example, assume that the countersign to be used in enciphering the message ONE DIVISION OF HORSEMEN ARRIVES TOMORROW is "In veritas vinces." The encipherment would proceed by matching the countersign with the plaintext, as shown below.

COUNTERSIGN:
i n v e r i t a s v i n c e s i n v e r i t a s

PLAINTEXT:
O N E D I V I S I O N O F H O R S E M E N A R R

This pattern tells the encipherer that the first letter of the plaintext (O) is to be enciphered using alphabet i, the second letter (N) by using alphabet n, the third letter (E) by alphabet v, and so on.

Belaso's countersign concept was an important contribution to the growth of cryptology for two reasons. First, it provided a mechanism for making use of polyalphabetic substitution at a time when the idea was just being developed. Second, it used a simple but effective technique—the familiar phrase—for employing a key, as it is now known, for such encipherments.

See also: polyalphabetic substitution.

BEOBACHTUNGS-DIENST (B-DIENST)

The cryptanalytic section of the German navy during World War II. The name means "observation services." The service's primary mission was to intercept and break enemy codes and ciphers, at which it was strikingly successful, one of the major reasons why the German navy dominated the early part of World War II.

One of the B-Dienst's early accomplishments took place in March 1940. The Germans planned to attack Norway, but had not been able to devise a scheme to get their ships to the Norwegian coast without meeting the more powerful British navy. As discussions about the invasion went forward, the B-Dienst intercepted a British message outlining plans to mine the port of Narvik in northern Norway. German officers decided to send a decoy fleet in the direction of Narvik, hoping to draw additional British naval support in that direction. Meanwhile, the main force of the German navy would be headed elsewhere, toward the southern coast of Norway.

The plan worked perfectly. When the British detected the movement of the decoy fleet toward the north, they concluded that the Germans were coming to interrupt the mining activity and sent the bulk of their ships toward Narvik, allowing the Germans to land on the southern coast without interference. The German conquest of Norway was completed in a matter of weeks.

That success was soon followed by many others. After British codebooks were impounded during the capture of the freighter *City of Baghdad* in July 1940, B-Dienst operators were routinely able to read messages enciphered in the British Broadcasting for Allied Merchant Ships (BAMS) code system. They were not only able to learn where British ships were located and which direction they were traveling, they also intercepted British messages telling their own warships the location of German U-boats. The B-Dienst was able to feed its own navy information not only on the location of likely targets for its U-boat attacks, but also how the U-boats could protect themselves against forthcoming British attacks.

Fortunately for the Allies, as the war continued the British rapidly improved their code and cipher systems, enveloping them in more efficient layers of secrecy. By the last year of the war, the B-Dienst was able to read only older and less important codes. The tables had also turned by then—British cryptanalysts routinely intercepted and read German codes and ciphers at the highest level.

For further reading: David Kahn, *The Codebreakers: The Story of Secret Writing*, New York: Macmillan, 1967, pp. 465–468.

BIBLICAL CRYPTOLOGY

Examples of cryptography and cryptanalysis found in the Bible. In his classic book on the history of cryptology, David Kahn mentions examples of the use of cryptology in biblical stories, primitive forms of the science and art for which he prefers the term *protocryptography* (or *precryptography*). Many writers on cryptology mention the story of Daniel, who was able to interpret handwriting on the wall that appeared before King Belshazzar. David explained to the king that the message, *mene mene tekel upharsin*, read: "God has numbered thy kingdom and found thee wanting." Although there is considerably more to this story than the cryptanalysis of writing that was not even a cipher, Kahn argues that Daniel can be thought of as "the first known cryptanalyst." Another frequently mentioned example of the use of cryptography in the Bible is found in the Book of Isaiah (chapter 7, verse 6), in which the names of Babel and Remaliah are encrypted as Sheshach and Tabeal.

For further reading: David Kahn, *The Codebreakers: The Story of Secret Writing*, New York: Macmillan, 1967, ch. 2.

BIFID

A type of cipher in which a pair of letters, numbers, or other symbols is used to represent a letter or number of plaintext. A Polybius square, for example, is a cipher system in which each letter of plaintext is represented by a pair of numbers determined by the position of the letter in a 5 x 5 matrix.

See also: Polybius.

For further reading: Brian Beckett, *Introduction to Cryptology*, Oxford: Blackwell Scientific Publications, 1988, pp. 50–53, 225–234; William M. Bowers, *Practical Cryptanalysis: Bifid*, Wilbraham, MA: American Cryptogram Association, 1960.

BIGRAM

A pair of letters in a cipher. A bigram is also known as a digraph. Bigrams are of importance in cryptanalysis because the frequency with which various two-letter combinations occur in English is well known and can be detected in coded messages. The most common two-letter combinations in English are, in order: TH, ER, ON, AN, RE, HE, IN, ED, ND, and HA. Thus, if a ciphertext of sufficient length contains the bigram xq most frequently, it might be guessed that xq codes for TH or, in other words, x = T and q = H. The phrase "of sufficient length" means that frequency counts can be applied only in relatively lengthy texts.

The location of bigrams in a message can also be informative. The two-letter combination HA is less likely to occur at the end of a word than at the beginning. A discovery that ej = HA, for example, helps in knowing where words in a ciphertext begin and end.

See also: frequency distribution.

BINARY NUMBER SYSTEM

The positional number system that uses base 2. In comparison with the decimal system, which makes use of ten digits (0, 1, 2, 3, 4, 5, 6, 7, 8, 9), the binary system makes use of only two digits, 0 and 1. The value of a digit in the binary system is determined by its position within a number, with each position representing some power of 2, as shown:

$$
\begin{array}{ccccccc}
0 & 0 & 0 & 0 & 0 & 0 & 0 \\
2^6 & 2^5 & 2^4 & 2^3 & 2^2 & 2^1 & 2^0 \\
\end{array}
$$

or

$$
\begin{array}{ccccccc}
64 & 32 & 16 & 8 & 4 & 2 & 1 \\
\end{array}
$$

The number 23 can be represented, then, as $2^4 + 2^2 + 2^1 + 2^0$, or as 10111. The binary number system is important because it can be used to represent systems, such as the elements that make up a computer, that can exist in only two states, such as on or off, or magnetized or nonmagnetized. Because computers are now widely used to encipher and store messages, a knowledge of binary number systems is critical for encipherers, decipherers, and cryptanalysts.

For further reading: Brian Beckett, *Introduction to Cryptology*, Oxford: Blackwell Scientific Publications, 1988, ch. 15.

BIOMETRIC DEVICE

Any system for measuring (*-metric*) a distinctive physical characteristic (*bio-*) such as a person's fingerprints or voice pattern. Biometric devices are one way of providing authentication in a communication between two individuals because they are usually very difficult to forge or disguise. One of the earliest and simplest forms of biometric-type devices was the distinctive touch of a telegraph operator during the transmission of messages. Some biometric devices currently in use are fingerprint, handprint, and voiceprint readers; retinal scanners; physical signatures; and keystroke timing.

An example of the possible application of biometric authentication is the use of fingerprints by banks to verify people who wish to make transactions but are not patrons of a given bank. In late 1996, two banks in Portland, Oregon, announced that henceforth they would require such individuals to provide a thumbprint before being permitted to cash a check or carry out any other transaction.

See also: fist.

For further reading: D. W. Davies and W. L. Price, *Security for Computer Networks: An Introduction to Data Security in Teleprocessing and*

Electronic Funds Transfer, Chichester: John Wiley & Sons, 1984, ch. 7; *Electronic Benefits Transfer: Use of Biometrics To Deter Fraud in the Nationwide EST Program,* Washington, DC: GAO, GPO #0546-D, 29 September 1995; Charlie Kaufman, Radia Perlman, and Mike Speciner, *Network Security: Private Communication in a Public World,* Englewood Cliffs, NJ: Prentice-Hall, 1995, pp. 221–222; Alan K. Ota, "Two Portland Banks Begin Fingerprinting," *The Oregonian* (14 September 1996): C7+.

BIRTHDAY PARADOX

A classic problem in probability theory that asks how large a group must be before two people within the group are likely to have the same birthday. Since there are 365 (or 366) possible birthdays from which to choose, the answer to this problem might be anticipated to be quite large. It might seem that well over a hundred people would have to assemble before two with the same birthday could be found.

In fact, the answer is quite different. First, the requirement that two people "are likely" to have the same birthday must be defined. For the sake of convenience, assume that this qualitative statement can be rephrased as "have a 50–50 chance" of having the same birthday. In other words, the problem is to find out how large the group must be that any two people will have a 50–50 chance of sharing the same birthday.

Mathematically, the answer can be determined quite easily. Suppose that the first person in the group states his or her birthday. What is the probability that the second person in the group does *not* share that birthday? The probability can be given as $n - 1$ (the number of days that have not yet been chosen as a birthday) divided by n (the total number of days that could be chosen as birthdays).

For the next person in the group, the probability of *not* sharing a birthday is $n - 2$ divided by n, and for the third person, the probability would be $n - 3$ divided by n. This trend can be summarized by saying that the probability of the rth student's

not sharing a birthday with previous members of the group is

$$p = n(n-1)(n-2)\ldots(n-r+1)/n^r$$

For $n = 365$ possible days of the year and $p =$ about 0.5, r turns out to be about 23. More precisely, for $r = 23$ exactly, $p = 0.493$. So the probability of the twenty-third member of the group *not* sharing a birthday with anyone else in the group is 0.493. Conversely, the probability of the twenty-third member *sharing* a birthday is 0.507, or just over 50–50. Thus, in a group of 23 people, the likelihood of two people sharing the same birthday is just over half.

The application of the birthday paradox to cryptology is that seemingly impossible mathematical tasks may not, in fact, be quite so daunting. One might calculate, as an example, that it would take 2^{64} trials to decrypt a ciphertext. As with the 365 days to be checked in the birthday paradox, however, that number of tests may not really be necessary. There may be reasons why only 2^{28} such tests will actually have to be performed to find the key to a cryptosystem. Now, 2^{28} is still a very large number, but it is certainly not as large as 2^{64}, and it is within the scope of any large computing machine available today.

See also: class P problem.
For further reading: D. W. Davies and W. L. Price, *Security for Computer Networks: An Introduction to Data Security in Teleprocessing and Electronic Funds Transfer,* Chichester: John Wiley & Sons, 1984, pp. 116–117; Charlie Kaufman, Radia Perlman, and Mike Speciner, *Network Security: Private Communication in a Public World,* Englewood Cliffs, NJ: Prentice-Hall, 1995, pp. 102–103; Carl H. Meyer and Stephen M. Matyas, *Cryptography: A New Dimension in Computer Data Security,* New York: John Wiley & Sons, 1982, app. B.

BIT

An acronym for binary digit. Computer systems operate with the binary number system, in which the only digits are 0 and

1. Every mechanical setting in a computer is either off or on, representing a binary digit of either 0 or 1.

See also: byte.

BIT COMMITMENT

A technique by which two users of a computer system can reach agreement on some issue without the risk of either user cheating. A bit commitment protocol requires that user A be able to commit himself or herself to some value of a variable without transmitting that information to user B and without permitting user A to change the selected value. Under these circumstances, user B can announce that he or she has made some choice with regard to an issue, and user A can announce, without risk of fraud, whether that choice corresponds to the decision user A has made with regard to the issue.

BIT-STREAM GENERATOR

An algorithm by which binary digits (bits) are produced for use in stream encipherment. The algorithm is written so as to produce a random sequence of bits (01001101001001010 . . .) that can be used as a key with which plaintext can be enciphered. The prototype of a bit-stream generator was the punched paper-tape key invented by Gilbert Vernam for use in his cipher machine in 1926. Today, bit-stream generators are computer programs that generate an endless sequence of binary numbers according to some program designed to maintain randomness in the sequence. The sequence of numbers is known as a key-stream or a cryptographic bit-stream.

See also: random number; stream encipherment; Vernam, Gilbert.
For further reading: Thomas Beth, ed., *Cryptography*, Lecture Notes in Computer Science Series, Berlin: Springer-Verlag, 1982, vol. 149, sec. 5; Carl H. Meyer and Stephen M. Matyas, *Cryptography: A New Dimension in Computer Data Security*, New York: John Wiley & Sons, 1982, p. 53.

BLACK

The name of a code designed for use by U.S. military attachés just prior to the beginning of World War II. The code drew its name from the color of the binder in which it was kept. Because the code had the additional advantage of providing a superencipherment component, military officers placed great confidence in its use for the conduct of their communications in every part of the world. In fact, however, the code was compromised even before the United States entered World War II. An Italian national, Loris Gherardi, appears to have broken into the office of the American military attaché in Rome and stolen the BLACK code. Shortly thereafter, the Italians passed the code on to their German allies.

With access to a top-level American code, German cryptanalysts were soon reading supposedly secret messages almost at will. The primary beneficiary of this breakthrough was Field Marshal Irwin Rommel, who was then pushing British forces back across the deserts of North Africa. He benefited to no small degree by knowing most of the details about the location, strength, movement, and plans of British forces, thanks to their ongoing correspondence with the American attaché in Cairo.

Fortunately for the Allies, the Americans found out that BLACK had been compromised. They used this information to send false cryptograms to their British allies, misleading Rommel and contributing to his ultimate defeat at El Alamein in October 1941.

For further reading: David Kahn, *The Codebreakers: The Story of Secret Writing,* New York: Macmillan, 1967, pp. 472–477.

BLACK CHAMBER

A secret room or building in which messages intercepted from an enemy are opened, cryptanalyzed (if necessary), and read. No exact or even approximate date can be given for the earliest black chambers because the interception of another party's correspondence has been a part of international (and even domestic) diplomacy for centuries, perhaps for as long as governments have existed. Some of the first black chambers were probably nothing more than a private room in which trusted aides were allowed to practice their eavesdropping.

By the eighteenth century, most European states had some form of a black chamber: the Cabinet Noir in France, the Geheime Kabinets-Kanzlei in Vienna, and the Decyphering Branch in Great Britain. A cryptanalysis group working for the U.S. government in 1919 was actually given the name the American Black Chamber.

Much of the work carried out in black chambers should be categorized as spying rather than as cryptanalysis. Workers developed ways of removing the wax seals that guaranteed the secrecy of letters. After opening and reading the letters, the wax was restored and imprinted with counterfeit seals. These activities inevitably led to cryptanalysis, however, because many of the letters were written in cipher or code. For this reason, black chambers were probably the training ground for a large fraction of cryptanalysts employed by governments.

The black chambers in the largest European nations died out around the middle of the nineteenth century. The Decyphering Branch closed in October 1844, and its French and Austrian equivalents closed four years later.

See also: American Black Chamber; cabinet noir; Geheime Kabinets-Kanzlei; Rossignol, Antoine.
For further reading: Peter Way, *Codes and Ciphers*. n.p.: Crescent Books, 1977, pp. 22–32.

BLETCHLEY PARK

A country estate used by the British Government Code & Cypher School (GC&CS) during World War II for a large portion of its most important cryptanalytical work. The town of Bletchley itself was, as author Andrew Hodges described it, "a small town of ordinary dullness." Bletchley Park, the country estate of stockbroker Herbert S. Leon, was a much more luxurious site. The GC&CS commandeered the estate partly to provide more space for its operations but, more importantly, to provide greater privacy for its code- and cipher-breaking activities.

Bletchley Park was the site of some of the most exciting intellectual activities of the war. Codebreakers at GC&CS were confronted with the daunting task of decrypting messages sent by means of the German Enigma code and, more generally, figuring out how the machine itself was constructed and how it worked. The project was known as ULTRA, and was successful beyond anyone's grandest hopes. Largely under the direction of Alan Turing, the secrets of the German Enigma machine were solved. By 1943, GC&CS was providing the British military with deciphered copies of German messages almost as quickly as German ships received them.

For nearly five years, Bletchley Park was home to some of the most brilliant mathematical, linguistic, and analytical minds in Great Britain. Included among them were Turing, Frank Lucas, Patrick Wilkinson, Dillwyn Knox, and many others who had been recruited from Cambridge, Oxford, and other universities across the country.

The living and working conditions were unexpected for such an important government activity. The mansion house was not large enough to house the scholars and staff, so quonset-type huts were built as work areas on the estate grounds. Villagers were unaware of the work going on at Bletchley Park, and often complained because such able-bodied men and women were not involved elsewhere in the war effort.

In fact, the world would not learn of the work conducted at Bletchley Park for three decades. The research, classified as top secret, was not revealed to the general public until 1974, and even then only certain details of the operation were released.

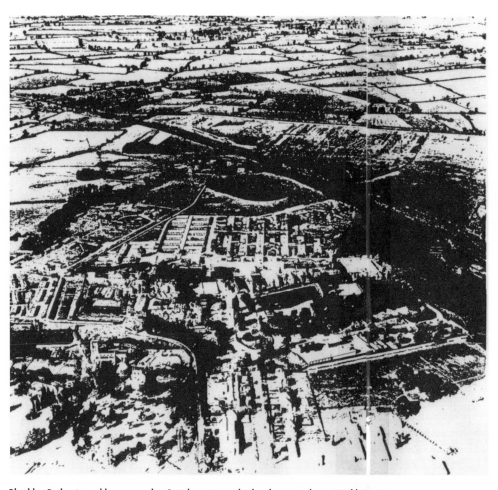

Bletchley Park, pictured here, served as British cryptographic headquarters during World War II.

See also: Enigma; Government Code & Cypher School; Turing, Alan; ULTRA.
For further reading: Francis H. Hinsley, *British Intelligence in the Second World War*, New York: Cambridge University Press, 1993; Hinsley, "The Enigma of Ultra: Britain's Breaking of Enemy Cyphers," *History Today* (September 1993): 15–20; F. H. Hinsley and Alan Stripp, eds., *Codebreakers: The Inside Story of Bletchley Park*, New York: Oxford University Press, 1993; Andrew Hodges, *Alan Turing: The Enigma*, New York: Simon & Schuster, 1983, passim.

BLOCK ENCRYPTION

A method for producing ciphertext by dividing plaintext into units (blocks) of set lengths. In the Data Encryption Standard (DES), for example, plaintext is divided into blocks 64 bits long. The plaintext is then combined with a key of fixed length, 56 bits in the case of DES. The resulting ciphertext block may or may not be 64 bits in length also.

The most important feature of block encryption is that every bit in the encrypted block is dependent on every bit in the plaintext block and every bit in the key, but not on anything else. When used in this fashion, block encryption is also known as Electronic Code Book (ECB). ECB may be the simplest and most obvious method for enciphering long messages. Suppose the message consists of 765 bits. It can be subdivided into 12 blocks of 64 bits each ($12 \times 64 = 768$) with three null bits added to complete the final block. Then each of the 12 blocks is enciphered, one at a time, to produce 12 blocks of ciphertext. Decipherment is simple because the key is applied to each of the 12 blocks in succession to recover the original plaintext.

The problem with ECB is that similar elements of plaintext in one block are enciphered exactly the same way in each block of ciphertext. In some cases, such repetitions may give a cryptanalyst the clue needed to discover the key or the algorithm by which the ciphertext was produced. To deal with this problem, three other kinds of algorithms were invented to deal with messages longer than 64 bits: cipher block chaining, cipher feedback, and output feedback modes.

See also: cipher block chaining; cipher feedback; data encryption standard; modes of operation; output feedback.

For further reading: Brian Beckett, *Introduction to Cryptology,* Oxford: Blackwell Scientific Publications, 1988, pp. 165–168; Henry Beker and Fred Piper, *Cipher Systems: The Protection of Communications,* New York: John Wiley & Sons, 1982, ch. 7; D. W. Davies and W. L. Price, *Security for Computer Networks: An Introduction to Data Security in Teleprocessing and Electronic Funds Transfer,* Chichester: John Wiley & Sons, 1984, ch. 4; Charlie Kaufman, Radia Perlman, and Mike Speciner, *Network Security: Private Communication in a Public World,* Englewood Cliffs, NJ: Prentice-Hall, 1995, ch. 3; Carl H. Meyer and Stephen M. Matyas, *Cryptography: A New Dimension in Computer Data Security,* New York: John Wiley & Sons, 1982, ch. 2.

BLUE

One of the codes used by the U.S. State Department for secret international communications from prior to World War I to after the beginning of World War II. The code was named for the color of the binding in which it was published. Both the BLUE code and its counterpart, the RED code, were almost childishly simple to decrypt. David Kahn pointed out that they were so easy to read that "the United States must have been the laughingstock of every cryptanalyst in the world."

BOMBE

A machine originally developed by Polish cryptanalysts in 1938 as a means of breaking the German Enigma code. The general principle was that because the Enigma was itself a machine, the best way to find out how it worked was to build one or more machines that would duplicate its operations. The complexity of the Enigma made it difficult to put this principle into operation, however.

The Poles were the first to mechanize the analysis of the Enigma because it was they who received the first models of the machine from French intelligence in 1936. Their approach was to construct a series of six Enigmalike machines—the bombes—that could simultaneously test all possible settings of the six rotors in an actual Enigma machine. The operation of the bombes was based on the discovery by Polish cryptologists that some letter combinations were physically possible (because of wiring within the machine) as keys in the Enigma and others were not. The function of the machines was to look for all possible combinations of letters and locate those that could physically be used as keys.

The wiring in the Enigma meant that the number of possible settings to be tested was 17,576. The set of six bombes required a maximum of about two hours to run through them all. Whenever the machines came to a combination of settings that might possibly be a key, they stopped. Human operators then read off the possible key from the machines and tried it on a sample of ciphertext to see if it could be deciphered to give a meaningful message. If it did, they had found a key for that message. If it did not, the machines were restarted to look for another possible key.

The source of the name for the machines—bombes—is not clear. Some authorities believe the name came from the ticking sound they made as they operated, a sound similar to the ticking of a time bomb. David Kahn hypothesizes that the name may have come from the

This American version of the original Polish bombe was used during World War II in an effort to crack the famous German Enigma code.

"rounded ice cream sundae" (*bomba*) their inventor was eating during the discussion of the design.

The Polish version of the bombe was a powerful tool in understanding the construction and operation of the original Enigma machine. But the really important breakthrough in making the bombe useful in rapid analysis of Enigma-encrypted messages was made by the brilliant English mathematician Alan Turing. Shortly after he arrived at Bletchley Park as a new recruit for the British Government Code & Cypher School, Turing suggested a new design for the bombe. Instead of searching for possible keys, Turing said, why not make a machine that compares possible keys with probable words? A familiar and widely used tool, probable words

are guesses by the cryptanalysts as to what a given plaintext word might be within any given ciphertext.

Turing's suggestion required a modification of the Polish bombe design in which the machines searched for certain possible matches between assumed key and assumed plaintext words or phrases. When a possible match was found, the bombes would send out a signal, and human operators took over the task of testing the assumed key to see if it could be used to decrypt a given passage of ciphertext. The new design turned out to be a spectacular breakthrough. Within a remarkably short period of time, cryptanalysts at Bletchley Park were reading a significant fraction of Enigma-enciphered messages sent to German ships and submarines in the Atlantic. Progress did not continue smoothly, however, because the Germans continually made modifications in the original Enigma machine and in the method by which ciphers were produced. Nonetheless, the British sufficiently kept pace with these revisions to make it possible for Allied ships to regain control of traffic in the Atlantic Ocean.

See also: Bletchley Park; Enigma; Government Code & Cypher School; Turing, Alan. For further reading: Robert I. Atha, "Bombe! 'I Could Harldly Believe It,' " *Cryptologia* (October 1985): 332–336; A. K. Dewdney, "On Making and Breaking Codes (I)," *Scientific American* (October 1988): 144–147; Andrew Hodges, *Alan Turing: The Enigma,* New York: Simon & Schuster, 1983, ch. 4; Marian Rejewski, "How Polish Mathematicians Deciphered the Enigma," *Annals of the History of Computing* 3 (1981): 213–234; Gordon Welchman, *The Hut Six Story,* New York: McGraw-Hill, 1982.

BOOK CODE ━━━━━━━━━━

A cryptosystem in which some set of numbers is used to indicate the words that make up a message. The first step in creating a book code is to choose some volume that is readily accessible to all who will be using the code. A dictionary is often selected because dictionaries contain all words likely to be used in a message. In addition, the words are arranged in alphabetical order, making them easy for the cryptographer to locate while enciphering a message.

In the book code's simplest form, the numbers used to encode the message represent the page, line, and word in a book. For example, the number set 173-14-3 refers to the third word on the fourth line of page 173 of the previously-agreed-on book.

Book codes are sometimes regarded as being close to perfect because anyone who does not know the key (the book used in enciphering) will have a great deal of trouble deciding where to start looking to attack the code. On the other hand, the physical problem of carrying around the key book sometimes makes the use of a book code unwieldy.

See also: Arnold-André codes.

BOOLEAN ALGEBRA ━━━━━━━━━━

A form of mathematics developed by English mathematician George Boole (1815–1864). Boole was inspired by the belief that it might be possible to represent simple logical propositions by means of symbols and then to manipulate those symbols to discover the logical consequences of the propositions.

As a simple example, suppose that the proposition "I will be home today" is represented by the symbol P, and the proposition "I will be home tomorrow" by the symbol Q. It is possible to determine mathematically the consequences of various combinations of these two propositions, P and Q.

Suppose, for example, one asks about the various possibilities of either P *or* Q being either true or false, OR of P *and* Q being either true or false. One way to carry out this analysis is to construct a "truth table," such as the one below.

P *or* Q: I will be home today OR I will be home tomorrow.

P *and* Q: I will be home today AND I will be home tomorrow.

P	Q	P or Q	P and Q
T	T	T	T
T	F	T	F
F	T	T	F
F	F	F	F

The simplicity of this table gives little sense of the vast number of ways in which Boolean algebra can be used in a variety of situations. For example, any proposition or concept that can be expressed in one of two distinct forms can be represented as true or false, yes or no, or mathematically in the binary system as 1 or 0. Such a concept can then be manipulated by standard mathematical operations. Boolean algebra is used today in the construction of computer and telephone circuitry.

See also: truth table.
For further reading: J. Eldon Whitesitt, *Boolean Algebra and Its Applications*, Reading, MA: Addison-Wesley, 1961.

BREAK

To decrypt a code or cipher.

BRIGHT, TIMOTHY

See shorthand.

BROOKS ACT OF 1965

An act passed in 1965 (Public Law 89-306) to provide for the "economic and efficient purchase, lease, maintenance, operation, and utilization of automatic data processing equipment by federal departments and agencies." Under the authority of this act, the National Bureau of Standards (now the National Institute of Standards and Technology) created a computer and communications security program in 1973. One important outcome of that program was the adoption of the Data Encryption Standard as a Federal Information Processing Standard for the safeguarding of unclassified but sensitive information.

See also: Computer Security Act of 1987; Data Encryption Standard; Federal Information Processing Standard.
For further reading: U.S. Congress, Office of Technology Assessment, *Information Security and Privacy in Network Environments*, OTA-TCT-606, Washington, DC: GPO, September 1994, pp. 134–136.

BROWN

A code developed for use by the U.S. State Department in the early 1930s.

BUCKET BRIGADE ATTACK

A system for breaking into correspondence between two individuals. Suppose that Alice and Bob wish to communicate with each other using a public-key cryptosystem. Each individual computes a number that will authenticate his or her own messages and exchanges that number with his or her partner. The system requires that a bad guy be able to intercept the correspondence between the two individuals and insert his or her own number for those used by Alice and Bob.

When Mr. Bad intercepts a message from Alice containing her secret number (3333, for example), he can substitute his secret number, 4444, and send the message on to Bob. Bob receives the message from Mr. Bad and responds with his own secret number, say 5555. Mr. Bad then replaces Bob's secret number with his own, 4444, and sends the reply back to Alice.

From this point on, Mr. Bad can read all communications between Alice and Bob because they are not using the secret number sent by the other (3333 or 5555) but the secret number chosen by Mr. Bad (4444).

This technique is given the name *bucket brigade* because it is similar to the process firefighters used in previous decades, passing buckets of water from one person to another. In this case, secret numbers are being passed from one person to another.

Of course, a bucket brigade attack works only when Mr. Bad is able to intercept a message and insert his or her own private number in place of those chosen by the legitimate correspondents.

See also: bad guy; Diffie-Hellman key exchange.
For further reading: Charlie Kaufman, Radia Perlman, and Mike Speciner, *Network Security: Private Communication in a Public World*, Englewood Cliffs, NJ: Prentice-Hall, 1995, pp. 149–150.

BUREAU DU CHIFFRE

The name given to various cipher offices in the French government. Included were those offices within the foreign ministry designed to handle correspondence among diplomats and within the French army intended for military communications.

BURR, AARON

Vice-president of the United States under Thomas Jefferson and later a political conspirator involving the recently purchased Louisiana Territory. Dissatisfied with his political career, in the early 1800s Burr (1756–1836) decided to strike out anew in the vast Louisiana Territory purchased from France in 1803. He allied himself with Gen. James Wilkinson, who was (unknown to Burr) an agent of Spain. Burr gathered together a small army, but it is not clear even today what Burr's intentions were in the new lands, whether he acted as a representative of the U.S. government or planned to become ruler of all or part of it himself.

In any case, Burr and Wilkinson agreed on a somewhat complex code for corresponding with each other. The code consisted of three parts, the first of which involved the use of symbols for words. A circle, for example, stood for the word *president.* The second part of the code made use of symbols for letters. The letter *a,* for example, was represented by a dash. The third part of the code was a traditional book code that used a standard dictionary of the time.

Burr's plans for the Louisiana adventure came to a bad end in 1806 when Wilkinson surrendered himself to the U.S. government and implicated Burr in a plot to take over the new lands. To support his claims against Burr, Wilkinson produced a letter sent to him by Burr supposedly inviting the general to join with him in an attack on Baton Rouge. The letter eventually reached President Thomas Jefferson, who ordered Burr's arrest. Burr was tried for treason and, although found not guilty, was ruined personally and politically.

See also: book code.
For further reading: Thomas Perkins Abernethy, *The Burr Conspiracy*, New York: Oxford University Press, 1954; Milton Lomask, *Aaron Burr,* 3 vols., New York: Farrar, Straus & Giroux, 1979, 1982, 1985.

BYTE

A series of bits, almost invariably numbering eight. Thus, the string of bits 01000010 is known as a byte.

See also: bit.

C

C-1

One of a series of codes (including the A-1, B-1, and D-1) developed for use by the U.S. State Department during the 1920s and 1930s. Like others in the series, the C-1 was capable of superencipherment, but it was relatively primitive both for the times and in comparison with ciphers and codes used by some other nations of the world.

CABALA

Also kabbalah; a system by which sacred writings are interpreted not simply by the letters in which they are expressed, but also by the numerical values and sequences in which those letters are arranged. Cabalistic interpretations were particularly important and widely studied in Jewish writings of the medieval period and, to a much lesser extent, in modern times. One of the simplest examples (although its structure is somewhat lost in English translations of the Bible) is Psalm 119. In its original Hebrew form, the psalm consisted of 22 sections of eight verses each. Each verse in each section began with the same letter: the first eight verses with the letter א (aleph), the second eight with the letter ב (beth), the next eight with the letter ג (gimel), and so on.

The focus of cabalistic teaching is the *Seifrot*, or the ten qualities of God. Cabalistic texts arrange the ten Seifrot in a pattern known as the Tree of Life. The ten Seifrot in the tree are connected to one another by means of 22 pathways, representing the 22 letters of the Hebrew alphabet. As one authority on cabala writes, "The resulting complexity of numbers, letters, names, and qualities provides a nearly inexhaustible source of study and manipulation."

For further reading: Elliot R. Wolfson, *Along the Path: Studies in Kabbalistic Myth, Symbolism, and Hermeneutics*, Albany: State University of New York Press, 1995.

CABINET NOIR

French for **black chamber.**

CABLEGRAM

A means of sending messages either along telephone lines or through underwater telephone cables. At one time, most important commercial and diplomatic communications were sent by cablegram. This fact is important to the history of cryptology because the cost of cablegrams was determined by the number of words in the message. Clearly, the fewer words, the less expensive the cablegram. Inventors and companies quickly learned that it was far more economical to use codewords for certain common phrases (depending on the activity discussed in the cablegram) than to send the complete message. With that realization came the development of codebooks and commercial codes.

See also: codebook.

Workers diligently enter cablegram messages on keypads. People quickly learned to encode their cablegrams to make them shorter and thus less expensive.

CAESAR, GAIUS JULIUS

Famous Roman general and statesman (100–44 B.C.), credited with inventing a simple cryptographic alphabet for the transmission of military communiqués to his troops in Gaul. In the Caesarean alphabet, any letter of plaintext is replaced by the third letter following. The substitution involved, therefore, would be of the following type:

PLAIN: A B C D E F G H I J K L M N O P Q R S T U V W X Y Z
cipher: d e f g h i j k l m n o p q r s t u v w x y z a b c

This substitution is not exactly correct, because the Roman (Latin) alphabet contained some letters different from those in the modern English alphabet.

Using this substitution code, the message CAESAR ARRIVES AT DAWN would be enciphered as: fdhvdu duulyhv dw gdzq.

Many authorities now use the term Caesar cipher or Caesar substitution to stand for any form of monoalphabetic substitution.

For further reading: Brian Beckett, *Introduction to Cryptology*, Oxford: Blackwell Scientific Publications, 1988, pp. 73–76; Christian Meier, *Caesar*, New York: Harper Collins, 1982; http://rschp2.anu.edu.au:8080/caesar.html.

CAESAR(EAN) CIPHER

See Caesar, Gaius Julius.

CAPSTONE CHIP

A microchip that implements the Skipjack algorithm used in computer network applications. The Capstone chip is contained in the U.S. Department of Defense's FORTEZZA card.

See also: Clipper chip; Skipjack.
For further reading: Lee Dembart, "Hide and Peek: Clipper Chip Proposal," *Reason* (No-

vember 1993): 40–45; U.S. Congress, Office of Technology Assessment, *Information Security and Privacy in Network Environments*, OTA-TCT-606, Washington, DC: GPO, September 1994, passim (*see* index).

CARDANO, GIROLAMO ━━━━━━

Italian physician, mathematician, popularizer of science, and author of more than 200 books who made two important contributions to the development of cryptology. He was born in Pavia on 24 September 1501 and died in Rome on 21 September 1576. An illegitimate son of a famous lawyer-mathematician, Cardano grew up to become, according to Isaac Asimov, "a thoroughgoing knave and rascal, a gambler, cheat, given to murderous rage, insufferably conceited and yet, withal, a first-class mathematician." Cardano was the first person to write a clinical description of the disease now known as typhus fever. He also developed a primitive concept of evolution, wrote the first book on the mathematics of chance, proposed the concept of the water cycle, described the importance of negative and imaginary numbers, and obtained from Niccolo Tartaglia his method for solving cubic equations, which Cardano published despite his promise not to do so.

Cardano's first important contribution to cryptology was the development of the concept of an autokey, a key that changes each time a new message is enciphered. Cardano chose to use the plaintext itself as the key, and began the key over each time a new plaintext word appeared. For example, in the message WAIT UNTIL DAWN, the key is the plaintext itself, and the encipherment of the message would be as follows:

```
key:        w a i t w a i t u w a i t
plaintext:  W A I T U N T I L D A W N
ciphertext: s a q m u n b b f z a e g
```

As proposed, Cardano's autokey resulted in cryptograms too easily solved by a cryptanalyst and too difficult for solution by a decipherer, conditions that led to the general dismissal of his system.

Cardano's second contribution was a steganographic device, the grille, which became more useful and more permanent than the autokey. A grille is constructed by cutting out rectangular pieces from sheets of stiff paper in patterns. A plaintext message (such as the one in Figure 6) is then written so that only certain words show through the openings in the grille. Thus, if the paper laid on top of the message, the hidden message would appear, as in Figure 7.

Perhaps the most serious drawback of the grille is the awkward phrasing that may develop in writing the cover message. In the example above, a skilled cryptanalyst might wonder about the prediction that passage of the river would not be possible for "nine or ten days" rather than "about a week," or some other more normal sounding phrase. Despite this defect, grille-like devices were widely used for cryptography even as late as World War II.

Dear Andres: I hear you have been able to gather a number of recruits for the army. I am delighted that you have been so hard at work, but it may have been for nought. The river has flooded its banks at Marne and it will be nine or ten days before anyone can cross again. I'll call tonight to suggest other plans. Sincerely, Eugene.

Figure 6

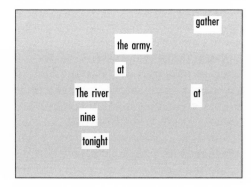

Figure 7

See also: autokey; grille; steganography.
For further reading: Myrtle Marguerite Cass, *The First Book of Jerome Cardano De Subtilitate*, Williamsport, PA: Bayard Press, 1934; Charles J. Mendelsohn, "Cardano on Cryptography," *Scripta Mathematica* (October 1939): 157–168; Oystein Ore, *Cardano—The Gambling Scholar*, Princeton, NJ: Princeton University Press, 1953; Peter Way, *Codes and Ciphers*, n.p.: Crescent Books, 1977, pp. 21–23.

CARD GAMES

Forms of recreation in which two or more players exchange signals about the cards they hold. Dishonest players have probably been around as long as card games have been played. Such players have developed an almost unlimited number and variety of techniques for letting their partners know the status of the hand they hold. In some cases, cards are actually marked on their backs so that a player can see what his or her partner is holding. In other cases, players may use words, phrases, or body signals to indicate the cards in their hands. Tugging on the right ear, for example, might indicate (although with not much imagination) that a player holds the ace of spades.

CARTIER, FRANÇOIS

Head of the French military cryptographic bureau during World War I. During this period, the quality of cryptographic and cryptanalytic skills varied greatly from nation to nation. France was generally conceded to have the finest of such bureaus, and Cartier's work was largely responsible for bringing the army's cryptologic ability to that level.

Early in the war, Cartier and his colleagues managed to break the ÜBCHI key used to encipher most of the German High Command's military communications. Gossip from frontline soldiers about this accomplishment prevented the French from making full use of it because the Germans soon overheard the French congratulating themselves on breaking the key and switched to another cryptosystem.

By the end of the war, Cartier became chief of the Bureau du Chiffre of the French army. He directed what David Kahn called "the first echeloned organization in the history of cryptology."

See also: Bureau du Chiffre; ÜBCHI.
For further reading: David Kahn, *The Code-breakers: The Story of Secret Writing*, New York: Macmillan, 1967, ch. 10.

CENTER FOR CRYPTOLOGIC HISTORY

An agency created in 1989 by order of William O. Studeman, then director of the National Security Agency (NSA). The center took over a number of already existing functions dealing with the history of American cryptology. Its current activities include research and publication projects focusing on the evolution of the cryptologic profession and the NSA; collection and storage of historical documents, photographs, slides, files, and other print and visual records; an oral history program; a videohistory project on the history of the NSA; the National Cryptologic Museum; *Cryptologic Quarterly*, a classified professional journal distributed among cryptologic professionals; a fellowship and intern program for NSA employees and members of the military; and an internal Cryptologic History Committee and a Cryptologic History Working Group.

The center is located at Fort George G. Meade, Maryland. The National Cryptologic Museum is open to the general public, but other center functions may be restricted to qualified researchers and users.

See also: National Cryptologic Museum.

CENTRAL INTELLIGENCE AGENCY (CIA)

The U.S. agency charged with collecting, evaluating, and disseminating information on political, military, economic, scientific, and other developments around the world with relevance to national security. The CIA was established in 1947 as an arm of the National Security Council (NSC) with the following specific responsibilities:

1. Advising the NSC on intelligence matters relating to national security
2. Making recommendations to the NSC regarding the coordination of intelligence gathering and evaluation activities within the federal government
3. Correlating and evaluating intelligence and providing for its appropriate dissemination
4. Performing any and all other activities determined by the NSC to be needed for the maintenance of national security
5. Performing any and all other activities dealing with intelligence as directed by the NSC.

The CIA has always operated as one of the most secretive organizations within the federal government. The statute by which it was established grants the agency the right to withhold the publication or other disclosure of "organization, functions, names, official titles, salaries, or numbers of personnel employed." The CIA is also one of the few federal agencies that is not required to make reports to the U.S. Congress.

Although the cryptologic role of the CIA is not well known, evidence shows that the agency carries out at least some cryptanalytic research of its own, as well as collecting and evaluating the results of such research in other departments and agencies.

See also: National Security Agency/Central Security Service.
For further reading: Harold C. Relyea, *Evolution and Organization of Intelligence Activities in the United States*, Laguna Hills, CA: Aegean Park Press, n.d., pp. 253–265; *United States Government Manual* (current ed.), "Central Intelligence Agency."

CERTIFICATION AUTHORITY (CA)

A trusted intermediary entity for public-key cryptographic systems. A certification authority maintains two types of public keys, its own and those of subscribing members. The public keys are maintained in some central storage location by the CA, or kept by individual nodes in a network and transmitted to the CA as needed.

A certification authority operates as follows. Alice wishes to send a message to Bob. Alice contacts the CA, indicating that she wishes to send a message to Bob and directing the CA to send Bob a copy of her public key. The CA sends a certificate to Bob providing Alice's name and her public key. The CA also sends Bob a copy of its own public key so that he can verify the legitimacy of the CA communication. Alice and Bob can then communicate with each other by established public-key cryptographic methods, with Bob confident that he is, in fact, communicating with the real Alice and not some impostor.

See also: Key Distribution Center; trusted intermediary.
For further reading: Charlie Kaufman, Radia Perlman, and Mike Speciner, *Network Security: Private Communication in a Public World*, Englewood Cliffs, NJ: Prentice-Hall, 1995, pp. 190–193; U.S. Congress, Office of Technology Assessment, *Information Security and Privacy in Network Environments*, OTA-TCT-606, Washington, DC: GPO, September 1994, pp. 53–56, passim.

CHAINING

A process by which individual characters or blocks of characters are treated together for the purposes of encipherment, decipherment, or authentication. The important feature of chaining is that it makes cryptanalysis of ciphertext more difficult by preventing a cryptanalyst from attacking individual units of which the ciphertext is made.

See also: cipher block chaining.

CHALLENGE-AND-RESPONSE PROTOCOL

A system of authentication by which one party in an electronic transaction is able to determine that the second party is legitimately identifying himself or herself. For example, a person may request information from a central data processing machine about some financial transaction. The machine must have some means of asking (challenging) the person to determine his or her true identity. One way to do this would be for the machine to transmit some random number to the person, asking him or her to perform a mathematical operation on that number using a key known only to the machine and to legitimate users of the system. The person then sends back his or her response, enciphered using the (supposedly) correct key. The machine can then check the enciphered response to see that it reflects the proper key.

See also: authentication; random number.
For further reading: Albrecht Beutelspacher, *Cryptology: An Introduction to the Art and Science of Enciphering, Encrypting, Concealing, Hiding and Safeguarding Described without Any Arcane Skullduggery but Not without Cunning Waggery for the Delectation and Instruction of the General Public,* Washington, DC: Mathematical Association of America, 1994, ch. 4; Warwick Ford, *Computer Communications Security,* Englewood Cliffs, NJ: Prentice-Hall, 1994; Jeffrey I. Schiller, "Secure Distributed Computing," *Scientific American* (November 1994): 72–76; U.S. Congress, Office of Technology Assessment, *Information Security and Privacy in Network Environments,* OTA-TCT-606, Washington, DC: GPO, September 1994, p. 32.

CHAMBER ANALYSIS

A primitive form of cryptanalysis in which a single person labors essentially alone to decrypt a single message. The technique is characteristic of the black chamber period of cryptology when one intercepted message, or a small number of such messages, was given to the "court cryptanalyst" or some other person skilled in decrypting messages.

Historian David Kahn uses the term *chamber analysis* to distinguish an early approach to decrypting messages from a more complex and sophisticated system that developed during World War I, particularly as cryptograms became more difficult to solve. In such cases, a relatively large volume of traffic was often necessary to give cryptographers the clues they needed to break enemy ciphers.

See also: cryptanalysis.
For further reading: David Kahn, *The Codebreakers: The Story of Secret Writing,* New York: Macmillan, 1967, pp. 348–349.

CHAMPOLLION, JEAN-FRANÇOIS

The French scholar (1790–1832) largely responsible for the translation of the Rosetta stone and the meaning of ancient Egyptian hieroglyphics it made possible.

See also: Rosetta stone.

CHARACTER SET

Any collection of symbols that have a generally-agreed-on meaning. For example, all the letters that make up an alphabet constitute a character set. So does the combination of letters, numbers, and control characters used in the operation of a typewriter, calculator, or computer. Character sets are said to be ordered if they are arranged in some meaningful sequence. An alphabet, for example, is not only a collection of symbols, it is arranged in sequence from *a* to *z* (in the English language).

See also: alphabet; control character.
For further reading: Brian Beckett, *Introduction to Cryptology,* Oxford: Blackwell Scientific Publications, 1988, ch. 1.

CHASE, PLINY EARLE

A graduate of Harvard University at the age of 19 and later professor of philosophy and logic at Haverford College in Pennsylvania. Chase (1820–1886) secured a place in cryptologic history with his discovery of fractionating ciphers. The discovery was announced in a short article published in the March 1859 edition of *Mathematical Monthly*.

The idea of representing letters by various combinations of numbers in a cipher was not new, of course. The Polybius square is one of the earliest and best known of such systems. Using a Polybius square, the word GO, for example, might be enciphered by the row and column numbers corresponding to each letter, *g* and *o*. Thus, if the letter *g* were in the third row and fourth column, and the letter *o* were in the first row and second column, GO would be enciphered as 34 12.

A common feature of all such systems prior to Chase's time, however, was that the numbers into which a message were enciphered were regarded simply as symbols. That is, 3, 4, 1, and 2 had no more *mathematical* meaning or function in the ciphertext 34 12 than did the letters *g* and *o*.

Chase suggested that the numbers in a ciphertext could be manipulated mathematically just like any other kinds of numbers. He proposed a system consisting of 30 letters from the English and Greek alphabets and other typographic symbols, as shown below.

	1	2	3	4	5	6	7	8	9	0
1	j	l	α	f	k	s	d	b	z	c
2	x	v	n	m	Θ	p	q	u	r	&
3	Ξ	o	e	i	y	Ψ	w	t	g	h

Suppose that the word to be enciphered is CAUTION. The first step in using Chase's cryptosystem is to represent each of the letters in the word by a pair of numbers taken from the table above, as shown below.

```
C A U T I O N
1 1 2 3 3 3 2
0 3 8 8 4 2 3
```

Notice that the first row under the plaintext word is taken from the row in which the letter occurs (C is in the first row), and the second row under the plaintext letter is taken from the column in which it occurs (C is in the 0 column).

Chase's method thus far contains nothing new in cryptology. In the next step, however, Chase suggests multiplying the bottom row above by the number 9:

$$
\begin{array}{r}
0\ 3\ 8\ 8\ 4\ 2\ 3 \\
\times\ 9 \\
\hline
3\ 4\ 9\ 5\ 8\ 0\ 7
\end{array}
$$

This process changes the number set beneath CAUTION to a new arrangement, namely:

```
C A U T I O N
1 1 2 3 3 3 2
3 4 9 5 8 0 7
```

The final step in Chase's method is to go back to the original checkerboard and find the letter equivalent for each of the new number pairs (13, 14, 29, 35, 38, 30, and 27). These are: a f r y t h q, which becomes the ciphertext for the plaintext word CAUTION.

Unfortunately, little interest was taken in Chase's cryptosystem. As a result, codes and ciphers used in the United States in succeeding generations were less secure than had the Chase system been adopted.

> See also: fractionating cipher; Polybius.
> For further reading: Brian Beckett, *Introduction to Cryptology*, Oxford: Blackwell Scientific Publications, 1988, pp. 56–57; *Quaker Biographies*, ser. 2, Philadelphia: Society of Friends, 1922.

CHAUCER, GEOFFREY

Famous English author who demonstrated in his writings that he had some familiarity with cryptography. In one of his books, *The Equatorie of the Planetis*, Chaucer (1340?–1400) includes six passages in ciphertext explaining how to use the equatorie, an early astronomical instrument. He uses symbols such as ^ and α to represent letters of the alphabet.

CHECKERBOARD

Any cryptosystem in which plaintext letters are laid out in a checkerboard-like arrangement. Because the English language contains 26 letters, the most common checkerboard is one with five squares in each direction, providing space for 25 letters. The twenty-sixth letter is accommodated by combining two letters that are unlikely to be confused with each other, such as *i* and *j*. The distinction between the two letters can almost invariably be made from the context of the message sent and received.

Probably the earliest form of the checkerboard cipher is the Polybius square, in which 25 letters are laid out in five rows of five columns each. Each row and each column are numbered so that each letter can be enciphered by a single two-digit number.

See also: bifid; Polybius.

CHECKSUM

Also known as check digits; a system for detecting errors that have occurred in data. The simple inputting of data by human operators inevitably results in errors. The most common are the transposition of two adjacent digits (e.g., inputting the number 78342 when the original number is 78432) and the replacement of one digit by another (e.g., inputting the number 000100 when the original number is 001100).

Computer programs typically include an additional digit that is not a data digit but a checksum calculated from the existing data digits. A variety of mathematical programs are available for calculating checksums, depending on the type and characteristics of data being inputted.

See also: error-correcting code.
For further reading: Henry Beker and Fred Piper, *Cipher Systems: The Protection of Communications*, New York: John Wiley & Sons, 1982, p. 323; D. W. Davies and W. L. Price, *Security for Computer Networks: An Introduction to Data Security in Teleprocessing and Electronic Funds Transfer*, Chichester: John Wiley & Sons, 1984, pp. 121–123; Charlie Kaufman, Radia Perlman, and Mike Speciner, *Network Security: Private Communication in a Public World*, Englewood Cliffs, NJ: Prentice-Hall, 1995, *see* index; William Stallings, *Network and Internetwork Security: Principles and Practices*, Englewood Cliffs, NJ: Prentice-Hall, 1995, ch. 4; Peter Wayner, "True Data," *Byte* (September 1991): 122–124+.

CHI SQUARE (χ^2) TEST

A statistical test invented to compare two or more cases or events with one another. The table below shows how the chi square test can be used. The data in the table come from a study on a new type of medication. One group of individuals (the drug group) has actually been given the medication. The second group (the control group) has been given a placebo (a capsule of starch that looks like the drug, for example). The numbers in the table show the number of individuals whose health improved or did not improve during the study.

	Cases who improved	Cases who did not improve	Total
Drug group	38	15	53
Control group	22	35	57
Totals	60	50	110

Now, if the two groups are really not different from each other in any way, then the fraction of people who improved during the research (60 ÷ 110 = 55 percent) would be expected to be the same for both drug and control groups. Of course, the percentage who improved might differ slightly between the two groups, but it should be very nearly 55 percent for both groups.

If the percentage of the drug group who actually improved is calculated, however, it is a quite different number: 38 out of 53, or 72 percent (38 ÷ 53). And the same is true for the number who improved in the control group: 22 of 57, or 39 percent.

The chi square test is a mathematical formula allowing the calculation of whether the observed percentages (72 and 39 percent) are *really* different from the percentage calculated by assuming no differences (55 percent). The actual calculation of chi square is a bit complicated because it depends on the number of variables being tested. The important point, however, is that the test gives a good indication as to whether those variables are related to one another purely by chance or whether an important difference exists among them.

The most obvious application of the chi square test in cryptanalysis is in matching the letter frequencies in a cryptogram with those in the ordinary English alphabet (or the alphabet of any other language). The results of the test provide some indication as to the kind of cipher being used. If the letter frequencies in the cryptogram are the same as those in the English language, the cipher may very well be a transposition cipher in which all of the letters of the plaintext are present, but in different sequences.

For further reading: Priscilla E. Greenwood and Mikhail S. Nikulin, *A Guide to Chi-Squared Testing*, New York: John Wiley & Sons, 1996; Lawrence C. Hamilton, *Modern Data Analysis: A First Course in Applied Statistics*, Pacific Grove, CA: Brooks/Cole, 1990, ch. 12.

CHOSEN PLAINTEXT ATTACK ▬▬▬

See attack.

CIFAX ▬▬▬▬▬▬▬▬▬▬▬▬▬

Any technique for altering a visual image by modifying the electrical signal into which that image is converted. As with written and spoken language, it may sometimes be necessary to encrypt a visual image, such as a photograph. In general, encryption of visual images can be accomplished in two ways. First, the image itself can be modified, as happens when a person looks into a curved mirror in the fun house of an amusement park. Second, the image can be converted into an electrical or electronic signal, which is then altered in some fashion. The

latter technique has been given the name *cifax* to reflect the en*ci*pherment of visual *facs*imiles.

One of the earliest cifax systems was devised by the French engineer Édouard Belin (1876–1963), who also invented the wirephoto process by which photographs are transmitted through telephone wires. In the Belin process, a photograph is placed on a rotating drum, above which is located a photoelectric cell. Light shining on the photograph is reflected to the cell, which converts light energy into electrical impulses. The type of impulses produced depends on the relative lightness and darkness on the photograph.

These impulses are sent into a telephone line as an electric current of varying frequency and amplitude. At the receiver end, the Belin process is reversed. Electrical impulses are converted to short bursts of light whose intensity corresponds to the amplitude of the electrical current. The original photograph reproduced on a rotating drum at the receiver's end is thus an exact match of the one at the sender's end.

Belin discovered during his research that the transmission of a photograph is unsuccessful unless the two rotating drums—at sending and receiving ends of the circuit—move at exactly the same speed. If the two drums rotate at different speeds, the receiver obtains only a smudged version of the original photograph.

But this discovery also revealed a method by which the original photograph could be enciphered. If the sender instructs the receiver that an image is being transmitted in such a way that the receiving drum must be set at a particular speed, the receiver can set his or her drum to that speed and receive a clear picture. But anyone who does not know the predetermined match of drum speeds (the "key" to this method of encipherment) will receive nothing but a smudged image.

The encryption of visual images was largely of academic interest until the last half century. Few people would have gone to the trouble to intercept a news photograph sent from one newspaper to another by means of the wirephoto machine, but with the development of television, the situation changed. When commercial stations began to send visual images through the air, it became desirable and profitable for individuals or "bandit stations" to intercept those images for their own viewing at no cost. As a result, television stations began to use scrambling techniques that made their visual images uninterpretable by viewers unless the viewers had a decoding system. For example, a station might split a transmission band on which its visual images are carried into two, three, or more smaller bands and then send the bands out in some scrambled form. Unless a viewer purchased or rented a decoder box, which restored the smaller bands to their proper position, he or she would receive only a scrambled image, or "snow" on a television receiver.

See also: ciphony; fiber optics.
For further reading: David Kahn, *The Codebreakers: The Story of Secret Writing*, New York: Macmillan, 1967, pp. 828–836; William Sheets, "TV Signal Descrambling," *Radio-Electronics* 1-9 (June 1986–July 1987): various pages.

CIPHER

A method of concealing the meaning of a word, phrase, sentence, or longer message in which the basic unit of concealment is the letter. In comparison, a code is a form of concealment in which the basic unit is the word. The term *cipher* refers to a message that has been encrypted by changing the sequence of letters in the plaintext (transposition) or by substituting a symbol (such as a number or some other letter) for the letters that make up the plaintext.

As an example, suppose that two people have agreed on a method of encipherment in which the letters of a message are simply reversed. The message ADVANCE TO HILL FIVE, then, becomes evif llih ot ecnavda or, as it would be more commonly written in groups of five letters, evifl lihot ecnav dazij, where the last three letters (zij) are added to fill out the final group of five. In this example, the final message produced is known as the cipher or, more commonly, the ciphertext. The system by which the plaintext is altered to produce the cipher is known as the algorithm. In many cases, some word, number, or other function is used to explain how an algorithm is to be used. Such functions are known as keys.

See also: algorithm; cipher alphabet; cipher letter; key; substitution; transposition.

CIPHER ALPHABET

The combination of letters, numbers, and/or other figures used to encipher a plaintext message.

CIPHER BLOCK CHAINING (CBC)

A form of block encipherment in which each block of ciphertext is dependent not only on the plaintext block and the key block but also on preceding blocks of ciphertext. For example, suppose that a key block is used to encipher plaintext block A to produce ciphertext block a. In the next step of the chaining process, plaintext block B is enciphered with the key block *and* with the ciphertext block just produced to form ciphertext block b. The third step is similar, involving the use of the key block, plaintext block C, and ciphertext block b to produce ciphertext block c.

This method of block encipherment can be compared with straightforward block encryption (electronic codebook) because every block of encrypted text in block chaining depends not just on the key and plaintext blocks for that segment of the message (as in ECB) but on all other ciphertext that precedes it. The problem encountered with ECB—repeated phrases in plaintext generating similar phrases in ciphertext—is not encountered with chaining.

See also: block encryption; cipher feedback; Data Encryption Standard; modes of operation.

For further reading: Henry Beker and Fred Piper, *Cipher Systems: The Protection of Communications,* New York: John Wiley & Sons, 1982, p. 288; D. W. Davies and W. L. Price, *Security for Computer Networks: An Introduction to Data Security in Teleprocessing and Electronic Funds Transfer,* Chichester: John Wiley & Sons, 1984, ch. 4; Charlie Kaufman, Radia Perlman, and Mike Speciner, *Network Security: Private Communication in a Public World,* Englewood Cliffs, NJ: Prentice-Hall, 1995, ch. 3; Carl H. Meyer and Stephen M. Matyas, *Cryptography: A New Dimension in Computer Data Security,* New York: John Wiley & Sons, 1982, pp. 62–85.

While many variations exist, this Confederate cipher disk shows the typical design.

CIPHER BUREAU
See MI8.

CIPHER DISK
A mechanical device for enciphering plaintext consisting of at least two circular pieces of metal, wood, or other rigid material pivoted at the center so that they can be turned independently of each other. The earliest such device was probably that of Leon Alberti. Further refinements made the device more versatile, but did not alter the basic concept.

One of the disks on the cipher disk always contains the plaintext alphabet, arranged either as a standard or mixed alphabet. At least one of the other disks contains the enciphering alphabet, such as another standard or mixed alphabet or a numerical alphabet. In order to encipher a message, the cipher-disk operator locates the first letter of the message on the plaintext disk, then writes down the corresponding cipher letter found on the enciphering disk. The operator next locates the second letter of the message on the plaintext disk and writes down the corresponding cipher letter found on the enciphering disk, and so on. In some cases, the two disks contain arms, like the hands on a clock, that are attached to each other through gears that move as the operator goes from one letter of plaintext to another.

One variation of the cipher disk is the "cylindrical cryptograph" originally designed by both Thomas Jefferson and Étienne Bazeries.

See also: Alberti, Leon Battista; Bazeries, Étienne; Jefferson, Thomas; Myer, Albert; Porta, Giovanni.

CIPHER FEEDBACK (CFB)
The use of ciphertext produced in one stage of an encipherment to produce ciphertext of later plaintext. Suppose that a plaintext message of 256 bits is subdivided into four cipher blocks of 64 bits each. Each block is then enciphered, one at a time, using a key block. Call the ciphertext blocks produced in this way A, B, C, and D.

In cipher feedback, ciphertext block A is produced by applying the key block to the first plaintext block. But ciphertext block B is obtained by combining the second plaintext block *and* the key block *and* ciphertext block B. Similarly, ciphertext block C is obtained from a combination of the key block plus the third plaintext block plus ciphertext block B.

Cipher feedback is a useful encryption technique because it tends to eliminate repetitive patterns in straightforward block encryption that could otherwise serve as clues to cryptanalysts.

See also: block encryption; cipher block chaining; Data Encryption Standard; modes of operation; output feedback mode.

For further reading: Henry Beker and Fred Piper, *Cipher Systems: The Protection of Communications,* New York: John Wiley & Sons, 1982, p. 287; D. W. Davies and W. L. Price, *Security for Computer Networks: An Introduction to Data Security in Teleprocessing and Electronic Funds Transfer,* Chichester: John Wiley & Sons, 1984, ch. 4; Charlie Kaufman, Radia Perlman, and Mike Speciner, *Network Security: Private Communication in a Public World,* Englewood Cliffs, NJ: Prentice-Hall, 1995, pp. 87–88; Carl H. Meyer and Stephen M. Matyas, *Cryptography: A New Dimension in Computer Data Security,* New York: John Wiley & Sons, 1982, pp. 91–98.

CIPHER LETTER

Any one of the letters, numbers, and/or other symbols that make up a cipher alphabet.

CIPHER MACHINE

Any mechanical device by which a message can be enciphered. In its broadest and most general sense, the cipher machine can be traced back more than 500 years to the cipher disk invented by Leon Battista Alberti. Alberti's cipher disk consisted simply of two concentric disks of different diameters, attached at their centers. One disk carried a standard alphabet and a few numbers, while the other disk carried a scrambled alphabet. Encipherment was accomplished by manually rotating the disks and writing down the cipher letter corresponding to each plaintext letter in the original message.

Generally speaking, the term *cipher machine* is reserved for devices that operate mechanically or electrically without the manual assistance (except for input) of humans. An example of such a device is the rotor, invented by Edward Hebern in the late nineteenth century. A rotor is a flat disk shaped somewhat like a hockey puck with two electrical contacts and internal electrical wiring. One of the electrical contacts represents a plaintext letter, and the other a ciphertext letter. When an electrical current enters the rotor at the plaintext letter contact, it travels through the internal wiring of the rotor and leaves through the ciphertext letter contact. The encryption of the letter from plaintext to ciphertext is thus made automatically.

Probably the most famous cipher machine was the German Enigma machine invented by Arthur Scherbius in about 1918. The Enigma consisted of a series of rotors plus a plugboard that reflected electrical currents internally within the machine. In its most advanced form, the Enigma was capable of more than 11 million different settings, creating a decryption nightmare for even the most proficient of cryptanalysts. The solution of the Enigma's wiring system, with the access to German codes that that solution made possible, is one of the great adventure stories in the history of cryptology.

See also: Alberti, Leon Battista; cipher disk; Enigma; Hebern, Edward H.; rotor; Scherbius, Arthur; ULTRA.

For further reading: Henry Beker and Fred Piper, *Cipher Systems: The Protection of Communications,* New York: John Wiley & Sons, 1982, ch. 2; D. W. Davies and W. L. Price, *Security for Computer Networks: An Introduction to Data Security in Teleprocessing and Electronic Funds Transfer,* Chichester: John Wiley & Sons, 1984, pp. 28–35; Peter Way, *Codes and Ciphers,* n.p.: Crescent Books, 1977, pp. 68–76.

CIPHERTEXT

A message intended to be secret obtained by applying some system of encipherment to a plaintext message. By applying simple transposition with a reversal of letter to the message S E L L, the ciphertext obtained would read L L E S.

CIPHERTEXT-ONLY ATTACK

See attack.

CIPHONY ━━━━━━━━━━━

Any method of scrambling oral speech. The term describes techniques that have been developed to make oral transmissions secret in much the same way encipherment makes written communications secret. The word itself reflects this intent, deriving from *cipher*, describing the intent to hide the message, and *telephony*, the science of telephonic communications. Just as encipherment involves the dissection of a word into its component parts (letters) and rearranging or substituting for those letters, ciphonic systems break apart speech patterns into their component elements and rearrange or substitute other sounds.

Ciphony became of interest almost as soon as long-distance oral communication between individuals was made possible. In 1881, five years after Alexander Graham Bell invented the telephone, the young American inventor James Harris Rogers proposed a method for scrambling oral communications over the new instrument. Rogers's method used the simple technique of transmitting a telephone message over two separate circuits alternately. Thus, for the first fraction of a second, the message would travel through circuit A, and for the next fraction of a second, through circuit B. The transmission would alternate so rapidly that anyone listening in on either circuit would hear only half the message. This amount of information, presumably, would be insufficient for the eavesdropper to interpret the message.

As telephones became more readily available over the next century, the need for ciphonic systems developed rapidly. In some cases, the need for secrecy in oral communications was a high government or military priority. As an example, President Franklin Roosevelt and Prime Minister Winston Churchill often found it necessary to speak with each other by trans-Atlantic telephone during World War II. They knew that enemy operatives could easily tap into their conversation and listen to their discussions; therefore, various ciphonic systems were developed to provide security for such discussions.

Ciphonic systems can be subdivided into a number of categories depending on how sounds are scrambled in a message. All such systems, however, operate on the two or three common characteristics of any spoken sound: the wavelength and/or frequency (which are reciprocally related to each other) and amplitude (loudness).

The sounds that make up human speech have frequencies in the range of 70–7,000 cps (cycles per second). Telephone equipment normally does not pick up the full range of the human voice, however, and usually consists of signals with frequencies in the range of 300–3,000 cps. The range of frequencies in either of these cases is known as the band over which the sound is expressed or detected.

One form of voice encipherment makes use of band-shifting. The term *band-shift* means that all of the sounds produced by a person speaking into a telephone are fed into a machine that increases their frequencies by some given amount. A sound with a frequency of 1,000 cps could be transformed into a 1,500-cps sound, for example. A sound with a frequency of 3,000 cps could be transformed into one with a frequency of 500 cps (3,000 cps + 500 cps = 3,500 cps, which is out of the range of the telephone and therefore shifted to the bottom of the scale). The result of band-shifting is that normal human words are transformed into unintelligible sounds.

The disadvantage of band-shifting, as with many of the primitive forms of voice scrambling, is that the enciphered sounds can be rather easily deciphered. All an eavesdropper need do is determine the method of scrambling and then, in the case of band-shifting, develop a device to reverse the shift.

Another primitive type of voice scrambler is the inverter. An inverter is a machine that reverses the frequency of a sound. For example, a letter spoken with a frequency of 400 cps is fed into a machine that "tips its frequency upside down," that is, gives it a high frequency rather than a low frequency. The 400-cps tone may exit the machine with a new frequency of 2,900 cps. (It was 100 cps above the lowest point of the telephone range to begin with, and is converted to a tone 100 cps below the highest point of the range.)

The inverter is an effective voice scrambler because each tone is changed by a relatively different amount. The 400-cps tone, for example, exits the scrambler with a new frequency 2,500 cps greater than its original value. However, a tone of 1,600 cps (1,300 cps above the lowest value in the range) will be converted to one with a frequency of 1,700 cps (1,300 cps below the highest value of the range). Any spoken message submitted to this type of scrambling is virtually impossible to understand.

As with band-shifting, however, inversion is a relatively simple process to detect electronically. Once an eavesdropper has discovered the system being used (inversion), the scrambled message can be fed into an unscrambling device that will reverse the original encipherment technique and decipher the message.

Another method of voice scrambling is band-splitting. In this system, the usual range of frequencies (300–3,000 cps for telephonic communication) is split or subdivided into some number of smaller ranges. The telephone range could be subdivided into one band consisting of frequencies from 300–1,200 cps, a second band with frequencies from 1,200–2,100 cps, and a third band with frequencies from 2,100–3,000 cps.

The scrambling process takes all the tones with frequencies within one of these three bands and substitutes frequencies from one of the other bands. The pattern might be, for example:

Band 1 replaces Band 3
Band 2 replaces Band 1
Band 3 replaces Band 2

Any message scrambled by this system will make virtually no sense at all to someone listening in on the transmission. On the other hand, all a legitimate receiver needs to know to unscramble the message is the pattern originally used in enciphering the message. By analogy, the oral message can be scrambled and unscrambled easily enough if both sender and receiver agree on the key to the scrambling process.

Yet another technique for scrambling oral communication is by altering the amplitude (loudness) of sounds that make up the message. Suppose that the first one-tenth second of a message is transmitted very quietly, the second one-tenth second very loudly, the third one-tenth at moderate volume, and so on. To an eavesdropper, the variations in amplitude would be so distracting as to make the actual words being spoken unintelligible. Again, the receiver need only know how volume changes are inserted into the original message in order to remove them and listen to the message in its original form.

The above systems illustrate the general principles of ciphony, but they are no longer widely used. Although the sounds produced are virtually unrecognizable to an eavesdropper simply by listening to them, they can be analyzed rather easily by electronic systems.

The options available to voice scramblers are nearly as limitless as to encipherers of the written word. For example, a spoken sentence might be thought of as a continuous sound wave that begins with the first word and ends with the last word. The frequency and amplitude of the wave is different at any given moment within the wave, depending on the sound (e.g., letter) that is being spoken.

One way to encipher such waves, then, is to break them apart horizontally. In other words, a machine breaks into the wave at each fraction of a second determined by the scrambler: once every tenth, hundredth, thousandth, or other fraction of a second. The wave that was originally continuous is now converted into a series of individual tones, each with its distinctive frequency and amplitude. An analogy would be a sentence, which can be broken into individual letters, numbers, and punctuation marks.

Just as any set of letters, numbers, and punctuation marks can be manipulated however the encipherer wants, the individual tones that make up the sound wave can be rearranged or substituted. The tone in position 1 can be moved to position 1,000, the tone in position 2 to position 500, the tone in position 3 to position 1,500, and so on. As always, the legitimate receiver can unscramble the message simply by knowing the pattern used to rearrange tones, while the eavesdropper may have no hint as to how the tones must be unscrambled to make a meaningful message. One of the systems that operates on this principle is known as time-division scramble because of the way it takes elements of an oral message and rearranges the temporal sequence in which they were spoken.

A final method for enciphering oral communications is by overlaying them with noise. Noise is usually defined as meaningless sound. If you are standing next to someone at a noisy party, you can probably carry on a reasonable conversation with that person. Indeed, everyone else in the room is also carrying on intelligible conversation with others around them.

But if you can stand back and listen to the sounds in the room as a whole, you will probably be unable to understand anything that is being said. In such a case, intelligible *sounds* have been replaced by unintelligible *noise*.

The same technique can be used to hide an oral message being transmitted by telephone. The sound wave on which the message is sent is combined with many other sound waves, each of which might have some meaning in and of itself but, when combined with all other sound waves, simply becomes noise. An eavesdropper trying to listen to the oral conversation is unlikely to be able to pick out the one sound wave that carries the message he or she is particularly interested in hearing.

For further reading: H. J. Beker, "Cryptographic Requirements for Digital Secure Speech Systems," *Electronic Engineer* 52:634 (1980): 37–46; Henry Beker and Fred Piper, *Cipher Systems: The Protection of Communications*, New York: John Wiley & Sons, 1982, ch. 9; Henry J. Beker and Fred C. Piper, *Secure Speech Communications*, London: Academic Press, 1985; Thomas Beth, ed., *Cryptography*, Lecture Notes in Computer Science Series, Berlin: Springer-Verlag, 1982, vol. 149, sec. 4; A. P. Gallois, "Communication Privacy Using Digital Techniques," *Electronics and Power* 22 (1976): 777–780; N. R. F. MacKinnon, "The Development of Speech Encipherment," *Radio and Electronic Engineer* 50:4 (1980): 147–155; Ivars Peterson, "Messages in Mathematically Scrambled Waves," *Science News* (20 July 1991): 37–38.

CIVIL WAR CRYPTOLOGY ━━━━━

Cryptosystems used by both Federal and Confederate military units during the U.S. Civil War. The war was especially important in the history of cryptology because it was the first major conflict to take place after the invention of the telegraph. For the first time, encrypted messages could be sent to large numbers of individuals over great distances. The possibilities offered by the telegraph became a critical impetus in the growth of both cryptography and cryptanalysis.

That having been said, it is probably true that cryptology had relatively little effect on the war's outcome. Neither side had yet developed the skills necessary to make the transmission or interception of encrypted messages of any great consequence.

On the Federal side, the most important type of cipher appears to have been the route transposition cipher, into which code was also inserted. For example, the encipherer might first replace certain words in the message by their code equivalents and then encipher the encoded message by route transposition. Even if a decrypter could discover the route used, the presence of codewords still made the message relatively secure. Federal officers also used monoalphabetic

Wooden signal towers, such as the Confederate tower pictured here, were often used to transmit cryptograms during the Civil War.

and polyalphabetic substitution ciphers, but not very effectively.

As weak as the Federal cryptographic systems were, they tended to be more than adequate in baffling the inexpert Confederates. It is said that the Rebels even published captured Federal ciphers in Southern newspapers in an effort to obtain their decipherment.

Confederate cryptographers tended to prefer the Vigenère square for their encipherments, yet they did so without much understanding of the cryptosystem's potential value. For example, they appear to have used only three different keys in the messages they sent (or at least of those

known). In addition, they apparently never (with one exception) enciphered a complete message, but mixed ciphertext with plaintext in the same transmission. This practice obviously made it much easier for their Federal counterparts to decrypt the messages.

A variety of other cryptosystems was employed during the war. Major Albert Myer developed a variety of signaling systems using torches and flags, as well as a cipher disk for enciphering messages. A sergeant in the Signal Corps, Edwin H. Hawley, invented a set of 26 wooden tablets, each containing its own cipher alphabet for a single plaintext letter, for use in polyalphabetic substitution ciphers. Hawley's invention was later granted the first U.S. patent for a cipher device.

See also: Morse code; Myer, Albert; route transposition; Stager, Anson; telegraph; Vigenère square.

For further reading: Wayne G. Barker, ed., *The History of Codes and Ciphers in the United States Prior to World War I*, Laguna Hills, CA: Aegean Park Press, 1978, ch. 3, 4; David Homer Bates, *Lincoln in the Telegraph Office*, New York: Century Co., 1907; David Kahn, *The Codebreakers: The Story of Secret Writing*, New York: Macmillan, 1967, ch. 7; William R. Plum, *The Military Telegraph during the Civil War in the United States*, Chicago: Jansen, McClurg, 1882; Paul J. Scheips, ed., *Military Signal Communications*, 2 vols., New York: Arno Press, 1980; Philip Van Doren Stern, *Secret Missions of the Civil War*, New York: Crown, 1959.

CLASS NP PROBLEM

See class P problem.

CLASS P PROBLEM

A set of problems that can be solved in polynomial time. That is, a class P problem can be given to a computer and an answer obtained from the machine within some given and reasonable period of time. As a simple example, once could ask the computer to find the product of 342,489,148,987 and 498,018,889,901,558. Or the computer could be directed to find the value of 8^{12} mod 261. Either of these problems might take the computer a certain amount of time to calculate, but it would eventually be able to find the answer. The "certain amount of time" needed to obtain an answer must meet the criterion that the computer would not have to run for many years or decades to do so.

Class NP problems, in contrast, are those that can be solved by a non-deterministic computer (that is, one that does not yet exist). The technique used to solve NP problems is searching. For example, a cryptosystem might exist in which the key can be found by searching systematically through 2^{60} possible options. The best possible computer can solve this problem by a trial-and-error approach if it works for about 366,000 years. Any cryptosystem with this characteristic would be considered *intractable*, or unbreakable, since it would take so long to find the correct option that it would be fruitless for a person to attack the system.

One of the most interesting and important questions in cryptologic theory today is whether there are NP problems that are *not* P problems. The question arises from the fact that any class P problem is obviously a class NP problem also. In the above example, if the cryptosystem in question contained 2^{40} options rather than 2^{60} options, the result would be quite different. A computer would require only about 13 days to search through all possible options, making the system a member of class P problems.

So far, no one has been able to prove whether P = NP or NP > P. The proof is of considerable importance because it would indicate, in the latter case, that some systems can be developed that are resistant to decryption given any reasonable time limit for the solution.

See also: algorithm; birthday paradox.

For further reading: Henry Beker and Fred Piper, *Cipher Systems: The Protection of Communications*, New York: John Wiley & Sons, 1982, pp. 224–225; "Cryptography," in *McGraw-Hill Encyclopedia of Science & Technology*, 7th ed., New York: McGraw-Hill, 1987, vol. 3, pp. 565–566; *Dictionary of Computing*, New York: Oxford University Press, 1983, p. 270; M. R. Garey and D. S. Johnson, *Computers and Intractability: A Guide to the Theory of NP-Completeness*, San Francisco: W. H. Freeman, 1979; Dominic Welsh, *Codes and Cryptography*, Oxford: Clarendon Press, 1988, pp. 140–148.

CLEAR

See cleartext.

CLEARTEXT

A message sent without encipherment. For example, a general might relay the message ATTACK AT DAWN in exactly that form to troops at the front, with no effort to mask its meaning from the enemy. Interestingly enough, messages are often sent "in clear" if there is any question that the enciphered message might be garbled or misunderstood by those who send it or for whom it is intended. The principle is that it may be more important to be sure that the message gets through than to be concerned about an enemy intercepting and reading the message.

CLIPPER CHIP

The computer microchip containing the Skipjack algorithm that implements the Escrowed Encryption Standard for telephonic communications.

> See also: Capstone chip; Escrowed Encryption Standard; FORTEZZA card.
> For further reading: *The Administration's Clipper Chip Key Escrow Encryption Program,* Hearing before the Subcommittee on Technology and the Law of the Senate Committee on the Judiciary, 103rd Congress, Second Session, 3 May 1994; Lee Dembart, "Hide and Peek: Clipper Chip Proposal," *Reason* (November 1993): 40–45; Dorothy E. Denning, "The Clipper Encryption System," *American Scientist* (July/August 1993): 319–323; Charlie Kaufman, Radia Perlman, and Mike Speciner, *Network Security: Private Communication in a Public World,* Englewood Cliffs, NJ: Prentice-Hall, 1995, pp. 465–469; http://www.epic.org/crypto/; http://cpsr.org/cpsr/privacy/crypto/clipper/clipper-faq.txt; http://cpsr.org/cpsr/privacy/crypto/clipperlatt_clipper_info_fax.txt.

CLOCK CODE

A system used by pilots during World War I to tell gunners where they should aim their weapons. The term *code* is not used here in its usual sense in that pilots were not attempting to hide or disguise information from anyone. Rather, it was a system by which information could be transferred from one part of a battlefield to another quickly and efficiently.

The clock code consisted of two parts, one providing the direction in which guns should be aimed and the second describing the distance from some given point. Imagine a series of concentric circles drawn around some central point. The distance between circles is taken to be some convenient number, such as 50 yards. The first circle, then, has a radius of 50 yards, the second a radius of 100 yards, the third a radius of 150 yards, and so on.

The orientation of the circles is taken by indicating the "top" of the circles (for example, a true north direction) as the 12 o'clock position. The "bottom" of the circles (or the true south direction) was then indicated as the 6 o'clock position. Other orientations around the circles could then be compared to the hours on the clock.

To specify a particular location, a pilot simply indicated the chosen circle (say, A for the innermost, B for the next circle outward, C for the next, and so forth) and the direction to be aimed. A transmission directing fire at the B9 position would mean that guns should be aimed in a due westward position (9 o'clock) within the 50- to 100-yard range.

CODE

A code is a word, number, or some other symbol used to represent a word, phrase, or syllable in plaintext. For example, a couple going to a party might agree to mention the word *chocolate* when one or the other wanted to leave the party. The word *chocolate,* then, is a codeword for the phrase "let's go home now."

Codes are one of the earliest forms of cryptography, having existed, according to David Kahn, as early as the first century B.C. in Assyria and Babylonia. They became widely popular in the fourteenth century with the rise of city states in Europe. Kahn traces the first modern code to about 1326, when Vatican writers introduced single letters to stand for commonly used names, such as A for king, D for Pope, and S for Marescallus. Before long, codes were a standard part of the nomenclators developed for sending secret messages throughout Europe.

After the invention of the telegraph in 1840, codes became popular for the transmission of commercial messages. A phrase such as "Buy 100 shares of Western Union" could be shortened by the use of codewords for "Buy 100 shares" and "Western Union." The actual message transmitted by telegraph might be 368 (for "Buy 100 shares") and 23 (for "Western Union"). The purpose of such codes was not primarily secrecy but cost savings. A message that reads 368 23 is obviously less expensive to send than one that reads "Buy 100 shares of Western Union."

In general, codes can be classified as one-part or two-part codes. In a one-part code, the plaintext terms are arranged in alphabetical order with their codegroups next to them. The codegroups may or may not also be arranged in alphabetical order. One-part codes are relatively much simpler to solve than two-part codes.

A two-part code is also known as a random code because it has two sections, one for encoding and one for decoding. The encoding section contains plaintext words arranged in alphabetical sequence, while the decoding section has the codewords or codegroups arranged in alphabetical or numerical sequence.

Codes can themselves be enciphered. Just as the phrase "Fight the good fight" can be enciphered, so can a coded transformation of the phrase (such as "Battlements can be embattled"). The result of such a process is known as enciphered code or encicode.

See also: codegroup; decode; encicode; encode; one-part code; two-part code.
For further reading: William F. Friedman, *Advanced Military Cryptography*, Laguna Hills, CA: Aegean Park Press, 1976, pt. E; Friedman, *Elementary Military Cryptography*, Laguna Hills, CA: Aegean Park Press, 1976, pt. 3; Friedman, *Elements of Cryptanalysis*, Laguna Hills, CA: Aegean Park Press, 1976, pt. 2; Laurence Dwight Smith, *Cryptography: The Science of Secret Writing*, New York: W. W. Norton, 1943, ch. 5.

CODEBOOK

Any document that can be used to encode and decode messages. One form of codebook is simply a book of any kind, such as a novel or a dictionary. A dictionary is a useful type of codebook because it contains all the words that might be used in a message. To use a book as a codebook, the sender and receiver of a message must agree on some type of coding system. One of the most common is to use a series of three numbers: the first designates the page of the book; the second number, the line on that page; and the third number, the word in that line. For example, the message DESTROY THE CODE could be represented as 342-21-5 40-3-2 152-15-5 if the fifth word in the twenty-first line on page 342 of some previously-agreed-on book is DESTROY, and the second word on the third line of page 40 is THE, and the fifth word on the fifteenth line of page 152 of the book is CODE.

A form of codebook commonly used by the military consists of numerical equivalents for terms often needed in a secret message. The following example is a section of such a codebook.

barrel	=	3245
barricade	=	8194
barrier	=	2045
base	=	0018
basement	=	3101
basin	=	2111

Written in this form, the codebook can be used to encode messages. The writer of the message simply looks down the list of terms in the codebook, finds the numerical equivalent of each term, and writes it down as the encoded message. A codebook arranged as shown above is a *one-part code*, because it shows only the conversion of plaintext to code. Such a codebook is difficult for the receiver to use because it is necessary to search through the whole list of numbers in the second column in order to decode a word or phrase.

To solve this problem, the *two-part codebook* was developed. This kind of codebook contains both an encoding section, like the one above, and a decoding section, in which the numerical (or literal or symbolic) codes are listed in some kind of logical order with their plaintext equivalents printed next to them. An example of a two-part code is shown below.

```
0000  =  general
0001  =  telegram
0002  =  front
0003  =  Monday
0004  =  1 P.M.
```

Two of the most widely used codebooks of this kind during World War I were *The American Trench Code* and *Front-Line Codes.*

Yet a third type of codebook is the commercial codebook. The principle behind a commercial codebook is identical to that of the military codebook described above, with common words encoded by means of numbers. The major difference between the two is that commercial codebooks are not designed primarily for sending *secret* messages but as a way of reducing the cost of transmitting a message.

For example, if a person can use the code 4482 for the expression "sell 100 shares of the following stock immediately," he or she could save money on a telegram containing this message. Codebooks of this type are also known as *public* codebooks, since they are not designed to be used for secret messages. Indeed, it is typical for thousands of copies of any one commercial codebook to be sold, with anyone in a field having access to any given code.

The first commercial codebook was probably that of William Clausen-Thue, *The ABC Codebook,* published in 1874. Over the next few decades, dozens of specific codebooks designed for use in either specific businesses (steel, coffee, coal, stockbroking, tobacco, and wool, for example) or commercial applications were published and sold.

The level of detail attained in commercial codebooks was quite remarkable. In Peycke and Fry's *The Economy Telegraphic Cipher Code Adapted to the Use of Brokers, Dealers, and Shippers of Green and Dried Fruit and Produce,* for example, the authors list specific codewords for a startling variety of California oranges ranging from Washington navels and seedlings to St. Michaels and bloods in 59 categories including fancy; extra choice; choice; standard; orchard run; Anaheim choice and standard; Arlington fancy, choice, and standard; Azusa fancy, choice, and standard; and so on.

See also: *The ABC Code;* one-part code; two-part code.

For further reading: William F. Friedman, "The International Telecommunication Convention," *Signal Corps Bulletin* (January–February 1934); David Kahn, *The Codebreakers: The Story of Secret Writing,* New York: Macmillan, 1967, ch. 22.

CODE COMPILATION SECTION ▬▬

A division of the U.S. Army Signal Corps created shortly after the United States became involved in World War I under authority of General Orders No. 8. The section was assigned the responsibility of generating code and cipher systems for the American Expeditionary Force stationed in France, and was headquartered in Paris.

At the war's outset, the United States had essentially no code or cipher capability of any consequence. Its armed forces were, to quote one official history of the period, "completely unprepared cryptographically." Yet, a number of factors made the role of cryptography more essential than in any previous conflict. As a result, an entirely new military division, the Code Compilation Section, was created to develop the cryptosystems necessary to provide the United States with a secret message capability comparable to that of its European allies and enemies.

During the course of the war, the Code Compilation Section developed and distributed a number of different codes for a variety of applications. Somewhat remarkably, the work of this section was accomplished by only a handful of men, five Signal Corps officers and three enlisted men. Among the codes developed by the section are the following:

1. The American Trench Code: Issued in 1918 for use as far down as companies on the front lines. The code was printed on paper 4½ x 7 inches, small enough to fit in a soldier's pocket. It was a one-part code consisting of about 1,600 codegroups. It was never actually used because officials regarded it as too insecure.
2. The Front Line Code: Printed in a book slightly smaller than the American Trench Code, it contained 500 two-letter codegroups. It may never have been used for anything other than training.
3. The "River Series" of Codes: A series of codes named after rivers, designed for communication within France. The first of these was the famous "Potomac Code" issued on 24 June 1918 in an edition of 2,000 copies. It was a two-part code containing approximately 1,800 entries and printed in a 7¼ x 9¾-inch booklet. The system used a trigraphic code. Other codes in this series included the "Mohawk," "Hudson," "Suwanee," "Wabash," "Allegheny," and "Colorado."
4. The "Lake Series" of Codes: A series of codes developed in the fall of 1918 and issued to the Second Army of the AEF, thereby reserving the "River Series" for the First Army. Codes in this series included the "Champlain," "Huron," "Osage," and "Seneca." Other "River" and "Lake" codes in preparation at the time of the Armistice were the "Niagara," "Michigan," and "Rio Grande."
5. Field Codes Nos. 1, 2, and 3: Three codes compiled and printed after the Armistice and, thus, never used.
6. The Staff Code: Released in June 1918, this code was intended primarily for upper-echelon officers. It contained 30,800 codegroups and was the largest and most comprehensive of the codebooks produced by the Code Compilation Section.
7. American Radio Service Code No. 1: Issued in 1918 to all radio stations and all military units having radio capabilities. It was a two-part code consisting of about 1,000 codegroups.

See also: codebook; U.S. Army Signal Corps. For further reading: Wayne G. Barker, ed., *The History of Codes and Ciphers in the United States prior to World War I*, Laguna Hills, CA: Aegean Park Press, 1978, ch. 7.

CODE CONDENSING

See compaction.

CODEGROUP

A word, number, or other symbol used to encode a plaintext message. For example, if the plaintext word *enemy* is to be represented by the number 187 in a code, then the number 187 is the codegroup for the plaintext word *enemy*. If a word is used for encoding, it is called the codeword, and if a number is used, it is called the codenumber.

See also: code; codebook.

CODENAME

A word selected to designate an event and intended to be used only by those privy to the event. The most common use of codenames is for military operations in which one side wishes to keep its intentions secret from the other side. Codenames are used at all levels of operations, from the planning of the most comprehensive strategic operations to the most detailed and specific tactical events.

Examples of some of the codenames used in World War II are as follows:

- *Forager:* The U.S. campaign to conquer the Marianas Islands between 15 June and 10 August 1944
- *Harpoon:* A British plan to deliver supplies to Malta during the first two weeks of June 1942
- *Herbstnebel* (Autumn Mist): The last major German offensive against the Western Allies in late 1944 and early 1945 (also known as the Battle of the Bulge)
- *Iceberg:* Invasion of Okinawa by U.S. forces on 1 April 1945
- *Ichi:* The yearlong offensive from May 1944 to May 1945 by Japanese forces attempting to destroy U.S. air bases in China

See also: Manhattan Project.
For further reading: Christopher Chant, *The Encyclopedia of Codenames of World War II*, London: Routledge & Kegan Paul, 1986.

CODENUMBER
See codegroup.

CODE TALKERS
See Navajo code talkers.

CODEWORD
See codegroup.

CODON
A set of three nitrogen bases in a molecule of messenger RNA that carries instructions for the manufacture of a particular amino acid.

See also: genetic code.

COINCIDENCE
See index of coincidence.

COLONIAL CRYPTOLOGY
Ciphers and codes used by the colonists and British during the century preceding the Declaration of Independence. Given the unsettled political climate in the newly formed United States of America, it should hardly be surprising that cryptology was extensively used by both the colonists and their allies and foes prior to and during the Revolutionary War. Most of these codes and ciphers were quite simple.

Monoalphabetic substitution, one of the simplest forms of cryptography, was extensively used by revolutionary leaders. Letters to and from Benjamin Franklin, John Jay, William Lee, Robert Morris, James Lovell, John Adams, Robert Livingston, Thomas Jefferson, James Madison, Edmund Randolph, and others all make use of such cryptograms.

Dictionary codes were among the most popular forms of cryptography. A number of writers made use of the well-known John Entick's *New Spelling Dictionary*. Jefferson and Monroe apparently carried out an extensive correspondence using such a code.

One of the best-known early cipher devices was invented during the colonial period. Thomas Jefferson's cypher wheel was ahead of its time, and was reinvented at least twice more, once by Étienne Bazeries about 1870 and again by Col. Parker Hitt about 1920.

Secret ink was another form of cryptology employed by both Federals and the British during this period. Messages to Benjamin Franklin in Paris, for example, often included sections written in invisible ink, a technique by which Franklin could be kept apprised of the state of affairs at home.

See also: cipher disk; invisible writing; Jefferson, Thomas; Lovell, James; Madison, James; monoalphabetic substitution.
For further reading: Wayne G. Barker, ed., *The History of Codes and Ciphers in the United States prior to World War I*, Laguna Hills, CA: Aegean Park Press, 1978, ch. 1, 2; Edmunch Cody Burnett, "Ciphers of the Revolutionary Period," *American Historical Review* (January 1917): 329–334; David Kahn, *The Codebreakers: The Story of Secret Writing*, New York: Macmillan, 1967, pp. 174–186; Victor Hugo Paltsits, "Use of Invisible Ink

for Secret Writing during the American Revolution," *Bulletin of the New York Public Library* 39 (1935): 227–264; Howard H. Peckham, "British Secret Writing in the Revolution," *Michigan Alumnus Quarterly Review* (26 February 1938): 126–131; Morton Pennypacker, *General Washington's Spies on Long Island and in New York*, Brooklyn: Long Island Historical Society, 1939; Michael L. Peterson, "The Church Cryptogram: To Catch a Tory Spy," *American History Illustrated* (November/December 1989): 36–43; Carl Van Doren, *Secret History of the American Revolution*, New York: Viking Press, 1941; Ralph E. Weber, *United States Diplomatic Codes and Ciphers, 1775–1938*, Chicago: Precedent Publishing, 1979.

COLOR CODES

The use of color to represent some object or idea. Throughout history, people have used various colors to stand for concepts that are understood by the general public or only by certain groups. As an example, Don Cameron Allen writes about the various ways in which writers used colors symbolically during the Renaissance. Some of the connections he makes include:

> black: sorrow and mourning
> blue: truth, hope, and fidelity in love
> green: infidelity or fickleness
> yellow: jealousy
> white: innocence and virginity

This phenomenon persists in the modern world, where scarlet may be associated with a tarnished moral character in women; purple, with royalty; and gray, with gloominess.

For further reading: Don Cameron Allen, "Symbolic Color in the Literature of the English Renaissance," *Philological Quarterly* (January 1936): 81–92 (*see* Allen's extensive notes on this topic); Ellen Conroy, *The Symbolism of Colour*, London: Rider, 1921.

COLOSSUS

An electronic machine built by cryptanalysts working at Bletchley Park during World War II to solve the German Enigma cryptosystem. In many respects,

the Colossi (two machines were built) were based on general principles proposed a decade earlier by British mathematician Alan Turing, although he was not directly involved in the construction.

The motivation for building the Colossi was the Germans' addition of a new cryptographic machine, the *geheimschreiber*, to their already powerful Enigma machine. British cryptanalytic machines known as bombes had been relatively successful in solving Enigma cryptograms, but the introduction of the much faster geheimschreibers meant that the Bletchley Park staff could not keep pace with the flow of enciphered machines between the German High Command and its ships at sea.

To solve this problem, a young engineer, T. H. Flowers, suggested the construction of a machine that operated with electronic valves rather than electromechanical relay switches used in the bombes. Such a machine would operate many times faster and with far fewer glitches than a machine using mechanical switches and electrical circuits.

More traditional engineers at Bletchley Park argued that the technology of electronic switches was not developed sufficiently to permit the construction of such a machine. Nonetheless, Max Newman, director of the laboratory, ordered that an attempt be made. The post office, which was also responsible for telephone and telegraph service, was instructed to provide Flowers and his staff with whatever resources he needed and, 11 months later, the first Colossus was ready for testing.

Almost from the outset, it was clear that an enormous breakthrough in cryptanalysis and electronic machinery had been made. The first Colossus was soon solving German ciphers at the rate of a few thousand characters per second, many times faster than even the most efficient bombes.

The importance of the Colossi extends far beyond its momentous role in breaking German ciphers during the war. In using electronic circuitry to solve logical problems, it represented the first "thinking" machine, which Turing had envisioned in the 1930s. As such, it is often regarded as the first modern computer.

See also: Bletchley Park; bombe; Enigma; Geheimschreiber; Turing, Alan.

For further reading: I. J. Good, "Pioneering Work on Computers at Bletchley," in N. Metropolis, J. Howlett, and G.-C. Rota, *A History of Computing in the Twentieth Century,* New York: Academic Press, 1980; Andrew Hodges, *Alan Turing: The Enigma,* New York: Simon & Schuster, 1983, ch. 5.

COLUMNAR TRANSPOSITION

A very popular form of transposition in which the columns in a rectangle or square are taken off in a sequence determined by a mutually-agreed-on key. Suppose that a cryptographer wishes to encipher the following message: MEET OUR AGENT AT THE GARDEN GATE AT NINE PM. The first step in enciphering this message is to write it in a block form, as shown below. The dimensions of the block are determined by the key. In this case, suppose that the key is the word VICTORY. The block is then written as shown with the keyword as the first line of the block:

```
V I C T O R Y
M E E T O U R
A G E N T A T
T H E G A R D
E N G A T E A
T N I N E P M
```

The message is enciphered by selecting the columns in the block in the same sequence as the alphabetic order of the letters in the key, C I O R T V Y, to give the ciphertext:

```
eeegl eghnn otate
uarep tngan matet rtdam
```

The message can then be deciphered, if the receiver knows the keyword, by rewriting the ciphered words into columns under the proper letters of the key.

Messages ciphered by means of columnar transposition can be made more difficult for an enemy to decipher if the process is repeated a second time. This approach is known as double columnar transposition. In the example above, for instance, the enciphered message could be rewritten in block form with a second keyword, as shown below.

```
C O N Q U E S T
E E E G I E G H
N N O T A T E U
A R E P T N G A
N M A T E T R T
D A M J Z S S I
```

In this case, five nulls—J, Z, S, S, and I—are added to fill out the block.

A variation of columnar transposition is interrupted columnar transposition, in which the ciphertext produced by columnar transposition is interrupted by omitting letters or introducing blanks into the ciphertext. The specific method to be used is indicated, of course, in the key. For example, the ciphertext generated from the first block above (key = VICTORY) might be generated by reading along diagonal lines in the block but omitting letters already introduced into the ciphertext. Reading from left to right along a diagonal beginning in the upper left corner of the block and then switching to a right-to-left diagonal, for example, would produce the following ciphertext from the VICTORY plaintext.

m g e a e u t (two g's omitted) n . . . etc.

In another method, blank spaces are inserted into the block to make it more difficult for the cryptanalyst to recognize letter patterns. The 7 x 5 VICTORY block shown above could be expanded to a 7 x 6 block by adding blank spaces, whose location would be indicated in the key. Notice that this produces a ciphertext differing from that obtained from the 7 x 5 block.

```
V I C T O R Y
M E E T   O U
R   A G E N
T A T T H E
  G A R D   E
N G A T E A T
N   I N E P M
```

The ciphertext obtained from this block would be as follows:

```
e a t a a   i e a g g   e h d e e
o e a p t   g t r t n   m r t n n   u n e t m
```

Note that this ciphertext is totally different from the one obtained from the uninterrupted columnar transposition above.

See also: transposition.
For further reading: William F. Friedman, *Advanced Military Cryptography,* Laguna Hills, CA: Aegean Park Press, 1976, pt. A; Friedman, *Elementary Military Cryptography,* Laguna Hills, CA: Aegean Park Press, 1976, sec. 2; Helen Fouché Gaines, *Cryptanalysis: A Study of Ciphers and Their Solution,* New York: Dover Publications, 1956, ch. 6; Donald D. Millikin, *Elementary Cryptography and Cryptanalysis,* Laguna Hills, CA: Aegean Park Press, n.d., ch. 8, 9.

COMBAT INTELLIGENCE UNIT (CIU) ━

A secret division of the U.S. Navy whose function was to provide intelligence information to the Pacific Fleet during World War II. At the war's outbreak, CIU had a small staff of three cryptanalysts and about two dozen secretaries, clerks, and assistants. Its job at the time was to break the Japanese navy's flag officer's code. After the attack on Pearl Harbor, however, CIU received a new assignment: cryptanalysis of JN25, the code system by which Japanese ships in the Pacific communicated with one another and with command officers in Japan.

The division's staff grew rapidly with the addition of recruits showing some talent for cryptology. By May 1942, the number of cryptanalysts had doubled, with another 50 just beginning to master

the subject. Overall, a staff of 120 worked in the unit's offices in the basement of the Fourteenth Naval District's administration building in Pearl Harbor.

During the summer of 1942, CIU broke through at least three versions of the JN25 cryptosystem, providing U.S. naval forces with critical information in advance of two major battles, the Battle of Coral Sea and the Battle of Midway. In the latter case, CIU was able to discover that the Japanese intended a fake attack on the Aleutian Islands in order to draw American ships away from the central Pacific. They then planned to focus all their naval firepower on the Midway Island area and complete their conquest of the Pacific, which had begun with the attack on Pearl Harbor six months earlier. Informed of the Japanese plans, Adm. Chester W. Nimitz was able to move the body of his forces to Midway, repulse the Japanese attack, and turn the tide of battle in the Pacific for the first time.

See also: Coral Sea, Battle of; J ciphers; Midway, Battle of.
For further reading: David Kahn, *The Codebreakers: The Story of Secret Writing,* New York: Macmillan, 1967, ch. 17.

COMINT ━━━━━━

An acronym for *communication intelligence,* a term that refers to any attempt to find out the location and/or movement of individuals and/or groups, as well as any messages being transmitted among them. As an example, a given station located in the United States might be assigned the task of listening in on communications being transmitted among ships at sea, as well as between those ships and their home bases, in a certain part of the Atlantic Ocean. That task would include finding the location of the ships to be monitored, counting the number of messages sent in a given period of time to and from each ship, identifying the nationality and names of the ships transmitting and/or receiving the messages, and copying down encrypted messages and sending them on for decryption.

In many cases, the messages monitored by COMINT are written or spoken communications. However, sometimes they consist of electronic transmissions between two or more mechanical devices. Radar signals sent out by stations in one nation to detect and observe the movement of planes from another nation, for example, can be monitored by a third party just like spoken messages. Characteristic electronic signals transmitted by satellites, rockets, or other unmanned objects can also be monitored and analyzed.

See also: SIGNIT; traffic analysis.
For further reading: Mario de Arcangelis, *Electronic Warfare: From the Battle of Tsushima to the Falklands and Lebanon Conflicts*, Poole, Dorset: Blandford Press, 1985.

COMMERCIAL CODEBOOK
See codebook.

COMMUNICATION INTELLIGENCE
See COMINT.

COMMUNICATION SECURITY
See COMSEC.

COMPACTION
In general, any process by which the number of items in a set is reduced, with or without losing any meaning contained within the set. For example, some computer programs will compact (compress) text by removing trailing spaces and/or by replacing strings of characters (such as -ing, -tion, the-) with a marker such as a flag. The text can be returned to its normal size by restoring the removed characters.

A plaintext message can be enciphered by removing characters from the message at certain intervals predetermined and understood by the sender and receiver. The removed characters and compacted text can then be transmitted separately and restored by the receiver according to the rule determined in advance (the key).

As an example, suppose that a text reads as follows:

THREE·SHIPS·ARRIVE·AT·6·PM·ON·TUESDAY
(where · represents a space between words)

This message can be encrypted by removing every fourth letter, as shown below:

THR E·S IPS ARR VE· T·6 PM· N·T ESD Y

The letters removed from the text are:

E H · I A · O U A

The enciphered message can then be sent in two parts, one of which is

THRE· SIPSA RRVE· T·6PM ·N·TE SDYRZ

where two nulls (R and Z) have been added to complete the final group of five characters, and

EH·IA ·OUAB

where one null, B, has been added.

The two segments can either be sent independently in the form shown, or they can be further enciphered by some other method, such as transposition or substitution.

Compaction can be used not only to add secrecy to a message but also as an economic measure. In sending cablegrams and telegrams, for example, the fewer number of words in the message, the less expensive the cablegram or telegram. This simple fact of economics led to the development in the late nineteenth century of code condenser books. The principle behind a code condenser is that a single position in the decimal numerical system can represent only ten different values (0 to 9), whereas a single position in an alphabetical system can have any one of 26 values (*a* to *z*).

Suppose that the message PUR-CHASE 500 TONS OF HIGH QUALITY ALUMINUM ORE is to be sent. A commercial codebook might offer the following codegroups:

359831 = PURCHASE
804038 = 500 TONS OF ALUMINUM ORE
991703 = HIGH QUALITY

The coded message, then, would be: 359831 804038 991703. This message could be further encoded by turning to a condenser codebook in which certain alphabetic equivalents are given for numbers and number combinations. Most commonly, such books convert a six-digit number into a five-letter word. The final message obtained from the code condenser in this case might read eqwlb jioce parer, a less expensive message because short words are charged at a different rate from long words. An added advantage of the literal code is that because letters are less likely to be misread than numbers, the message is less subject to error.

COMPOSITE NUMBER

Any number that can be expressed as the product of two or more prime numbers. The *fundamental theorem of arithmetic* says that every positive composite number can be expressed as the product of some unique collection of prime numbers. The composite number 450, for example, can be expressed as the product of $2 \times 3^2 \times 5^2$. The relationship between prime and composite numbers plays an important role in cryptology because the mathematical operation involved in calculating composite numbers from their primes is an easy function, while the inverse process, the determination of the prime factors of a composite number (particularly a very large one), is much more difficult. This relationship is exploited in various one-way functions such as the trap-door and knapsack functions.

See also: knapsack problem; one-way function; prime number; trap-door function.

COMPRESSED ENCODING

A method for converting plaintext messages of various lengths into ciphertexts of fixed length. Compressed encoding can be used to convert messages of 256, 312, 482, and 648 bits (for example) into ciphertexts of all the same length, say 256 bits. This is useful because a cryptanalyst must examine a very large number of ciphertext samples in order to decrypt messages. In general, for a compressed encoding function that produces a ciphertext of m, the number of trials that must be made to find two matches is 2^{m-1}. In the case of an m of 64, for example, it would require 9,223,372,036,854,775,808 trials.

See also: hashing algorithm.
For further reading: Carl H. Meyer and Stephen M. Matyas, *Cryptography: A New Dimension in Computer Data Security*, New York: John Wiley & Sons, 1982, pp. 398–409.

COMPUTATIONAL COMPLEXITY

Also computational difficulty; a measure of the number of mathematical operations that must be performed to solve a given problem, such as decrypting a ciphertext. In cryptology, computational complexity is a specialized area of study within the field of mathematics known as complexity theory.

It stands to reason that some mathematical operations are more complex than others. In general, finding n^2 is simpler than finding n^3, which is simpler than finding n^{100}. However, this statement may not be strictly true, depending on the value of n. Complexity theory provides a way of comparing the mathematics of various problems such as these and indicating which are more likely to be complex.

Computational complexity is important in cryptology because it provides an indication of the strength of an enciphering algorithm. Given some situation in which $n = 100,000$, for example, it is clear that an algorithm requiring n^{100} choices is stronger than one requiring n^3

choices. Complexity theory permits calculation of the upper limits of the computational complexity involved with the use of various algorithms. It can predict that, at most, x hours will be required to obtain a solution for such algorithms. It would be even more useful to know the lower limit. If it is known, say, that an algorithm can be broken in ten years *at most*, what is the least time in which the algorithm can be broken? The answer to this question provides an even better indication of the strength of the algorithm than the maximum time required for solution. Unfortunately, mathematicians do not as yet have a way of determining such lower limits.

See also: class P problem; knapsack problem; strong algorithm.

For further reading: Brian Beckett, *Introduction to Cryptology*, Oxford: Blackwell Scientific Publications, 1988, pp. 126–130; "Cryptography," in *McGraw-Hill Encyclopedia of Science & Technology*, 7th ed., New York: McGraw-Hill, 1987, vol. 3, p. 565; D. W. Davies and W. L. Price, *Security for Computer Networks: An Introduction to Data Security in Teleprocessing and Electronic Funds Transfer*, Chichester: John Wiley & Sons, 1984, pp. 255–257; Dominic Welsh, *Codes and Cryptography*, Oxford: Clarendon Press, 1988, ch. 9.

COMPUTATIONALLY SECURE

Safe from being decrypted under any practical circumstances. Some cryptosystems are known to be subject to cryptanalysis if enough tests are made on them. For example, one might calculate that a ciphertext can be broken if 2^{128} trials are made on the text. The point is, even with the most sophisticated modern computational equipment available, such tests would take far more time than any person, machine, or agency would be willing to devote to the decrypting process. The system would therefore be computationally secure for all practical purposes.

For further reading: D. W. Davies and W. L. Price, *Security for Computer Networks: An Introduc-*

tion to Data Security in Teleprocessing and Electronic Funds Transfer, Chichester: John Wiley & Sons, 1984, pp. 41–42; Claude E. Shannon, "Communication Theory of Secrecy Systems," *Bell System Technical Journal* (October 1949): 656–715.

COMPUTER

A device capable of carrying out a sequence of operations according to a distinct and explicit set of instructions. Computers normally have the capability to accept data from an external source (input function), manipulate that data (processing function), and report the results of the manipulation (output function).

Computers have had an effect on cryptology in the last half of the twentieth century somewhat analogous to the invention of the telegraph in the 1830s. In the years following World War II, computer technology was largely restricted to the use of very large machines operated by the federal government for defense and intelligence purposes and, to a lesser extent, by a few large corporations involved in information gathering and processing. In such settings, protecting the security of computer-based information was a matter of limited interest to a small number of individuals. The cryptosystems needed to assure the security of such information were relatively simple.

The development of inexpensive personal computers and networking in the last half of the twentieth century has dramatically changed the situation. Today, personal computers are ubiquitous. They are found in homes, offices, schools, factories, and other settings everywhere in the world. Because of networking systems such as the Internet and the World Wide Web, an individual sitting in his or her own den can access information about an almost unlimited number of subjects from nearly anywhere in the world.

Protecting the security and privacy of information has necessarily become a critical issue in the modern world. Some individuals (hackers) break into computer systems just to demonstrate their

The most powerful supercomputers currently available, Cray computers, such as this one at the National Security Agency, are often used to crack the most difficult codes.

own skills or "for the fun of it." Others have more serious goals, such as interfering with financial transactions for their own benefit, or capturing corporate or government information that might compromise corporate or national security.

A rather remarkable amount of break-in activity has taken place in recent years. A study reported in May 1996, for example, found that nearly half of 400 organizations polled admitted to "electronic intrusions" or "unauthorized probes" of their computer systems on the part of disgruntled employees or competitors within the previous 12 months. The prime source for such break-ins was the Internet. A second study showed that hackers break into computers at the Pentagon more than 160,000 times each year. These break-ins represent a 65 percent success rate, or more than a quarter million attempts by unauthorized individuals. In the vast majority of cases, the military neither detects nor investigates these electronic intrusions.

As a result of these changes, cryptography has taken on a very different role in the 1990s. Most government agencies and a large number of businesses now find it necessary to encrypt information they possess and/or transmit. A drug manufacturer located in Switzerland, for example, will encrypt proprietary information about a new product before sending the information on to its New York office to prevent competitors from learning about the product. A bond seller in Tokyo will encrypt an order to a London financial office to ensure that unauthorized individuals do not find out about his (or the buyer's) financial condition. An embassy officer in New Delhi will encrypt a status report on the state of politics in the Kashmir before transmitting it to her home office in Djakarta.

The use of computers and networks to store and transfer information raises a number of difficult issues for cryptography. On the one hand, a great deal of computer information is crucial to corporate or national security, and therefore must be protected from eavesdroppers. On the other hand, both corporations and government agencies may be tempted to be overly protective of information that, especially in an open society like the United States, may not need to be secured.

Similarly, companies and the government may find it necessary or desirable to collect large quantities of data about individuals—medical records, legal information, and the like. But in open societies, individuals have a fundamental right to privacy about their own affairs. This dichotomy raises important questions as to how individual privacy can be protected in a society where so much personal information is already available to large numbers of people.

See also: Computer Security Act of 1987; Computer System Security and Privacy Advisory Board; confidentiality; Escrowed Encryption Standard; hacker; password sniffing; Privacy Act of 1974; security; spoofing.
For further reading: J. A. Cooper, *Computer and Communications Security: Strategies for the 1990s*, New York: McGraw-Hill, 1989; D. W. Davies and W. L. Price, *Security for Computer Networks: An Introduction to Data Security in Teleprocessing and Electronics Funds Transfer*, New York: John Wiley & Sons, 1984; P. Denning, ed., *Computers under Attack: Intruders, Worms, and Viruses*, Reading, MA: ACM Press, 1990; Asael Dror, "Secret Codes: Encryption," *Byte* (June 1989): 267–270; Editors of Time-Life Books, *Computer Security*, Alexandria, VA: Time-Life Books, 1986; H. Feistel, "Cryptography and Computer Privacy," *Scientific American* (May 1973): 15–23; W. Ford, *Computer Communications Security: Principles, Standard Protocols, and Techniques*, Englewood Cliffs, NJ: Prentice-Hall, 1994; Keith M. Jackson and Jan Hruska, eds., *Computer Security Reference Book*, Boca Raton, FL: CRC Press, 1992; Carl H. Meyer and Stephen M. Matyas, *Cryptography: A New Dimension in Computer Data Security*, New York: John Wiley & Sons, 1982; http://www.itd.nrl.navy.mil/ITD/5540/ieee/cipher/cipher-archive.html.

COMPUTER SECURITY ACT OF 1987 ▬

An act (Public Law 100-235) to establish a computer security program for the federal government that would protect sensitive information and provide for the development of standards and guidelines for unclassified federal computer systems. The need for such an act became obvious during the 1980s as the number of federal agencies responsible for computer security grew rapidly, concerns about computer security became more apparent, and questions developed about the control of information stored in and transmitted through computers and networks.

Another important impetus for this act was the growing feeling in the 1980s that the National Security Agency (NSA) was assuming too large a role in setting standards for computer systems in all areas of federal government, including nonmilitary as well as military. One of the specific actions that most concerned observers was a document issued in 1986 by National Security Adviser John Poindexter entitled "National Telecommunications and Information Systems Security Policy Directive No. 2." This document proposed an expansion of NSA's responsibility for controlling the security of government communications far beyond its traditional role of defense and national security. It proposed restricting access to any information that "could adversely affect other governmental interests" including information in fields such as economics, finance, technology, industry, agriculture, and law enforcement. One critic noted that Poindexter's directive was so comprehensive that "[t]here is no data that anyone would spend money on that is not covered by that definition."

To deal with such concerns, Congress passed and President Ronald Reagan signed the Computer Security Act establishing a civilian authority whose responsibility was to develop standards relating to sensitive but unclassified data. That authority was to reside in the National Bureau of Standards (NBS), now the National Institute of Standards and Technology (NIST). In its report on the bill, the House Committee on Science, Space, and Technology made very clear its intention in writing the act.

> While supporting the need for a focal point to deal with the government security problem, the Committee is concerned about the perception that the NTISSC [National Telecommunications and Information Systems Security Committee] favors military and intelligence agencies. It is also concerned about how broadly NTISSC might interpret its authority over "other sensitive national security information" [the Poindexter directive]. For this reason, H.R. 145 creates a civilian counterpart, within NBS, for setting policy with regard to unclassified information. . . .

In addition to establishing a program for protecting all sensitive unclassified data, the act provided for the development of Federal Information Processing Standards (FIPS), training personnel in the protection of secure information, creation of a Computer System Security and Privacy Advisory Board, and identification of computer systems that contain sensitive information along with the development of security plans for such systems.

Considerable controversy has arisen since passage of the Computer Security Act of 1987. One fundamental problem is that NIST has been inadequately funded to carry out its mandates fully. As a result, the NSA, which is less likely to experience funding problems, has expanded its activities to fill the vacuum left by NIST's incomplete efforts. The Office of Technology Assessment (OTA) reflected on this state of affairs in a 1994 review of security policies. OTA recommended that Congress consider setting funding for the Department of Commerce (in which NIST is located) at levels that would assure that agencies have "sufficient resources to safeguard information assets." OTA also suggested that Congress "ensure that the Department of Commerce assigns sufficient resources to the National Institute of Standards and Technology (NIST) to support its Computer Security Act responsibilities. . . ."

The complete text of the Computer Security Act of 1987 can be found in Office of Technology Assessment, *Information Security and Privacy in Network Environments,* 1994, pp. 190–196.

For further reading: U.S. Congress, House of Representatives, Committee on Government Operations, *Computer Security Act of 1987: Hearings on H.R. 145 before the Subcommittee on Legislation and National Security of the House Committee on Government Operations,* 100th Congress, First Session, 26 February 1987; U.S. Congress, House of Representatives, Committee on Government Operations, *Computer Security Act of 1987: Report To Accompany H.R. 145,* House Report 100-153, pt. II, 100th Congress, First Session, 11 June 1987; U.S. Congress, House of Representatives, Committee on Science, Space, and Technology, *Computer Security Act of 1987: Hearings on H.R. 145 before the Subcommittee on Science, Research, and Technology and the Subcommittee on Transportation, Aviation, and Materials of the House Committee on Science, Space, and Technology,* 100th Congress, First Session, 11 June 1987; U.S. Congress, Office of Technology Assessment, *Information Security and Privacy in Network Environments,* OTA-TCT-606, Washington, DC: GPO, September 1994, pp. 139–150, 164–171, 190–196; U.S. Congress, Office of Technology Assessment, *Issue Update on Information Security and Privacy in Network Environments,*

OTA-BP-ITC-147, Washington, DC: GPO, June 1995, passim; http://www.epic.org/crypto/.

COMPUTER SYSTEM SECURITY AND PRIVACY ADVISORY BOARD ▬▬

A board established by the Computer Security Act of 1987 with two primary functions. First, the board was assigned the responsibility of analyzing issues related to the security of information stored in and transmitted by way of computer systems. Second, it was to advise and report to the secretary of commerce, the director of the Office of Management and Budget, and the director of the National Security Agency on its findings with regard to the security of computer information. The board is appointed by the secretary of commerce.

See also: Computer Security Act of 1987.
For further reading: U.S. Congress, Office of Technology Assessment, *Information Security and Privacy in Network Environments*, OTA-TCT-606, Washington, DC: GPO, September 1994, pp. 176–177, 218–219.

COMSEC ▬▬▬▬▬▬▬

An acronym for *com*munications *sec*urity, the protecting of messages sent by means of public communication systems. A major purpose of ciphers and codes is to provide such security. The principle behind communications security is that most messages are transmitted along telephone lines, telegraph lines, electronic signals, or other means that can be intercepted and read by almost anyone. If such messages are intended to be read by only certain individuals, they must be enciphered or encoded to make them unintelligible to those for whom they are not intended.

COMSEC is also a government acronym for the Office of Communications Security of the National Security Agency.

See also: file security.

For further reading: David Kahn, *The Code-breakers: The Story of Secret Writing*, New York: Macmillan, 1967, pp. 709–718; Orville C. Lewis, "COMSEC in Transition," *Signal* (August 1985) (also reprinted in Marshall D. Abrams and Harold J. Podell, eds., *Tutorial Computer and Network Security*, Washington, DC: IEEE Computer Society Press, 1987); Carl H. Meyer and Stephen M. Matyas, *Cryptography: A New Dimension in Computer Data Security*, New York: John Wiley & Sons, 1982, ch. 5, 7; Lt. Gen. Charles R. Myer, "Viet Cong SIGNIT and U.S. Army COMSEC in Vietnam," *Cryptologia* (April 1989): 143–150.

CONCEALMENT CIPHER ▬▬▬▬▬

A message sent in clear by some hidden means. The term is somewhat misleading, because no enciphering actually takes place. The sender makes the assumption that the message can be transmitted in plaintext because the means by which it is carried and delivered is safe enough to prevent discovery by an enemy.

For example, one might want to send the message BUY ONE HUNDRED SHARES TODAY by composing a paragraph like the following:

"Buy that stock?" Not on your life! One would have to be foolish to make such a decision. And why? A hundred reasons can be given. What if the stock should collapse tomorrow? Shares would be worth next to nothing. Who wants to be involved in such a deal? Today, people are much wiser than that.

If the sender and receiver of this message agree that the first word in every second sentence (ignoring articles such as a, an, and the) is to be part of the secret transmission, the message becomes obvious.

See also: steganography.
For further reading: Helen Fouché Gaines, *Cryptanalysis: A Study of Ciphers and Their Solution*, New York: Dover Publications, 1956, ch. 2.

CONDENSING, CODE ▬▬▬▬▬

See compaction.

CONFIDENTIALITY

The disclosure of information only to individuals and entities for whom it is meant. Confidentiality is an important issue in modern society in general and cryptology in particular. At one time, information given to a personal physician could reasonably be expected to be retained in that physician's private office. With the widespread use of computer data banks and the ease with which information is transferred from one computer to another, that assumption is no longer valid. An individual's personal health records may very well be sent to computers in a local hospital, a health insurance company, one or more government agencies, and other locations. As a consequence, many experts recommend a greatly improved system by which confidential records, either personal or corporate, can be protected from unauthorized snooping. An obvious mechanism for obtaining confidentiality is to encipher the information in a format that cannot be read by the general public or by eavesdroppers.

See also: authentication; digital signature; eavesdropper; security.

For further reading: U.S. Congress, Office of Technology Assessment, *Information Security and Privacy in Network Environments,* OTA-TCT-606, Washington, DC: GPO, September 1994, pp. 3–5, 35–39, 82–83.

CONTACT CHART

A device used by cryptanalysts to recognize cipher letters in a text by comparing other letters with which they occur. An example of a contact chart is shown in Figure 8. The numbers in the first column show the frequency with which the given cipher letter appears in the text. The letters in the second column are the cipher letters. The letters across the top of the chart are the other cipher letters in the text. The hash marks in the table indicate the number of times each combination appears. Thus, the combination ZW occurs seven times, as indicated by the

		W	B	F	Y	X	Q	J
41	Z	ЖII		II		II		III
32	R		II		I	II	III	
28	W	II	III	Ж		I	II	III
25	E		II	II	I	IIII	I	
22	C	II		III	II	I	ЖI	II
20	X	III	I	I	III	II	II	I
19	P	I	III	II	Ж	II	I	III

Figure 8

seven hash marks. (The chart shown here is incomplete, showing only seven letters in each direction.

The value of the contact chart is that it helps the cryptanalyst recognize certain two-letter combinations, or digraphs. In the above chart, the digraph ZW occurs more frequently than any other, and therefore has a high probability of corresponding to *th* or *er*, the two most common digraphs in English. Since the letter Z has already been identified tentatively as *e* because of its high frequency, ZW is likely to correspond to *er*, making the cipher letter W equivalent to plaintext letter *r*.

See also: bigram; frequency distribution.

For further reading: Fred B. Wrixon, *Codes and Ciphers,* New York: Prentice-Hall, 1992, pp. 41–42.

CONTENT ANALYSIS

An attack on ciphertext by examining various characteristics of the text itself. Two common and simple approaches used in content analysis are determination of letter frequencies and the search for probable words. Content analysis is the most fundamental aspect of cryptanalysis.

Additional information useful in decryption is often available from sources other than the ciphertext itself.

For example, the cryptanalyst might be able to make use of the fact that the message being studied was sent by Mr. A to Miss B from point C to point D during a particular time period. The use of information gathered from sources other than the ciphertext itself is known as *context analysis.*

See also: frequency distribution; probable word; side information; traffic analysis.

CONTEXT ANALYSIS

See content analysis.

CONTROL CHARACTER

A symbol in a character set that causes a machine to perform a function, such as to shift from upper- to lowercase, or vice versa. Codes and ciphers sent by mechanical, electrical, or electronic means so that a message is printed or otherwise reproduced must include encryption for control characters in the message.

See also: character set.
For further reading: Carl H. Meyer and Stephen M. Matyas, *Cryptography: A New Dimension in Computer Data Security,* New York: John Wiley & Sons, 1982, pp. 204–206.

CORAL SEA, BATTLE OF

An important engagement between U.S. and Japanese ships in the Pacific Ocean northeast of Australia. American naval commanders received advance notice of Japanese plans to attack Port Moresby, New Guinea, as a means of establishing a launching site for an eventual attack on Australia. They were able to send two aircraft carriers, the *Lexington* and the *Yorktown,* to engage the Japanese fleet led by the carrier *Shokaku.* The battle itself was something of a standoff; the Americans

The USS *Lexington* explodes as the Battle of Coral Sea rages. The skill of U.S. intelligence in cracking the Japanese fleet's secret codes concerning a planned attack on Port Moresby, New Guinea, gave U.S. Admiral Nimitz the upper hand in positioning his forces, leading to a strategic victory for the Allies.

lost the *Lexington,* and the Japanese the light carrier *Shoho.* For the United States, the most important element of the engagement was the thwarting of Japanese plans to take Port Moresby. The battle is also of historical interest because it was the first naval engagement to be conducted entirely with aircraft. The surface vessels of the two navies never made visual contact with one another.

See also: Combat Intelligence Unit.
For further reading: David Kahn, *The Codebreakers: The Story of Secret Writing,* New York: Macmillan, 1967, ch. 17.

CRACK
To **decrypt** a code or cipher.

CRACKER
See hacker.

CRIMINAL CODES
See argot.

CRYPTANALYSIS
The art and science of deciphering a message by someone for whom it is not intended. The word was originally suggested by William Friedman in 1920. Terms such as cryptanalysis, decryption, deciphering, and decoding are sometimes used synonymously with one another, but each term has a unique meaning. For example, decryption normally refers to the process by which a person for whom a message *is* intended extracts the plaintext from the ciphertext or codetext of the message. In contrast, cryptanalysis involves a similar action by someone for whom the message is *not* intended. Cryptanalysis obviously requires a great deal more skill than does decryption; in the latter case, the person has the key that allows decryption of the message, while in the former, the cryptanalyst must work out the key as well as the algorithm by which the message was enciphered.

See also: attack; cryptology.
For further reading: Brian Beckett, *Introduction to Cryptology,* Oxford: Blackwell Scientific Publications, 1988, ch. 3; Carl H. Meyer and Stephen M. Matyas, *Cryptography: A New Dimension in Computer Data Security,* New York: John Wiley & Sons, 1982, pp. 21–23; Abraham Sinkov, *Elementary Cryptanalysis: A Mathematical Approach,* New York: Random House, 1968.

CRYPTANALYST
A person who practices cryptanalysis.

CRYPTOEIDOGRAPHY
A term suggested by David Kahn to describe any method of disguising the appearance of a visual image. In general, two methods are available: altering the physical image itself, or altering the electrical pattern produced when the image is converted into some type of electrical signal. Probably the most common example of the former technique is the use of fiber optics to encrypt a visual image. The various methods used to garble electrical signals are classified under the rubric of cifax.

See also: cifax; fiber optics.

CRYPTOGRAM
A secret message.

See also: ciphertext.

THE CRYPTOGRAM
Journal of the American Cryptogram Association.

See also: American Cryptogram Association.

CRYPTOGRAPHER
A person who practices cryptography.

CRYPTOGRAPHY

From the Greek κρυπτς, for "hidden," and γραφια, for "writing"; the art and science of secret writing. More precisely, cryptography is the practice of enciphering or encoding a message so that it can be read by someone for whom it is intended, but not by anyone for whom it is not intended. An even more exact definition is that cryptography is the process of providing secure communications over insecure channels. This definition emphasizes the fact that people often have to transmit secret messages to one another (secure communications) by means of communication systems like telephone and telegraph lines to which many people have access.

Messages can be enciphered by either of two general methods: substitution or transposition. Substitution is the process by which individual letters in a message are replaced by other letters, numbers, or symbols. If a single plaintext letter is replaced by one and only one ciphertext letter, the process is known as monoalphabetic substitution. If more than one letter, number, or symbol is used to substitute for a single plaintext letter, the process is known as polyalphabetic substitution.

Transposition may take many forms, including the rearrangement of letters within a word or message, or the rearrangement of words themselves.

Some general rules for cryptography have been summarized by Donald D. Millikin in his book *Elementary Cryptography and Cryptanalysis*. In abbreviated form, they are:

1. Study carefully, understand thoroughly, and adhere strictly to the instructions in each codebook or supplied with each cipher.
2. Exercise care to prevent the loss or compromise of a codebook or a cipher key. . . .
3. Messages to be sent in code or cipher should be as short as possible. . . .
4. Never repeat a message in a code or a cipher other than the one in which it was originally transmitted. . . .
5. Never send in code or cipher a message that has been transmitted previously in clear.
6. Never send in clear a message previously sent in code or cipher.
7. Never mix clear text and secret text. . . .
8. To avoid errors, capital letters should be used in writing cryptograms. . . .
9. In cryptographing and decryptographing all work must be checked by another person for accuracy. . . .

See also: cryptology; monoalphabetic substitution; polyalphabetic substitution; transposition.

For further reading: Henry Beker and Fred Piper, *Cipher Systems: The Protection of Communications*, New York: John Wiley & Sons, 1982, ch. 1; D. W. Davies and W. L. Price, *Security for Computer Networks: An Introduction to Data Security in Teleprocessing and Electronic Funds Transfer*, Chichester: John Wiley & Sons, 1984, ch. 2; D. Denning, *Cryptography and Data Security*, Reading, MA: Addison-Wesley, 1983; Carl H. Meyer and Stephen M. Matyas, *Cryptography: A New Dimension in Computer Data Security*, New York: John Wiley & Sons, 1982, ch. 7; Jennifer Seberry and Joseph Pieprzyk, *Cryptography: An Introduction to Computer Security*, Englewood Cliffs, NJ: Prentice-Hall, 1989; U.S. Congress, Office of Technology Assessment, *Information Security and Privacy in Network Environments*, OTA-TCT-606, Washington, DC: GPO, September 1994, pp. 112–128, 174–183; *see also* items listed in the general bibliography.

CRYPTOLOGIA

A quarterly journal of cryptology published by the Rose-Hulman Institute of Technology in Terre Haute, Indiana. The journal was established in 1977 and deals with a wide variety of cryptologic topics, including computer security, history, codes and ciphers, mathematics, military science, espionage, cipher devices, literature, and ancient languages. Journal articles range from the simple and mundane to the difficult and esoteric. Annual subscriptions are $40 and are available from *Cryptologia*, Department of Mathematical Sciences, United States Military Academy, West Point, NY 10996-9902.

CRYPTOLOGY

From the Greek κρυπτς, for "hidden," and λογοσ, for "word" or "reason." The meaning of the term *cryptology* itself has a long and checkered history. It was long used by most writers as a synonym for *cryptography*. Only in the last half century has its modern definition—those arts and skills associated with both cryptography and cryptanalysis—become widely adopted.

The association of cryptography and cryptanalysis within the general rubric of cryptology reflects a reality about the relationship of encipherment and decryption. That is, the purpose of cryptography is to write messages that can be read only by those for whom they are intended. The purpose of cryptanalysis is to intercept and translate messages by someone for whom they are *not* intended.

Development in either of these two fields obviously reflects development in the other. As methods of cryptography improve, the need for better methods of cryptanalysis grows. Conversely, as cryptanalysts become more adept at breaking into messages, cryptographers must look for better ways to encipher them.

The origins of cryptology go back to the earliest written human records, although not in the form that we associate with the subject today. Early scribes apparently altered words not to hide meanings, but for religious, scholarly, mystical, or other reasons. David Kahn credits Muslim scholars in the seventh century A.D. as being the first true cryptologists, that is, the first people to formulate specific rules of cryptography and cryptanalysis.

The flowering of cryptology in Western society can be traced to the seventeenth and eighteenth centuries, when political intrigue among states required the distribution of secret messages, along with the concomitant need for interception and decryption of those messages. This period was marked by the development of the black chambers in Europe, small groups of scholars whose job it was to encipher, decipher, and decrypt messages. The most popular form of cryptography used at the time was the nomenclator, a combination of code and cipher that largely fell into disuse by the end of the eighteenth century.

One of the most dramatic turning points in the history of cryptology can be traced to the invention of the telegraph by Samuel F. B. Morse in the 1830s. The telegraph made it possible to send messages over long distances to a large number of individuals. Methods for protecting the content of these messages from those for whom they were not intended became a matter of considerable interest. As a result, cryptography and cryptanalysis flourished during the U.S. Civil War, the first major armed conflict to take place after Morse's invention.

Another critical event in the history of cryptology was the growing realization of the importance of mathematics in enciphering messages. Some of the most significant early work in this field was that of Lester S. Hill in the late 1920s. Although Hill's ideas were important, the potential of mathematical cryptology was not fully appreciated until the invention of sophisticated cipher machines and the development of information theory in the 1950s.

Cipher machines also have a long history. Some of the earliest mechanical devices for enciphering and deciphering messages can be traced to the inventions of Leon Battista Alberti in the early fifteenth century. Not until cryptologists found ways to use electromechanical and then electronic systems for the design of cipher machines in the twentieth century, however, did such devices begin to have a significant impact on cryptography and cryptanalysis. Today, with the wide availability of the modern computer, any type of cryptology that does *not* make use of a sophisticated cipher machine is nothing more than an amateur amusement.

Perhaps the greatest revolution in the history of cryptology has taken place within the past few decades: the invention of public-key cryptography. Until the 1970s, the general assumption behind cryptography was that one individual could transmit an enciphered message to a second individual provided that both had secret information known only to themselves, the "key" as to how the message was enciphered.

In the 1970s, a number of mathematicians proposed a new type of cryptography, one in which at least part of the key was public knowledge. This form of encipherment became known as public-key cryptography.

The basis for public-key cryptography is that large volumes of correspondence must now be distributed to large numbers of individuals over vast networks that are essentially open to anyone who wants to listen in. In such cases, traditional forms of cryptography are hopelessly inadequate, and new techniques, such as public-key cryptography, are needed to protect the privacy of messages.

The widespread use of electronic systems to carry out many kinds of transactions has also affected the nature of modern cryptology. For example, many purchases can now be made without the direct involvement of two humans or the use of physical evidence such as checks, credit card slips, or cash. In these cases, many forms of authentication may be necessary, including evidence as to the identities of the individuals involved in the transaction, accuracy of the transaction itself, and confirmation of its having been conducted.

See also: Alberti, Leon Battista; authentication; biblical cryptology; black chamber; cipher machine; Civil War cryptology; colonial cryptology; computer; decipher; decrypt; encipher; Enigma; Hill, Lester; information theory; key; Morse code; Muslim cryptology; network; nomenclator; privacy; public-key cryptography; telegraph.

For further reading: David Kahn, "Modern Cryptology," *Scientific American* (July 1966): 38–46; A. Lempel, "Cryptology in Transition," *ACM Computing Surveys* 11:4 (1979): 285–303; G. J. Simmons, "Cryptology: The Mathematics of Secure Communications," *Math Intelligencer* 1:4 (1979): 233–246. *See also* general references in the bibliography.

CRYPTOPHONY

A term describing any method for disguising the message contained in a spoken message (*crypto-* = "hidden" + *-phony* = "sound").

See also: ciphony.

CRYPTOSYSTEM

Any set of procedures by which plaintext is converted to ciphertext. The Baconian and Caesarean codes are examples of simple cryptosystems. Cryptosystems can be subdivided into two general categories: those for which the underlying procedures for enciphering and deciphering are intended to remain secret, and those for which these procedures are made generally available. The former are known as restricted-use cryptosystems and the latter as general-use cryptosystems.

Throughout much of history, most cryptosystems were of the first type. Cryptographers did *not* want anyone other than a potential recipient to know the cryptosystem being used. In recent years, general-use cryptosystems have become more widely employed. In these systems, no attempt is made to keep secret the general rules for enciphering and deciphering, but the key employed is available only to a select number of individuals and only for a short period of time.

See also: public-key cryptography.

CRYPTOTYPER

See Damm, Arvid.

CYCLOMETER

A mechanical device built to solve the construction of the Enigma machine and the ciphers it produced. The device was first constructed by the Polish radio manufacturing company Wytwornia Radiotechniczna AVA (AVA Radio Manufacturing) at the request of Polish cryptanalysts in 1936. It consisted of two rotors, similar to those used in the Enigma machine, linked to each other. For a period of two years, the cyclometer was marginally useful in helping the Poles better understand the Enigma machine and crack at least some of its keys. By 1938, however, Polish cryptanalyst Marian Rejewski had devised a better device for working on the Enigma, a device later given the name *bombe*.

> See also: Bletchley Park; bombe; Enigma; ULTRA.
> For further reading: M. K. Dziewanowski, "Polish Intelligence during World War II: The Case of Barbarossa," *East European Quarterly* (September 1994): 381–391; Marian Rejewski, "How Polish Mathematicians Deciphered the Enigma," *Annals of the History of Computing* 3 (1981): 213–234.

CYPHERPUNKS

An informal group of men and women interested in computers who are battling against government attempts to monitor electronic communications, particularly with regard to the use of President Clinton's Escrowed Encryption Standard (EES). EES is a system of encryption in which users are required to deposit a copy of their private key with an escrow agent to which the federal government has access. The government therefore has the capability to listen in on any communications carried out using that key. The purpose of this arrangement is to allow the government to monitor communications that are potentially illegal, dangerous, or harmful, such as those between terrorist groups or drug sellers.

Cypherpunks argue that EES gives the government too much latitude to listen in on communications among innocent private citizens. Users of electronic networks have no way of knowing whether their correspondence is being monitored, they say, which is a frightening interference with privacy. They argue that the EES system will result in the United States becoming a "cyberspace police state," in which anyone's and everyone's private communications can be monitored. Even if the EES allows the government to keep track of dangerous individuals and organizations, they say, that does not give the government the right to eavesdrop on private citizens who have been accused of no crime.

Cypherpunks were originally mobilized in early 1994 when President Bill Clinton announced approval of the Clipper chip technology on which EES is based. In response, a civil liberties group called Computer Professionals for Social Responsibility was able to produce 47,000 electronic messages objecting to the president's announcement. "The war is upon us," said Tim May, cofounder of the Cypherpunks. "Clinton and Gore folks have shown themselves to be enthusiastic supporters of Big Brother."

Cypherpunks are likely to be a part of the cryptologic landscape for some time to come. The issues raised by EES are fundamental to the nature of enciphered public communications, and are not likely to be resolved within the foreseeable future.

> See also: Clipper chip; Escrowed Encryption Standard.
> For further reading: Dan Lehrer, "Clipper Chips and Cypherpunks," *The Nation* (10 October 1994): 376–380; Steven Levy, "Battle of the Clipper Chip," *New York Times Magazine* (12 June 1994): 44–51+.

D

D-1

One in a series of codes (along with A-1, B-1, and C-1) used by the U.S. State Department during the 1930s. The codes were not particularly secure and were largely replaced in the late 1930s by the M-138 strip cipher.

DAMM, ARVID

A Swedish textile engineer, entrepreneur, amateur cryptologist, and inventor. Damm is famous, according to David Kahn, because he founded a cipher machine company that went on to become "the only commercially successful one in the world."

Damm was a prolific inventor. He designed controls for his office lights that could be operated from his desk, and armrests and footrests on his chairs that could be adjusted with the touch of a button. In 1919, he invented a cipher machine that included a primitive form of the rotor. The machine itself was apparently so poorly designed that it was never built. Nonetheless, Damm continued to explore various designs for cipher machines.

In 1921, Damm and Olof Glydén founded a company called Aktiebolaget Cryptograph (Cryptograph, Inc.) with the purpose of marketing Damm's cipher machines. One of the first devices produced was the Mecano-Cryptographer Model A 1, also called the Cryptotyper. This machine appears to have found no market, although a later model, the Electro-Crypto Model B 1, was modestly successful. One copy of the B 1 was purchased by the Swedish government for use in the main office of its telegraph bureau, and orders were received for demonstration models from a number of other wireless companies.

Aktiebolaget Cryptograph's real success, however, came not with the B 1 or any of Damm's other inventions, but with a device created by B. C. W. Hagelin, son of one of the company's investors. Hagelin found ways to modify one of the Damm machines to make it operate effectively and efficiently, and offered it to the Swedish army. The army was sufficiently impressed to place a large order for the machine, named the B-21. At the moment that Aktiebolaget Cryptograph was about to achieve financial success, however, Damm died. The company was taken over by Hagelin's relatives and business partners, and reorganized as Aktiebolaget Cryptoteknik. A decade later, the company achieved the breakthrough that had always eluded Damm, selling 5,000 cipher machines to the French government and making Hagelin a millionaire.

See also: cipher machine; Hagelin, Boris Caesar Wilhelm; rotor.
For further reading: David Kahn, *The Codebreakers: The Story of Secret Writing*, New York: Macmillan, 1967, pp. 422–425; C. G. McKayy, "From the Archives: Arvid Damn Makes an Offer," *Cryptologia* (July 1994): 243–249.

DANTE ALIGHIERI ━━━━━

Italian poet (1265–1321) whose most famous work may be the *Divina Commedia* (Divine Comedy). In 1921, American writer and critic Walter Arensberg published a book, *The Cryptography of Dante*, in which he claimed to have discovered nearly 500 examples of cryptographic allusions in the *Divine Comedy*. He divides these into nine types of cryptograms: acrostics, anagrams, cabalas, interior sequence ciphers, letter sequence ciphers, puns, string ciphers, plays on separate letters, and telestics.

As just one example, Arensberg points to lines 25 through 63 of the twelfth canto of the *Purgatorio*. Every third line of this passage begins with the letters V V V V O O O O M M M M. Arensberg argues that this "strikingly symmetrical arrangement" of the first letters of the lines could be, but almost certainly is not, accidental. Instead, he suggests that the letters represent an acrostic for the Italian word for "man": *uom* (*v* being equivalent to *u* in Latin and medieval Italian). Further, Arensberg argues that the acrostic provides a critical clue to an unidentified figure in the poem, a person Arensberg believes may be Dante himself.

See also: acrostic; anagram; cabala.
For further reading: Walter Arensberg, *The Cryptography of Dante*, New York: Alfred A. Knopf, 1921.

DATA ENCRYPTION ALGORITHM (DEA)
See Data Encryption Standard.

DATA ENCRYPTION STANDARD (DES)
A method for providing security for unclassified computer files maintained by the U.S. government. DES was created as a result of Public Law 89-306 and Executive Order 11717, in which the secretary of commerce was authorized to establish uniform standards for automatic data processing. The original solicitation for such a method was published in the *Federal Register* on 15 May 1973 and 27 August 1974. An algorithm meeting the specified requirements was developed by the International Business Machines Corporation (IBM) and published for comment in the *Federal Register* of 17 March 1975. It was originally expected that DES would be useful for a period of up to 15 years. Although it was decertified for use with classified documents within the federal government by the National Security Agency in 1988, it continues to have a number of important applications.

The formal announcement of the Data Encryption Standard was published in Federal Information Processing Standards Publication 46 on 15 January 1977, which is included as an appendix to this book.

The details of the DES algorithm are rather complex, although the general outline of the system is relatively easy to understand. The main steps are as follows.

1. The original data to be enciphered are divided into cipher blocks of 64 bits each in size.
2. The 64 bits in each block are subjected to an initial permutation according to a pattern specified by the algorithm. For example, the bit originally located in position 58 is moved to position 1; the bit originally in position 50 is moved to position 2; the bit originally in position 42 is moved to position 3; and so on. The reason for this step is not entirely clear since the permutation step does not add to the security of the DES algorithm.
3. The DES algorithm generates a group of 16 different keys, each 48 bits in size, from a single key block of 64 bits. Of the 64 bits in the block, 56 are used to generate the keys and the other 8 are used as checks. The first step in this process is to do a permutation on the 56 generating bits in the initial key block, somewhat similar to the process described in step 2 above.
4. The initial 64-bit data block is split into two 32-bit blocks, which can be called L_0 and R_0. The R_0 block is then

subjected to an operation known as the mangler function. The mangler function combines the 32-bit R_0 block with the first 48-bit key, K_0, to produce a new data block (which we will call the F_0 block) consisting of 32 bits. The new F_0 block is then combined with the L_0 block to form the right-hand block of the next round of the algorithm, R_1.

5. At the same time, the original 32-bit R_0 block also becomes the new 32-bit L_1 block of the next round.

6. Steps 4 and 5 constitute the first iteration of the DES algorithm. These steps are repeated 15 times before a final 64-bit ciphertext block is obtained.

7. In order to decipher a text enciphered by DES, the above sequence of steps is simply reversed through the 16 iterations.

The development and use of DES have been deeply embroiled in a host of economic and political issues. One fundamental question is the extent to which DES technology should be sold outside the United States. For the most part, the federal government has placed strict restrictions on such sales, arguing that the availability of DES technology would provide foreign military forces and terrorists with access to secret U.S. information. The vast majority of American businesspeople respond that such information will find its way overseas in any case, and private U.S. companies are at a severe disadvantage in not being able to provide DES-based technology to international buyers.

An interesting piece of data in this dispute was provided in a 1994 report by the Software Publishers Association, which found that 170 software products (98 made in the United States and 72 made overseas) and 237 hardware products (152 made in the U.S. and 85 in foreign countries) made use of the DES algorithm.

See also: algorithm; cipher block chaining; Escrowed Encryption Standard; export controls; iteration.

For further reading: Wayne G. Barker, *Introduction to the Analysis of the Data Encryption Standard (DES)*, Laguna Hills, CA: Aegean Park Press, n.d.; Brian Beckett, *Introduction to Cryptology*, Oxford: Blackwell Scientific Publications, 1988, ch. 16; Eli Biham and Adi Shamir, *Differential Cryptanalysis of the Data Encryption Standard*, New York: Springer-Verlag, 1993; Don Coppersmith, "The Data Encryption Standard (DES) and Its Strength against Attacks," *IBM Journal of Research and Development* (May 1994): 243–250; D. W. Davies and W. L. Price, *Security for Computer Networks: An Introduction to Data Security in Teleprocessing and Electronic Funds Transfer*, Chichester: John Wiley & Sons, 1984, ch. 3; A. K. Dewdney, "On Making and Breaking Codes (II)," *Scientific American* (November 1988): 142–145; M. E. Hellman, "DES Will Be Totally Insecure within Ten Years," *IEEE Spectrum* (July 1979): 32–39; Charlie Kaufman, Radia Perlman, and Mike Speciner, *Network Security: Private Communication in a Public World*, Englewood Cliffs, NJ: Prentice-Hall, 1995, pp. 60–73; Carl H. Meyer and Stephen M. Matyas, *Cryptography: A New Dimension in Computer Data Security*, New York: John Wiley & Sons, 1982, ch. 3; Mikael J. Simovits, *The DES—An Extensive Documentation and Evaluation*, Laguna Hills, CA: Aegean Park Press, n.d.; William Stallings, *Network and Internetwork Security: Principles and Practices*, Englewood Cliffs, NJ: Prentice-Hall, 1995, ch. 1; Mark D. Uehling, "Cracking the Code," *Popular Science* (January 1993): 71–74+; U.S. Congress, Office of Technology Assessment, *Information Security and Privacy in Network Environments*, OTA-TCT-606, Washington, DC: GPO, September 1994, pp. 118–123, 129–130, and passim; U.S. Congress, Office of Technology Assessment, *Issue Update on Information Security and Privacy in Network Environments*, OTA-BP-ITC-147, Washington, DC: GPO, June 1995, passim (*see* index).

DECIPHER

The process by which a person extracts the plaintext of a message from its enciphered form. A military officer, for example, might send instructions about a battle to a frontline officer in cipher. The frontline officer must be familiar with the enciphering system and have the key that will allow conversion of the ciphertext to its original plaintext.

See also: decrypt.

DECIPHERING ALPHABET

The cipher alphabet arranged to convert ciphertext into plaintext.

See also: alphabet.
For further reading: Donald D. Millikin, *Elementary Cryptography and Cryptanalysis*, Laguna Hills, CA: Aegean Park Press, n.d., pp. 6–7.

DECODE

The process by which a person to whom a coded message is sent retrieves the plaintext from the coded message. The terms *decipher, decode,* and *decrypt* are sometimes used synonymously, although incorrectly so. The first two terms refer to the recovery of ciphertext or coded text, respectively, by someone for whom the message *is* intended. The last term refers to the recovery of such messages by someone for whom they are *not* intended.

DECRYPT

The process by which a person for whom a message is *not* intended extracts the meaning of the enciphered message. The process of decryption is different from that of decipherment because, in the latter case, the person who receives the messages knows the system by which the message was enciphered and is able, with relative ease, to extract the plaintext from the ciphertext. A person who is *not* supposed to receive the message (the cryptanalyst) is forced to use a variety of techniques to convert the obtained ciphertext to the plaintext from which it was originally derived.

See also: decipher.

DECYPHERER

A term used in the early eighteenth century for officials of the English government who were responsible for the decryption of secret messages. Apparently the first person to hold this title was William Blencowe, grandson of John Wallis. Throughout the century, the Decypherer's responsibilities became more extensive, and he eventually became head of a Decyphering Branch of the government. The branch operated as the British equivalent of the black chambers that were so predominant in European politics at the time. Among its other activities, the Decyphering Branch was active during the revolutionary period in the United States, reading many of the messages transmitted back and forth among the colonists and their allies. By 1812, the Decyphering Branch and the Decypherer (like other black chambers) were no longer regarded as important to the government, and their positions were abolished.

See also: black chamber.
For further reading: David Kahn, *The Codebreakers: The Story of Secret Writing*, New York: Macmillan, 1967, ch. 5; Peter Way, *Codes and Ciphers*, n.p.: Crescent Books, 1977, pp. 27–28.

DELASTELLE, FÉLIX MARIE

A functionary in the French government, Delastelle (1840–1902) wrote an important book on cryptology, *Traité Élémentaire de Cryptographie*, in which he proposed a promising form of fractionating cipher that used transposition.

See also: fractionating cipher.
For further reading: Brian Beckett, *Introduction to Cryptology*, Oxford: Blackwell Scientific Publications, 1988, pp. 50–51; William M. Bowers, "F. Delastelle—Cryptologist," *The Cryptogram* (March–April and May–June 1963): 79–82, 85, 101, 106–109.

DENNING, DOROTHY

Professor of computer science at Georgetown University and a strong supporter of the Clinton administration's Clipper chip escrowed encryption initiative. Denning (1945–) is one of a relatively small number of professional cryptologists who support the concept of key escrow as a way of allowing the federal government to monitor potentially harmful or dangerous encrypted messages.

Denning was born 12 August 1945 in Grand Rapids, Michigan. She was awarded her A.B. and A.M. degrees in mathematics from the University of Michigan in 1967 and 1969, respectively, and earned a Ph.D. in computer science at Purdue University in 1975. She served as associate professor of computer science at Purdue, senior staff scientist at SRI International, and researcher at Digital Equipment Corporation before accepting her current position at Georgetown.

Denning has held a number of important professional and advisory positions, including president of the International Association for Cryptologic Research, chair of the National Research Council Forum on Rights and Responsibilities of Participants in Networked Communities, cochair of the Association of Computing Machinery's (ACM) Conference on Computer and Communications Security, and chair of the International Cryptography Institute. She is author of the book *Cryptography and Data Security* and numerous professional papers. In 1990, she was awarded the Distinguished Lecture in Computer Science Award of the ACM.

See also: Escrowed Encryption Standard; export controls.
For further reading: http://www.cosc.georgetown.edu/~denning/.

DE RERUM VARIETATE

One of the two books in which the Italian cryptologist Girolamo Cardano laid out some of the fundamental principles of cryptography.

See also: Cardano, Girolamo.

DES

See Data Encryption Standard.

DE SUBTILITATE

A book by Girolamo Cardano in which the author outlined some of his fundamental ideas about cryptology.

See also: Cardano, Girolamo.

DIFFERENCE METHOD

A technique of cryptanalysis used when a message or series of messages is believed to consist of code enciphered by means of a numerical additive. For example, suppose that the plaintext word ARMAMENT is encoded according to some system by means of the codenumber 59147. The cryptosystem in use may then require some additive function, such as 11213, to produce the encicode 60350.

To recover the original codenumber from this encicode, obviously the decrypter must first discover the additive function used to encipher the codenumber. One approach is to collect as much encicode text as possible and look for hints or external clues that would suggest the nature of the additive function. Portions of text are then manipulated to discover the additive function and subtract (find the difference of) that function from the encicode to obtain the original codenumbers in the text.

For further reading: For a full description of the technique, *see* David Kahn, *The Codebreakers: The Story of Secret Writing,* New York: Macmillan, 1967, pp. 440–444. *See also* Wayne G. Barker, *Cryptanalysis of an Enciphered Code Problem Where an "Additive" Method of Encipherment Has Been Used,* Laguna Hills, CA: Aegean Park Press, n.d.

DIFFIE, WHITFIELD

One of the most famous names in the field of public-key cryptography. In 1977, Diffie coauthored a now-famous paper, "New Directions in Cryptography," with Martin Hellman. The paper describes a cryptosystem by which two individuals can correspond with each other secretly even though they use a public communications system.

Whitfield Diffie received his bachelor of science degree in mathematics from the Massachusetts Institute of Technology in 1965. He worked for more than a decade at Northern Telecom, where he was manager of secure systems research as well as responsible for the development of security technologies for the company. In 1991, Diffie was appointed Distinguished Engineer at Sun Microsystems in Mountain View, California, a post he still holds.

In 1996, Diffie was awarded a doctorate in Technical Sciences (Honoris Causa) by the Swiss Federal Institute of Technology in recognition of his work on public-key cryptography. He has also been awarded the IEEE Information Theory Society Best Paper Award for 1979 and the IEEE Donald E. Fink Award for 1981.

See also: public-key cryptography.

DIFFIE-HELLMAN KEY EXCHANGE

A method for generating an encryption key that can be shared between two individuals. The method was developed by Stanford University researchers Whitfield Diffie and Martin Hellman and announced in 1976.

Figure 9 illustrates the Diffie-Hellman key exchange process. One individual, designated here as Alice, creates a key-pair that consists of her own public key, which is published and available to anyone who wants to examine it, and a private key, whose identity she keeps to herself. A second individual, designated here as Bob, mirrors that process, using his own public and private keys. The two then exchange their public keys.

In the next step, both Bob and Alice generate a new kind of key, known as a *session key*, consisting of his or her own private key and the other person's public key. The session key generated by both individuals is the same, and can be used from then on to encrypt and decrypt messages to each other.

When the two have completed their communications, the session keys are destroyed. If they choose to have further communications at another time in the future, they repeat the process and generate new session keys.

Note that the process described here can be used for the generation of *keys*, but cannot be used to encrypt messages themselves.

The process described above can be expressed more concisely mathematically as follows. Alice and Bob wish to communicate secretly with each other over channels that are open to the general public. The first thing they must do is select two numbers, one being any large prime, p, and the second, any integer smaller than p. Call the second number s. (Some conditions may apply to the selection of s, but they will be ignored in this discussion.) The numbers selected, p and s, can be published publicly.

Alice and Bob each select a secret number known only to themselves. Call these secret numbers a for Alice and b for Bob. Both Alice and Bob then calculate a new number, called T_A for Alice and T_B for Bob. These numbers are calculated as follows:

$$T_A = s^a \bmod p$$
$$T_B = s^b \bmod p$$

The two correspondents then exchange their T's with each other. Alice sends T_A to Bob and receives in return his T_B.

Each person now performs another computation, raising the value of the T they have received to their own secret number, s. That is,

$$k_A = T_B^a \bmod p$$
$$k_B = T_A^b \bmod p$$

At this point, both correspondents should have found the same value for k. The reason for this identity is that

$$k_A = T_B^a \bmod p = (s^b)^a \bmod p = s^{ba} \bmod p$$
$$k_B = T_A^b \bmod p = (s^a)^b \bmod p = s^{ab} \bmod p$$

Since $s^{ba} \bmod p = s^{ab} \bmod p$, k_A must also equal k_B.

See also: key; prime number; public-key cryptography.

For further reading: Albrecht Beutelspacher, *Cryptology: An Introduction to the Art and Science of Enciphering, Encrypting, Concealing, Hiding and Safeguarding Described without Any Arcane Skullduggery but Not without Cunning Waggery for the Delectation and Instruction of the General Public,* Washington, DC: Mathematical Association of America, 1994, pp. 120–124; Gilles Brassard, *Modern Cryptology: A Tutorial,* New York: Springer-Verlag, 1988, pp. 23–26; D. W. Davies and W. L. Price, *Security for Computer Networks: An Introduction to Data Security in Teleprocessing and Electronic Funds Transfer,* Chichester: John Wiley & Sons, 1984, pp. 231–234; Whitfield Diffie and Martin Hellman, "New Directions in Cryptography," *IEEE Transactions on Information Theory* (November 1976): 644–645; Charlie Kaufman, Radia Perlman, and Mike Speciner, *Network Security: Private Communication in a Public World,* Englewood Cliffs, NJ: Prentice-Hall, 1995, pp. 147–152; Alan G. Konheim, *Cryptography: A Primer,* New York: John Wiley & Sons, 1981, p. 288+; William Stallings, *Network*

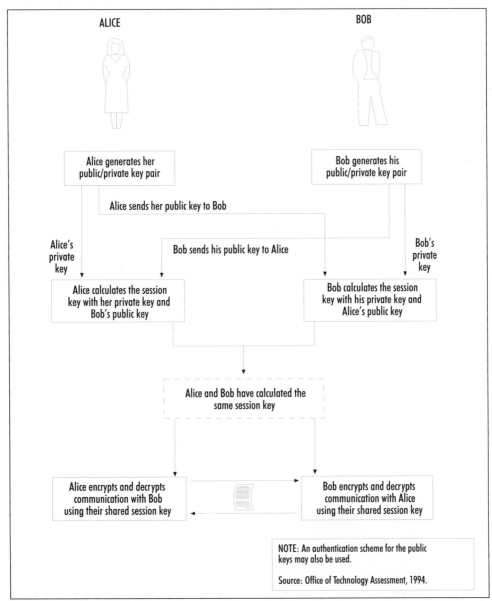

ALICE

BOB

Alice generates her public/private key pair

Bob generates his public/private key pair

Alice sends her public key to Bob

Alice's private key

Bob sends his public key to Alice

Bob's private key

Alice calculates the session key with her private key and Bob's public key

Bob calculates the session key with his private key and Alice's public key

Alice and Bob have calculated the same session key

Alice encrypts and decrypts communication with Bob using their shared session key

Bob encrypts and decrypts communication with Alice using their shared session key

NOTE: An authentication scheme for the public keys may also be used.

Source: Office of Technology Assessment, 1994.

Figure 9

and *Internetwork Security: Principles and Practices*, Englewood Cliffs, NJ: Prentice-Hall, 1995, ch. 7.

DIGITAL SIGNATURE

Any form of encipherment by which one user of a computer system is able to confirm his or her identity to any other user of the system and by which the receiver of the signature would be able to prove to a disinterested third party that the signature is authentic. A digital signature is an electronic counterpart to the handwritten system by which people commit themselves to legal documents, such as purchases or sales of land, stock, objects, or services.

An important step in the implementation of digital signature systems was the Utah Digital Signature Act, signed into law on 10 March 1995. This act provides a mechanism by which computer documents can be signed and other transactions authenticated through electronic means. The act also created a state Digital Signature Agency with the responsibility of licensing and regulating certification systems. The act defines the private key held by any subscriber as that person's private property, thus providing a means by which theft or misuse of the key can be prosecuted.

The Utah statute is important beyond its state applications because it was specifically drawn as a proposed model for other states. It is so written that it can be adapted and applied by other states and at the national and international levels.

See also: Digital Signature Standard; RSA algorithm.

For further reading: Brian Beckett, *Introduction to Cryptology*, Oxford: Blackwell Scientific Publications, 1988, pp. 136–140; Albrecht Beutelspacher, *Cryptology: An Introduction to the Art and Science of Enciphering, Encrypting, Concealing, Hiding and Safeguarding Described without Any Arcane Skullduggery but Not without Cunning Waggery for the Delectation and Instruction of the General Public*, Washington, DC: Mathematical Association of America, 1994, pp. 103–106; D. W. Davies and W. L. Price, *Security for Computer Networks: An Introduction to Data Security in Teleprocessing and Electronic Funds Transfer*, Chichester: John Wiley & Sons, 1984, ch. 9; D. E. R. Denning, "Digital Signatures with RSA and Other Public-Key Cryptosystems," *Communications of the ACM* 27 (1984): 388–392; Steven Levy, "Sign Here," *Macworld* (February 1995): 175–176; Stephen Matyas, "Digital Signatures—An Overview," *Computer Networks* 3 (1979): 87–94; Carl H. Meyer and Stephen M. Matyas, *Cryptography: A New Dimension in Computer Data Security*, New York: John Wiley & Sons, 1982, ch. 9; M. O. Rabin, "Digital Signatures," in R. A. DeMillo, et al., eds., *Foundations of Secure Computation*, New York: Academic Press, 1978, pp. 155–168; R. L. Rivest, A. Shamir, and L. Adleman, "A Method for Obtaining Digital Signatures and Public-Key Cryptosystems," *Communications of the ACM* (February 1978): 120–126; Bruce Schneier, "Digital Signatures," *Byte* (November 1993): 309–312; William Stallings, *Network and Internetwork Security: Principles and Practices*, Englewood Cliffs, NJ: Prentice-Hall, 1995, ch. 4; U.S. Congress, Office of Technology Assessment, *Information Security and Privacy in Network Environments*, OTA-TCT-606, Washington, DC: GPO, September 1994, pp. 35–39, 124–125, 215–216, and passim; Dominic Welsh, *Codes and Cryptography*, Oxford: Clarendon Press, 1988, ch. 12.

DIGITAL SIGNATURE STANDARD (DSS)

A federally designed cryptographic system for generating and verifying digital signatures. As shown in Figure 10, to use the DSS, a sender first uses a hashing system to create a message digest of the original message. The DSS is then attached to the message digest, providing a unique form of authentication for the message. A person who receives a message encrypted by this system uses the sender's public key and the known hashing method to verify that the person who claims to have sent the message is indeed that person. DSS is different from certain other forms of digital signature authentication because it is not reversible, and therefore cannot be used for secret-key cryptograms.

As of the mid-1990s, the federal government planned to use DSS throughout most of its agencies, but a number of problems have arisen. Questions have been raised about patent violations in the development of the system, and many agencies already use other forms of digital signatures, including variations of the RSA system.

See also: hashing algorithm; RSA algorithm. For further reading: "Adopting a Digital Signature Standard," *Science News* (11 June 1994): 383; Charlie Kaufman, Radia Perlman, and Mike Speciner, *Network Security: Private Communication in a Public World*, Englewood Cliffs, NJ: Prentice-Hall, 1995, pp. 152–157; Ivars Peterson, "Digital Security Signed, Sealed, Delivered," *Science News* (7 September 1991): 148; William Stallings, *Network and Internetwork Security: Principles and Practices*, Englewood Cliffs, NJ: Prentice-Hall, 1995, ch. 7; U.S. Congress, Office of Technology Assessment, *Information Security and Privacy in Network Environments*, OTA-TCT-606, Washington, DC: GPO, September 1994, pp. 167–168, 215–222; http://www.epic.org/crypto/.

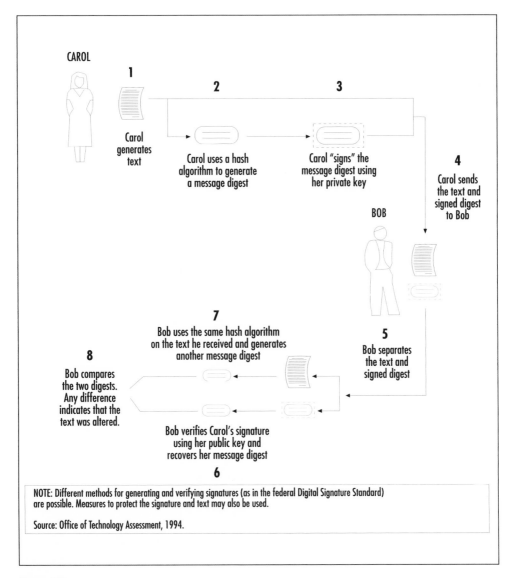

CAROL

1 Carol generates text

2 Carol uses a hash algorithm to generate a message digest

3 Carol "signs" the message digest using her private key

4 Carol sends the text and signed digest to Bob

BOB

5 Bob separates the text and signed digest

6 Bob verifies Carol's signature using her public key and recovers her message digest

7 Bob uses the same hash algorithm on the text he received and generates another message digest

8 Bob compares the two digests. Any difference indicates that the text was altered.

NOTE: Different methods for generating and verifying signatures (as in the federal Digital Signature Standard) are possible. Measures to protect the signature and text may also be used.

Source: Office of Technology Assessment, 1994.

Figure 10

DIGRAM

See bigram.

DIGRAPH

See bigram.

DIGRAPHIC SUBSTITUTION

See substitution.

DIRECT STANDARD ALPHABET

A monosubstitution alphabet in which the cipher alphabet is shifted by some constant number of letters to the left or right from the plaintext alphabet. An example of a direct standard alphabet is the Caesarean cipher, in which the cipher alphabet is shifted by three places from the plaintext alphabet. A direct standard alphabet can be represented mathematically by the formula $C = P + K$, in which C represents any letter in the cipher alphabet, P any corresponding letter in the plaintext alphabet, and K the constant number by which the cipher alphabet is shifted to the right $(+K)$ or left $(-K)$ from the plaintext alphabet.

See also: reverse standard alphabet.

DISCRETE LOGARITHM

Any integer x that satisfies the equation $y = a^x \bmod n$ for any given value of y, a, and n.

See also: logarithm.

DOLL CODE

A cryptosystem used by Valvalee Dickinson during World War II to provide information to the Japanese government about the location and movement of American warships by using spurious messages about dolls. Mrs. Dickinson owned a doll shop on Madison Avenue in New York City and was a fervent supporter of Japan during the war. She obtained information about U.S. naval plans and then encoded that information in a jargon code in which various ships were referred to by doll names and descriptions (such as the "Siamese Temple Dancer" and "the broken doll in a hula grass skirt"). Mrs. Dickinson was finally trapped when a letter addressed to Buenos Aires was returned to a person whose name was listed as the sender, but who knew nothing about the letter. She pleaded guilty to violating wartime censorship laws and was sentenced to ten years in prison and assessed a $10,000 fine.

See also: jargon code.
For further reading: Don Whitehead, *The FBI Story: A Report to the People*, New York: Random House, 1956, pp. 194–195.

DOUBLE TRANSPOSITION

See columnar transposition.

DRAKE, FRANK D.

American astronomer who has long been one of the primary investigators in the U.S. search for intelligent life outside our solar system. Drake (1930–) was born in Chicago and received his bachelor's degree in engineering physics in 1952 and his doctorate in astronomy from Harvard University in 1958.

His area of special interest is radio astronomy, but early in his career he began to focus on the search for intelligent life elsewhere in the universe. While working at the National Radio Astronomy Observatory in Green Bank, West Virginia, he carried out one of the seminal research projects in the search for extraterrestrial intelligence (SETI). The group he headed was called Project Ozma after the princess in L. Frank Baum's science fiction story *Ozma of Oz*. The project produced no definitive information that such life exists.

This finding did not discourage Drake and his colleagues, however. In the mid-1970s, he collaborated with Carl Sagan in a project that made use of the 300-meter radio telescope at Arecibo, Puerto Rico, to listen for signals from outer space. Again, the project failed to discover signals that could be construed as coming from other intelligent beings.

Drake has by no means abandoned his belief in the existence of intelligent life outside our solar system. He has written two books about SETI for the general public, *Intelligent Life in Space* (1967) and *Is Anyone Out There?: The Scientific Search for Extraterrestrial Intelligence* (1992). He also collaborated with Sagan to produce plaques attached to the Pioneer 10 and Pioneer 11 space probes launched in 1972 and 1973, respectively, and destined to travel throughout interstellar space for years into the future.

Drake is currently dean of natural sciences at the University of California at Santa Cruz.

For further reading: Brian Beckett, *Introduction to Cryptology*, Oxford: Blackwell Scientific Publications, 1988, pp. 99–101; Roy Gallant, *Beyond Earth: The Search for Extraterrestrial Life*, New York: Four Winds Press, 1977.

DRESDEN CODEX

See Mayan hieroglyphics.

DUMMY TRAFFIC

Messages transmitted by one side in a conflict, designed to confuse an enemy who intercepts such messages. Dummy traffic is meant to mislead an enemy as to when, where, and how an attack is to be launched on enemy territory. One of the most dramatic and effective examples of the use of dummy traffic was the planning that preceded the landing of Allied military forces on the beaches of Normandy in 1944. This operation was given the codename FORTITUDE.

Prior to the attack, Allied commanders sent out a number of false messages (which they knew German operators would intercept) indicating that an imminent attack would occur at Calais, in southern Norway, or in North Africa. The messages were apparently very successful, and German forces were taken by surprise when the Allied attack actually took place at Normandy.

In today's world, traffic analysis is a crucial element in conducting military maneuvers. As a result, efforts to deceive an enemy concerning a military force's real intentions have become a critical part of planning movements.

See also: traffic analysis.

EAVESDROPPER

A person who attempts to decipher an enciphered message for whom the message is not intended.

See also: enemy.

For further reading: Charlie Kaufman, Radia Perlman, and Mike Speciner, *Network Security: Private Communication in a Public World*, Englewood Cliffs, NJ: Prentice-Hall, 1995, passim (*see* index); Carl H. Meyer and Stephen M. Matyas, *Cryptography: A New Dimension in Computer Data Security*, New York: John Wiley & Sons, 1982, p. 2.

EFT

See electronic funds transfer.

ELECTION OF 1876

A contest for the presidency of the United States between Republican candidate Rutherford B. Hayes and Democratic candidate Samuel J. Tilden, in which cryptology first came to the attention of the American public as a factor in political contests. When all votes had been counted, Tilden appeared to be the winner of the election, having received about a quarter-million more votes than his Republican opponent. However, this overwhelming popular victory was worth only 184 electoral votes, one short of the number needed to elect Tilden president.

The election was tarnished by claims of corruption and fraud on both sides, and serious disputes remained in four states—Florida, Louisiana, Oregon, and South Carolina—even after final popular vote tallies had been announced. These disputes were to be resolved by a supposedly balanced committee consisting of five Supreme Court justices, five members of the Senate, and five members of the House of Representatives. In fact, the committee's vote on all four contested elections followed a strict party line, with eight Republicans outvoting seven Democrats in all cases. All contested electoral votes were awarded to Hayes, giving him the presidency.

Having lost the contest in the Electoral College, the Democrats attempted to salvage their reputation by accusing the Republicans of widespread treachery both during and after the election. They hoped that such a strategy, although having no effect on that election, might sway voters in future elections.

The party's plans backfired, however, when word of Democratic attempts to bribe electoral voters in the four disputed states came to light. Two years after Hayes's election, the *New York Tribune* released reports of messages sent in cipher from Democratic Party leaders to their associates in the four disputed states. The messages were encrypted in various ways; some were in code, others used monoalphabetic substitution, and still others were in checkerboard ciphers.

One message sent to Democratic leaders in Oregon, for example, read:

> By vizier association innocuous to negligence cunning minutely previously readmit doltish to purchased afar act with cunning afar sacristy unweighed afar pointer tigress cuttle superannuated syllabus dilatoriness misapprehension contraband kountze bisculous top usher spinerferous answer.

Coded messages implicated Rutherford B. Hayes and the Democratic Party in political scandal during the 1876 presidential election. This newspaper scene of the time depicts initial public reaction to the story.

The message turned out to be a book code based on the popular *Household English Dictionary,* in which the first word of the code, *by,* indicates the page and word to which to turn to search for the next word of the message. Each subsequent cipher word was then to be found in the same position on the fourth following page of the dictionary. The final decryption of the message was:

Certificate will be issued to one Democrat. Must purchase Republican elector to recognize and act with Democrat and secure vote and prevent trouble. Deposit ten thousand dollars my credit Kountze Brothers, Twelve Wall Street. Answer.

The message was signed by J. N. H. Patrick, an agent of the Democratic Party.

Another cryptosystem used by the Democrats was a simplified version of transposition that had been used during the Civil War. In this system, an enciphering key consisting of numbers from 1 to 15, 20, 25, or 30 was selected. A key for a 20-word message might comprise the following sequence:

18 7 14 3 20 11 2 19 10 8
15 13 1 4 17 6 12 5 9 16

To encipher the following message (not an actual message from the election), each word is assigned a number, as shown below:

1	2	3	4	5
REQUIRE	YOU	SEND	TEN	THOUSAND
6	7	8	9	10
DOLLARS	TO	EUGENE	IMMEDIATELY	TO
11	12	13	14	15
COVER	COST	OF	OBTAINING	VOTE
16	17	18	19	20
OF	HANSON	AND	HIS	ALLY.

The enciphered message, following the key sequence given above, would be:

and to obtaining send washington cover you his to wolverine wardrobe of require black philadelphia dollars cost strawberry immediately of.

An attempt was made to make the message more secure by using codewords for certain key terms, such as Washington for ALLY, wolverine for EUGENE, wardrobe for VOTE, black for TEN, Philadelphia for HANSON, and strawberry for THOUSAND.

Revelation of the Democrats' own "dirty tricks" during the Tilden-Hayes election meant that, rather than gaining sympathy in its campaign to discredit the Republicans and build goodwill for the next election, the party suffered a second

defeat in 1880. Winfield S. Hancock, the Democratic candidate, lost to James A. Garfield, the Republican candidate, by 7,000 votes out of 9 million cast, but by 155 to 214 in the Electoral College. Historian Alexander C. Flick observed that "As a result of the cipher telegrams the Republicans won an advantage which probably gave them the national election of 1880."

See also: book code; checkerboard; Civil War cryptology; code; monoalphabetic substitution; transposition.
For further reading: D. Beaird Glover, *Secret Ciphers of the 1876 Presidential Election*, Laguna Hills, CA: Aegean Park Press, n.d.; David Kahn, *The Codebreakers: The Story of Secret Writing*, New York: Macmillan, 1967, ch. 7.

ELECTRIC CODE MACHINE

A cipher machine designed and built by Edward Hebern.

See also: Hebern, Edward.

ELECTRO-CRYPTO MODEL B 1

See Damm, Arvid.

ELECTRONIC CODE BOOK (ECB)

See block encryption.

ELECTRONIC COUNTER-COUNTERMEASURES

See electronic security.

ELECTRONIC COUNTERMEASURES

See ELINT.

ELECTRONIC FUNDS TRANSFER (EFT)

Financial transactions that take place electronically without the use of paper documents. Traditionally, purchases have been made, bills paid, and funds moved from one account to another manually. For example, a person might write a check to a store for the purchase of a book. The store presents that check to a local bank, where it is processed. The check writer's account is debited the amount of the check, and the store is credited for the same amount. If the check writer and the bookstore use different banks, the transaction becomes more complicated.

In recent decades, the disadvantages of paper transactions have become more apparent. For one thing, huge amounts of paper are needed to carry out such transactions. Also, paper transactions are highly insecure. As an example, people may forge checks or alter the amount for which they are written. Also, the handling of large volumes of paper by human workers—even when aided by computers—is a very large expense for financial institutions.

To overcome some of these problems, many financial institutions have developed systems for moving funds from consumer to retailer and back, and from one financial institution to another, by sending messages electronically. In some cities, a person can pay bills simply by calling a single telephone number, inputting some form of identification, and requesting that payments be made in certain amounts to certain accounts. Perhaps the most familiar form of electronic funds transfer for most consumers is the use of automatic teller machines (ATMs), at which money can be deposited or withdrawn, or funds transferred from one account to another, all without the involvement of paper or another human.

An advantage of electronic funds transfer is that such transactions can generally be more secure than traditional transactions taking place between two humans and/or involving the use of paper documents. The invention of the ATM made the need for security very obvious, and sophisticated cryptographic systems were developed at the same time the technology of ATMs was introduced. Today, as intruders develop more sophisticated techniques for breaking into EFT networks, the operators of those networks attempt to stay one step ahead by developing more and more secure systems.

See also: authentication; automatic teller machine; password; personal identification number.

For further reading: Henry Beker and Fred Piper, *Cipher Systems: The Protection of Communications,* New York: John Wiley & Sons, 1982, pp. 315–325; D. W. Davies and W. L. Price, *Security for Computer Networks: An Introduction to Data Security in Teleprocessing and Electronic Funds Transfer,* Chichester: John Wiley & Sons, 1984, ch. 10; Carl H. Meyer and Stephen M. Matyas, *Cryptography: A New Dimension in Computer Data Security,* New York: John Wiley & Sons, 1982, ch. 11.

ELECTRONIC MAIL (E-MAIL) ━━━

Communications among two or more individuals sent by electronic means, such as over the Internet. Electronic mail has many advantages over more traditional forms of mail delivery (such as the U.S. Postal Service, also known as "snail-mail"). Foremost among these is the speed with which a message can be sent from one node of a network to another. By its very nature, however, electronic mail presents a number of concerns about privacy, security, and related issues. It is relatively easy, for example, for an eavesdropper to intercept and read a message sent by Alice to Bob. Such security concerns have made cryptology an issue of everyday significance for a substantial fraction of the nation's population.

One proposal for dealing with security in electronic mail comes from the U.S. Postal Service (USPS) itself. In late 1996, the USPS announced that it was designing a system to provide electronic postmarks for e-mail. The first step in this system would be for correspondents to submit their messages electronically to a USPS computer or some other trusted intermediary. The message would be stamped with a date and time, enciphered, and signed with a digital signature. The enciphered message would then be sent to the intended recipient. The recipient would decipher and read the message simply by clicking on a key that enables a program called the USPS Mail Reader. USPS officials estimate transmission time for the system to be of the order of eight minutes and the projected cost at 22 cents for the first 50 kilobytes of message.

See also: anonymity; authentication; envelope technology; integrity; privacy; public-key cryptography.

For further reading: Charlie Kaufman, Radia Perlman, and Mike Speciner, *Network Security: Private Communication in a Public World,* Englewood Cliffs, NJ: Prentice-Hall, 1995, ch. 12; Alan Phelps, "Business as Usual: E-mail Puts a New Twist on Old Debates," *PC Novice* (September 1995): 86–88; Bruce Schneier, "Protect Your E-mail," *Macworld* (November 1995): 112–115; William Stallings, *Network and Internetwork Security: Principles and Practices,* Englewood Cliffs, NJ: Prentice-Hall, 1995, ch. 8; U.S. Congress, Office of Technology Assessment, *Information Security and Privacy in Network Environments,* OTA-TCT-606, Washington, DC: GPO, September 1994, pp. 36–37.

ELECTRONIC SECURITY

A subdivision of signal security whose purpose is to prevent a foreign nation from intercepting and identifying electronic signals sent out by one's own sources. For example, operators at a U.S. radar station in Alaska are aware that other nations will be listening in on their transmissions, attempting to learn their location and nature. Therefore, the operators devise methods to interfere with those detection efforts. A common technique is to shift the frequency at which radar signals are transmitted so that outside observers cannot obtain a "fix" on any one transmission.

A second function of electronic security is to counteract the countermeasures of foreign observers. As another example, the Alaska radar observers are also aware that outside observers will attempt to jam their radar transmission so that U.S. observers cannot locate and identify their counterparts. The U.S. observers employ techniques for breaking through the foreign observers' defenses, trying to overcome the jamming process and track the foreign observers. Such techniques are known as counter-countermeasures.

The fields of electronic security and electronic intelligence are intimately involved with each other. Every major nation in the world is searching for new ways to locate and intercept foreign electronic transmissions and, at the same time, looking for ways of responding to exactly the same efforts by the nations on whom they are spying. This interaction of electronic security and electronic intelligence is sometimes known as electronic warfare. As with the nuclear weapons and space races between the United States and the Soviet Union, electronic warfare appears to have a built-in life of its own. Every technological development by one side requires a corresponding solution by the other, plus a new development of its own. The ultimate consequences of continuing electronic warfare are unlikely to have the potentially disastrous consequences of the nuclear weapons race on the one hand nor the beneficial technological effects of the space race on the other.

See also: COMINT; ELINT; signal security.

ELECTRONIC WARFARE

See electronic security.

ELINT

A military acronym for *electronics intel*ligence, one of the two major divisions of signal intelligence. The purpose of electronics intelligence, or ELINT, is to collect data from foreign sources transmitting anywhere within the electromagnetic spectrum. Some of the more obvious examples of such transmissions are those from radar sources and from telemetry messages sent between foreign satellites and bases in their home country. Two common techniques for collecting such data are high-flying spy airplanes and spy satellites that can listen in on foreign communications.

ELINT does not have a direct major cryptanalytic function in terms of listening in for cryptograms sent out by foreign nations. However, it has an indirect function in that it provides cryptanalysts with information about the source of messages, the frequency with which they are sent, and the locations to which they are delivered.

ELINT also has a second function, that of disrupting the electronic signals coming from a foreign source. As an example, a U.S. airplane might not only listen in on radar transmissions coming from a Russian station, but also might attempt to jam those transmissions to protect its own presence and identity. Devices and techniques employed to interfere with foreign electronic transmissions are known as countermeasures.

See also: COMINT; signal security.
For further reading: Mario de Arcangelis, *Electronic Warfare: From the Battle of Tsushima to the Falklands and Lebanon Conflicts*, Poole, Dorset: Blandford Press, 1985.

E-MAIL
See electronic mail.

ENCICODE
An abbreviation for enciphered code. Encicode is a form of superencipherment in which a codeword or codenumber is enciphered to produce a more secure message. In theory, one way to do this is to take a codeword and encipher it to form a new cipherword, as in the example below.

PLAINTEXT WORD: BATTALION
CODEWORD: dandelion
ENCIPHERED CODEWORD: noilednad

In this example, the unenciphered codeword (dandelion) is also known as the placode (short for plaincode).

In practice, this process is seldom used with codewords because it alters the words themselves. Codenumbers, on the other hand, are easily modified through superencipherment. For example, suppose that the codenumber of BATTALION is 38241. One way to superencipher this codenumber is by simple transposition: reverse the digits in the number. The encicode in this case would be 14283.

Other, more sophisticated techniques are used to encipher codes. For example, a constant term known as the additive might be added to each codenumber in a code. Suppose that the additive for the message in which the word BATTALION appears is 48293. The placode for this codeword, 38241, would be further enciphered by adding to it the additive 48293, as shown below:

PLACODE: 38241
ADDITIVE: 48293
ENCICODE: 86534

The first example of encicodes is found in the writings of Leon Battista Alberti, who provided space on his cipher disk for this purpose. The practice did not gain popularity, however, until the invention of the telegraph. Then, the need to reduce long messages to short codes and ciphers in order to save money increased the popularity of superencipherment and encicodes.

See also: additive; Alberti, Leon Battista; superencipherment; telegraph; transposition.
For further reading: Wayne G. Barker, *Cryptanalysis of an Enciphered Code Problem— Where an "Additive" Method of Encipherment Has Been Used*, Laguna Hills, CA: Aegean Park Press, n.d.; William F. Friedman, *Advanced Military Cryptography*, Laguna Hills, CA: Aegean Park Press, 1976, pp. 102–113.

ENCIPHER
The process of converting plaintext into ciphertext.

ENCIPHERER
A person who enciphers.

ENCIPHERING ALPHABET

The alphabet used in converting plaintext into ciphertext.

See also: alphabet.
For further reading: Donald D. Millikin, *Elementary Cryptography and Cryptanalysis*, Laguna Hills, CA: Aegean Park Press, n.d., pp. 6–7.

ENCODE

The process of converting plaintext into code.

ENCRYPTION

The process of converting plaintext into ciphertext or into code. The term is sometimes used synonymously with *encipherment*.

ENEMY

In wartime, a person or group of individuals against whom a nation is fighting. The term is used in cryptology also to refer to anyone for whom a message is not intended.

See also: eavesdropper.

ENIGMA

In everyday usage, the term *enigma* refers to something that is mysterious or puzzling. In its capitalized form, the term refers to a machine used for coding and decoding messages, originally invented by the German electrical engineer Arthur Scherbius in 1918.

The Enigma machines contain three basic components: (1) a typewriterlike keyboard on which the plaintext is typed, (2) an internal electromechanical system that converts plaintext to ciphertext, and (3) a display system in which the ciphertext is displayed. During the decoding process, the ciphertext is typed into the machine and the plaintext displayed on the screen.

The key to encipherment and decipherment systems within an Enigma is a series of rotors by which one letter is

One of the most powerful cryptographic tools, the German Enigma machine produced a code that had cryptanalysts puzzled for more than 20 years.

transcribed into another letter. In Scherbius's original design, three rotors were included, each capable of transposing a letter. For example, if an operator pressed the letter *h* on the keyboard, an electrical current would travel through the first rotor, transcribing the *h* into (for example) a *y*.

A wire between the first and second rotors allows the flow of electricity from the *y* position on the first rotor to a position (say, the *t*) on the second rotor. Within the second rotor, the *t* would also be transcribed, suppose to a *b*. Yet another connection between the second and third rotors would transcribe the *b* on the second rotor to (for example) the *x* position on the third rotor, where it would be converted to an *m* (for example).

Certain features of the original Enigma made it a particularly powerful ciphering device. For example, each time the operator pressed a key, the second rotor would rotate by one position. Thus, the sequence h → y → t → b → x → m would *not* be repeated if the *h* were pressed a second time. If the second rotor were to advance by one position, the new coding sequence might be something like: h → y → u → r → q → v. That is, knowing that plaintext *h* is equal to ciphertext *m* in the first step says nothing about how *h* is encoded in the next step of the message.

Over a period of two decades, the Enigma was constantly changed and improved by German inventors. One of the most important changes was the addition of a half-rotor or reflector to the machine. The half-rotor did not perform any encipherment, but simply sent the electrical current coming from the third rotor back into the rotor at a different contact. The half-rotor added thus one more step to the encoding of a letter.

As the Enigma machine grew in complexity, it also became easier to use physically. Scherbius's original model stood 15 inches high and weighed more than 100 pounds. In its final version, it was only 4 inches high and weighed 15 pounds.

When first introduced, the Enigma was of relatively little interest to business, the German military, or the foreign service, all of whom Scherbius had initially contacted. A decade later, however, the government began to appreciate the value of electro-mechanical encipherment of messages and purchased copies of the machine for the air force, army, navy, and diplomatic service. By 1926, the first messages encoded by the Enigma were being transmitted by the navy from its central headquarters to surface ships and U-boats.

Breaking the Enigma code was a matter of high priority for Allied intelligence agencies, especially the British, during World War II. Great Britain's very survival depended on supplies obtained from all parts of the world, usually by ship across the Atlantic. Protecting those shipping lanes meant finding out where the German navy lay in wait in the Atlantic. And the key to that information lay in being able to read instructions encoded by Enigma sent from the German High Command to its ships at sea.

The earliest breakthrough in solving the Enigma code came when a worker in the German Cipher Center, Hans-Thilo Schmidt, offered to sell information about the machine to French intelligence. That information was later passed on to Polish intelligence agents, who had been working on the Enigma for a number of years, and eventually to the British Government Code & Cypher School at Bletchley Park. There, largely through the work of a young genius named Alan Turing, the Enigma code was broken as early as 1940. Although continual modifications in the Enigma machine created ever-changing challenges for Allied cryptologists, German coded messages never again proved an insurmountable task for the Allies.

See also: Bletchley Park; cipher machine; Government Code & Cypher School; rotor; Scherbius, Arthur; Schmidt, Hans-Thilo; Turing, Alan.

For further reading: A. K. Dewdney, "On Making and Breaking Codes (I)," *Scientific American* (October 1988): 144–147; M. K. Dziewanowski, "Polish Intelligence during World War II: The Case of Barbarossa," *East European Quarterly* (September 1994): 381–391; J. Garlinski, *Intercept: The Enigma War*, London: J. M. Dent, 1979; Francis H. Hinsley, *British Intelligence in the Second World War*, New York: Cambridge University Press, 1993; Andrew Hodges, *Alan Turing: The Enigma*, New York: Simon & Schuster, 1983, passim; David Kahn, "An Enigma Chronology," *Cryptologia* (January 1993): 237–246; Michael Kernan, "The Object at Hand," *Smithsonian* (May 1990): 22+; Wladyslaw Kozaczuk, *Enigma*, trans. by Christopher Kasparek, University Publications of America, 1984; Marian Rejewski, "How Polish Mathematicians Deciphered the Enigma," *Annals of the History of Computing* 3 (1981): 213–234; Gordon Welchman, *The Hut Six Story: Breaking the Enigma Codes*, New York: McGraw-Hill, 1982; Richard Woytak, "Polish Military Intelligence and Enigma," *East European Quarterly* (March 1991): 49–57.

ENTROPY

A term from physics that refers to the amount of disorder in a system. Consider a large crystal of table salt, for example.

The particles of which the crystal is composed have been arranged into a highly ordered form that gives the crystal its characteristic shape. If the crystal is smashed or crushed, some of that order is lost. The single ordered crystal is broken down into smaller pieces, many of which can easily be seen to constitute smaller ordered particles. The disorder in the system (the sample of salt) has increased, and so has the entropy. The illustration can be carried one step farther by dissolving the salt in water. The particles of which the salt is made are totally dispersed among water molecules. Both disorder and entropy of the system are at a maximum.

Entropy is of considerable interest in the field of physics because it has been demonstrated that all natural systems tend to increase in entropy, that is, they tend toward disorder. The end of the universe is thought to result in a maximum level of entropy, in which all forms of matter and energy are equally distributed throughout space.

The concept of entropy has been profitably applied to the field of cryptology. In this case, it concerns the amount of disorder that exists within a language and within the messages sent using that language. Any language (including English, of course) has a relatively low level of entropy. For example, the letter q in English is always followed by the letter u. There is no uncertainty, no disorder, with regard to the arrangement of these two letters.

This fact is reflected in frequency tables for individual letters, digraphs, and trigraphs. If one sees the letters t and h in a three-letter word, there is virtually no doubt as to the identity of the third letter.

Students of information theory have developed a number of mathematical formulas that reflect the amount of entropy within a given message. These formulas are based on the probability of various occurrences within the message. For example, suppose that a message consists of 26 letters that can be designated as x_1, $x_2, x_3, \ldots, x_{26}$. If no information at all is

available about these letters, then the probability of any one is simply 1/26. More generally, for a message containing r letters, the probability of encountering any one of the letters is $1/r$.

A similar analysis can be applied to the variety of ciphertext messages that can be generated from a given cryptosystem. Suppose an individual knows that 100 such ciphertexts are possible. If any one such ciphertext is intercepted, the probability of its being one of the 100 is simply 1/100.

In actual experience, many clues may be available to indicate that the probability of encountering some one letter in 26 or some one message in 100 is greater than a random choice. For a monoalphabetic substitution ciphertext generated from the English language, for example, one letter (the cipher letter equivalent for plaintext e) will occur more often than any other letter. This statement simply says that cryptanalysis makes use of the fact that probabilities of letters, words, and messages in ciphertext are seldom randomly distributed.

The basic formula used in expressing the amount of probability (or entropy) in any message is $H(M) = S\, p_i \log(p_i)$, where $H(M)$ is the entropy for the message and p_i is the probability of the ith element of the message.

The mathematics of this discussion rapidly extend beyond the limits of this book. However, one conclusion from the above expression can be pointed out. It can be demonstrated that the entropy, $H(M)$, is a maximum when the probability of all p_i is equal. This mathematical conclusion merely confirms the commonsense observation pointed out above that a message in which all letters are equally likely is one of maximum disorder and one about which the observer knows the least.

See also: bigram; frequency distribution; information theory; probability; probable word; trigram.

For further reading: Henry Beker and Fred Piper, *Cipher Systems: The Protection of*

Communications, New York: John Wiley & Sons, 1982, pp. 151–153; Carl H. Meyer and Stephen M. Matyas, *Cryptography: A New Dimension in Computer Data Security,* New York: John Wiley & Sons, 1982, pp. 627–629; J. Reeds, "Entropy Calculations and Particular Methods of Cryptanalysis," *Cryptologia* 1 (1977): 235–254.

ENVELOPE TECHNOLOGY

A proposed method for protecting information now generally available on the Internet. Envelope technology has been suggested as a way of making sure that people who create items for the Internet get paid for their work, just as authors, songwriters, and other kinds of artists are paid a royalty for the works they create. At present, an item that appears on the Internet is usually in the public domain. Anyone who calls up the item on his or her screen is then able to copy and/or print the information displayed there.

At the end of 1996, envelope technology was still being discussed by professionals and users of the Internet, and it was not yet clear whether the system would really work. Critics point out that for each person who can create an envelope, there is at least one other person who can find a way to break into it. They remind proponents of envelope technology of the failed attempts by television broadcasters to scramble signals during the 1970s. As fast as those systems were put into place, other inventors found ways to unscramble the signals and put their products on the market for purchase by the general public.

Still, research on envelope technology goes forward. The principle is that a person could protect his or her work on the Internet by putting it inside a sealed "envelope" (or Digibox) that is protected cryptographically and that could be "opened" only by having the correct key. Rights to the key and access to the material inside the envelope could then be purchased. Part of the purchase price would be returned to the inventor of the material in the form of a royalty.

See also: Internet; password; security.
For further reading: Tom Abate, "Sealing Fate of Free Content on the Net?" *San Francisco Examiner* (8 September 1996): C-1+.

ERROR-CORRECTING CODE

A mechanism by which someone who receives an enciphered message is able to determine whether one or more errors have been introduced during transmission. Errors are a familiar feature of message transmission. Disturbances in the atmosphere, for example, can cause a television picture, radio signal, or telephone message to become garbled. When messages are sent in binary code, errors are especially likely to occur. In the sequence 100101101100, the change of a single bit (to produce, say, 100111101100) can result in a totally different meaning for the message.

For this reason, enciphered messages typically include some physical or mathematical operation that allows the recipient to check for errors. One method is to repeat the digits one or more times. A sequence such as 1010 can be transmitted as 111000111000, with each of the four original digits repeated three times.

More commonly, some mathematical operation is performed on the digits that make up the message. For example, the digits might be enciphered to add up to some given number. The first seven bits in a byte might be written in such a way that they always add up to 0. A message in which the product of the first seven bits in a sequence did *not* sum to 0 would then be known to have an error in it. The mathematical operations devised to detect errors in a transmitted message are generally complex and beyond the scope of this book. Suffice it to say that a number of such systems permit recipients to recognize the presence of an error in a received transmission.

A fundamental consideration in writing error-detection codes is the trade-off between efficiency of error detection and economy of transmission time. That is, simply repeating each digit a number of times (as in the first example above) is a relatively effective way of detecting errors, but it requires the use of many more digits. The challenge for theorists is to find a means of detecting errors without increasing message length any more than absolutely necessary.

See also: binary number system.
For further reading: Henry Beker and Fred Piper, *Cipher Systems: The Protection of Communications*, New York: John Wiley & Sons, 1982, pp. 307, 323–325; R. E. Blahut, *Theory and Practice of Error Control Codes*, Reading, MA: Addison-Wesley, 1983; V. D. Goppa, "A New Class of Linear Error-Correcting Codes," *Problems of Information Transmission* 6:3 (1970): 207–212; F. J. MacWilliams and N. J. A. Sloane, *The Theory of Error-Correcting Codes*, Amsterdam: North-Holland Publishing, 1978; Ivars Peterson, "Policing Digits: New Keys for Keeping Digital Data Straight," *Science News* (12 March 1994): 170–171; W. W. Peterson and E. J. Weldon, *Error-Correcting Codes*, 2nd ed., Cambridge, MA: MIT Press, 1972; V. Pless, *Introduction to the Theory of Error-Correcting Codes*, New York: John Wiley & Sons, 1982; N. J. A. Sloane, "Error-Correcting Codes and Cryptography," in *The Mathematical Gardener*, ed. by D. A. Klarner, Belmont, CA: Wadsworth, pp. 346–382; Scott A. Vanstone and Paul C. van Oorschot, *An Introduction to Error Correcting Codes with Applications*, Boston: Kluwer Academic Publishers, 1989.

ESCROW AGENT

In general, the person or entity holding something in escrow for a third party. In the field of cryptology, the term refers to the person or entity who holds the key or keys used in an asymmetrical cryptosystem. The escrow agents originally designated by Attorney General Janet Reno for the Escrowed Encryption Standard in 1994 were the Automated Systems Division of the U.S. Treasury Department and the National Institute of Standards and Technology.

See also: Escrowed Encryption Standard.
For further reading: Dorothy E. Denning and Dennis Branstad, "A Taxonomy for Key Escrow Encryption," available from the author at denning@cs.georgetown.edu; Steven Levy, "Scared Bitless," *Newsweek* (10 June 1996): 49–50+; U.S. Congress, Office of Technology Assessment, *Information Security and Privacy in Network Environments*, OTA-TCT-606, Washington, DC: GPO, September 1994, passim (*see* index); http://world.std.coml~franl/crypto/policy.html.

ESCROWED ENCRYPTION STANDARD (EES)

A Federal Information Processing Standard (FIPS-185) that uses the classified Skipjack algorithm for enciphering data. EES was proposed as an FIPS by the Clinton administration on 30 July 1993 as an alternative to the older Data Encryption Standard (DES) for use with unclassified voice, fax, and data communications transmitted through telephone systems. EES is sometimes referred to as Clipper because the Skipjack algorithm was also used with a microchip of that name.

EES has been the focus of an ongoing and vigorous debate from its inception, at the outset met with almost universally negative comments. Among the complaints were concerns that the encrypting algorithm was classified and therefore not available for public scrutiny, that no information about its testing was available, that the algorithm had been developed by the National Security Agency (rather than some nonmilitary agency), that it may infringe some existing patent rights, that it required escrowing of keys, and that it was not as cost-effective as the older but still useful DES.

Some of the strongest objections to the EES system have come from an informal group of computer engineers, administrators, hackers, and others interested in the use of electronic technology. Known collectively as Cypherpunks, these individuals argue that EES is a mechanism by which the federal government can listen in on the private conversations of innocent men and women around the world.

The Clinton administration has consistently argued that key-escrowing is essential at a time when potentially massive amounts of illegal business are being transacted through telephone and computer networks, and is also crucial to maintaining national security functions.

From the outset, the Clinton administration made it clear that EES is a *voluntary* system for both government agencies and the private sector. The concern among some observers, however, is that future administrations (or even the Clinton administration at a later time) may decide to make EES mandatory. Without the resolution of issues such as those outlined above, such an action would meet with heated opposition by many of those now working in the field of cryptography.

The debate over the implication of EES continues today. The Clinton administration has made some efforts to make the program more palatable to its many critics. In August 1995, for example, it agreed to increase the amount of encryption materials that U.S. companies were allowed to export to other nations. Companies would have to agree, however, to make their private keys to such materials available to the U.S. government under court order.

In early 1996, the government agreed to consider even further relaxations, acknowledging that existing rules governing EES put U.S. companies at a serious economic disadvantage in dealing with encipherment schemes from other nations. Relaxing the use of EES-related programs is likely to meet continuing objections from the National Security Agency and various law-enforcement agencies, however, out of concerns that terrorists and criminals would benefit at least as much as legitimate businesspeople from such changes in U.S. encryption policies.

See also: Cypherpunks; export controls.
For further reading: *The Administration's Clipper Chip Key Escrow Encryption Program*, Hearing before the Subcommittee on Technology and the Law of the Senate Committee of the Judiciary, 103rd Congress, Second Session, 3 May 1994; Lee Dembart, "Hide and Peek," *Reason* (November 1993): 40–45; Dan Lehrer, "Clipper Chips and Cypherpunks," *The Nation* (10 October 1994): 376–380; Steven Levy, "Battle of the Clipper Chip," *New York Times Magazine* (12 June 1994): 44–51+; National Research Council press release (30 May 1996), available on http://www.epic.org/crypto/reports/nrc_release.html; Ivars Peterson, "Encrypting Controversy," *Science News* (19 June 1993): 394–395; U.S. Congress, Office of Technology Assessment, *Information Security and Privacy in Network Environments*, OTA-TCT-606, Washington, DC: GPO, September 1994, pp. 120–123, 161–163, 173–182; U.S. Congress, Office of Technology Assessment, *Issue Update on Information Security and Privacy in Network Environments*, OTA-BP-ITC-147, Washington, DC: GPO, June 1995, passim (*see* index); http://www.epic.org/crypto/.

EUCLIDEAN ALGORITHM

A method of finding the greatest common divisor (gcd) of two numbers. The algorithm was first discovered by the great Greek mathematician Euclid and was included in the seventh book of his *Elementa* (Elements) in about 300 B.C. In essence, the algorithm requires progressively reducing the size of the integers whose gcd is being sought.

Suppose that the greatest common divisor of 184 and 516 is sought. The first step is to divide the larger of these integers by the other:

$$516 \div 184 = 2 \text{ with a remainder of } 148$$

The process is then repeated, taking the smaller of the two original numbers and dividing by the remainder:

$$184 \div 148 = 1 \text{ with a remainder of } 36$$

The process is repeated again:

$$148 \div 36 = 4 \text{ with a remainder of } 4$$

And again:

$$36 \div 4 = 9 \text{ with a remainder of } 0$$

Now, according to the Euclidean algorithm the last nonzero remainder is the greatest common divisor. In this example, that remainder is 4, so 4 is the gcd of 184 and 516. To prove this result: $184 \div 4 = 46$ and $516 \div 4 = 129$.

Euclid's algorithm is important in cryptology because it can also be used to determine the multiplicative inverse of a number. That is, if $A \times B = 1 \pmod{n}$, and A is known, Euclid's algorithm can be used to calculate B. This process is important because in some public-key cryptographic systems (such as the RSA algorithm), public and private keys are related to each other as multiplicative inverses. In the RSA algorithm, for example,

$$\text{(public key)} \times \text{(private key)} = 1 \pmod{n}$$

See also: algorithm; relative primes; RSA algorithm.
For further reading: Brian Beckett, *Introduction to Cryptology,* Oxford: Blackwell Scientific Publications, 1988, pp. 101+; Henry Beker and Fred Piper, *Cipher Systems: The Protection of Communications,* New York: John Wiley & Sons, 1982, pp. 377–380; Charlie Kaufman, Radia Perlman, and Mike Speciner, *Network Security: Private Communication in a Public World,* Englewood Cliffs, NJ: Prentice-Hall, 1995, pp. 165–168; Carl H. Meyer and Stephen M. Matyas, *Cryptography: A New Dimension in Computer Data Security,* New York: John Wiley & Sons, 1982, pp. 38–41; Dominic Welsh, *Codes and Cryptography,* Oxford: Clarendon Press, 1988, pp. 138–140.

EXCLUSIVE OR OPERATION

An alternate term for modulo 2 addition. Exclusive OR operations are indicated by the symbol $\oplus$ and follow the general rules of modulo 2 arithmetic, namely:

$$0 + 0 = 0 \quad 0 + 1 = 1 \quad 1 + 0 = 1 \quad 1 + 1 = 0$$

See also: binary number system; modulo arithmetic.

EXHAUSTIVE SEARCH

A method for solving a ciphertext simply by trying every conceivable possibility, one at a time. As a simple example, suppose that an enemy has intercepted a ciphertext message and suspects that the key for the message may be any one of 2^{32} possible options. One approach to decrypting the ciphertext is to try key 1, then key 2, then key 3, and so on to key 2^{32}. At each step, the possible key is applied to the ciphertext to see if recognizable plaintext is obtained.

Of course, it is possible that the cryptanalyst may obtain the correct answer on the very first try with key 1. On the other hand, he or she might not find the key until trial 2^{32}. Making this number of trials by hand is, of course, impossible. But modern high-speed computers can go through a very large number of trials in manageable time (a few hours or days, perhaps).

See also: algorithm.

EXPONENTIAL TIME FUNCTION
See algorithm.

EXPORT CONTROLS

Regulations established by the federal government setting limitations on the types, amounts, and destinations of products that can be shipped to other nations. The issue of export controls has been arguably the single most contentious problem in the field of practical cryptography in the United States during the 1990s. The reason for the debate is that two critical aspects of national policy collide over the issue.

In the first place, the U.S. government is very much concerned about the kind of cryptographic hardware and software made available to other nations. Some of those nations may decide to use the materials to learn about American defense readiness, break ciphered messages transmitted among American diplomats, and, in general, eavesdrop on private and secure communications of importance to national security. Controlling the export of cryptographic systems and materials is therefore a matter of profound concern to the Department of Defense, the State Department, the Central Intelligence Agency, the National Security Agency, and other agencies of the administration.

On the other hand, the export of cryptographic materials and systems is vitally important to American business. Many companies that operate in this country are now multinational corporations with offices all over the world. These companies often wish to send enciphered messages to their worldwide offices and can do so only if the most up-to-date cryptography is available to all of its branches to which messages will be sent.

In addition, companies that make cryptographic systems and materials are eager to market their products overseas. It makes no sense to them that they are prevented from competing with foreign corporations in a world where multinational business has become a way of life.

The type of control exerted over exports varies depending on the product. At the least restrictive end of the spectrum are general licenses granted to companies for the export of products that have no military or sensitive civilian use and/or are already widely available from foreign companies. The next most restrictive license is for "dual-use" products—products that have both military and civilian applications. Licenses in this category fall under the jurisdiction of the U.S. Commerce Department, which carries out the provisions of the Export Administration Act (50 U.S.C. App 2401-2420) and the Export Administration Regulations. Finally, products with a primarily or exclusively military application are administered by the State Department acting under the authority of the Arms Export Control Act (22 U.S.C. 2751-2794) and the International Traffic in Arms Regulation (22 C.F.R. 120-130).

Cryptographic materials are included under Category XIII(b)—Auxiliary Military Equipment, Information Security Systems and Equipment—of the Munitions List, and include items such as cryptographic and key-management systems, cryptanalytic systems, and other hardware and software used in generating and maintaining information secrecy systems.

Almost any product that contains the Data Encryption Standard (DES) falls under Category XIII(b) and requires a license from the State Department, a license that is often difficult to obtain because of the power of DES as an encryption tool. Yet, business executives argue, products containing the DES cryptosystem are already available almost universally from other nations, so U.S. controls are essentially ineffective in preventing enemies from obtaining the program. Furthermore, they question the logic of developing the most powerful encryption tool in the world right here in the United States, then not permitting its use by private businesses in a multinational business climate.

See also: Data Encryption Standard; Escrowed Encryption Standard; National Security Agency/Central Security Service. **For further reading:** Charlie Kaufman, Radia Perlman, and Mike Speciner, *Network Security: Private Communication in a Public World,* Englewood Cliffs, NJ: Prentice-Hall, 1995, passim (*see* index); Steven Levy, "Battle of the Clipper Chip," *New York Times Magazine* (12 June 1994): 44–51+; Levy, "Scared Bitless," *Newsweek* (10 June 1996): 49–50+; Stuart J. D. Schwartzstein, "Export Controls on Encryption Technologies," *SAIS Review* (Winter/Spring 1996): 13–34; U.S. Congress, Office of Technology Assessment, *Information Security and Privacy in Network Environments,* OTA-TCT-606, Washington, DC: GPO, September 1994, passim (see index); U.S. Congress, Office of Technology Assessment, *Issue Update on Information Security and Privacy in Network Environments,* OTA-BP-ITC-147, Washington, DC: GPO, June 1995, app. C; F. Weingarten, "Controlling Cryptographic Publication," *Computers & Security* 2 (1983): 41–48; http://www.epic.org/crypto/.

FABYAN, GEORGE

American businessman, philanthropist, and proponent of the theory that many, if not all, of William Shakespeare's works were actually written by Sir Francis Bacon. Fabyan (1867–1936) had no formal education beyond high school, but he proved to be an adept businessman and made his fortune in the textile industry. At a relatively young age, he built an estate on 500 acres of land near Geneva, Illinois, where he established a variety of laboratories whose primary function was to find evidence for his theory about the origin of Shakespeare's works.

Fabyan's name is important in the history of cryptology primarily because of two employees he hired to work at his laboratories, Elizabeth and William Friedman. He asked the Friedmans to use their skills in cryptology to look for evidence of Bacon's authorship of the Shakespearean works. After more than two years of research, the Friedmans came to the conclusion that the evidence for which Fabyan was searching did not exist: Shakespeare, not Bacon, wrote the works attributed to him.

The work at Riverbank marked the beginning of an illustrious career in cryptology for the Friedmans. While still at the estate in 1917, William Friedman taught a class in cryptology for army officers. In addition, he put together many of the concepts on cryptography and cryptanalysis that he had developed while working on the Shakespeare project in a series of publications that later became known as the Riverbank Publications.

See also: Friedman, Elizebeth Smith; Friedman, William; Shakespeare ciphers.

For further reading: David Kahn, *The Codebreakers: The Story of Secret Writing,* New York: Macmillan, 1967, ch. 12; Fred W. Kranz, "Early History of Riverbank Acoustical Laboratories," *Journal of the Acoustical Society,* vol. 42, no. 2, part I (1971), pp. 381–384; Louis Kruh, "A Cryptological Travelogue: Riverbank—1992," *Cryptologia* (January 1993): 80–94; *The National Cyclopedia of American Biography,* Clifton, NJ: James T. White, 1938, vol. 26, pp. 93–94; *Who Was Who in America, 1897–1942,* Chicago: A. N. Marquis, 1942, p. 380.

FACTORING

Also called factorization; the mathematical process of discovering which two numbers have been multiplied together to give some larger number. As a trivial example, it is obvious that the factors of 6 are 2 and 3 because 2 x 3 = 6. Factoring has become an important issue in modern cryptology because some public-key cryptographic systems are based on the presumption that it is easy to find the product of two large prime numbers (where "large" means 50 digits or more), but very difficult to find the prime factors that make up some large composite number (where "large" means 100 digits or more).

It is easy for a high-speed computer to find the product of 841,983,932,791,901 x 428,327,667,103,337. But finding out which prime numbers are the two factors of a composite number such as

187,293,384,649,241,377,519,382,312,397 is very difficult.

See also: composite number; prime number; RSA algorithm.
For further reading: H. C. Williams, "Factoring on a Computer," *Math Intelligencer* 6 (1984): 29–36.

FAIR CRYPTOGRAPHY

Proposed systems of cryptography based on the principle that keys for public-key cryptographic systems can be placed in escrow with one or more trusted intermediaries. These systems have been suggested as alternatives to the Escrowed Encryption Standards (EES) proposed by the Clinton administration in 1993. EES met with almost unanimous objection when it was first proposed, and a number of cryptologists began working on other schemes for key-escrow that would meet the objective of allowing government agencies access to keys without compromising the privacy of individuals, corporations, and other entities.

In one form of fair cryptography, a user might split the secret key into two or more parts, each of which would be distributed to an agency of the federal government and a trusted intermediary, such as a bank, a certification authority, or a Key Distribution Center. When a request was made for access to the cryptosystem, the user could sign a request and send a key component plus its "shadow" to the escrow agents. The "shadow" would provide enough of the key to allow the escrow agents to confirm that the key is legitimate without actually revealing the details of the key to every agent. The key would therefore remain secret, yet allow legitimate users access to all of its parts.

In another variation of fair cryptography, a secret key might be subdivided into four or more parts, with some number less than the total being sufficient for decryption. Thus, a company might use an algorithm with four parts divided among itself and three trusted intermediaries and an agency of the federal gov-

ernment. When a demand was made for access to the key, the company, the federal government, and one of the trusted intermediaries might provide the portions of the key needed for decryption. Decryption could occur without any of the four entities knowing all four parts of the key.

See also: certification authority; escrow agent; Escrowed Encryption Standard; Key Distribution Center; trusted intermediary.
For further reading: U.S. Congress, Office of Technology Assessment, *Information Security and Privacy in Network Environments*, OTA-TCT-606, Washington, DC: GPO, September 1994, p. 67.

FEDERAL BUREAU OF INVESTIGATION (FBI)

A division of the U.S. Department of Justice established in 1908 as the Bureau of Investigation for the department. The bureau was charged with "investigating all violations of Federal law except those that have been assigned by legislative enactment or otherwise to another Federal agency." Its jurisdiction covers the six crime areas that most affect society: organized crime, drugs, counterterrorism, white-collar crime, foreign counterintelligence, and violent crime.

The first two decades of the bureau's history were somewhat undistinguished. By the early 1920s, its reputation had been severely damaged by widespread corruption among its agents. In 1924, 29-year old J. Edgar Hoover was appointed its new director, with instructions to clean up the bureau's operations. Over the next half century, Hoover did just that, making the bureau's agents models of efficiency and incorruptibility. Hoover himself, however, operated at the edges, and perhaps just beyond the limits, of legality in achieving this transformation.

The FBI's involvement in cryptologic activities has traditionally been rather modest. Their efforts tend to focus on intelligence-gathering and counter-espionage activities. One important ex-

The FBI's cryptographic department, pictured during the 1930s.

ception is the analysis of criminal codes and ciphers within its Cryptanalytical and Translation Section (CTS). In this section, the FBI has one of the few cryptanalytical services available to and within law enforcement agencies in the United States. State and local law officers commonly transmit to the CTS requests for assistance with the breaking of codes and ciphers used in illegal betting operations, smuggling, and large-scale theft activities.

Two notable cryptanalytic cases in which the FBI was involved concerned the decryption of codes being used by rumrunners during the Prohibition Era and the solution of the new microdot technology developed by Soviet espionage agents in the 1950s.

See also: Friedman, Elizebeth Smith; microdot.
For further reading: Don Whitehead, *The FBI Story: A Report to the People,* New York: Random House, 1956.

FEDERAL INFORMATION PROCESSING STANDARD (FIPS)

A standard established to provide security and privacy for communications within and between government and nongovernment agencies. The Computer Security Act of 1987 assigned responsibility to the National Institute of Science and Technology (formerly the National Bureau of Standards) for developing guidelines and training programs for ensuring the security and privacy of computer system communications. In general, those standards do not apply to so-called Warner Amendment systems, those with a national security function such as the Department of Defense, the National Security Agency, and the Central Intelligence Agency. One of the most controversial FIPS regulations concerns the Escrowed Encryption Standard promulgated by the administration of President Bill Clinton in 1993.

For further reading: U.S. Congress, Office of Technology Assessment, *Information*

Security and Privacy in Network Environments, OTA-TCT-606, Washington, DC: GPO, September 1994, passim (*see* index).

FEEDBACK FUNCTION ━━━━━━━━

Any operation in which the final product is used to affect the beginning stages of the operation. Feedback functions are common in the everyday world. Consider the circulation of water vapor through the atmosphere. When the air above a lake is very dry, water evaporates from the lake and becomes water vapor in the air above the lake. As long as the concentration of water vapor is relatively low, evaporation will continue. Eventually, the water vapor in the air becomes so concentrated that water droplets condense in the air; it rains, water falls back into the lake, and the air is once again dry.

Various cryptosystems make use of feedback programs in the encipherment of plaintext. The ciphertext generated in one round of encipherment is used as the starting point in the next round of encipherment.

See also: cipher feedback; Data Encryption Standard.

FIBER OPTICS ━━━━━━━━━━

A form of technology in which beams of laser light are carried through very thin strands (about the size of a human hair) of high-quality glass. Fiberglass technology was first envisioned by Narinder Singh Kapany in the 1950s. The principle on which the technology is based is that a beam of light can be made to travel through a very long strand of glass without losing any of its fundamental characteristics in the process. Essentially the beam is contained within the strand by means of internal reflections.

In order to transmit a message, a large number of glass strands are joined to one another to form a glass cable. The glass cable is roughly analogous to a cable consisting of many copper wires bound together in a transmission line. Light shone

on an object at one end of the cable is reflected off various segments of the picture into discrete strands of the optical cable. The picture is then transmitted, essentially dot-by-dot, through the glass cable to its opposite end. The collection of dots emerging from the end of the cable is a true and accurate replica of the original object. Optic fibers of this design have revolutionized the communications industry because of their ability to transmit images and data far more efficiently and accurately than telephone wires or other forms of metal connections.

Kapany recognized from the outset that the principle of optical fibers is inherently adaptable to the transmission of coded images. The image that enters one end of an optical cable (the plaintext image) is first broken down into thousands of discrete units (points of light). To obtain a true picture of the original object, one need only maintain the proper orientation of individual strands in the optical fiber at the end of the cable.

However, there is no reason that the cable cannot be cut at some point along its length and its segments rearranged. For example, one end of the cut cable might simply be rotated through 90 degrees. The image formed at the end of the cable would not look like the original object. In fact, it might not look like anything at all. The cutting of the cable could be compared to encrypting the data (plaintext image) originally input to the cable.

To decipher the scrambled visual message, a receiver would have to know what operation had been performed on the cable (in this case, cutting and rotating it through 90 degrees). Reversing that operation would result in a deciphered image of the original object.

The technique for encrypting fiber-optic data is not quite as simple as it sounds. The glass fibers are so small that cutting and manipulating them is very difficult and can result in distortions of the original data. One successful approach is to work with groups of fibers rather than with individual fibers. Physical damage to the glass strands is minimized and encryption occurs much more efficiently.

See also: cryptoeidography.
For further reading: Elizabeth Corcoran, "Light-Talk: Goal of Putting Optical Fibers in the Home," *Scientific American* (October 1989): 74+; Narinder S. Kapany, "Fiber Optics," *Scientific American* (November 1960): 72–81; Arthur J. Zuckerman, "Optical Fibers Are Taking Over Telecommunications," *Popular Science* (October 1987): 70–74.

FIELD CIPHER

A cryptosystem that is designed and largely used for the transmission of military messages during wartime. Prior to the invention of the telegraph, most cryptograms were designed to be delivered from one person to another with only a modest consideration for speed of transmission. Once the telegraph became available, however, the same message could rapidly be sent at the same time to many military units. In such a context, it became important to have ciphers that military commanders and their subordinates could use relatively easily. Those ciphers became known as *field ciphers*.

One of the first cryptologists to recognize the need for and importance of field ciphers was Auguste Kerckhoffs. In his famous book *La Cryptographie militaire*, Kerckhoffs laid down the six fundamental requirements for any usable field cipher: (1) it must be unbreakable; if not in theory, at least in practice; (2) any compromise to the system should not inconvenience correspondents using it; (3) the key used in the system should be easy to remember and easy to change when necessary; (4) the ciphertext should be capable of transmission by means of the telegraph; (5) the apparatus to be used in enciphering and deciphering messages should be easily portable and usable by a single person; and (6) the system should be simple, requiring no unusual effort or strain on the part of the users.

See also: Kerckhoffs, Auguste; telegraph.

For further reading: William F. Friedman, *American Army Field Codes in the American Expeditionary Forces during the First World War*, Washington, DC: War Department, 1942.

FIELD CODES NOS. 1, 2, AND 3

See Code Compilation Section.

FILE SECURITY

Protection of data stored in some medium, such as a computer, from use by some unauthorized individual or from accidental loss. One way to provide file security is with physical mechanisms, such as placing a computer in a locked room protected from fire, water damage, theft, and other possible intrusions. A second way to provide security is to encipher the data itself, such as by using the Data Encryption Standard. File security is also known as *file protection*.

See also: Data Encryption Standard.
For further reading: Carl H. Meyer and Stephen M. Matyas, *Cryptography: A New Dimension in Computer Data Security*, New York: John Wiley & Sons, 1982, pp. 278–299.

FILL

See initializing vector.

FIREWALL

A barrier installed in an information network to prevent unauthorized users from gaining access to that network. For example, a given firewall might deny access to any incoming message except those coming from or going to specific locations in the network. Firewalls have been designed and implemented by the U.S. Department of Defense in its Information Warfare initiative.

See also: active intrusion-detection system.
For further reading: W. Cheswick and S. Bellovin, *Firewalls and Internet Security: Repelling the Wily Hacker*, Reading, MA: Addison-Wesley, 1994; Warwick Ford, *Computer Communications Security*, Englewood Cliffs, NJ: Prentice-Hall, 1994; Jeffrey I. Schiller,

"Secure Distributed Computing," *Scientific American* (November 1994): 72–76; U.S. Congress, Office of Technology Assessment, *Information Security and Privacy in Network Environments*, OTA-TCT-606, Washington, DC: GPO, September 1994, pp. 34–35.

FIST

The characteristic technique used by telegraph operators in the transmission of messages. No two operators touch the telegraph key with precisely the same speed, force, or other characteristic. Some operators may work very rapidly with a very light touch, while others operate the key more slowly but with a heavier touch.

Identifying an operator's fist has some important cryptologic significance. Suppose that an enemy agent wishes to send a false message to a listening post. An experienced observer at the listening post is usually able to tell whether the message is indeed being sent from a friendly operator or from an unknown individual.

Identifying fists can also assist in traffic analysis. Simply by recognizing the fist of a foreign operator, an observer can tell where the operator is located and/or whether the operator has moved positions.

See also: biometric device; telegraph; traffic analysis.

FORSCHUNGSAMT

A cryptanalytic division of the German Air Ministry established by Field Marshal Hermann Göring in 1933. The agency had little or nothing to do with air force activities; rather, it was used by Göring to spy on correspondence between the German government and other nations as well as his rivals for power within the Nazi Party.

For further reading: David Kahn, *The Codebreakers: The Story of Secret Writing*, New York: Macmillan, 1967, pp. 446–450.

FORTEZZA CARD

A Personal Computer Memory Card Industry Association (PCMCIA) card that has the capability of implementing the Skipjack algorithm, digital signature, and key exchange functions. The U.S. Department of Defense uses the card in its Defense Message System for the transmission of secure messages. In general, PCMCIA cards are slightly larger than a credit card. They contain a microprocessor chip such as the Capstone chip, and have connectors on one end that plug into a computer or card reader.

See also: Capstone chip; Escrowed Encryption Standard.

FORTITUDE

The codename given to the plan devised by Allied commanders to confuse the German military command as to the target of its planned invasion in June 1944.

See also: dummy traffic.

FRACTIONATING CIPHER

A cryptosystem in which a plaintext message is first converted into a bifid cipher, which is then rearranged and reenciphered by some other means, such as monoalphabetic substitution or transposition. David Kahn attributes to Pliny Earle Chase, American professor of natural history and philosophy, the modern refinement of the fractionating cipher, whose origins probably go back at least to the time of Polybius.

As an example of a fractionating cipher, imagine a checkerboard constructed like the one below.

```
    1  2  3  4  5
1   b  a  c  k  g
2   r  o  u  n  d
3   e  f  h  ij l
4   m  p  q  s  t
5   v  w  x  y  z
```

The keyword used in constructing this checkerboard is BACKGROUND.

Now assume that the message to be enciphered is BREAK CAMP NOW. The first step is to locate the numerical bifid corresponding to each letter of the message:

B = 11 R = 21 E = 31 A = 12 K = 14 C = 13
A = 12 M = 41 P = 42 N = 24 O = 22 W = 52

Now each bifid is rewritten in vertical sequence, as follows:

B R E A K C A M P N O W
1 2 3 1 1 1 1 4 4 2 2 5
1 1 1 2 4 3 2 1 2 4 2 2

This numerical arrangement can be rearranged in any number of ways. For example, one could construct a new set of bifids by reading off the numbers above horizontally from left to right. This approach would give the bifids 12 31 11 14 42 25 11 12 43 21 24 22. Finally, the original checkerboard could be used to reencipher these bifids into new cipher letters, as follows:

12 = a 42 = p 43 = q
31 = e 25 = d 21 = r
11 = b 11 = b 24 = n
14 = k 12 = a 22 = o

The cipher message produced, then, would be aebkp dbaq rno.

See also: bifid; Chase, Pliny Earle; monoalphabetic substitution; Polybius; superencipherment; transposition.
For further reading: Brian Beckett, *Introduction to Cryptology*, Oxford: Blackwell Scientific Publications, 1988, pp. 49–53; Helen Fouché Gaines, *Cryptanalysis: A Study of Ciphers and Their Solution*, New York: Dover Publications, 1956, ch. 22.

FREEMASONS' CIPHER

A system of cryptography developed and used by the Freemasons beginning in the early 1700s. The Freemasons originated as a group of stoneworkers who were not affiliated with craft guilds like those to which many other workingmen

belonged. Over time, the association evolved into a business and social club, the Free and Accepted Masons, with many secret rituals. Chapters of the Masons continue to exist today throughout the United States and in other parts of the world.

To keep their business secret from general scrutiny, the Freemasons adopted a form of the pigpen cipher for their correspondence and record-keeping. The pigpen cipher uses two tic-tac-toe–like boxes and two cross-hatched squares. Each of the 26 letters of the alphabet can be accommodated in one of the boxes formed by these four geometric figures, as shown in the diagram.

To encipher a message using the Freemasons' cipher, locate the position of each letter in the message in one of the figures and sketch that portion of the figure, as shown below.

The Freemasons' cipher was revealed to the general public long ago, and the club no longer uses it for correspondence or record-keeping.

FREQUENCY DISTRIBUTION

The frequency with which any letter, pair of letters, set of three letters, or other combination of letters occurs within a particular language. Frequency counts are one of the most important tools in the cryptanalysis of a message. If the following message were intercepted, for example, a first step in cryptanalyzing it would be to see which letters occur most frequently.

wopqz ijoot cyrwx kmeoe fhotz tvoem ceoto wsloj

In this example, the most frequently occurring letters are *o* (found nine times), *t* (found four times), and *w* (found three times). If the message is assumed to be a monoalphabetic substitution cipher, it would be reasonable to expect that the letter occurring most frequently in the cipher *(o)* is equivalent to the most frequently occurring letter in the English language, which is *e*. Similarly, the second most common letter in the ciphertext might be expected to represent the second most frequently occurring letter in English, *t*, and so on.

Some important caveats must be considered, however. The message shown above is quite short, and its frequency distribution of letters may not correspond to the frequency distribution of letters in the English language as a whole. Secondly, the message may not be enciphered in a monoalphabetic system, but in a polyalphabetic system. In such a case, the cipher letter *o* might not represent the same plaintext letter each time it is used. Despite these and other hazards in using frequency distributions, it is a commonly used and potentially powerful tool for cryptanalysis.

The frequency distribution of letters against which a message like the one above can be compared varies for a number of reasons. First, as indicated previously, frequency distributions differ slightly according to the length of a document, although that variation is much less than might be predicted. Second, the frequency distribution of letters depends on the language. The Hawaiian language, for example, contains only 12 letters (a, e, h, i, k, l, m, n, o, p, u, and w) and has a very different distribution than English. Third, the type of document examined affects the frequency distribution of letters. A poem might have a slightly differ-

ent distribution of letters than a treatise on quantum physics.

Over the years, many authorities have prepared tables of frequency distribution of letters by the brute-force technique of counting the letters in a given passage. These tables show a remarkable similarity, differing only slightly from expert to expert. The tables printed below were originally prepared by Parker Hitt for his *Manual for the Solution of Military Ciphers*, published in 1915. They show the count of 10,000 letters taken from military orders and reports, and are arranged from the most frequently used letter to the least frequently used:

Frequency of Letters

E	1,277	C	296
T	855	M	288
O	807	P	223
A	778	Y	196
N	686	W	176
I	667	G	174
R	651	B	141
S	622	V	112
H	595	K	74
D	402	J	51
L	372	X	27
U	308	Z	17
F	297	Q	8

Hitt's manual also contains a list of the most common bigrams and trigrams, as shown in the table below.

Most Frequent Bigrams

TH	50	IN	31
ER	40	ND	30
ON	39	ED	30
AN	38	HA	26
RE	36	AT	25
HE	33	EN	25

Most Frequent Trigrams

THE	89	FOR	33
AND	54	NDE	31
THA	47	HAS	28
ENT	39	NCE	27
ION	36	EDT	27
TIO	33	TIS	25

See also: bigram; trigram.
For further reading: Brian Beckett, *Introduction to Cryptology*, Oxford: Blackwell Scientific Publications, 1988, pp. 39–45; William F.

Friedman, *Elements of Cryptanalysis*, Laguna Hills, CA: Aegean Park Press, 1976, pt. 1; Helen Fouché Gaines, *Cryptanalysis: A Study of Ciphers and Their Solution*, New York: Dover Publications, 1956, passim; Donald D. Millikin, *Elementary Cryptography and Cryptanalysis*, Laguna Hills, CA: Aegean Park Press, n.d., ch. 3; Laurence Dwight Smith, *Cryptography: The Science of Secret Writing*, New York: W. W. Norton, 1943, ch. 6.

FRIEDMAN, ELIZEBETH SMITH ━━━▶

American cryptologist and wife of cryptologist William Friedman. Elizebeth's mother, Sophia Smith, is said to have chosen the unusual spelling to avoid having her youngest child called "Eliza," a nickname she obviously did not like. Elizebeth's father was John M. Smith, a dairyman and banker who also served on the county Republican committee.

Elizebeth (1892–1980) earned a degree in English at Michigan's Hillsdale College, and accepted a position at the Newberry Library in Chicago. There she met George Fabyan, a wealthy businessman with an intense interest in the origins of William Shakespeare's works. Fabyan was convinced that all or most of Shakespeare's writings had been produced by Sir Francis Bacon. He created a substantial research institute on his estate at Riverbank in Geneva, Illinois, to search for evidence to support his theory. In 1916, Fabyan offered Elizebeth a job at Riverbank working on the Shakespeare/Bacon project.

Elizebeth learned about the efforts of some staff members to locate ciphers in Shakespeare's work that would prove they had been written by Bacon. Although she had no previous experience with cryptology, she rapidly developed an interest in the subject. In pursuing this interest, she became acquainted with another Riverbank staffer with a similar story, William Friedman.

Friedman had been hired off the campus at Cornell University by Fabyan to work as a geneticist at Riverbank. He too had been caught up in the cryptologic

studies going on there, and William and Elizebeth were soon working together on the supposed Baconian ciphers in Shakespeare. They fell in love and eventually married in May 1917. They would become, according to David Kahn, "the most famous husband-and-wife team in the history of cryptology."

The cryptologic work for which Elizebeth Friedman is probably most famous was her decryption of cryptograms used by rumrunners during Prohibition. The importing of illegal alcoholic beverages after adoption of the Eighteenth Amendment in 1919 had become big business involving enormous profits. Handling the details of getting liquor from off-shore "mother ships" to smaller delivery boats and thence to ports on land required an organizational genius for which most legal businesses would be thankful. The rumrunners' task was made even more difficult by the fact that they not only had to make deliveries, they had to avoid federal agents in the process.

As part of this operation, the rumrunners developed cryptosystems even more advanced and sophisticated than those used by the U.S. military during and after World War I. They employed these systems to transmit messages among mother ships, delivery boats, landing ports, and individuals involved in the importing process. The Coast Guard had no problem intercepting the encrypted messages being sent by rumrunners, but they experienced no success whatsoever in decrypting them. Thus, a potentially powerful tool in stopping the flow of illegal liquor into the United States was useless to the Coast Guard.

Then, in April 1927, the task of decrypting the intercepted messages was turned over to Elizebeth Friedman. Within months, she had broken the cryptosystem used by the rumrunners.

The system consisted of four steps, illustrated in the example below. The first step involved the use of the well-known codebook, *The ABC Code*. The first word

American cryptanalysts William and Elizebeth Friedman both made incredible contributions to cryptology.

or phrase of the plaintext message was looked up in *The ABC Code* and its comparable codenumber written down. The additive 10000 was then added to that codenumber. The new codenumber was looked up in a second codebook, the *Ajax*, and its corresponding codeword written down. Finally, the *Ajax* codeword was further enciphered by means of a simple monoalphabetic substitution.

Step 1: Plaintext ARRIVING ON TUESDAY = codenumber 82193
Step 2: Add 10000 to codenumber: 92193
Step 3: 92193 in *Ajax* = NZKLW
Step 4: Monoalphabetic substitution: NZKLW = QDOPC

This final word (along with the rest of the message) was then transmitted.

Later in life, Elizebeth Friedman and her husband returned to the subject that had brought them together at Riverbank:

the Shakespearean ciphers. By this time, they had long since concluded that no evidence existed to support the contention that Shakespeare's works had been written by Bacon. They presented and supported this conclusion with voluminous evidence in a book they jointly published in 1957, *The Shakespearean Ciphers Examined.* Elizebeth Friedman died in Plainfield, New Jersey, on 31 October 1980.

See also: Fabyan, George; Friedman, William. For further reading: James R. Chiles, "Breaking Codes Was This Couple's Lifetime Career: W. and E. Friedman," *Smithsonian* (June 1987): pp. 128–130+; *The Friedman Legacy: A Tribute to William and Elizebeth Friedman,* Fort George G. Meade, MD: Center for Cryptologic History, 1992; "Key Woman of the T-Men," *Reader's Digest* (September 1937): 51–55; Peter Way, *Codes and Ciphers,* n.p.: Crescent Books, 1977, pp. 126–131; Malcolm Willoughby, *Rum War at Sea,* Washington, DC: GPO, 1964.

FRIEDMAN, WILLIAM ━━━━━━▶

American cryptologist, described by cryptology historian David Kahn as the greatest figure in his field, a man whose "theoretical contributions and . . . practical attainments exceed those of any other cryptologist."

Friedman was born in Kishinev, Russia, on 24 September 1891. When he was less than a year old, his family emigrated to the United States. After graduating from high school in 1909, he enrolled at the Michigan Agricultural College in East Lansing, but left at the end of the first term when he decided that farming was not a field in which he was interested. He enrolled instead at Cornell University, where he majored in genetics.

After receiving his bachelor's degree in genetics, Friedman stayed on at Cornell's graduate school. His work there was interrupted in 1915 by the arrival of George Fabyan, a wealthy industrialist and proponent of the theory that all or most of Shakespeare's works had been written by Sir Francis Bacon. Fabyan had established an impressive school at his estate, Riverbank, in Geneva, Illinois, with the objective of collecting evidence to support his Baconian theories. He invited Friedman to accept a position as head of its genetics department, and Friedman accepted in June 1915.

Friedman had not been at Riverbank long before he was drawn into the ubiquitous discussions over authorship of the Shakespearean works. He quickly became fascinated about the efforts going on around him to break the supposed ciphers in Shakespeare/Bacon's work. He later wrote that cryptology (a term he himself first defined) became an "outlet" for him.

Joining him in his growing enthusiasm was a young woman also working at Riverbank, Elizebeth Smith. Before long, the two found they had more than cryptology in common, and they were married in May 1917. The Friedmans became the most famous couple in the history of cryptology.

Soon after Friedman was appointed head of the Department of Ciphers at Riverbank, the United States entered World War I. The government began sending him ciphers to decrypt and young officers to train in the principles of cryptography and cryptanalysis. One consequence of these assignments was a series of publications, called Riverbank Publications, on a wide variety of topics in cryptology. These included such subjects as *A Method of Reconstructing the Primary Alphabet from a Single One of the Series of Secondary Alphabets* (the first in the series), *Methods for the Solution of Running-Key Ciphers, An Introduction to Methods for the Solution of Ciphers, Methods for the Reconstruction of Primary Alphabets*, and *Index of Coincidence and Its Applications in Cryptography*. A number of these publications have been reissued by and are now available from Aegean Park Press (Laguna Hills, California).

The last of the publications cited above, *Index of Coincidence*, must be regarded, according to Kahn, "as the most important single publication in cryptology." The reason for this accolade is that Friedman illustrated in careful detail for the first time how mathematical principles could be used in ciphering and deciphering messages. In particular, he showed how well-known principles of statistics could be used to decrypt a message for which little or no other information was available.

After the war, Friedman accepted an interim position with the Signal Corps and then moved over to the War Department, where one of his first assignments was to teach a course in codes and ciphers at the Signal School. In connection with that course he wrote a textbook, *Elements of Cryptanalysis*, that, according to Kahn, "for the first time, imposed order upon the chaos of cipher systems and their terminology."

In 1922, Friedman was appointed chief cryptanalyst at the Signal Corps, where he was in charge of the Code and Cipher Compilation Section, Research and Development Division. Seven years later, when the American Black Chamber was dissolved, the range of cryptologic responsibilities in the Signal Corps was greatly expanded, and Friedman was chosen to be director of the Corps' new Signal Intelligence Service (SIS). As the SIS went through a number of permutations, he remained in that position, or a comparable one, as part of the Army Security Agency's G-2 office and later as a consultant and technical adviser in the National Security Agency.

Friedman officially retired from government work in 1955, but continued to serve as a consultant and adviser. In 1955, he was awarded the Medal for Merit by CIA Director Allen W. Dulles for his work in the field of cryptology. He died in Washington, D.C., on 21 November 1969.

See also: Fabyan, George; Friedman, Elizebeth Smith.
For further reading: James R. Chiles, "Breaking Codes Was This Couple's Lifetime Career: W. and E. Friedman," *Smithsonian* (June 1987): 128–130+; *The Friedman Legacy: A Tribute to William and Elizebeth Friedman*, Fort George G. Meade, MD: Center for Cryptologic History, 1992; James L. Gilbert and John P. Finnegan, *U.S. Army Signals Intelligence in World War II: A Documentary History*, Washington, DC: Center of Military History, 1993; David Kahn, *The Codebreakers: The Story of Secret Writing*, New York: Macmillan, 1967, ch. 12; *Who's Who in America, 1962–63*, Chicago: A. N. Marquis, 1962, vol. 32, p. 1,077.

FRONT LINE CODE ━━━━━━━

See Code Compilation Section.

FUNKSPIEL ━━━━━━━

A German term that translates literally to "radio" (*funk-*) "game" (*-spiel*). Although the word itself suggests a harmless and entertaining activity involving radio transmissions, the reality is quite differ-

ent. In actual practice, funkspiel is used by one intelligence agency to send out false and misleading messages to an enemy agency.

As an example, Allied forces during World War II depended heavily on information and assistance provided by underground operatives in resistance movements throughout Europe. Messages were sent to such operatives describing intended air strikes and other military operations and, in return, information was received about the number, location, and nature of military forces in the area, possible targets, and other topics of interest to Allied forces.

From time to time, underground operators were captured and their code and cipher books and radio equipment impounded by the Germans. This gave the Germans a golden opportunity to continue the underground station's operations, listening to incoming Allied messages and sending out whatever information they chose to relay.

Funkspiel was not a simple operation. It could not be successful, for example, if code and cipher books were destroyed before or during capture of an underground radio station. Also, German operatives had to be sure that they could match the fist of radio operators who worked out of the station. In many cases, Allied listening posts recognized that messages were no longer coming from an underground operative with whom they were familiar but from someone else— presumably an enemy operator.

By no means was funkspiel limited to the Germans. On a number of occasions, counterintelligence agents were able to locate radio operators working out of London, New York, and other cities, sending messages to Germany, Italy, or Japan. This gave them the opportunity to turn the tables on the Germans and employ funkspiel activities themselves.

See also: fist.

G

G.2 A.6

A cryptanalytic section of the American Expeditionary Forces (AEF) formed as a result of General Orders No. 8, issued 5 July 1917. The section's name came from the fact that it was section 6 of the Military Intelligence Division (the A part of the acronym), which in turn was section 2 (the Intelligence Section) of the General Staff (G). G.2 A.6 was assigned primary responsibility for the interception, analysis, and decryption of enemy messages on the Western Front. It consisted of five sections, whose duties were cryptanalysis, traffic analysis, enemy telephone monitoring, tracking of enemy air artillery spotters, and monitoring of U.S. communication transmissions for possible security violations.

At first, G.2 A.6 operated under a distinct disadvantage; its personnel were trained largely in decipherment when, in fact, most German messages were being sent in code. The unit rapidly developed the necessary decryption skills and was soon providing the U.S. command with valuable information about the location and movement (and in some cases, the existence) of German army units.

As the war progressed, G.2 A.6 became a far more efficient organization, often providing decryptions of German messages within hours of interception. Perhaps the culmination of its work came in late 1918 when it intercepted and decrypted a message from Field Marshal August von Mackensen, then leading the German army of occupation in Rumania. The message told of the army's imminent withdrawal from its restless foe. The news was of enormous value to Allied armies deciding how to deal with its enemies on the Balkan front.

G.2 A.6 remained in existence after the completion of World War I, albeit with a much diminished mission. On 15 September 1945, it was merged with other military intelligence agencies into the newly formed Army Security Agency.

See also: Army Security Agency; Military Intelligence Division.
For further reading: David Kahn, *The Codebreakers: The Story of Secret Writing*, New York: Macmillan, 1967, ch. 11.

GADSBY: A STORY OF OVER 50,000 WORDS WITHOUT USING THE LETTER E

A novel written by Ernest Vincent Wright in 1939. The feature of interest about this work is that it does not contain the letter *e* anywhere in its text. Cryptanalysts often cite the novel to illustrate the point that frequency counts can be misleading when dealing with texts of atypical character, such as foreign languages, scientific works, or books written without the letter *e!*

For further reading: Ernest Vincent Wright, *Gadsby: A Story of Over 50,000 Words without Using the Letter E,* Los Angeles: Wetzel Publishing, 1939.

GARBLE

The introduction of an error in a transmission. In some cases, a message is garbled by accident, with potentially harmful results. A telegraph operator who omits a dot or a dash from a message can change the meaning of a single letter and, by extension, a word. Errors of transmission are so common and so nearly unavoidable that most important messages include some form of check that allows the receiver to determine whether changes have occurred in the process of transmission.

Errors can also be introduced into transmissions intentionally by someone wishing to cause confusion. For example, an operator can send out radar signals that will garble the comparable signals being transmitted by an enemy tracking station. By garbling the station's radar, friendly aircraft may be able to escape detection.

See also: electronic security.

GEHEIME KABINETS-KANZLEI

The Austrian black chamber that operated during the eighteenth century, generally recognized as the most efficient operation of its kind during the period.

See also: black chamber.
For further reading: Peter Way, *Codes and Ciphers,* n.p.: Crescent Books, 1977, pp. 30–32.

GEHEIMSCHREIBER

A class of enciphering machines produced by the German company of Siemens and Halske during World War II. The Geheimschreiber was used largely for communications between German naval commanders and their U-boats in the Atlantic. It used a variation of the Baudot code in which an operator first typed a plaintext message into a teletype machine. The machine then enciphered the message onto a paper tape in the form of holes (or no holes), overlaid with a Vernam cipherlike key. An operator at the receiving end of the message passed the enciphered message through a teleprinter that reversed the enciphering process and printed out the original plaintext message.

In 1942, British cryptanalysts at Bletchley Park began noticing that their intercepts contained a type of cipher different from the Enigma messages with which they were thoroughly familiar. They decided that these messages were being enciphered by a new type of machine (the Geheimschreiber), to which they gave the name Fish. They employed machines similar to those used in solving the Enigma cipher machine and its messages in order to break the Fish cryptosystem, with comparable success.

See also: Bletchley Park; Enigma; ULTRA.
For further reading: Andrew Hodges, *Alan Turing: The Enigma,* New York: Simon & Schuster, 1983, pp. 228–278, passim; Wolfgang Mache, "Geheimschreiber," *Cryptologia* (October 1986): 230–242.

GENERAL-USE CRYPTOSYSTEM

See cryptosystem.

GENETIC CODE

The arrangement of nitrogen bases in a molecule of deoxyribonucleic acid (DNA) that directs the formation of proteins in a living organism. A DNA molecule is a long, spaghettilike molecule that consists of alternating fragments of sugar and phosphate molecules. Attached to each sugar fragment is one of four possible nitrogen bases: adenine (A), cytosine (C), guanine (G), or thymine (T). During mitosis, a new molecule of messenger RNA (mRNA) is formed, using

A computer-generated graphic of DNA, one of nature's most complicated cryptographic puzzles.

the DNA molecule as a template. An mRNA molecule is also a long, spaghetti-like molecule with a backbone of sugar and phosphate groups, to which is attached some combination of four nitrogen bases: adenine (A), cytosine (C), guanine (G), and uracil (U), but not thymine. The sequence of bases in mRNA is determined by the sequence of bases in the "master molecule" of DNA. That is, for each A in a DNA molecule, a U is generated in the corresponding mRNA; for each C in a DNA, a G is generated, and so on.

The mRNA molecule's job is to travel to mitochondria in cells, from which it directs the synthesis of protein molecules. Each group (triplet or codon) of three nitrogen bases calls for a specific amino acid. For example, the presence of the grouping AUC in an mRNA molecule directs that the amino acid iso-leucine is to be constructed. The CCG codon, in contrast, codes for the construction of the amino acid proline. The complete "dictionary" of 64 codons from all possible combinations and permutations of the four nitrogen bases is called the genetic code.

For further reading: Harold Hart, *Organic Chemistry: A Short Course*, 8th ed., Boston: Houghton Mifflin, 1991, ch. 18; David E. Newton, *The Chemistry of Carbon Compounds*, 2nd ed., Portland, ME: J. Weston Walch, ch. 13; Marshall W. Nirenberg, "The Genetic Code: II," *Scientific American* (March 1963): 80–94; T. W. Graham Solomons, *Organic Chemistry*, 2nd ed., New York: John Wiley & Sons, 1980, Special Topic P.

GEOMETRICAL TRANSPOSITION

A very old form of cryptography in which plaintext is enciphered by making use of some geometric figure into which the plaintext letters are inserted. Squares, diamonds, and rectangles are among the most popular geometric figures.

As an example, suppose that one wishes to encipher the plaintext MEET THE COMMANDER AT THE TOP OF THE HILL. One approach would be to first arrange the letters of the message in a square:

```
M E E T T H
E C O M M A
N D E R A T
T H E T O P
O F T H E H
I L L X V G
```

Notice that the message contains only 33 letters, but 36 letters are required to complete the square. The final three letters, X, V, and G, are nulls, added to fill out the square.

The ciphertext can now be created by reading through the square in any number of ways. For example, one ciphertext can be created by reading down the columns, from left to right. The ciphertext produced by this method would be

```
m e n t o i e c d h f l e o e e t l t m
r t h x t m a o e v h a t p h g r c w p
```

Again, nulls have been added at the end of the message to provide a complete set of five letters for the last word of the ciphertext.

The receiver can decipher this message only if he or she is familiar with the key (the pattern from which the ciphertext was originally constructed). The receiver knows that the first five letters in the ciphertext, m e n t o, constitute the first column of the 6 x 6 square from which the message was constructed. By reconstructing that square, the receiver can decipher the message.

A different ciphertext could be produced by traveling through the 6 x 6 square in some other pattern as, for example, by reading down the first column, up the last column, down the second column, up the next-to-last column, down the third column, and up the third-to-last column. The ciphertext obtained in this case would be:

```
m e n t o i g h p t a h e c d h f l v e
o a m t e o e e t l x h t r m t j n n i
```

Geometric transposition is also known as *route transposition*, with the word *route* suggesting that a particular route or path is followed in taking off the ciphertext.

In his book *Manual for the Solution of Military Ciphers*, Colonel Parker Hitt outlines eight of the most common forms of route transposition: simple vertical (like the first example above); simple horizontal; alternate vertical; alternate horizontal; simple diagonal; alternate diagonal; spiral, clockwise; and spiral, counterclockwise. These eight do not exhaust the number of other routes possible.

See also: null; transposition.
For further reading: William F. Friedman, *Advanced Military Cryptography*, Laguna Hills, CA: Aegean Park Press, 1976, pt. A; Helen Fouché Gaines, *Cryptanalysis: A Study of Ciphers and Their Solution*, New York: Dover Publications, 1956, ch. 4, 5; Donald D. Millikin, *Elementary Cryptography and Cryptanalysis*, Laguna Hills, CA: Aegean Park Press, n.d., ch. 7; Laurence Dwight Smith, *Cryptography: The Science of Secret Writing*, New York: W. W. Norton, 1943, ch. 3.

GII
See global information infrastructure.

GLOBAL INFORMATION INFRASTRUCTURE (GII)
A term used to describe all of the hardware and software by which worldwide communications are made possible. The term reflects a major change that has taken place in the commercial world since the end of World War II. Prior to the war, most (although certainly not all) companies conducted business primarily in their own native country. The demand for lines of communication between Brazil and Japan, for example, or between Germany and Iran was relatively modest.

Today, the situation is very different. The world economic market is dominated by multinational companies, corporations with their "home" in one nation but doing business in all parts of the world. Such companies find it essential to have the means to buy, sell, and carry on other transactions in every part of the world without delay. The tools needed for this kind of operation—computers, electronic networks, satellite networks, and the like—are the infrastructure on which the global information economy depends.

Cryptography is the key to a successful global information infrastructure. As a report by the Computer Systems Policy Project puts it:

> The GII will not flourish without effective security mechanisms to protect commercial transactions. Consumers and providers of products and services, particularly those involving health care and international commerce, will not use GII applications unless they are confident that electronic communications and transactions will be confidential, that the origin of messages can be verified, that personal privacy can be protected, and that security mechanisms will not impede the transnational flow of electronic data.

The report points out that nations will often be tempted to develop security systems for commercial transactions that are consistent with those developed for and used by the government (as has been the case with DES and EES), but that "government needs should not be used as reasons to replace or overwhelm the private sector standards processes."

For further reading: *ICC Position Paper on International Encryption Policy,* Paris: International Chamber of Commerce, 1994; *Perspectives on the Global Information Infrastructure,* Washington, DC: Computer Systems Policy Project, February 1995.

"THE GOLD BUG" ━━━━━━━━

Perhaps the most famous of all literary works in which cryptology plays a central role. The work was written by Edgar Allan Poe in 1843 for *Graham's Magazine* and reprinted in the *Dollar Newspaper* (twice) and the *Saturday Courier* before appearing in book form in Poe's *Tales of the Grotesque and Arabesque.* The story tells about the discovery of an unusual golden beetle found by a naturalist, William Legrand, on Sullivan's Island in South Carolina. Legrand makes a sketch of the beetle for a friend, the narrator of the

story. When the narrator later holds the sketch inadvertently in front of a flame, Legrand notices that words begin to appear on the paper. With further heating, a cryptogram appears that contains directions for finding a hidden treasure. The cryptogram reads as follows:

```
  5 3 ‡ ‡ † 3 0 5 ) ) 6 *
; 4 8 2 6 ) 4 ‡ .
  ) 4 ‡ ) ; 8 0 6 * ; 4 8
† 8 6 0 ) ) 8 5
;
    l ‡ ( ; : ‡ * 8 † 8 3
( 8 8 ) 5 * † ; 4 6
  ( ; 8 8 * 9 6 ? ; 8 ) ‡
( ; 4 8 5 ) ; 5
  * † 2 ; * ‡ ( ; 4 9 5 6
* 2 ( 5 * - 4 ) 8
  8 * ; 4 0 6 9 2 8 5 ) ;
) 6 ‡ ‡ ; l
  ( ‡ 9 ; 4 8 0 8 l ; 8 :
‡ l ; 4 8 ‡ 8 5
  ; 4 ) 4 8 5 † 5 2 8 8 0
6 * 8 l ( ‡ 9 ; 4 8
  ; ( 8 8 ; 4 ( ‡ ? 3 4 ;
4 8 ) 4 ‡ ; l 6 l
  ; ; l 8 8 ; ‡ ? ;
```

Using a frequency count of letters in the cryptogram, Legrand deciphers the message. It reads:

> A good glass in the bishop's hostel in the devil's seat—forty-one degrees and thirteen minutes—northeast by north—main branch seventh limb east side—shoot from the left eye of the death's head—a beeline from the tree through the shot fifty feet out.

From these directions, Legrand and the narrator search for and discover the treasure, that of pirate captain William Kidd. A number of flaws exists both in the cryptanalysis of the message, as described by Poe, and in the plotline itself. However, both the magazine articles and the book form of the story were widely popular and successful, and are still read with pleasure by people of all ages today.

See also: frequency distribution.
For further reading: "The Gold Bug" was originally published in Edgar Allan Poe, *The Murders in the Rue Morgue and Other Tales,* Philadelphia: Porter & Coates, 18??, but has since been republished in many anthologies. *See* especially E. C. Stedman and

G. E. Woodberry, eds., *The Works of Edgar Allan Poe,* Chicago: Stone & Kimball, 1905, 10 vols., which includes some of Poe's own commentaries on his cryptologic works.

GOUZENKO, IGOR ━━━━━

A cipher clerk in the Russian embassy in Ottawa whose 1945 defection to the West provided valuable information on the operation of the Soviet espionage system. Gouzenko (1919–1982) supplied Canadian officials with the meaning of a number of codenames used by the Soviets, information on their use of one-time pads, and clues to some important Canadian and British figures involved in espionage for the Soviet Union.

For further reading: *The Defection of Igor Gouzenko: Report of the Canadian Royal Commission,* 4 vols., Laguna Hills, CA: Aegean Park Press, n.d.; Fred B. Wrixon, *Codes and Ciphers,* New York: Prentice-Hall, 1992, pp. 80–81.

GOVERNMENT CODE & CYPHER SCHOOL (GC&CS) ━━━━

A division of the British Foreign Office whose responsibility was to "study the methods of cypher communication used by foreign powers" and "advise on the security of British codes and cyphers." GC&CS was created at the end of World War I out of the British Admiralty's famous cryptology bureau, Room 40, and its functions were transferred from the Admiralty to the Foreign Office. In anticipation of possible hostilities with the Germans, in August 1938 the service was moved from offices in London to the beautiful country estate of Bletchley Park, about 45 miles northwest of London. It remained active there until the war's conclusion in 1945.

GC&CS experienced some noteworthy successes during the 1920s, including the interception and decryption of important Russian communications that led to the fall of the Labor government in 1924. However, it was constantly hampered by lack of funds from a government that was unable to see its value during peacetime. As a result, the service was inadequately prepared to respond to the emerging threat posed by Nazi Germany in the 1930s. In fact, not until the outbreak of the war did funds once more begin to flow at levels that would give the British at least a modest cryptologic presence in the forthcoming conflict.

Without question, the accomplishment for which GC&CS is best known is its breaking of the Enigma cipher machine and cryptosystem. At the start of 1938, the service's attempts to decrypt Enigma-enciphered messages were completely unsuccessful. Workers at GC&CS came to the conclusion that the Enigma was essentially unbreakable. Whether it was or not, the government had still not provided the service with the funds needed to hire the personnel required to solve the cipher machine and its cryptosystem.

Then, in the summer of 1938, a breakthrough occurred that totally changed the service's prospects for solving the Enigma. Polish cryptanalysts passed on to their British counterparts priceless information about the Enigma machine that had been given to them by the French, and showed them a decrypting machine they thought could be used to break the Enigma. Fortunately, the information fell into the hands of Alan Turing, one of the world's greatest mathematicians and creative intellects of the day. With the information provided by the Poles and Turing's leadership, the GC&CS staff was eventually able to solve the Enigma, an attainment that, except for the discovery of radar, was perhaps the single most important scientific accomplishment responsible for the Allies' winning of World War II.

See also: Bletchley Park; Enigma; Turing, Alan.
For further reading: William F. Clarke, "Government Code and Cypher School: Its Foundation and Development with Special Reference to Its Naval Side," *Cryptologia* (October 1987): 219–226; Francis H.

Hinsley, *British Intelligence in the Second World War,* New York: Cambridge University Press, 1993; Hinsley, "The Enigma of Ultra: Britain's Breaking of Enemy Cyphers," *History Today* (September 1993): 15–20; Andrew Hodges, *Alan Turing: The Enigma,* New York: Simon & Schuster, 1983, passim; Gordon Welchman, *The Hut Six Story: Breaking the Enigma Codes,* New York: McGraw-Hill, 1982.

GRAY

A diplomatic code introduced in 1919 that David Kahn described as "the best known and longest lived of American diplomatic codes." Like the GREEN code it replaced, the GRAY code was a one-part code consisting of five-letter codegroups of the form CUCUC, where C represents a consonant and U a vowel.

Although GRAY was the cryptosystem by which American diplomats communicated with one another about their most secret business, the code was anything but secure. One code clerk described the GRAY and other systems used by the State Department as "quaint transparencies dating back to the time when Hamilton Fish was Secretary of State under President Grant." As an example of this transparency, the clerk pointed out that, in GRAY, the codeword for LOVE was lovve.

The GRAY and other diplomatic codes of the time were so well known to cryptanalysts in other nations that the United States was essentially incapable of conducting any type of secure diplomatic correspondence. As Japan began its expansionist policies of the 1930s, for example, they apparently read every communication between Washington and its representatives throughout Asia and the rest of the world. Despite its obvious inadequacies, the GRAY code remained in use among U.S. diplomats until the early 1940s.

For further reading: David Kahn, *The Codebreakers: The Story of Secret Writing,* New York: Macmillan, 1967, pp. 490–492; Fred B. Wrixon, *Codes and Ciphers,* New York: Prentice-Hall, 1992, p. 81.

THE GREAT CRYPTOGRAM

A book written by Ignatius Donnelly summarizing his evidence that the plays credited to William Shakespeare were in fact written by Sir Francis Bacon. The book was published in 1888 by R. S. Peale & Company of Chicago. Donnelly's book is based on a massive misreading of textual materials that he regarded as ciphers indicating the real author of the so-called Shakespearean plays. Donnelly's arguments were thoroughly refuted in a later book by William and Elizabeth Friedman.

See also: Shakespeare ciphers.
For further reading: Ignatius Donnelly, *The Great Cryptogram: Francis Bacon's Cipher in the So-Called Shakespeare Plays,* Chicago: R. S. Peale, 2 vols., 1988; William F. Friedman and Elizabeth S. Friedman, *The Shakespearean Ciphers Examined,* Cambridge: Cambridge University Press, 1957.

GREATEST COMMON DIVISOR (GCD)

The largest integer that divides evenly into two or more other integers. For example, the greatest common divisor of 6, 15, 18, and 24 is 3, since 3 is the largest number that divides into all four integers evenly. The gcd of 18, 30, and 42, in contrast, is 6.

Finding the gcd of a set of numbers is a fundamentally important operation in the cryptanalysis of many public-key cryptographic algorithms.

See also: Euclidean algorithm; relative primes; RSA algorithm.

GREEN

A diplomatic code introduced by the U.S. State Department in 1910 as a replacement for the BLUE code. The GREEN was a one-part code consisting of five-letter codegroups. Like most other U.S. codes before World War II, the GREEN was not a particularly sophisticated cryptosystem, and apparently it was soon being read by cryptanalysts in many nations, both friend and foe.

For further reading: Fred B. Wrixon, *Codes and Ciphers,* New York: Prentice-Hall, 1992, pp. 81–82.

GREEN BOOK

Brief name for the *Green Book on the Security of Information Systems.* The Green Book was produced as the result of a decision by the European Council in May 1992 to establish a Senior Official's Group to advise the council on a plan of action to be taken and strategies to be developed for the security of information systems in European communications. The Green Book examines the issues involved in this` area, suggests a range of options available, and lists requirements for actions. The three general areas with which the Green Book is concerned are trust services, international developments, and technical harmonization.

For further reading: U.S. Congress, Office of Technology Assessment. *Information Security and Privacy in Network Environments,* OTA-TCT-606, Washington, DC: GPO, September 1994, pp. 91–92.

GRILLE

A steganographic device by which plaintext messages are hidden by some geometric means. The concept was first described by Girolamo Cardano in about 1550. Cardano's grille consisted of a piece of stiff paper or metal into which rectangular holes were cut. When the holes were placed over an otherwise innocent-looking message, a hidden message would appear. (*See* the example under Cardano, Girolamo). Cardano's grille had some fundamental flaws, but in one form or another it remained a popular tool of cryptographers for more than four centuries.

One variation of the Cardano grille was suggested by an Italian general, Luigi Sacco, in the early twentieth century. The Sacco grille consists of a rectangular sheet of paper divided into 12 columns and six rows, producing a matrix of 72 squares.

Squares are cut out of each column in the matrix at random. A portion of such a grille is shown below.

To use the grille, the cryptographer writes a message on a sheet of paper the same size as the grille. The message must contain all the letters of the hidden message. An example taken from William F. Friedman's text on *Advanced Military Cryptography* (Aegean Park Press, 1976) illustrates how the grille can be used:

```
I  H  A  V  E  W  O  R  K  E
D  V  E  R  Y  W  E  L  L  A
L  L  D  A  Y  T  R  Y  I  N
G  T  O  G  E  T  E  V  E  R
Y  T  H  I  N  G  S  T  R  A
I  G  H  T  E  N  E  D  U  P
B  E  F  O  R  E  G  O  I  N
G  O  N  M  Y  N  E  X  T  T
R  I  P  S  O  U  T  H  B  U
T  I  N  S  I  D  E  T  E  N
```

The grille, whose construction is known to both encipherer and decipherer, is placed over the message so that only certain letters in the message show through holes in the grille. For example, the grille might be placed so that only the boldface letters in the above message show through. The message can then be read from left to right, top to bottom, through the grille.

As an additional step in encipherment, the revealed message shown above (ALL DESTROYERS OUTSIDE) could be enciphered by taking off the letters from top to bottom in each column, producing the ciphertext lrtad tsser yoids eloeu. Knowing the shape of the grille, the decipherer could simply insert the cipher letters in their proper position in the openings of the grille and read the original message.

A further variation of Cardano's idea is the turning (or revolving or rotating) grille. Such a grille might consist of six columns and six rows, giving a total of 36 squares. The nine letters of a message might be written in the first nine squares that make up the upper left quadrant of the grille before the grille is rotated through 90 degrees. The next nine letters are written in the new upper left quadrant of the grille before it is turned once more through 90 degrees. The process is repeated twice more until the complete message has been written into all four quadrants of the grille, but in different sequence, of course. The message can then be taken off letter-by-letter in any manner predetermined by encipherer and decipherer. The exact dimensions of the turning grille and how it is to be used in enciphering (and deciphering) a message can be changed in a number of ways.

See also: Cardano, Girolamo; geometrical transposition; Sacco, Luigi; steganography. For further reading: William F. Friedman, *Advanced Military Cryptography*, Laguna Hills, CA: Aegean Park Press, 1976, sec. 5; Helen Fouché Gaines, *Cryptanalysis: A Study of Ciphers and Their Solution*, New York: Dover Publications, 1956, ch. 3-5, passim.

GRONSFELD CIPHER

A cryptosystem invented in the seventeenth century by the count of Gronsfeld. The cipher became best known in the 1890s when it was used by a group of anarchists to transmit messages to one another. The cipher was solved by the brilliant French cryptologist Étienne Bazeries, and its messages were used in the trial and conviction of the anarchists.

The Gronsfeld cipher is an abbreviated form of the Vigenère cipher, in which the key consists of a series of numbers, such as 829351. The number sequence indicates the alphabet to be used in enciphering each of the letters in the plaintext. For example, if the first word of a message is REVOLT, the first letter (R) would be advanced by eight letters to give the cipher letter *z*. The second letter (E) would be advanced by two letters to give the cipher letter *g*, and so on. The enciphered word produced for REVOLT

with the keynumber of 829351 would be zgerqu.

See also: Bazeries, Étienne; Vigenère square.

GYLDÉN, YVES

A Swedish businessman and cryptologist, Gyldén (1895–1963) is perhaps best remembered today as the author of an important book dealing with the use of codes and ciphers during World War I, *Chifferbyråernas insatser i världskriget till lands.* The book was not only highly regarded in Sweden but other nations as well. The U.S. Army Signal Corps reprinted it under the title *The Contribution of the Cryptographic Bureaus in the World War.* The book is currently available in reprint form from Aegean Park Press, Laguna Hills, California.

Gyldén's interest in cryptology grew through a natural course of events. His father, Olof, was a business partner of Arvid Damm in the formation of Aktiebolaget Cryptograph, a company established to manufacture cipher machines invented by Damm. Gyldén devoted considerable time and effort to speaking and writing about the importance of cryptology in his native Sweden, and he is credited with arousing interest in the subject among many of the Scandinavian countries. He also served the Swedish government in cryptanalyzing secret messages dealing with illegal business activities and, during the war, breaking ciphers sent by belligerent nations on both sides of the conflict.

See also: Damm, Arvid. For further reading: Yves Gyldén, *The Contribution of the Cryptographic Bureaus in the World War,* Washington, DC: GPO, 1936 (reprinted by Aegean Park Press, Laguna Hills, CA, 1978); David Kahn, *The Codebreakers: The Story of Secret Writing,* New York: Macmillan, 1967, pp. 478–483.

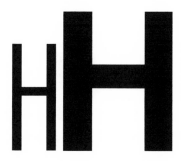

HACKER

An unauthorized person who attempts to break through the security program on a computer program or system in order to obtain information to which he or she is not entitled. In some cases, the hacker may want the information for private use and/or gain. In other cases, the person attempts to break computer security simply to demonstrate intellectual skill—to "beat the system" as a kind of game.

See also: computer.
For further reading: P. Denning, ed., *Computers under Attack: Intruders, Worms, and Viruses*, Reading, MA: ACM Press, 1990; Katie Hafner and John Markoff, *Cypherpunk: Outlaws and Hackers on the Computer Frontier*, New York: Simon & Schuster, 1991; Steven Levy, *Hackers—Heroes of the Computer Revolution*, New York: Doubleday, 1984; Bruce Sterling, *The Hacker Crackdown: Law and Disorder on the Electronic Frontier*, New York: Bantam Books, 1992.

HAGELIN, BORIS CAESAR WILHELM

Swedish businessman, entrepreneur, and cryptologist. Hagelin (1892–1983) was born in Russia, where his father was consul-general. He was educated in St. Petersburg and graduated from the Royal Institute of Technology in Stockholm with a degree in mechanical engineering. He held jobs with the Swedish electrical manufacturing company ASEA and the Standard Oil Company of New Jersey.

Hagelin's family had planned to return to Russia after communism failed and the czarist government was returned to power. When that did not happen, Hagelin was sent to Sweden to work in the company established by Arvid Damm and Olof Gyldén, Aktiebolaget Cryptograph, a company in which his father had made a substantial investment.

In 1925, Hagelin learned that the Swedish army was thinking about purchasing the German Enigma cipher machine for its own cryptographic use. He decided that one of Damm's inventions, later named the B-21, could be modified to meet Swedish specifications. He demonstrated the device to Swedish officials and was awarded a substantial contract. At about this time, Damm died, and Hagelin's family and financial associates bought out Damm's firm and renamed it Aktiebolaget Cryptoteknik.

For about a decade, the B-21 was the most compact cipher machine capable of printing out ciphertext then available. In 1934, the French government expressed an interest in purchasing the machine for its own military forces, but insisted that it be reduced to pocket size. The challenge seemed unrealistic; the B-21 was the size of a standard typewriter and weighed 37 pounds. Hagelin nonetheless tackled the assignment and managed to shrink the device to a box about the size of an ordinary telephone receiver with a weight of just under 3 pounds. The French were delighted with the final product and placed an order for 5,000 of the machines.

The French contract set Hagelin and Aktiebolaget Cryptoteknik on the road to financial success. As David Kahn writes, Hagelin eventually became "the first—

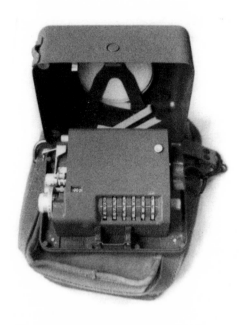

This minicipher device is the result of Boris Hagelin's efforts to shrink cipher machines.

and the only—man to become a millionaire from cryptology."

Hagelin followed up his successful agreement with the French with visits in 1937 and 1939 to the United States, where the American military was also interested in his C-36 (as it was then called) machine. During the prolonged negotiations that followed, Hagelin heard that Germany had invaded Norway. He decided that he would have to leave Sweden for the United States immediately. All travel to the United States had been canceled because of Germany's conquest of France, Holland, and Belgium. Hagelin decided instead to travel across Europe to Italy. He and his wife set sail from Genoa with blueprints and a disassembled model of the cipher machine hidden in their luggage. The trip was well worthwhile. The U.S. Army purchased Hagelin's design and, under the name M-209, made it the army's primary cipher machine during the war. In the first year of production, the Smith & Corona Company turned out 400 M-209s a day. By the end of the war, more than 140,000 were manufactured.

Hagelin died on 7 September 1983.

See also: Damm, Arvid; M-209.

For further reading: Boris C. W. Hagelin, "The Story of the Hagelin Cryptos," edited by David Kahn, *Cryptologia* (July 1996): 204–222. David Kahn, *The Codebreakers: The Story of Secret Writing*, New York: Macmillan, 1967, pp. 425–434.

HANDSHAKING

Any system by which users desiring to transmit information back and forth between themselves can obtain verification of the users and the information transmitted between them. One way to create a handshaking system is for two users to agree upon a given key or set of keys that they will use in their correspondence and sign a formal contract defining this key or keys.

See also: authentication.
For further reading: Carl H. Meyer and Stephen M. Matyas, *Cryptography: A New Dimension in Computer Data Security*, New York: John Wiley & Sons, 1982, pp. 351–354.

HASHING ALGORITHM

An algorithm that can be used to produce a condensed version of a message, which can then be signed electronically by the sender. The hashing algorithm is a one-way function, which means that the condensed version of the message cannot be decrypted in order to obtain the original message. The hashing process is used for the purpose of authenticating a message sent by means of public-key cryptography. A hash is also known as a message digest.

See also: digital signature; one-way function; public-key cryptography.
For further reading: D. W. Davies and W. L. Price, *Security for Computer Networks: An Introduction to Data Security in Teleprocessing and Electronic Funds Transfer*, Chichester: John Wiley & Sons, 1984, pp. 137, 280–281; Charlie Kaufman, Radia Perlman, and Mike Speciner, *Network Security: Private Communication in a Public World*, Englewood Cliffs, NJ: Prentice-Hall, 1995, ch. 4; William Stallings, *Network and Internetwork Security: Principles and Practices*,

Englewood Cliffs, NJ: Prentice-Hall, 1995, ch. 4; U.S. Congress, Office of Technology Assessment, *Information Security and Privacy in Network Environments*, OTA-TCT-606, Washington, DC: GPO, September 1994, pp. 39, 124–125.

HAYHANEN, REINO

Soviet espionage agent and later defector. Hayhanen (1920–1961?) worked as a courier and communications agent for Soviet spy Rudolph Ivanovich Abel. The working relationship between the two Soviet agents apparently began to disintegrate about 1957 when Abel suggested that Hayhanen return to the Soviet Union for a "vacation." Hayhanen interrupted his return trip to Moscow in Paris, where he defected to the U.S. embassy. His testimony was later crucial in convicting Abel of espionage. The place, date, and circumstances of Hayhanen's death have never been confirmed.

For further reading: Louise Bernikow, *Abel*, New York: Trident Press, 1970; James B. Donovan, *Strangers on a Bridge: The Case of Colonel Abel*, New York: Atheneum, 1964.

HEBERN, EDWARD H.

American businessman and inventor of cryptographic machines. Hebern was born in Streator, Illinois, on 23 April 1869. After graduating from high school, he moved to California, where he worked in the lumber industry before turning to home building and sales as a career. At some time during this period he became interested in cryptology in general, and in the construction of cryptographic machines in particular.

One of his earliest inventions consisted of a pair of typewriters whose keys were randomly joined to each other by means of electrical wires. When an operator struck any given key on the first typewriter, an electrical current passed through the connecting wire and activated a second key on the other typewriter. Typing in the letter *p* on the first machine, for example, might cause the letter *c* to print out on the second machine. Thus, the device was an electromechanical system of monoalphabetic substitution.

The two-typewriter system itself was not nearly as important as its concept, which Hebern refined in the development of the rotor. A rotor is a hockey puck–shaped disk of hard rubber, Bakelite, or some other material, with 26 electrical contacts on each of the disk's faces. The contacts on each side were joined by means of electrical wires imbedded within the disks.

The first patent for the rotor concept was issued in 1919 to the Swedish inventor Arvid Damm, but evidence indicates that Hebern developed the idea at least two years earlier. His own patent for the device was issued in 1924.

By 1921, Hebern incorporated the rotor into the design of a cryptographic machine in which he tried to interest the U.S. Navy. His presentation came at just the right time, because the navy was looking for a new cryptosystem for its secret communications. Their response was sufficiently positive to encourage Hebern to return to California and incorporate the first cipher machine company in the United States, the Hebern Electric Code.

Initial response by prospective investors was enthusiastic. Hebern was able to sell $1 million worth of stock with almost no trouble, and construction on the company's first plant began 21 September 1922.

In many ways, the first few months of the company's existence were its finest. The navy was apparently committed to purchasing the machine, and new investors were eager to join in Hebern's venture.

But the company began going downhill almost immediately. Sales were much slower than anticipated, and the company could not keep up mortgage payments on the ambitious building opened in 1922. Stockholders became nervous about their investment, and the state of California filed charges against Hebern, claiming he had conducted improper financial transactions. Although he was eventually acquitted of the charges, the company did not survive, and it filed for bankruptcy in 1926.

Hebern never gave up his hope of selling a usable cryptographic machine to the U.S. military. For the next 15 years, he filed for new patents, developed new machines, and made new presentations to the military services. In 1947, he filed suit for $50 million against the army, navy, and air force, claiming that they had stolen his ideas for cipher machines without actually buying anything from him. His suit was later settled out of court for $30,000, in a decision that David Kahn calls "tragic, unjust, and pathetic, [one that] does his country no honor."

Hebern died of a heart attack in Oakland, California, on 10 February 1952.

See also: rotor.
For further reading: Wayne G. Barker, ed., *The History of Codes and Ciphers in the United States during the Period between the World Wars, Part II: 1930–1939*, Laguna Hills, CA: Aegean Park Press, 1978, pp. 48–54; David Kahn, *The Codebreakers: The Story of Secret Writing*, New York: Macmillan, 1967, pp. 415–420.

HELLMAN, MARTIN E.

Coauthor with Whitfield Diffie of one of the seminal papers in public-key cryptography, "New Directions in Cryptology," published in 1976. Diffie and Hellman (1945–) outlined a method by which two individuals could agree on a key that they would share with each other, which would allow them to exchange secret messages by means of public systems of communication. In 1976, Diffie and Hellman again collaborated on a critical survey paper entitled "Privacy and Authentication: An Introduction to Cryptography."

Martin Hellman was born in New York City on 2 October 1945. He earned his bachelor's degree in electrical engineering from New York University in 1966; his master of science in 1967 and Ph.D. in 1969 were both in electrical engineering and earned from Stanford University. He was a member of the research staff at IBM's Watson Research Center from 1968 to 1969 and on the faculty of electrical engineering at the Massachusetts Institute of Technology from 1969 to 1971. In 1971, he returned to the Stanford faculty and is now professor emeritus at the university.

Hellman is the author or coauthor of over 60 technical papers and has been awarded five U.S. patents and many additional patents from foreign nations. Among his honors are the California State Psychological Association's Award for Distinguished Contribution to Consumer Protection in 1978 and the IEEE Centennial Medal in 1984. In addition to his work in cryptology, Hellman is interested in ethical issues arising out of technological development.

See also: public-key cryptography.
For further reading: http://ee.stanford.edu/ee/faculty/Hellman_Martin.html.

HEXADECIMAL NOTATION

A numerical system based on the number 16 (*hexa-* = "six"; *decimal* = "ten"). Each of the positions in a number, then, represents some power of 16. The digit farthest to the right represents 16^0; the next digit to the left, 16^1; the next digit to the left, 16^2; and so on. Hexadecimal notation is a very efficient system for representing large numbers.

See also: binary number system; octal notation.

HIEROGLYPHICS

A written language used in ancient Egypt in which written symbols are used to represent sounds. The subject of hieroglyphics is of interest in the history of cryptology primarily for two reasons. First, the earliest examples of intentional textual modifications can be traced to hieroglyphic texts from about 1900 B.C. Such modifications apparently were not designed to hide the meaning of text but to indicate the importance of the text's writer.

Egyptian hieroglyphic messages may be the earliest examples of written text that employ cryptograms.

The second feature of hieroglyphics of interest to cryptologists is the use of the Rosetta stone to understand the meaning of hieroglyphics. The Rosetta stone is a slab of rock discovered in 1801 by French engineers in an Egyptian town of that name. The stone contains the same text written three times—once in hieroglyphics, once in Greek, and once in a colloquial Egyptian language known as demotic.

See also: Rosetta stone.

HILL, LESTER

U.S. mathematician, cryptographer, and one of the creators of algebraic cryptography. Cryptography has never been limited to the use of letters in codes and ciphers. Numerals and other symbols (such as *, &, and #) have been used to encipher plaintext almost as commonly as letters. Indeed, the cryptosystem suggested by Polybius in the second century B.C. used pairs of numbers to represent plaintext letters.

But the notion of manipulating numbers in ciphertext according to math-ematical rules is a relatively new concept. Polybius thought of the ciphertext 11 34 32 21 as a series of letterlike number combinations, not as a problem in mathematics to be solved by addition, subtraction, or some other operation. Today, the encipherment of letters as numbers is carried out *for the purpose of* performing mathematical operations on those numbers. One of the pioneers in this changing conception of cryptography was Lester Hill. Hill was born in New York City in 1891. He received his Ph.D. in mathematics from Yale University in 1926 and taught at the University of Montana, Princeton, the University of Maine, Yale, and Hunter College. In 1929 and 1931, Hill published two papers, both in *The American Mathematical Monthly,* describing systems for enciphering plaintext so that it could be manipulated by familiar algebraic processes.

Hill began his first paper by suggesting that a series of four plaintext letters, $x_1, x_2, x_3,$ and $x_4,$ could be enciphered into ciphertext letters $y_1, y_2, y_3,$ and y_4 by means of four simultaneous linear equations of the form:

$$y_1 = 8x_1 + 6x_2 + 9x_3 + 5x_4$$
$$y_2 = 6x_1 + 9x_2 + 5x_3 + 10x_4$$
$$y_3 = 5x_1 + 8x_2 + 4x_3 + 9x_4$$
$$y_4 = 10x_1 + 6x_2 + 11x_3 + 4x_4$$

(Simultaneous linear equations are equations in which the variables are raised to no higher power than the first and in which those variables all have the same value at the same time.)

The first step in the actual encipherment process is to assign numerical values randomly to each plaintext alphabet letter as illustrated in the example below:

A	B	C	D	E	F	G	H	I	J	K	L	M
5	22	11	16	3	25	12	20	6	23	8	19	1

N	O	P	Q	R	S	T	U	V	W	X	Y	Z
13	24	14	7	18	10	0	4	2	15	17	21	9

Now suppose that the first word in the plaintext message is SELL. The numerical values of these letters from the above chart are:

$$S = 10 \quad E = 3 \quad L = 19 \quad L = 19$$

These values are then substituted in the above equations to give:

$$y_1 = 8(10) + 6(3) + 9(19) + 5(19)$$
$$y_2 = 6(10) + 9(3) + 5(19) + 10(19)$$
$$y_3 = 5(10) + 8(3) + 4(19) + 9(19)$$
$$y_4 = 10(10) + 6(3) + 11(19) + 4(19)$$

The calculations performed give new equations, as follows:

$$y_1 = 80 + 18 + 171 + 95$$
$$y_2 = 60 + 27 + 95 + 190$$
$$y_3 = 50 + 24 + 76 + 171$$
$$y_4 = 100 + 18 + 209 + 76$$

At this point, a new problem arises. Although numbers are manipulated mathematically in this algorithm, those numbers must still represent real letters of the English (or some other) language. In fact, the number 10 has already been assigned the value S in this example.

But what does the number 80 in the first equation above represent? Since there are only 26 letters in the English alphabet, 80 has no meaning for encipherment.

The solution Hill used is to operate in modular arithmetic, using modulo 26. That means that every number must have a value of 0 to 25, which can then represent all 26 letters of the English alphabet. Any number greater than 26 in modulo 26 is represented by the remainder after the number is divided by 26. For example, the number 29 is represented by 3 because

$$29 \div 26 = 1 \text{ with a remainder of 3.}$$

Similarly, the number 100 is represented by 22 because

$$100 \div 26 = 3 \text{ with a remainder of 22.}$$

The variables in the four equations above can now be converted to their modulo 26 values and the equations solved for y, as follows:

$$y_1 = 2 + 18 + 15 + 17 = 52$$
$$y_2 = 8 + 1 + 17 + 8 = 34$$
$$y_3 = 24 + 24 + 24 + 15 = 87$$
$$y_4 = 22 + 18 + 1 + 24 = 65$$

Finally, the values for y are converted to their modulo 26 equivalents and enciphered in their literal form:

$$y_1 = 52 = 0 \text{ modulo } 26 = t$$
$$y_2 = 34 = 8 \text{ modulo } 26 = k$$
$$y_3 = 87 = 9 \text{ modulo } 26 = z$$
$$y_4 = 65 = 13 \text{ modulo } 26 = n$$

The decipherment of ciphertext produced by this system involves, as would be expected, a series of mathematical operations that are the reciprocal of those used during encipherment. Hill specified a group of deciphering equations in his article, for example, that would be used with the enciphering equations given above:

$$x_1 = 23y_1 + 20y_2 + 5y_3 + y_4$$
$$x_2 = 2y_1 + 11y_2 + 18y_3 + y_4$$
$$x_3 = 2y_1 + 20y_2 + 6y_3 + 25y_4$$
$$x_4 = 25y_1 + 2y_2 + 22y_3 + 25y_4$$

In his 1931 article, Hill suggested a second and even more elegant method for enciphering and deciphering by using algebraic operations. He proposed converting the plaintext letters of a message into numbers (as in the above example) and then writing out the message in a matrix. A matrix is a set of numbers arranged in some kind of square, such as a 4 x 4 or 5 x 5 arrangement.

The advantage of this method is that a significantly larger number of plaintext letters can be enciphered at one time within a matrix than by means of simultaneous linear equations. Further, matrix operations are relatively simple to work with, no more complex than a set of linear equations. The second paper therefore promised to provide an even more interesting technique for using mathematical operations to encipher and decipher messages.

Unfortunately, Hill's cryptosystems had only a modest impact on cryptography in succeeding years. Perhaps the main problem was that the mathematical work required to implement his systems was fairly time-consuming. Hill himself recognized this drawback, and he attempted to design a machine that would do the calculations necessary for enciphering and deciphering. However, the machine was not very successful either.

Hill's real contribution to cryptology, then, was in the realm of theory. He foresaw and suggested some of the ways in which cryptology would move away from an art dependent on the brilliance of one or two individuals to a mathematical science in which machines could be designed to use complex mathematical operations to encipher and decipher messages. Hill retired from his teaching position at Hunter College in 1960 and died the following year in Bronxville, New York.

See also: matrix; modulo arithmetic.
For further reading: Brian Beckett, *Introduction to Cryptology*, Oxford: Blackwell Scientific Publications, 1988, pp. 172–181; David Kahn, *The Codebreakers: The Story of Secret Writing*, New York: Macmillan, 1967, pp. 404–410; "Lester Hill Dies: A Mathematician," *New York Times* (10 January 1961): 47. Hill's original papers are "Concerning Certain Linear Transformation Apparatus of Cryptography," *American Mathematical Monthly* (March 1931): 135–154, and "Cryptography in an Algebraic Alphabet," *American Mathematical Monthly* (June–July 1929): 306–312.

HITT, PARKER

Colonel in the U.S. Army Signal Corps and cryptologist. Hitt was born in 1877 in Indianapolis, Indiana, and attended Purdue University as a student in civil engineering. He interrupted his college studies in 1898 when the Spanish-American War broke out, serving in the Philippines, Alaska, and California before being sent to the U.S. Army Signal School at Fort Leavenworth, Kansas. There he discovered that he had a real interest in and knack for cryptography, and was soon given the task of solving cryptograms intercepted from Mexican revolutionaries fighting under Pancho Villa.

Hitt's greatest contribution to cryptology may well be the book he published in 1915, the *Manual for the Solution of Military Ciphers.* According to David Kahn, the 101-page booklet was the first on the subject published in the United States. It contained not only the information Hitt gained from his own studies in cryptology but also knowledge he gathered by reading European books on the subject. The first printing of Hitt's book (4,000 copies) was soon sold out, and a second printing of 16,000 copies was ordered. When World War I broke out, the book was used as a training manual for soldiers in the American Expeditionary Forces. It has since been reprinted by and is available from Aegean Park Press (P.O. Box 2837, Laguna Hills, CA 92654; item #C-1).

Hitt also made important contributions in the field of cipher machines. He was, according to Kahn, "aghast" at the device designated as the official cipher machine by the U.S. Army during World War I. The device was a Portalike cipher disk with a reversed cipher alphabet on the inner wheel and a standard plaintext alphabet on the outer wheel. It was a very primitive mechanism for enciphering messages, even less useful than Porta's original invention.

As an improvement on the army cipher disk, Hitt proposed using variations of the Bazeries cylindrical cryptograph. One of these variations, later called the M-138, was essentially an updated version of the instrument developed by Bazeries and Thomas Jefferson. The second, the M-94, was an expanded version of the cylindrical cryptograph, in which letter sequences on the disks were written out on long sheets of paper, which were then arranged so they could be shifted back and forth in relationship to each other.

After retiring from the army, Hitt joined the International Telephone and Telegraph Company (IT&T), where he served as vice-president of the firm's cryptographic subsidiary, International Communication Laboratories. While employed at IT&T, he invented a printing telegraph cipher machine for the State Department. Hitt died in 1971 at the age of 94.

See also: Bazeries, Étienne; cipher disk; Jefferson, Thomas; M-94; M-138.
For further reading: Parker Hitt, *Manual for the Solution of Military Ciphers*, Fort Leavenworth, KS: Press of the Army Service Schools, 1916; David Kahn, *The Codebreakers: The Story of Secret Writing*, New York: Macmillan, 1967, ch. 11.

HOBO CODES

A form of jargon code used by poor, homeless people to pass information to others of their kind. Hobo codes consisted of both written and spoken signals. For example, homeless people looking for a handout often left marks on the door stoops or other parts of a home to indicate whether the homeowner was likely to be receptive to begging or not. Hoboes also used spoken words to describe the important elements of their environment, such as *open* for a friendly home or town, and *sally* for the Salvation Army. Although still in use to some extent today, hobo codes are much less common than they were in the 1930s.

See also: jargon code.
For further reading: Godfrey Irwin, *American Tramp and Underworld Slang*, New York: Sears Publishing, 1934.

HOLMES, SHERLOCK

Perhaps the most famous fictional detective in the world, immortalized by Sir Arthur Conan Doyle in a series of four novels and 56 short stories written between 1879 and 1930. Holmes's friend, Dr. Watson, is the narrator of the tales.

Cryptanalysis is one of the skills that would be expected in Holmes's repertoire, and indeed it is. At one point, he acknowledges to Watson that he is "fairly familiar with all forms of secret writing, and am myself the author of a trifling monograph upon the subject in which I analyse one hundred and sixty separate ciphers."

In fact, cryptology is mentioned in Holmes's cases on only a handful of occasions, the most famous of which is the code used in "The Adventure of the Dancing Men." A segment of that code is shown below in Figure 11. The code is used by Chicago gangster Abe Slaney to communicate with a former girlfriend named Elsie who has, since her Chicago

Figure 11

days, married a wealthy English squire. The squire finds messages apparently intended for Elsie written in chalk on various parts of the manor house and its outbuildings. He copies the coded messages and brings them to Holmes. Holmes successfully solves the ciphertext, but not in sufficient time to prevent the murder of the squire. He is able, however, to write to Slaney in the American's own code, asking him to return to the manor house. Since Slaney assumes that no one other than a member of the Chicago gang would know the code, he comes back to the scene of the crime and is arrested.

Holmes's cryptanalysis of the "dancing men" code has been the subject of considerable discussion and analysis by devotees of Conan Doyle's work, and especially by members of the "Baker Street Irregulars," an informal organization of Sherlock Holmes fans. The debate centers on the fact that the cipher in printed versions of the story cannot be enciphered as described by Holmes; some error has crept into the ciphertext. David Kahn discusses at length the possible sources of that error, and comes to the conclusion that it was Holmes's chronicler, Dr. Watson, who introduced the error.

For further reading: Sir Arthur Conan Doyle, *The Complete Sherlock Holmes: The A. Conan Doyle Memorial Edition*, 2 vols., Garden City, NY: Doubleday Doran & Co., 1930; David Kahn, *The Codebreakers: The Story of Secret Writing*, New York: Macmillan, 1967, pp. 794–798.

HOMOPHONES

Two or more letters, numbers, or other symbols used as cipher letters for a single plaintext letter. For example, suppose that a particular cryptosystem uses polyalphabetic substitution in which the letter *a* is represented in various parts of the cipher by the following cipher letters: $b, j, k, r, 17$, and @. In that case, b, j, k, r, 17, and @ are all homophones. A substitution cipher con-

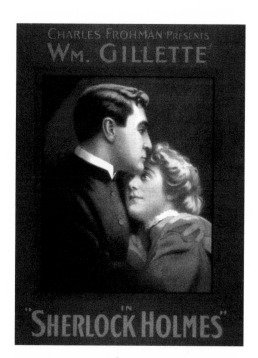

A 1903 theater poster advertises the stage production "Sherlock Holmes." Among his several talents, Sir Arthur Conan Doyle's fictional detective was a skilled cryptanalyst.

structed using homophones is also known as *homophonic substitution.*

See also: polyalphabetic substitution.
For further reading: Brian Beckett, *Introduction to Cryptology,* Oxford: Blackwell Scientific Publications, 1988, pp. 3–6; Carl H. Meyer and Stephen M. Matyas, *Cryptography: A New Dimension in Computer Data Security,* New York: John Wiley & Sons, 1982, pp. 733–740.

HOMOPHONIC SUBSTITUTION
See homophones.

HOST (COMPUTER)
A computer that is part of a network and provides services to other units within the network. For example, large banks have one or more host computers that store information on customers. Peripheral computers in the banks' computer network can access the information by contacting the host, establishing the authenticity of their requests, and collecting and using that information as needed.

See also: network.

HOST PROCESSING CENTER (HPC) ━━

The primary computer or computers at a financial institution that manages and controls financial transactions taking place within the institution. For example, the transfer of funds that takes place when an individual deposits, withdraws, or transfers money through an automatic teller machine (ATM) is authorized and managed by computers at the host processing center for the financial institution or institutions involved.

See also: automatic teller machine; electronic funds transfer; network.
For further reading: Carl H. Meyer and Stephen M. Matyas, *Cryptography: A New Dimension in Computer Data Security*, New York: John Wiley & Sons, 1982, ch. 11.

HUTS AT BLETCHLEY PARK ━━━━━

Quonset hut–type buildings constructed at Bletchley Park during World War II for use by the British Government Code & Cypher School (GC&CS). British intelligence operations were moved from London to Bletchley Park at the beginning of the war, but facilities at the suburban estate were far from adequate for housing the hundreds of new employees taken on by GC&CS. As a result, temporary buildings similar to U.S. quonset huts were erected and assigned to the various research teams. Before long, each research team became known by the number of the hut it occupied.

Hut 8 was occupied by Alan Turing's team, which worked on cryptanalysis of the German naval codes. Next to it was Hut 4, where decrypted texts from Hut 8 were analyzed by naval intelligence experts. Cryptanalysts working on the German army and air force cryptograms were housed in Hut 3, and their companion team of intelligence analysts worked next door in Hut 6. Hut 10 was reserved for the meteorological staff, while Hut 11 housed the bombes devised by Turing and his staff for the solution of the Enigma ciphers. Other huts were used for housing and offices.

See also: Enigma; Turing, Alan; ULTRA.
For further reading: Andrew Hodges, *Alan Turing: The Enigma*, New York: Simon & Schuster, 1983, passim; Gordon Welchman, *The Hut Six Story: Breaking the Enigma Codes*, New York: McGraw-Hill, 1982.

I.D. 25

See Room 40.

INDEX OF COINCIDENCE

A test, also known as the Kappa test, that determines the likelihood that any pair of letters in a message are equal to each other. The index of coincidence for the 26 letters of the English alphabet randomly chosen is 0.0385, a value known as k_r, while the index of coincidence for the 26 letters of the alphabet as used in a typical plaintext message (that is, a series of coherent sentences rather than a random mixture of letters) is 0.0667, a value known as κ_p. The index of coincidence is a standard tool used by cryptanalysts in determining the key in a polyalphabetic substitution cipher.

For further reading: Henry Beker and Fred Piper, *Cipher Systems: The Protection of Communications,* New York: John Wiley & Sons, 1982, pp. 39–43; William F. Friedman, *The Index of Coincidence and Its Applications in Cryptanalysis,* Laguna Hills, CA: Aegean Park Press, n.d.

INFORMATION PROTECTION SYSTEM (IPS)

A cryptosystem developed at International Business Machines (IBM) in the 1970s in an effort to improve security at the company's Thomas J. Watson Research Center in Yorktown Heights, New York. The system makes use of the Data Encryption Standard, which was also developed at IBM for the federal government and later made available to IBM facilities around the world for protection of the company's data. The strength of IPS as a cryptosystem lies in a number of special features such as the absence of any key within the system itself (keys are created and used only for individual transactions) and protection against repetitive patterns in plaintext reappearing in ciphertext.

INFORMATION THEORY

The description of communication by means of mathematical symbols and laws. The first person to attempt a mathematical description of the written word appears to have been R. V. L. Hartley in 1928. However, the man regarded as the father of modern information theory is Claude Shannon. Shannon laid out the fundamental concepts of information theory in two articles published in 1948 and 1949.

The essential tenet of Shannon's theory is that information can be thought of as the inverse of uncertainty. The more uncertainty existing in a given message (a portion of ciphertext, for example), the less we know about the message; that is, the less information we have about the message. Conversely, the less uncertainty in a message, the more information the message contains.

Consider the sequence of letters EICOW MBXCI PQZHE CCNIW, for example. Knowing nothing else about this string of characters, the uncertainty contained in the message is very high. However, the addition of even one piece of information can change the situation. If it were somehow known that the frequency of letters in this short message is the same as the frequency of letters in the English language, then it could be said with some certainty that C = e (since e is the most common letter in the English language and C is the most common letter in the message).

The most common method for expressing uncertainty about a message in information theory is with the concept of entropy. Entropy is a measure of the amount of disorder in a system. The more disorganized a system, the greater its entropy. The concept of entropy has been well studied in physics for more than a century, so a considerable body of theory is available to apply to this new communication field.

The specific field of mathematics used to discuss the uncertainty (and, hence, the information) in a message is probability theory. The argument is that the more certainty about a particular piece of information, the greater the probability that the information is true. The level of certainty about, say, the meaning of a specific letter in a message can be designated by expressing its probability within the range of 0 (complete uncertainty) to 1 (complete certainty).

Once this agreement has been reached, the well-known laws and theorems of probability theory can be applied to the message units that make up a ciphertext or other piece of written language. For example, it can be shown that the amount of information (I) in a message (M) is given by

$$I(M) = -S(p_m \log_2 p_m)$$

where p_m is the probability of a given value for any one unit of the message m. In words, the above formula simply says that the total amount of information in a message $[I(M)]$ is equal to the sum (S) of all the probabilities of the individual units

of the message (p_m), each multiplied by the logarithm to the base 2 of those probabilities $(\log_2 p_m)$. (The negative sign in the formula is needed to make the value of $I(M)$ positive.)

The base 2 is selected for the logarithm used here to make it consistent with the most common method now used for transmitting communications: the computer bit. Most data and messages are now encoded in the binary number system (0 or 1) so that they can be processed by computers. The base 2 is selected for the definition of entropy and information, therefore, to make these concepts consistent with computer mathematics.

See also: entropy; logarithm; probability; Shannon, Claude.
For further reading: N. M. Abramson, *Information Theory and Coding*, New York: McGraw-Hill, 1963; A. Feinstein, *Foundations of Information Theory*, New York: McGraw-Hill, 1958; R. G. Gallager, *Information Theory and Reliable Communications*, New York: John Wiley & Sons, 1968; S. Guiasu, *Information Theory with Applications*, New York: McGraw-Hill, 1977; R. V. L. Hartley, "Transmission of Information," *Bell Systems Technical Journal* 7 (1928): 535–563; B. McMillan, "The Basic Theorems of Information Theory," *Annals of Mathematical Statistics* 24:2 (1953): 196–219; Carl H. Meyer and Stephen M. Matyas, *Cryptography: A New Dimension in Computer Data Security*, New York: John Wiley & Sons, 1982, pp. 627–629; G. Raisbeck, *Information Theory: An Introduction for Scientists and Engineers*, Cambridge, MA: MIT Press, 1964; Claude Shannon, "Communication Theory of Secrecy Systems," *Bell Systems Technical Journal* 28 (1949): 657–715; Shannon, "A Mathematical Theory of Communication," *Bell Systems Technical Journal* 27 (1948): 379–423, 623–656; Shannon, "Prediction and Entropy of Printed English," *Bell Systems Technical Journal* 30 (1951): 50–64; D. Slepian, ed., *Key Papers in the Development of Information Theory*, New York: IEEE Press, 1974; Warren Weaver, "The Mathematics of Communication," *Scientific American* (July 1949): 11–15; Dominic Welsh, *Codes and Cryptography*, Oxford: Clarendon Press, 1988, p. 10, passim.

INFORMATION WARFARE (IW)

Activities by the U.S. Department of Defense designed to deal with the opportunities and risks that have evolved as the military develops an increasing reliability on widespread electronic distribution of information. One aspect of Information Warfare is that the military now collects, creates, uses, and distributes much larger volumes of information than ever before. Much of that information is of interest to both friends and foes of the United States.

Another aspect of IW is that this information is stored in computers and transmitted from computer to computer along lines that are readily available to individuals and entities for whom the information is not intended. As part of its IW planning, the Department of Defense (DOD) has developed a number of active and passive mechanisms to deal with the potential theft of military information, mechanisms such as firewalls and active intrusion-detection systems.

One issue that has developed as a result of DOD IW activities is that the military may take too prominent a role in the control of information flow through circuits over which the military has no control. For example, although the Internet was originally created as a U.S. governmental information highway, it is now generally available to nonmilitary users. The Computer Security Act of 1987 was passed at least partly to prevent the military from assuming a predominant role in the control over the flow of information in nonmilitary settings.

See also: active intrusion-detection system; firewall.
For further reading: Winn Schwartau, *Information Warfare: Chaos on the Electronic Superhighway*, New York: Thunder's Mouth Press, 1994.

INITIALIZING VECTOR

Also initializing variable; some function needed to start an encipherment process. Initializing vectors are needed for a number of reasons. For example, should two plaintext messages begin with the same words, they would be enciphered by the same ciphertext if both were exposed to the same algorithm. However, if one or both were first combined with a string of random numbers, their encipherments would be different.

Some systems also depend on the encipherment of "the previous cipher block." But at the beginning of the encipherment process, there is no "previous cipher block." In this case, plaintext can be combined with an initializing vector to initiate the encipherment process.

In general, an initiating vector must meet one of three criteria. First, it can be a truly random number so that it does not introduce recognizable patterns into the ciphertext created. Second, it can be a pseudorandom number provided that any number regularities it exhibits are too difficult to discover. Finally, it can be a repeating number if the period of repetition is sufficiently great to avoid recognition by a cryptanalyst.

Initializing vectors are also known as *seeds* or *fills*.

For further reading: Brian Beckett, *Introduction to Cryptology*, Oxford: Blackwell Scientific Publications, 1988, pp. 84–87; D. W. Davies and W. L. Price, *Security for Computer Networks: An Introduction to Data Security in Teleprocessing and Electronic Funds Transfer*, Chichester: John Wiley & Sons, 1984, pp. 93–95; Charlie Kaufman, Radia Perlman, and Mike Speciner, *Network Security: Private Communication in a Public World*, Englewood Cliffs, NJ: Prentice-Hall, 1995, pp. 82–84, 109–110; Carl H. Meyer and Stephen M. Matyas, *Cryptography: A New Dimension in Computer Data Security*, New York: John Wiley & Sons, 1982, pp. 56–61, 92–93.

INTEGRITY

With regard to data and communications, the term refers to the fact that a particular message has been stored and/or transmitted without change. This property is very important because it allows someone who receives a message to be certain that the message is exactly the same as the one transmitted by the sender. Imagine that a person wishing to buy stocks sends an electronic message to a stockbroker telling the broker to purchase 100,000 shares of a given stock. Then imagine that an error occurs during transmission resulting in the addition of a single zero to the purchase order, calling for 1,000,000 shares rather than 100,000. Such an error would be disastrous.

Errors occur during message transmission primarily for two reasons. The first, and least likely, is because of accidents. The person sending the message might unintentionally introduce an error into the message. Second, and more commonly, the message may be changed intentionally by some eavesdropper. A person may wish to cause harm to another person or entity by introducing false or harmful information into the transmitted message.

Electronic transactions are reliable and useful only if two criteria are met. First, they must retain their integrity: The person who receives a message must be confident that the message is no different from the one originally sent. Second, messages must be authentic; that is, they must actually have come from the person who claims to have sent them.

See also: message authentication code.
For further reading: Albrecht Beutelspacher, *Cryptology: An Introduction to the Art and Science of Enciphering, Encrypting, Concealing, Hiding and Safeguarding Described without Any Arcane Skullduggery but Not without Cunning Waggery for the Delectation and Instruction of the General Public,* Washington, DC: Mathematical Association of America, 1994, ch. 4; Charlie Kaufman, Radia Perlman, and Mike Speciner, *Network Security: Private Communication in a Public World,* Englewood Cliffs, NJ: Prentice-Hall, 1995, passim (*see* index); U.S. Congress, Office of Technology Assessment, *Information Security and Privacy in Network Environments,* OTA-TCT-606, Washington, DC: GPO, September 1994, pp. 28, 31–37; U.S. Congress, Office of Technology Assessment, *Issue Update on Information Security and Privacy in Network Environments,* OTA-BP-ITC-147, Washing-

ton, DC: GPO, June 1995, pp. 46–47; Peter Wayner, "True Data," *Byte* (September 1991): 122–124+.

INTELLECTUAL PROPERTY

Possessions that consist primarily of ideas rather than physical objects. A new software program for making financial calculations is an example of intellectual property. The person or persons who have developed this process are considered to "own" the process in the same way that a person who constructs a new house is considered to own that building. Intellectual property can sometimes be protected by a patent.

Protection of intellectual property from theft is an important issue in commerce. Ideas are commonly stored in computer systems and transmitted from one location to another by electronic means that are relatively accessible to eavesdroppers, hackers, and others not authorized to use them. Cryptography is now widely used to encipher such ideas while they are stored in a computer to protect them from break-in, and during transmission to protect them from being intercepted by an enemy.

For further reading: U.S. Congress, Office of Technology Assessment, *Information Security and Privacy in Network Environments,* OTA-TCT-606, Washington, DC: GPO, September 1994, passim; U.S. Congress, Office of Technology Assessment, *Issue Update on Information Security and Privacy in Network Environments,* OTA-BP-ITC-147, Washington, DC: GPO, June 1995, pp. 71–73, 130–131.

INTELLIGENCE

Information about an enemy or a potential enemy that has been analyzed and assessed with regard to its accuracy and potential significance. For example, a spy satellite might detect the fact that ten warships from nation A have come from all parts of the world to assemble off the coast of the Yucatán in Mexico. The data can be described as information: a set of facts about a particular situation or event.

But what is the meaning and/or significance of the assembling of these ten warships? The answer to that question cannot be obtained from the information itself but must be gleaned from other sources: communications sent back and forth among the ships and their home commander; other indications of military forces being collected; current relationships between nation A, our own nation, Mexico, and other nations; and so on.

The relationship between information and intelligence can be illustrated by the work carried out by the British Government Code & Cypher School at Bletchley Park during World War II. British intelligence officers were divided into two discrete groups: those who collected information obtained by the cryptanalysis of German ciphers and those who decided on the importance and value of this information.

See also: Huts at Bletchley Park.
For further reading: Harold C. Relyea, *Evolution and Organization of Intelligence Activities in the United States*, Laguna Hills, CA: Aegean Park Press, n.d., passim.

INTERNATIONAL ASSOCIATION FOR CRYPTOLOGIC RESEARCH (IACR)

An international organization dedicated to the furthering of research in cryptology. The association was organized in 1983 and currently has about 800 members worldwide. Members come from a wide variety of fields, including mathematics, computer science, electrical and electronic engineering, manufacturing, and government service. The association holds an annual meeting in the United States known as CRYPTO '97 (the nu-

meral indicates the year of the conference), another meeting somewhere in Europe known as EUROCRYPT '97, and other occasional regional meetings (such as ASIACRYPT '95).

The official journal of the organization is the *Journal of Cryptology*, published quarterly by Springer-Verlag (ISSN 9033-2790). The journal contains highly technical research articles on topics such as "On the Distribution of Characteristics in Bijective Mappings," "Necessary and Sufficient Conditions for Collision-Free Hashing," and "Short RSA Keys and Their Generation."

Business offices of IACR are located at Aarhus Science Park, Gustav Wieds Vej 10, DK-8000 Aarhus C, Denmark.

For further reading: http://www.iacr.org/~iacr/.

INTERNATIONAL CODE OF SIGNALS

A system by which ships at sea are able to communicate with one another. The system had its origins in the British Board of Trade code originally announced in 1857. That code was later modified and adopted by every nation with a navy and/or merchant marine fleet. The code consists of two parts: one is a visual code relayed by means of colored flags and the other is a written code transmitted by telegraph.

Some examples of the visual code are shown in Figure 12.

INTERNATIONAL DATA ENCRYPTION ALGORITHM (IDEA)

An encryption system invented by Xuejia Lai and James L. Massey of ETH Zuria and first published in 1991. IDEA

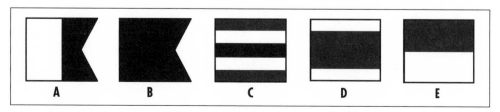

A B C D E

Figure 12

operates in much the same way as the Data Encryption Standard (DES), in that plaintext is divided into 64-bit blocks and then encrypted with a 128-bit key. As with DES, IDEA also passes data through 16 iterations before producing a final set of ciphertext.

As of this writing, IDEA appears to be a secure system (no one has yet published a method for breaking it).

See also: Data Encryption Standard.
For further reading: Charlie Kaufman, Radia Perlman, and Mike Speciner, *Network Security: Private Communication in a Public World*, Englewood Cliffs, NJ: Prentice-Hall, 1995, pp. 74–80; William Stallings, *Network and Internetwork Security: Principles and Practices*, Englewood Cliffs, NJ: Prentice-Hall, 1995, ch. 6; http://rschp2.anu.edu.au:8080/idea.html.

INTERNET ●━━━━━━━

A network of computers and other electronic systems that allows individuals, groups, corporations, government agencies, and other entities to exchange information with one another. The Internet was originally created by the U.S. Defense Advanced Research Projects Agency (DARPA) to link defense research centers in the United States and Europe. It consisted of a network of Department of Defense (DOD) host computers, satellite networks, and a number of local area networks. By the strictest definition, the term *Internet* refers only to those entities operating within the conditions specified by the Transmission Control Protocol/Internet Protocol. In actual fact, it often includes a much larger number of operating systems.

Over the past decade, the Internet has expanded greatly to include individual and corporate users, as well as nondefense users from various government bodies. By one recent estimate, more than 30 million users worldwide now access information stored on the Internet. While the Internet is an invaluable information tool in modern society, its existence also creates a number of is-

Nowadays people can check e-mail over drinks or access the World Wide Web during dinner at places such as the @ Café in New York City.

sues concerning the personal privacy of users and the security of information available on the network.

As an example, the U.S. Defense Information Systems Agency conducted mock attacks on 8,932 DOD computers in 1993–1994. The agency was able to break into 7,860 of those computers, and more than 95 percent of the time the break-in was not detected by the host computer. The risk to national security reflected by this exercise and the need for increased security against such attacks are obvious.

See also: computer; World Wide Web.
For further reading: Ed Krol, *The Whole Internet User's Guide and Catalog*, Sebastapol, CA: O'Reilly and Associates, 1992; Michael Neubarth, et al., "Internet Security" (Special Section), *Internet World* (February 1995): 31–72; U.S. Congress, Office of Technology Assessment, *Information Security and Privacy in Network Environments*, OTA-TCT-606, Washington, DC: GPO, September 1994, passim.

INTRACTABLE
See class P problem; unbreakable cipher.

INVERSION
See ciphony.

INVISIBLE WRITING
A form of steganography in which a message is inscribed on (usually) paper in a form invisible to the human eye, but which can later be made visible by some physical or chemical means. The literature on invisible writing is enormous and goes back to the earliest days of cryptology. The first widespread use of invisible writing seems to have occurred among Muslim correspondents in the seventh century.

The many forms of invisible writing can be subdivided into physical and chemical processes. One example of a physical process is well known to devotees of detective stories. A person writes a note on a pad of paper, leaving an impression on the next sheet of paper, and then removes the note. The readability of the impression depends on various factors: the type of paper used, the pressure of the writer, and the angle at which the impression is examined. The impression can often be read more clearly by rubbing the sheet lightly with the edge of a pencil lead.

Another physical form of invisible writing involves the use of certain colorless chemicals that glow when exposed to ultraviolet (or "dark") light. The page on which such messages are written appears to be blank, but when exposed to a dark light, the hidden words glow and become easily readable.

Probably the most common form of invisible writing involves the reaction between two chemicals, one of which is colorless, to produce a colored product. For example, a solution of iron sulfate is colorless, and an invisible ink can be made from it. To reveal the message, the paper is swabbed with a solution of potassium cyanate. The potassium cyanate reacts with the iron sulfate to form a blue compound known as ferric ferrocyanide, or Prussian blue. Many such chemical combinations, called *sympathetic inks*, are known and have been used throughout history.

A second type of invisible ink is known as an *organic* ink. Milk, fruit juices, and vinegar are examples. The common property of such inks is that they char when heated, leaving behind a thin layer of black carbon. For example, an invisible message could be written on a piece of paper with a fountain pen filled with vinegar. To read the message, the paper is gently heated above a flame, causing the dried vinegar to char, leaving a visible message on the paper.

One of the great advantages of invisible inks is that they can be used on any sheet of paper, whether or not it already contains printing or writing. For example, a message can be written in invisible ink on the page of a book and sent through the mails to a correspondent who is expecting the message. Anyone who intercepts the page is unlikely to be aware that it also contains a hidden message.

History is replete with stories of diplomats who found invisible inks an ideal way to communicate with each other, even when they used no other form of steganography or cryptography. For example, the first news received by the Continental Congress of Great Britain's plans to bring about the "total submission" of the American colonies came by means of a letter written in invisible ink from Sir James Jay, an English physician writing in 1776 from London to his brother, John Jay. Similar messages were sent by the elder Jay from London to Benjamin Franklin in Paris.

See also: colonial cryptology; steganography. For further reading: Martin Gardner, *Codes, Ciphers and Secret Writing*, New York: Dover Publications, 1972, ch. 6; David Kahn, *The Codebreakers: The Story of Secret Writing*, New York: Macmillan, 1967, pp. 522–525, passim; Victor Hugo Paltsitis, "Use of Invisible Ink for Secret Writing during the American Revolution," *Bulletin of the New York Public Library* 39 (1935): 227–264.

ITERATION

The process of repeating a mathematical operation more than once. A message might be enciphered, for example, by transposing the letters and/or numbers of which the message is made in order to make it more difficult for an unauthorized person to read. But the message can be made even more difficult to decrypt if the letters and/or numbers in the first encipherment are transposed a second, third, and fourth time. In most iterative processes, the output obtained from one step in the algorithm is used as the input for the next step. The algorithm used in the Data Encryption Standard (DES) makes use of 16 such iterations during the encryption of a message.

See also: Data Encryption Standard.

JARGON CODE

A system in which an apparently innocent word, phrase, or sentence has a totally different meaning to anyone familiar with the code. David Kahn points out that jargon codes can be traced to the earliest days of cryptology. A papal code used in the fourteenth century, for example, substituted the words EGYPTIANS for Ghibellines and SONS OF ISRAEL for Guelphs in the ongoing conflict between those two groups.

The great advantage of jargon codes is that they can be used very openly, often without arousing any suspicion among uninitiated listeners. A drug dealer could call a customer on a telephone known to be tapped, for example, with the message that "The new book you ordered has arrived. It can be picked up at our office tomorrow at ten A.M." That seemingly innocent message might mean to the customer that "The marijuana that you ordered has arrived. It will be delivered to your car at midnight tonight."

Jargon codes are generally very easy to use and, in many cases, quite safe. In addition to their use in illegal activities, they have also been employed for military purposes. Many of the plans for the invasion of Normandy in June 1944, for example, were broadcast openly in jargon code by the BBC. Underground fighters on the continent were kept informed daily as to the date, time, and location of the forthcoming invasion.

See also: argot; open code.
For further reading: Don Ethan Miller, *The Book of Jargon: An Essential Guide to the Inside Language of Today*, New York: Macmillan, 1981.

J CIPHERS

The name given by U.S. cryptanalysts to a series of codes and ciphers used by the Japanese diplomatic service prior to and during World War II. The ciphers used an interrupted columnar transposition system in which blanks were inserted into columns to change the length of enciphered plaintext. Columns were copied off according to a keynumber system that designated the sequence of the columns to be used. The various arrangements of blanks within columns were designated by U.S. cryptanalysts as K versions of a J cipher. Thus, a particular message might be recognized as a K3 transposition of the J12 cipher.

See also: Code Compilation Section; Coral Sea, Battle of; Midway, Battle of.
For further reading: John Costello, *The Pacific War*, New York: Rawson, Wade, 1981; Edwin T. Layton, with Roger Pineau and John Costello, *"And I Was There": Pearl Harbor and Midway—Breaking the Secrets*, New York: William Morrow, 1985; Takeo Yoshikawa, "Prelude in the Pacific: Attempts to Intercept and Crack Japanese Codes Prior to Pearl Harbor Attack," *American History Illustrated* (September/October 1991): 52–63.

JEFFERSON, THOMAS

Statesman, scholar, and third president of the United States. Most Americans know of Jefferson (1743–1826) in terms of his political accomplishments, but fewer realize that he was also a scholar of considerable attainments, including those in the field of science. He was very interested in

Among his many achievements, Thomas Jefferson made valuable contributions to the field of cryptology.

paleontology, for example, and studied and classified fossils found in New York State. He also studied agriculture and experimented with new varieties of grains.

Probably because of his activities in the field of international politics, Jefferson also developed an interest in cryptology. In the 1780s, he and James Madison corresponded using a nomenclator that had been invented by Robert Livingstone, then U.S. secretary of foreign affairs. Jefferson is probably best remembered, however, for his invention of a wheel cypher that could be used in enciphering and deciphering messages.

The Jefferson cipher wheel consisted of a cylindrical piece of wood six to eight inches long and about two inches in diameter. A hole was bored through the middle of the cylinder and a metal rod inserted into the hole. The diameter of the rod had to be just large enough to allow the wood cylinder to rotate around it.

Next, a standard alphabet was inscribed on the outer face of the cylinder with *a* at one end of the cylinder and *z* at the other. Inscribed below the standard alphabet were 25 more alphabets, all randomly mixed. The cylinder was cut cross-

wise to produce 26 separate disks, each with its own alphabet arranged around the circumference of its face. If the face of the cylinder could be unwrapped and laid out on a flat piece of paper, it would look something like this:

```
a b c d e f g h i j k l m n o p q r s t u v w x y z
p l m k o n j i u h b v g y t f c x d r e s z a w q
t h n y j m u k i l o p b g r v f e c d w x s q z a
z m x n c b v a l s k d j f h g p q o w i e r u t y
(etc.)
```

To encipher a message with the Jefferson cipher wheel, first the plaintext message was arranged on one of the wheels. To encipher the message THE TREATY IS SIGNED, for example, the first wheel at the left of the cylinder is turned to the letter *t*, and the second wheel turned so that the letter *h* is immediately adjacent to the *t*. The third wheel is turned to bring an *e* next to the *h*, and the first word (the) is enciphered. This process continues until the complete plaintext can be read on the cylinder.

At this point, the plaintext has also been enciphered in the 25 other alphabets that lie below it on the wheel. The encipherer can choose to take off and transmit any one of them. Suppose that the enciphered message reads uxipm qiscf ssnge noliw. The person who receives the message must have a cipher wheel identical to the one used for encipherment, of course. The enciphered message is set on any continuous line of letters, just as the plaintext message was. The decipherer then looks for some other row on the wheel on which some intelligible message can be found; the message would be, of course, THE TREATY IS SIGNED. The chances of finding more than one intelligible message is virtually zero.

Interestingly enough, Jefferson apparently thought so little of his invention that he made no effort to promote its use. It lay in a drawer for more than a century before being rediscovered in 1922. Ironically, that was the same year in which the U.S. Army adopted the M-94 cipher device as its official cipher machine. In the years after Jefferson made his invention, the same idea was reinvented at least twice, once by Étienne Bazeries in 1890, and again by Colonel Parker Hitt in 1914.

See also: Bazeries, Étienne; cipher disk; Hitt, Parker; M-94.

For further reading: Louis Kruh, "The Genesis of the Jefferson/Bazeries Cipher Devices," *Cryptologia* 5:4 (1981): 193–208; *The National Cyclopedia of American Biography*, Clifton, NJ: James T. White, 1938, vol. 26, pp. 93–94; Norman K. Risjord, *Thomas Jefferson*, Madison, WI: Madison House, 1994.

JN CIPHERS

The designation given by U.S. cryptanalysts to a series of Japanese naval codes used prior to and during World War II.

See also: J ciphers.

JOURNAL OF CRYPTOLOGY

Official journal of the **International Association for Cryptologic Research.**

For further reading: http://www.swcp.com/~iacr/jofc/jofc.html.

KAHN, DAVID

Journalist, author, and historian of cryptology. Probably more than any other individual, Kahn (1930–) is responsible for inspiring public interest in an arcane, mysterious, and poorly understood field: cryptology. In his classic book *The Codebreakers,* Kahn traces the origin of cryptology from its earliest appearances in Egypt, China, India, and other civilizations. He provides a detailed analysis of the major events in the field of cryptology up to the publication date of the book (1967). The book is such a tour de force that no person can be considered informed about the subject of cryptology without having read and studied it.

David Kahn was born in Great Neck, New York, received his B.A. from Bucknell University, and worked from 1955 to 1963 as a reporter for the Long Island newspaper *Newsday.* After spending two years in research on *The Codebreakers,* he became a news desk editor for the European edition of the *New York Herald Tribune* in Paris. He returned to Great Neck, where he has written articles for magazines and journals ranging from *Playboy* to the *New York Times.* He developed an interest in cryptology early in life and has served as president of the American Cryptogram Association. In addition to *The Codebreakers,* Kahn has written two other important books, *Kahn on Codes* (Macmillan, 1983) and *Seizing the Enigma* (Houghton Mifflin, 1991).

KAPPA TEST

See index of coincidence.

KASISKI EXAMINATION

A method of cryptanalysis devised by Prussian army officer and cryptanalyst Friedrich Kasiski in the early 1860s. Kasiski was born 29 November 1805 in Schlochau, West Prussia (now Czluchow, Poland), enlisted in the army at the age of 17, and spent the rest of his life in the military. He died 22 May 1881.

Kasiski's great contribution to cryptanalysis is found in a book he published in 1863, *Die Geheimschriften und die Dechiffrir-kunst* (Secret Writing and the Art of Deciphering), in which he gives a method for cryptanalyzing a polyalphabetic cipher enciphered with a repeating keyword or phrase. Consider the case shown below, where the repeating key is ARMY.

KEY:
A R M Y A R M Y A R M Y A R M Y A R M Y A R M Y
PLAINTEXT:
T H I S P A T H I S B E T T E R T H A N A N Y O T H E R
CIPHERTEXT:
q z d g i x f e d j h d n q m c q z b y w s l k q z m c

Notice that any repetition of a letter sequence in both the key and the plaintext produces a comparable repetition of letter sequences in the ciphertext. In the message above, a repetition of AR in the key with TH in the plaintext results in the encipherment of *qz* in the ciphertext (italicized in the example). Similarly, a repetition of MY in the key with ER in the plaintext produces **mc** in the ciphertext (boldface).

Kasiski's genius was in the recognition of how this kind of pattern could be used to break a cipher. He counted the spaces

151

between the first and each subsequent repetition of a distinctive letter sequence. In the case of the *qz* sequence above, the number of spaces before a repeat (known as the *interval*) is 16 and 8. For the **mc** sequence, the interval is 12.

Kasiski's argument is that the interval between repetitions gives a clue to the length of the keyword. Specifically, he suggests breaking up the intervals into their smallest factors and then finding out which of those factors represents the actual length of the keyword. In the example above, the factors of the intervals are:

$$16 = 2 \times 2 \times 2 \times 2$$
$$8 = 2 \times 2 \times 2$$
$$12 = 2 \times 2 \times 3$$

The only length that can satisfy all three of these conditions is 2×2, or 4, so the keyword must have a length of four letters.

The Kasiski examination, as this procedure is known, is not necessarily quite as "clean" as this description would imply. Repetition of letters within a message can confuse the analysis, but identifying the true length of the keyword can usually be accomplished even with such additional factors. Once the keyword is found, familiar techniques for discovering monoalphabetic substitutions can be used and, eventually, the polyalphabetic extensions determined.

See also: polyalphabetic substitution.
For further reading: Henry Beker and Fred Piper, *Cipher Systems: The Protection of Communications*, New York: John Wiley & Sons, 1982, pp. 46 et seq.; Albrecht Beutelspacher, *Cryptology: An Introduction to the Art and Science of Enciphering, Encrypting, Concealing, Hiding and Safeguarding Described without Any Arcane Skullduggery but Not without Cunning Waggery for the Delectation and Instruction of the General Public*, Washington, DC: Mathematical Association of America, 1994, ch. 2; William M. Bowers, "Major F. W. Kasiski—Cryptologist," *The Cryptogram* (January–February 1964): 53–54, 58–60; David Kahn, *The Codebreakers: The Story of Secret Writing*, New York: Macmillan, 1967,

pp. 207–213; Helen Fouché Gaines, *Cryptanalysis: A Study of Ciphers and Their Solution*, New York: Dover Publications, 1956, ch. 14.

KERBEROS

A service based on the use of secret keys for providing authentication in network communications. The system was originally developed by R. M. Needham and M. D. Schroeder at the Massachusetts Institute of Technology in the late 1970s. A complete description of two later versions of the system, Kerberos V4 and Kerberos V5, is available in *Network Security: Private Communication in a Public World* by Charlie Kaufman, Radia Perlman, and Mike Speciner, Englewood Cliffs, NJ: Prentice-Hall, 1995, chs. 10 and 11.

For further reading: Jeffrey I. Schiller, "Secure Distributed Computing: Project Athena," *Scientific American* (November 1994): 72–76.

KERCKHOFFS, AUGUSTE

Author of one of the most important books in the history of cryptology, *La Cryptologie militaire*. Born in Nuth, Holland, on 19 January 1835, Kerckhoffs was christened Jean-Guillaume-Hubert-Victor-Françoise-Alexandere-Auguste-Kerckhoffs von Niuewenhof; he later changed his name to a more manageable form. Kerckhoffs graduated from the University of Liège with degrees in science and letters, and taught at high schools in Holland and France before becoming professor of German at the Ecole des Hautes Etudes Commerciales and the Ecole Arago, both in Paris. From 1887 to 1895, he was also secretary of the French Association for the Propagation of Volapük (World Speak), an international language that was widely popular during the period. He died in 1903.

David Kahn praises Kerckhoffs's *La Cryptologie militaire* as one of the two great nineteenth-century books on cryptology. Its significance, according to

Kahn, is that it "sought answers to the problems thrust upon cryptology by new conditions, and that the solutions he proposed were valid, well-grounded, and meritorious." One of the enduring features of *La Cryptologie* is the set of six ground rules for cryptology that he established. Any cryptosystem, he said, must have the following characteristics:

1. It must be unbreakable, if not in theory, at least in practice.
2. Any compromise to the system should not inconvenience correspondents using it.
3. The key used in the system should be easy to remember and easy to change when necessary.
4. The ciphertext should be capable of transmission by means of the telegraph.
5. The apparatus to be used in enciphering and deciphering messages should be easily portable and usable by a single person.
6. The system should be simple, requiring no unusual effort or strain on the part of those who have to use it.

For all practical purposes, these six principles remain as relevant to military communications today as they did more than a hundred years ago when Kerckhoffs wrote his book.

Kerckhoffs's name is also retained in the fundamental rule of cryptanalysis, namely that "The security of a cryptosystem must not depend on keeping secret the algorithm used in the system, but only on keeping the key secret."

KEY

Any set of instructions that establish the method by which messages are to be encrypted and decrypted within a particular cryptosystem. In general, keys are of two kinds: secret or public. The most familiar is the secret key, which is revealed only to specific individuals for whom secret messages are designed. When the German High Command sent messages to its submarines at sea, for example, it took great care to make sure that only members of the German navy had access to its keys. To a large extent, the process of cryptanalysis is the effort by individuals for whom keys are *not* intended to discover what those keys are and, with that information, decrypt otherwise secret information.

In recent years, the concept of a public key has been introduced. A public key is one that is published for anyone to see and use. Secret messages can still be sent between two or more individuals if the public key is combined with a private key held by each of the individuals for whom the messages are intended.

The most common types of keys are keywords, keyphrases, and keynumbers. A keyword is a single word that establishes the specific enciphering alphabet to be used in writing a given cipher. For example, a Vigenère table, as shown on page 294, consists of a 26 x 26 matrix used for polyalphabetic ciphering. If the keyword to be used in a particular cryptosystem is VIRTUE, then the plaintext message HONOR IS ITS OWN REWARD can be enciphered as follows:

```
KEY:    VIRTUEVIRTUEVIRTUEV
PLAIN:  HONORISITSOWNREWARD
CIPHER: cwehlmnqkliaizvpuvy
```

A keyphrase is used in much the same way as a keyword except that a collection of words (the phrase) rather than a single word is used as the key. The same message above (HONOR IS ITS OWN REWARD) can be enciphered with the keyphrase GOD SAVE THE KING as follows:

```
KEY:    GODSAVETHEKINGGODSA
PLAIN:  HONORISITSOWNREWARD
CIPHER: ncqgrdwbawyeaxkkdjd
```

Many variations of keywords and keyphrases have been developed. In some cases, the letters that make up a message are themselves used as the keyphrase for enciphering the plaintext. A key of this type is called an autokey.

A keynumber is a number that indicates the sequence in which some enciphering operation is to take place. For example, in columnar transposition, a keynumber indicates to the encipherer the order in which the columns are to be taken off in writing the cipher. With the message ALL GOOD MEN WILL COME TO THE AID OF THEIR KING and the keynumber 52143, the encipherment would take place as follows:

```
5  2  1  4  3
A  L  L  G  O
O  D  M  E  N
W  I  L  L  C
O  M  E  T  O
T  H  E  A  I
D  O  F  T  H
H  E  I  R  K
I  N  G  Q  X
```

CIPHERTEXT: lmlee figld imhoe nonco ihkxg eltat rqaow otdhi

Many types of keys are now in use, depending on the specific purpose for which they are intended. At least three different types of keys are used in communication systems. The *session key* is generated and used for a single exchange of data and/or information among two or more people or groups. The session key is generated specifically for that session, and is destroyed following the session.

A session key generally has to move along lines of communication, however. For that reason, the session key itself is enciphered by means of the *terminal key*. A terminal key is generally used for a longer period of time than a session key, but it is also eventually destroyed.

Finally, the key used to generate the terminal key, the *master key*, is stored in the central computer of a network system. The master key is a relatively permanent fixture of the system and can be used to generate terminal keys whenever needed. There is, therefore, a hierarchy of keys: master keys are used to generate

terminal keys, which in turn are used to generate session keys.

The language used to describe keys may differ also. For example, in their discussion of the use of cryptography for protecting file and communication security, Meyer and Matyas list more than a dozen types of keys. These include a *primary key* (or *data-encrypting* and *data-decrypting key*) for enciphering and deciphering data, a *primary communication key* (or simply a *communication key*) for providing communication security, a *session key* for use in a specific communication session, a *file security key* for protection of file data, a *secondary key* for the encrypting of a primary key, and *secondary communication* and *secondary file keys*, used to protect keys for both communication and files. For more details on the large variety of keys now used in various systems, see the references at the end of this entry.

See also: autokey; progressive key; public-key cryptography; running key; secret-key system, Vigenère square.

For further reading: Henry Beker and Fred Piper, *Cipher Systems: The Protection of Communications*, New York: John Wiley & Sons, 1982, pp. 292–303; Gilles Brassard, *Modern Cryptology: A Tutorial*, New York: Springer-Verlag, 1988, ch. 2; William F. Friedman, *Elementary Military Cryptography*, pt. 2: Cipher Systems, Laguna Hills, CA: Aegean Park Press, 1976; Helen Fouché Gaines, *Cryptanalysis: A Study of Ciphers and Their Solution*, New York: Dover Publications, 1956, passim; Charlie Kaufman, Radia Perlman, and Mike Speciner, *Network Security: Private Communication in a Public World*, Englewood Cliffs, NJ: Prentice-Hall, 1995, ch. 10, passim; Carl H. Meyer and Stephen M. Matyas, *Cryptography: A New Dimension in Computer Data Security*, New York: John Wiley & Sons, 1982, ch. 4, passim; Donald D. Millikin, *Elementary Cryptography and Cryptanalysis*, Laguna Hills, CA: Aegean Park Press, n.d., ch. 2; William Stallings, *Network and Internetwork Security: Principles and Practices*, Englewood Cliffs, NJ: Prentice-Hall, 1995, ch. 3; Fred B. Wrixon, *Codes and Ciphers*, New York: Prentice-Hall, 1992, pp. 108–110.

KEY CARD

A device used in place of a traditional lock-and-key system to allow access to a particular room or building. The card assigned to any one employee contains magnetically coded information that contains a cipher identifying the specific facility for which it is valid plus a second cipher identifying the employee who is permitted access to the building. When the card is inserted into the card reader at the door to the facility, the magnetic code is read by the host computer and compared to a master list of permitted entrants and to a second list of stolen or lost cards. If the card is valid, the door automatically unlocks to permit access.

KEY DISTRIBUTION

Any and all systems by which the key for some cryptosystem is made available to all who need to use it. In earlier days, keys could be transmitted between cryptographers and decrypters rather easily, often by personal messenger. Today, many cryptosystems require that a great many different individuals have access to a key, often in a relatively short period of time. Therefore, key distribution becomes an important practical problem.

See also: key management.
For further reading: William Stallings, *Network and Internetwork Security: Principles and Practices,* Englewood Cliffs, NJ: Prentice-Hall, 1995, ch. 2; Dominic Welsh, *Codes and Cryptography,* Oxford: Clarendon Press, 1988, pp. 170–171, ch. 11.

KEY DISTRIBUTION CENTER (KDC)

An entity that holds master keys for all nodes in a network and is able to generate conversation keys between any two of those nodes. Assume that network security is based on a private-key cryptosystem. To understand how a KDC works, think of it as the hub of a wheel, and the connections between it and individual nodes as spokes in the wheel. When node A wishes to communicate with node B, it contacts the KDC and requests a session key with which it can communicate with B. KDC first authenticates A by checking the private key that it shares with A. It then encrypts a session key using A's secret key and some random number, R, and passes that key on to A. At the same time, KDC encrypts the session key for B using the private key shared by B and KDC and sends that key on to B. A and B are then able to communicate securely with each other by using the shared secret key generated by KDC.

KDCs solve perhaps the most difficult single problem of secret-key cryptography today, which is making sure that everyone who wants to communicate securely within a network has access to an acceptable secret key.

But KDCs have a number of serious drawbacks. One obvious problem is that the KDC has the private (secret) key for every node in the network. If the KDC is compromised, the private keys become available to the hacker or other person who has broken into the KDC. That individual can then read secure communications generated at any or all nodes in the network.

KDCs also present the problem of potential bottlenecks if the network becomes very busy. Because every node must communicate with a single trusted intermediary, nodes may have to wait to obtain the session keys they need to carry on communications.

See also: certification authority; node; trusted intermediary.
For further reading: Charlie Kaufman, Radia Perlman, and Mike Speciner, *Network Security: Private Communication in a Public World,* Englewood Cliffs, NJ: Prentice-Hall, 1995, pp. 189–190, 243–249.

KEY-ESCROW ENCRYPTION

A cryptosystem in which the key for the system is deposited with some third party. The term *escrow* in general refers to the depositing of something (such as money) with a third party while a transaction between two other parties is being accomplished. During the sale of a house, for example, money is deposited in an escrow account while the sale is being completed between buyer and seller. Key-escrow encryption might be compared to the practice of leaving a spare key to your home with a good friend in case you happen to lose your own key.

Key escrow has become an increasingly important issue in modern-day cryptography because of the necessity and/or desirability of government and law enforcement bodies to monitor certain computer-based or other electronic transactions. For example, a police department might be interested in knowing the details of illegal and encrypted money transfers taking place between two individuals or entities. If the two individuals or entities have been required to deposit a spare key with the government in advance, law enforcement agencies may be able to eavesdrop on their conversations.

See also: Escrowed Encryption Standard.

KEY MANAGEMENT

The generation, storage, cataloging, distribution, and destruction (when appropriate) of an encryption key. Key management is one of the most crucial functions in cryptography today. In the first place, a key is of little or no value if it is produced without imagination and intelligence. A system will not be very secure if the key can be easily broken.

Second, encryption keys must be monitored as carefully as physical keys that protect a home or office. If employees are careless in their use of keys, the keys will be of little value no matter how ingeniously they were prepared. One report on key management stresses that "a well-thought-out and secure key-management infrastructure is necessary for effective use of encryption-based safeguards in network environments." Such an infrastructure would include

specific mechanisms for issuing keys, registering the public keys of users, and authenticating owner keys.

See also: key; key distribution.
For further reading: Henry Beker and Fred Piper, *Cipher Systems: The Protection of Communications*, New York: John Wiley & Sons, 1982, pp. 303–305; D. W. Davies and W. L. Price, *Security for Computer Networks: An Introduction to Data Security in Teleprocessing and Electronic Funds Transfer*, Chichester: John Wiley & Sons, 1984, ch. 6; William Stallings, *Network and Internetwork Security: Principles and Practices*, Englewood Cliffs, NJ: Prentice-Hall, 1995, ch. 3.

KEYNUMBER
See key.

KEYPHRASE
See key.

KEYWORD
See key.

KINSEY, ALFRED C.
The pioneer of research on human sexuality in the United States. Between 1938 and 1948, Kinsey (1894–1956) and his colleagues interviewed tens of thousands of men and women in order to gain basic information on their sexual histories. At the time, Kinsey was professor of zoology at Indiana University.

The issue of asking people about their sexuality was fraught with all manner of ethical, psychological, social, and procedural questions. In order to guarantee that an individual's responses were as secure as possible, Kinsey developed an elaborate coding system by which responses were recorded. A typical response sheet consisted of a grid containing about 40 rows and 7 columns, with additional space for other comments and notes. The nearly 300 spaces on the record sheet corresponded to questions asked by Kinsey and his associates about sexual histories.

An individual's responses to questions from Kinsey or his colleagues were recorded by means of numbers ("7 - 12" or "30 (-40)"), letters ("HSŸP" or "C - d"), or symbols of various kinds ("o" or "ü"). Only a handful of Kinsey's staff was able to understand the meaning of these coded symbols.

For further reading: Alfred C. Kinsey, Wardell B. Pomeroy, and Clyde E. Martin, *Sexual Behavior in the Human Male*, Philadelphia: W. B. Saunders Company, 1948, pp. 71–73.

KNAPSACK PROBLEM

A classic problem in number theory that has important applications to public-key cryptography. The knapsack problem originally got its name from the following situation. Suppose that a knapsack is filled with a number of stones of different weights, say 1, 2, 4, 8, 16, and 32 pounds each. The problem is to find out which stones are actually in the knapsack when its total weight is some given number, such as 27 pounds.

Knapsack problems can usually be subdivided into *easy* and *difficult* problems. The example above is an "easy" problem. Of the possible stones to be found in the knapsack, the heaviest (32 pounds) can be eliminated immediately (the filled knapsack weighs less than this stone). It takes relatively little imagination to see that a weight of 27 pounds can be obtained by choosing stones that weigh 16 pounds (to start with the heaviest of those remaining), 8 pounds, 2 pounds, and 1 pound. Or, to state the case mathematically, $27 = 16 + 8 + 2 + 1$.

The reason this problem is "simple" is that the numbers selected for the weights of the stone have a special relationship to one another; namely, each number in the series is greater than the sum of all those that precede it. For example, $16 > 8 + 4 + 2 + 1$. Knapsacks in which the stones are *not* arranged in some obvious sequence and which do *not* have some such relationship present "difficult" problems. For example, what combination of numbers in the set [235, 91, 684, 473, 199, 897] add to give a total of 1,248? The solution is by no means impossible or even very difficult. But it is clearly more difficult than the "easy" example given above. More to the point, the problem becomes more and more difficult as the set of numbers to be considered increases in size and the number to be matched (the total weight of the knapsack) increases.

The use of the knapsack problem for encryption was first envisioned by M. C. Merkle and M. E. Hellman in 1978. The first step in the Merkle-Hellman algorithm is to express the plaintext in the binary number system. Suppose a portion of that message reads 0 0 1 1 0 1. The plaintext is encrypted by combining it with a set of numbers such as those used in the "easy" knapsack example given above (1, 2, 4, 8, 16, 32). The combination of plaintext and knapsack set would produce:

$$0 \times 1 + 0 \times 2 + 1 \times 4 + 1 \times 8 + 0 \times 16 + 1 \times 32$$
$$= 0 + 0 + 4 + 8 + 0 + 32$$
$$= 44$$

The message 0 0 1 1 0 1, then, would be enciphered as 44.

Decipherment or decryption of this cipher would be relatively simple, as it was in the first example above. Merkle and Hellman, however, proposed a method by which the cipher could be made secure as a public-key cryptogram. Their suggestion was to convert the "easy" knapsack (such as 1, 2, 4, 8, 16, 32 used above) to a much more difficult knapsack (say, 493, 912, 388, 479, 101, 358) and then use the more difficult knapsack as a public key that can be published anywhere. Messages can be enciphered easily using the public key, but decipherment is much more difficult, as it was in the "difficult" example given above. In fact, for all practical purposes, Merkle and Hellman believed, this knapsack was sufficiently secure to use for secret messages. They calculated that a cipher constructed with 64 bits of plaintext and 64 knapsack numbers would produce

2^{64}, or 1.8×10^{19} possible combinations. An enemy or eavesdropper attempting to examine all possible combinations working at the rate of one per microsecond would require more than 570,000 years to try all possibilities.

On the other hand, a legitimate recipient of the enciphered message could decipher the message rather easily. The recipient would know the relationship between the "easy" and the "difficult" knapsack sets, and could convert the latter to the former without much difficulty. Once the enciphered message was restated in the "easy" form, it could be deciphered quickly and unambiguously.

As it turns out, the Merkle-Hellman cryptosystem is not as secure against decryption as it would at first appear. A number of mathematicians have demonstrated techniques by which messages encrypted using the knapsack approach can be broken within a reasonable period of time using high-speed computers. The system still holds promise, however, for the encipherment of messages for which a lower level of security is permissible.

See also: binary number system; public-key cryptography.

For further reading: Brian Beckett, *Introduction to Cryptology*, Oxford: Blackwell Scientific Publications, 1988, pp. 327–335; Henry Beker and Fred Piper, *Cipher Systems: The Protection of Communications*, New York: John Wiley & Sons, 1982, pp. 373–380; D. W. Davies and W. L. Price, *Security for Computer Networks: An Introduction to Data Security in Teleprocessing and Electronic Funds Transfer*, Chichester: John Wiley & Sons, 1984, pp. 246–250; R. C. Merkle and M. E. Hellman, "Hiding Information and Signatures in Trapdoor Knapsacks," *IEEE Transactions on Information Theory* 24 (1978): 525–530; Carl H. Meyer and Stephen M. Matyas, *Cryptography: A New Dimension in Computer Data Security*, New York: John Wiley & Sons, 1982, pp. 48–53; Luke J. O'Connor and Jennifer Seberry, *Cryptographic Significance of the Knapsack Problem*, Laguna Hills, CA: Aegean Park Press, n.d.; M. R. Schroeder, *Number Theory in Science and Communication*, Berlin: Springer-Verlag, 1984, ch. 14; "Shredded Knapsack:

Work of Ernest F. Brickell," *Scientific American* (January 1985): 56–57.

KNIGHT'S TOUR

A geometric form of transposition based on the movements made by the knight in a game of chess. According to the rules of chess, a knight can move in only one pattern: two spaces horizontally or vertically and then one space vertically or horizontally, in an L shape. Following this pattern, it is possible for a knight to move across a chessboard in such a way as to cover every space once but no space more than once. In fact, a number of such tours are possible. The tour shown below is only one of many:

1	4	53	18	55	6	43	20
52	17	2	5	38	19	56	7
3	64	15	54	31	42	21	44
16	51	28	39	34	37	8	57
63	14	35	32	41	30	45	22
50	27	40	29	36	33	58	9
13	62	25	48	11	60	23	46
26	49	12	61	24	47	10	59

A knight's tour can be used as the basis for enciphering a message if the message is written horizontally or vertically on the 64 chessboard spaces and then taken off according to the specific tour agreed on in advance by the encipherer and decipherer.

See also: geometrical transposition.

For further reading: William F. Friedman, *Advanced Military Cryptography*, Laguna Hills, CA: Aegean Park Press, 1976, pp. 39–40; Donald D. Millikin, *Elementary Cryptography and Cryptanalysis*, Laguna Hills, CA: Aegean Park Press, n.d., pp. 99–102.

KNOCK CIPHER

A method of transmitting secret messages by sound. A person knocks on a board, a piece of metal, or some other material in a manner somewhat similar to the way in which a telegraph operator taps on a key. The difference is that the knock code makes use of a Polybius square of the form below. Thus, the letter *h* would be represented by two knocks followed immediately by three knocks.

	1	2	3	4	5
1	a	b	c	d	e
2	f	g	h	ij	k
3	l	m	n	o	p
4	q	r	s	t	u
5	v	w	x	y	z

The advantage of the knock cipher is that two people who cannot see each other or who cannot pass messages back and forth can still communicate in cipher. Prisoners are one example of this situation.

See also: Nihilist cipher; Polybius.

KNOT CIPHER

A very old cryptosystem in which messages are enciphered as knots in a piece of rope or string. Imagine that the letters of the alphabet are written out on a sheet of paper, wood, or some other material. The alphabet can be in either standard form or mixed, as shown below.

F L D K S J A H A T Y R U E I W O Q P V B C N X M Z

To encipher the message SMITH LEAVES TODAY, lay one end of the rope at the extreme left end of the above alphabet, pull the rope tightly, and tie a knot at a position on the rope that corresponds to the letter *S* in the alphabet. Next, move the knot just tied to the left end of the alphabet and locate the position of the second letter in the message, the *M*, on the alphabet. Tie a second knot in the rope at a position corresponding to this letter. Place the second knot at the left end of the alphabet, and repeat the process, this time tying a knot for the letter *I*, and so forth until the complete message is tied into the rope.

The advantage of such a system, of course, is that a third party is unlikely to realize that a rope full of knots is really being used to transmit a secret message.

KNOWN PLAINTEXT ATTACK

See attack.

KRYPTOKNIGHT

A network authentication system developed by International Business Machines (IBM) in the mid-1990s. Its official name is Network Security Program, or NetSP. A description of KryptoKnight can be found in *Network Security: Private Communication in a Public World* by Charlie Kaufman, Radia Perlman, and Mike Speciner, Englewood Cliffs, NJ: Prentice-Hall, 1995, ch. 17.

KULLBACK, SOLOMON

American mathematician and cryptologist. Kullback was born in 1907 in New York City, earned his Ph.D. from Columbia University in mathematics, and taught briefly in high schools of the city. He was good friends with Abraham Sinkov, with whom he later worked as a cryptanalyst in the Signal Intelligence Service (SIS) of the U.S. Signal Corps.

In 1931, Kullback was invited by William Friedman to join the newly established SIS. The opportunity was a challenging one, because the U.S. military was just beginning to appreciate the potential value of cryptography and cryptanalysis. At first, SIS's mission was somewhat vague and involved developing codes and ciphers for the U.S. military, decrypting intercepted enemy messages, and carrying out training and research in cryptology.

As the Japanese threat in Asia grew, however, the attention of SIS staffers turned toward the Far East. Kullback focused particularly on ciphers in the Japanese J series (as they were called by American cryptanalysts) and, with his colleagues at SIS, was eventually successful in solving both the RED and PURPLE Japanese codes.

As the SIS went through a series of bureaucratic transitions, Kullback served with its successors, the Armed Forces

Security Agency and the National Security Agency (NSA). He served from 1952 to 1962 in the latter organization as director of the Office of Research and Development.

After his retirement from the NSA, Kullback taught at George Washington University, Florida State University, and Stanford University. He died 5 August 1994.

See also: Friedman, William; Signal Intelligence Service.

For further reading: Wayne G. Barker, ed., *The History of Codes and Ciphers in the United States during the Period between the World Wars, Part II: 1930–1939,* Laguna Hills, CA: Aegean Park Press, 1978, passim; "In Memoriam: Solomon Kullback," *Cryptologia* (April 1995): 149–150.

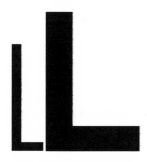

LAFAYETTE-WASHINGTON CODE

A handwritten code used by George Washington and the Marquis de Lafayette to communicate with each other during the Revolutionary War. The code was revealed to the general public in 1996 as part of 25,000 items from Lafayette's papers loaned to the U.S. Library of Congress by their present owner, Count Rene de Chambrun. The items are now available for use by researchers on microfilm in the reading room of the library.

The Lafayette-Washington code is a simple numerical code in English in which numbers represent individuals, institutions, and objects. As an example, the numbers 12 and 14 stand for *France,* 73 stands for *liberty,* and 1,000 stands for *revolution.*

At the age of 19, Lafayette purchased his own ship and sailed to the aid of the American revolutionaries in 1777. Washington made him a major general in the U.S. Army and his own personal aide. On the numerous occasions when Lafayette was away from Washington's headquarters, the numerical code was used to transmit messages between the two men.

See also: code.

"LAKE SERIES" OF CODES

See Code Compilation Section.

LAW ENFORCEMENT ACCESS FIELD (LEAF)

A feature of the Escrowed Encryption Standard (EES) that permits authorized law enforcement agencies to decrypt a message when authorized to do so by an appropriate court. The LEAF chip is embedded along with the Skipjack chip into integrated chips, which are built into large, tamperproof hardware used in the storage and transmission of data. These chips are manufactured by VLSI Logic and programmed by the Mykotronx Company under the supervision of escrow agents from the National Institute of Standards and Technology and the Automated Systems Division of the U.S. Treasury Department.

To understand how LEAF can be used, imagine that a certain law enforcement agency has been given permission by a court to intercept a message encrypted with the EES standard. The encrypted message is transmitted in conjunction with the Law Enforcement Agency Field, which includes information as to the owner of the escrowed keys. This information allows the law enforcement agency to request those keys from the escrow agent in order to decrypt the message in question.

See also: Escrowed Encryption Standard.
For further reading: Dorothy E. Denning, "The Clipper Enforcement System," *American Scientist* (July–August 1993): 319–322;

Denning, "Encryption and Law Enforcement," available from the author at denning@cs.georgetown.edu; Charlie Kaufman, Radia Perlman, and Mike Speciner, *Network Security: Private Communication in a Public World*, Englewood Cliffs, NJ: Prentice-Hall, 1995, pp. 466–468; U.S. Congress, Office of Technology Assessment, *Information Security and Privacy in Network Environments*, OTA-TCT-606, Washington, DC: GPO, September 1994, pp. 116–120, passim; Peter Wayner, "Should Encryption Be Regulated?" *Byte* (May 1993): 129–130+.

LITERAL ALPHABET ━━━━━

See alphabet.

Literature is the perfect medium in which to hide deeper meanings. Rudyard Kipling, portrayed at his desk in this undated painting, made use of cryptology in his writing.

LITERARY CRYPTOLOGY ━━━━━━━

The use of cryptology in poems, novels, short stories, and other works of literature. A number of important examples of literary cryptology can be cited. Geoffrey Chaucer was among the earliest authors to invent and use a cipher alphabet in his works. Lewis Carroll, the author of *Alice's Adventures in Wonderland* and a famous mathematician in his own right, published a Vigenère-type table in 1868 with instructions for its use in enciphering and deciphering messages. Sir Arthur Conan Doyle, Dante, Walter Gibson, Rudyard Kipling, Arthur Koestler, Edgar Allan Poe, William Makepeace Thackeray, and Jules Verne were only a few of the famous authors who made use of cryptology in their works.

The examples that can be cited of the use of cryptography in world literature are almost endless. In many instances, writers use some form of concealment cipher to convey a message that extends beyond the obvious words in a poem, novel, or some other piece of literature. As an example, the Elizabethan poet George Herbert wrote a poem entitled "Our Life Is Hid with Christ in God," in which a second message is concealed within the poem. The hidden message is indicated in the following version of the poem by means of italicized words:

> *My* words and thoughts do both express this notion,
> The *Life* hath with the sun a double motion.
> The first *Is* straight, and our diurnal friend;
> The other *Hid*, and doth obliquely bend.
> One life is wrapt *In* flesh, and tends to earth:
> The other winds towards *Him*, whose happy birth
> Taught me to live here so *That* still one eye
> Should aim and shoot at the one which *Is* on high;
> Quitting with daily labour all *My* pleasure,
> To gain at harvest an eternal *Treasure*.

See also: Chaucer, Geoffrey; "The Gold Bug"; Holmes, Sherlock; Poe, Edgar Allan.

For further reading: Raymond T. Bond, *Famous Stories of Code and Cipher*, New York: Collier Books, 1965; Maxwell Grant, "Chain of Death," *Shadow Magazine* (15 July 1934): 8–97; Dorothy L. Sayers, *Have His Carcase* (a Lord Peter Wimsey mystery that makes extensive use of ciphers), London: Brewer, Warren & Putnam, 1932; Peter Sears, *Secret Writing*, New York: Teachers & Writers Collaborative, 1986, ch. 14.

LOGARITHM ━━━━━━━

The exponent to which a number must be raised to obtain some given number. Mathematically the term *logarithm* can be defined as $x = A^y$, where y is the logarithm or exponent, A is the base or the number to which y is raised, and x is the given number. Although any number can be taken as the base, most logarithmic systems use the number 10 or the transcendental number e, having the value 2.71828183 (to eight decimal places). Logarithms using the base 10 are known as common logarithms, and those using the base e are known as natural logarithms.

As an example, what is the logarithm of 100 in the common system of logarithms? That is, to what exponent must 10 be raised to produce the given number of 100? The answer in this case is simple; the logarithm of 100 in base 10 is 2. That is, $10^2 = 100$, so 2 is the exponent or logarithm of 10.

Logarithms are an essential part of some public-key cryptographic systems. The general principle is that some numbers can quite easily be raised to some exponent if one or the other of these two numbers is or contains a secret number known only to the user of the cryptographic system. However, anyone who does not know the secret number will have a very difficult problem reversing the process; that is, finding the logarithm of some given number. For more details, see **Diffie-Hellman key exchange.**

For further reading: D. W. Davies and W. L. Price, *Security for Computer Networks: An Introduction to Data Security in Teleprocessing and Electronic Funds Transfer*, Chichester: John Wiley & Sons, 1984, pp. 225–236.

LOGIC BOMB

See malicious software.

LOGOGRAM

Also logograph; a letter, symbol, or sign used to represent an entire word or phrase. The term is retained in modern usage in the form of literal or pictorial logos used to identify a particular company. The earliest logograms can be traced to ancient Egypt, where hieroglyphic-like symbols were used in writing to represent actual objects, locations, or actions.

LOVELL, JAMES

Delegate to the Continental Congress, cryptologist, customs collector, and naval officer. Born into a Loyalist family in Boston, Lovell's allegiance was with the colonies. He was arrested by the British as a spy in 1775, and a year later exchanged for a British officer. Shortly after, he was elected to the Continental Congress. David Kahn repeats a comment that attests to Lovell's loyalty to the new nation, reporting that "he never once in the next five years visited his wife and children."

Lovell (1737–1814) developed an interest in both cryptography and cryptanalysis during his tenure with the Continental Congress's Committee on Foreign Affairs. He invented a Vigenèrelike cryptosystem that made use of a combination of letters and numbers for enciphering messages. The system was apparently not very successful because of what Fred Wrixon calls "numerous problems," one of which was Lovell's tendency to make mistakes in enciphering a message.

Lovell's claim to fame (Kahn calls him the "Father of American Cryptanalysis") rests on his success in breaking a cipher system then in use among British generals. In the fall of 1781, some dispatches between British general Charles Cornwallis and his subordinates were captured and delivered to the Continental Congress. They were handed over to Lovell, who broke the ciphers in a matter of days. Lovell wrote General George Washington that the system he had solved might well be in regular use among other British officers.

Lovell's guess was soon confirmed. Letters between Cornwallis at Yorktown and General Henry Clinton in New York were intercepted and found to be enciphered in the same system. The messages Lovell was thereby able to read revealed British plans to send reinforcements to Cornwallis by sea. This news enabled Washington's forces and the French fleet off New York, commanded by Admiral Count de Grasse, to intercept British reinforcements and ensure the defeat of Cornwallis. Cornwallis's surrender at Yorktown on 19 October 1781 can therefore be largely attributed to James Lovell's success in knowing British strategy almost as soon as the enemy.

See also: Vigenère square.
For further reading: Dumas Malone, *Dictionary of American Biography*, New York: Charles Scribner's Sons, 1933, vol. 11, pp. 438–439; David Kahn, *The Codebreakers: The Story of Secret Writing*, New York: Macmillan, 1967, pp. 181–184; Fred B. Wrixon, *Codes and Ciphers*, New York: Prentice-Hall, 1992, pp. 116–117.

LUCIFER CIPHER

An encipherment algorithm developed by International Business Machines (IBM) in the early 1970s that was later used as the basis for the creation of the Data Encryption Standard (DES) in 1974.

See also: Data Encryption Standard.
For further reading: D. W. Davies and W. L. Price, *Security for Computer Networks: An Introduction to Data Security in Teleprocessing and Electronic Funds Transfer*, Chichester: John Wiley & Sons, 1984, pp. 51–53; Dominic Welsh, *Codes and Cryptography*, Oxford: Clarendon Press, 1988, pp. 162–165.

M

M-94

A cipher machine originally conceived by Col. Parker Hitt and developed by Maj. Joseph Mauborgne, both of the U.S. Signal Corps, in 1917. The device was an updated version of the cylindrical cryptograph invented by Étienne Bazeries of the French army and Thomas Jefferson's wheel cypher. Hitt proposed it because of the inadequacy of the existing Signal Corps cipher systems at the outset of World War I.

The M-94 consisted of 25 aluminum disks attached to an aluminum rod four and one-half inches long so that they could be rotated. The disks were held in place by a nut at the end of the rod. The sequence in which the disks were arranged could be changed easily by removing the nut and the disks and putting them back on the rod in a different order. Each disk contained a mixed alphabet stamped around its circumference.

A cryptogram could be produced by arranging the disks in some sequence so that the plaintext message could be read from left to right along one row of the disks. The ciphertext could then be taken off from any one of the other rows of letters found on the disks. Any message of 25 letters or less could be enciphered in one setting of the device. For messages of more than 25 letters, the M-94 could be reset in groups of 25 letters each. To decipher a message, the receiver needed a device exactly like the one used to encipher the message; the disks were set to correspond with the ciphertext received, and the other rows of the machine

examined for a sequence of letters that could be read as a plaintext message.

The M-94 was officially adopted by the U.S. Army in 1922. In addition, the machine was widely used by the U.S. Navy (under the name *CSP 488*), the U.S. Coast Guard, and military attachés until 1943. At that point, it was replaced by sophisticated electronic and electromechanical cipher machines.

See also: Bazeries, Étienne; Hitt, Parker; Jefferson, Thomas; M-138; Mauborgne, Joseph.
For further reading: Wayne G. Barker, ed., *The History of Codes and Ciphers in the United States during the Period between the World Wars, Part II: 1930–1939*, Laguna Hills, CA: Aegean Park Press, 1978, pp. 38–40, passim; William F. Friedman, *Advanced Military Cryptography,* Laguna Hills, CA: Aegean Park Press, 1976, sec. 13; Greg Mellen and Lloyd Greenwood, "The Cryptology of Multiplex Systems," *Cryptologia* vol. I, no. 1 (1977): 4–16.

M-134-C

See SIGABA.

M-134 SERIES

See SIGABA.

M-138

A cipher machine first suggested by Col. Parker Hitt of the U.S. Army Signal Corps just prior to World War I. Hitt was very much concerned that cryptographic systems then in use by the U.S. military would be inadequate if the United States were drawn into the war. As a result, he proposed two variations of devices originally invented by French general Étienne Bazeries and Thomas Jefferson, known respectively as the cylindrical cryptograph and the wheel cypher.

In both the Bazeries and Jefferson devices, a sequence of letters was printed along the circumference of a set of disks attached to a central rod, around which they could be turned. In his design of the M-138, Hitt proposed "peeling off" the sequence of letters and laying it out on a long, narrow strip of paper. One strip of paper would be required for each of the disks in both devices.

The strips of paper were mounted within a frame through which they could be moved up and down. Hitt originally hoped to have the strips and frame made of aluminum, but the necessary technology was not yet available, so the first models of the device were made of laminated Bakelite, a tough plastic.

In Hitt's original design, the frame held 25 strips of paper, each containing two mixed alphabets. To encipher a plaintext message, the strips were arranged so that the letters along any one row spelled out the first 20 letters of the message. The ciphertext, then, consisted of the horizontal sequence of letters along any one of the other rows in the device selected for this purpose.

In the 1930s, the army adopted a variation of the device described above, the M-138A. The M-138A had 100 strips, 30 of which could be used at any one time. The frame in which the strips were held was also modified to fold in the middle, making it easier to carry, and by this time, both slides and frame were made of aluminum. Because of the construction of the M-138 and M-138A, both devices were also known as "strip cipher devices."

See also: Bazeries, Étienne; Jefferson, Thomas; M-94; Mauborgne, Joseph.
For further reading: Wayne G. Barker, ed., *The History of Codes and Ciphers in the United*

States during the Period between the World Wars, Part II: 1930–1939, Laguna Hills, CA: Aegean Park Press, 1978, pp. 38–40, 52–54.

M-209

A cipher machine invented by Swedish inventor Boris Hagelin and marketed originally as the Hagelin C-48. Hagelin purchased the Swedish cipher machine manufacturing corporation Aktiebolaget Cryptograph in 1927 after the death of its founder, Arvid Damm. Hagelin reorganized the firm and gave it the name Aktiebolaget Cryptoteknik. Just as the company appeared to be on the verge of economic success, selling thousands of its Type C-36 cipher machines to the French army, World War II intervened.

After fleeing to the United States, Hagelin tried to interest the U.S. military in another version of the C-36, the C-48. After lengthy negotiations and testing by U.S. cryptanalytic experts, the Signal Corps decided to purchase the rights to Hagelin's machine (by then known as model type B-360). Under its new name, M-209, Hagelin's machine became the mainstay of everyday cryptography for the Signal Corps. The machine was later called by David Kahn "the most ingenious mechanical creation in all cryptography."

In its final form, the M-209 was a box-like device measuring 3¼ x 5½ x 7 inches containing repair and maintenance materials, such as extra ink pads, paper tape, lubricating oil, and a screwdriver. It weighed six pounds and was amazingly rugged for an instrument of its sophistication, supposedly able to withstand shock, drops, dust, sand, high humidity, and low temperatures. It was able to encipher or decipher at a rate of about 15 to 30 letters per minute. At peak production, the Smith & Corona Typewriter Company turned out 400 machines a day. By the end of the war, nearly 150,000 were in use in the military.

The key elements of the M-209 include a hamster cage–like cylinder containing 27 rods. The cylinder rotates horizontally when a power handle at the right of the machine is turned. Each of the 27 rods on the cylinder contains metallic projections known as lugs, which can be set in various positions on the rod.

Slightly below and in front of the cylinder is a set of six keywheels, each of which has a different number of letters on its circumference. One contains 26 letters, and the others 25, 23, 21, 19, and 17. Each of the six keywheels controls the movement of a guide arm situated between it and the cylinder. As a keywheel turns, it comes into contact with a guide arm that, in turn, may or may not come into contact with one of the lugs on a rod.

The rods in the rotating cylinder are attached to a variable gear, whose number of teeth is determined by the position of the lugs on the rod. As the keywheel rotates, it moves a guide arm that may or may not come into contact with a lug, which may or may not move a rod into the variable gear. As the gear rotates, it displays the ciphertext letter corresponding to the inputted plaintext letter for that given combination of movements. At the same time, it moves a print wheel into a position to print out the displayed letter on a paper tape moving beneath the print wheel.

To begin the actual enciphering process, the operator of the machine must set the keywheels in some specific position, a setting that the decipherer, of course, must also know. Following that process, the operator turns a wheel at the left of the machine until the first plaintext letter in the message can be seen in a window at the left side of the device. The operator then turns the power handle, which initiates the sequence of operations within the machine described above. The operator reads off the enciphered letter in the window next to the enciphering wheel and, at the conclusion of the enciphered process, removes the paper tape carrying the enciphered message.

The decipherment process is, of course, just the reverse. The receiving operator first sets the keywheels at the agreed-on position and enters the cipher-

text letters, one by one, into the machine. Each time the power wheel is turned, the plaintext equivalent of the ciphertext letter is read off in the display window and printed on a new paper tape.

The arrangement of six keywheels with different numbers of letters on each means that the machine has 101,405,850 different settings (26 x 25 x 23 x 21 x 19 x 17). It obviously established the M-209 with enormous potential as a safe enciphering device.

See also: cipher machine; Enigma; Hagelin, Boris Caesar Wilhelm.
For further reading: Wayne G. Barker, *Cryptanalysis of the Hagelin Cryptograph*, Laguna Hills, CA: Aegean Park Press, n.d.; Henry Beker and Fred Piper, *Cipher Systems: The Protection of Communications*, New York: John Wiley & Sons, 1982, pp. 63–124; David Kahn, *The Codebreakers: The Story of Secret Writing*, New York: Macmillan, 1967, pp. 426–432; H. Paul Greenough, "Cryptanalysis of the Uncaged Hagelin," *Cryptologia* (April 1990): 145–161; Robert Morris, "The Hagelin Cipher Machine (M-209)," *Cryptologia* (July 1978): 267–289.

MADISON, JAMES

Fourth president of the United States. As was the case with many other leaders of the early American republic, Madison (1751–1836) made extensive use of codes and ciphers for correspondence during the later colonial and revolutionary periods. For example, his correspondence with Edmund Randolph during the summer and fall of 1782 employed a monoalphabetic substitute cipher devised by James Lovell. An official cryptologic history of this period called the Madison-Randolph letters "the most noteworthy series of letters in this cipher."

A number of encipherment errors introduced by Madison did not prevent decipherment of the letters, but rather provided the first example of the use of probable words in the solution of ciphers in the United States. The sequence of cipher letters in one of Madison's letters suggested the probable word *commission*, an assumption that proved correct and provided the key to the cipher.

Madison also used both a dictionary code and a numerical code in his correspondence with Randolph, Thomas Jefferson, and James Monroe.

See also: colonial cryptology; Jefferson, Thomas; Lovell, James.
For further reading: Wayne G. Barker, ed., *The History of Codes and Ciphers in the United States prior to World War I*, Laguna Hills, CA: Aegean Park Press, 1978, ch. 1.

MAGDEBURG

See Room 40.

MAGIC

Spelled as both MAGIC and Magic; a name given to information obtained from decrypted Japanese diplomatic correspondence by American cryptanalysts just prior to and during World War II. The name is reputed to have been invented by Rear Adm. Walter S. Anderson, who, according to David Kahn, was inspired by "the mysterious daily production of the information and by the aura of sorcery and the occult that has always enveloped cryptology."

That flow of information depended not at all on supernatural powers, of course, but rather on the intense efforts of U.S. cryptanalysts in the navy's cryptanalytic section, OP-20-GY, and its counterpart in the army, the Signal Intelligence Service (SIS). The two agencies worked largely in isolation from each other during the prewar years but, following Pearl Harbor, joined efforts to break through codes and ciphers used for Japanese diplomatic and (later) naval communications.

The cryptosystems of greatest interest to U.S. cryptanalysts were the PURPLE ciphers, in which the diplomatic messages of highest secrecy and importance were transmitted, and the JN series of naval codes. The PURPLE ciphers were enciphered in an advanced Japanese cipher machine known as the Alphabetical Type-writer 97, which had been mechanically duplicated by William Friedman and his colleagues at SIS as early as August 1940. By the beginning of World War II, the SIS was decrypting 50 to 75 messages a day and sending their results to the offices of the president; the secretaries of state, war, and navy; the chief of staff; the chief of naval operations; and the heads of the army and navy war plans divisions and intelligence offices.

Despite this relatively extensive chain of distribution, many MAGIC decryptions never reached the individuals best able to make use of them or, if they did, much too late to be of any value. In fact, questions about the timely delivery of messages concerning the attack on Pearl Harbor were sufficiently serious to require a series of congressional hearings on the whole process following completion of the war.

MAGIC successes in reading JN ciphers had a significant impact on the outcome of the war. Cryptanalysts were able to inform naval commanders of Japanese plans for attacks in the Coral Sea and on Midway Island sufficiently in advance to allow the U.S. Navy to avoid potentially disastrous consequences in both instances.

See also: Coral Sea, Battle of; J ciphers; Midway, Battle of; OP-20-G; PURPLE; Signal Intelligence Service.
For further reading: John Costello, *The Pacific War*, New York: Rawson, Wade, 1981; David Kahn, *The Codebreakers: The Story of Secret Writing*, New York: Macmillan, 1967, ch. 1; Edwin T. Layton, with Roger Pineau and John Costello, *"And I Was There": Pearl Harbor and Midway—Breaking the Secrets*, New York: William Morrow, 1985; Bruce Lee, *Marching Orders: The Untold Story of World War II*, New York: Crown Publishers, 1995; Ronald Lewin, *The American Magic: Codes, Ciphers, and the Defeat of Japan*, New York: Farrar, Straus & Giroux, 1982; Bradley F. Smith, *The Ultra-Magic Deals and the Most Secret Special Relationship, 1940–1946*, Novato, CA: Presidio Press, 1993; Ronald H. Spector, *Listening to the Enemy*, Wilmington, DE: Scholarly Resources, 1988.

MAGIC SQUARE

A square grouping of numbers arranged so that they add up to the same sum in every direction: horizontal, vertical, and diagonal. One of the most famous magic squares was devised by German painter Albrecht Dürer and inserted into his etching *Melencolia I,* which is reproduced on the next page. Notice that in addition to adding to 34 in the directions indicated, the sum of the four middle boxes is also 34. Finally, Dürer managed to include the date of his painting in the middle two boxes of the bottom row.

16	3	2	13
5	10	11	8
9	6	7	12
4	15	14	1

The construction of magic squares has long been of interest to amateur mathematicians, but they are also relevant to cryptology because they provide a simple method of establishing the key for a route transposition. Suppose that a magic square of 5 x 5 dimensions is laid out and agreed on by encipherer and decipherer. The position of the numbers within the magic square provides a key to the sequence in which plaintext letters are to be taken off during encipherment of a message.

See also: knight's tour.
For further reading: Helen Fouché Gaines, *Cryptanalysis: A Study of Ciphers and Their Solution,* New York: Dover Publications, 1956, ch. 1.

MALICIOUS SOFTWARE

A computer program whose sole or primary purpose is to cause some harm or inconvenience to other computer users. One author refers to such programs as *digital pests.* The more common forms of digital pests are:

- *bacteria*—programs that replicate themselves within a computer, using up memory space and interfering with normal computer operations
- *logic bomb*—a program that at some given time in the future sets off harmful instructions that interfere with computer operations
- *Trojan horse*—instructions included within an otherwise useful program that may have harmful effects on computer operations
- *virus*—a program that makes copies of itself and inserts them into other computer programs
- *worm*—a program that, like a bacterium, replicates itself, but rather than being confined to a single computer is distributed throughout a computer network

For further reading: Peter J. Denning, ed., *Computers under Attack: Intruders, Worms, and Viruses,* New York: Addison-Wesley, 1990; Lance J. Hoffman, ed., *Rogue Programs: Viruses, Worms and Trojan Horses,* New York: Van Nostrand Reinhold, 1990; Charlie Kaufman, Radia Perlman, and Mike Speciner, *Network Security: Private Communication in a Public World,* Englewood Cliffs, NJ: Prentice-Hall, 1995, pp. 18–24; William Stallings, *Network and Internetwork Security: Principles and Practices,* Englewood Cliffs, NJ: Prentice-Hall, 1995, ch. 5; U.S. Congress, Office of Technology Assessment, *Information Security and Privacy in Network Environments,* OTA-TCT-606, Washington, DC: GPO, September 1994, pp. 26, 36.

MANHATTAN PROJECT

A codename given to the effort by Allied scientists to harness nuclear energy in the production of atomic bombs during the early 1940s. A decade earlier, scientists discovered that energy stored in atomic nuclei is released during one of two kinds of reactions: atomic fission and atomic fusion. In the first type of reaction, large atomic nuclei (such as those of uranium atoms) are broken into two or more smaller nuclei with the release of large amounts of energy. In nuclear fusion,

Albrecht Dürer's 1514 engraving *Melencolia I* features a magic square in the upper right-hand corner.

small atomic nuclei (such as hydrogen nuclei) are combined with one another to form larger nuclei, also with the release of large amounts of energy. The first reaction forms the basis of an atomic (or fission) bomb, and the second, the basis of a hydrogen (or fusion) bomb.

The wartime effort to find out whether such weapons were possible, and if so, how they could be built, was arguably the most closely guarded secret of its magnitude in human history. Even the U.S. Congress was not informed of the project, and funds for its operation—some $2 billion—were taken from a presidential discretionary budget. It should hardly be surprising, therefore, to learn that codes were an integral part of the project.

Indeed, the project's formal name—the Manhattan Engineering District—gave no hint whatsoever of its purpose. Most of the research was done in Tennessee; Chicago, Illinois; New Mexico; and other locations far from New York City. Individuals involved in the project were also assigned codenames: *Relief* or *99* for Gen. Leslie R. Groves, director of the project; *Nicholas Baker* for Niels Bohr; *Henry Farmer* for Enrico Fermi; and *A. H. Comas* or *A. Holly* for Arthur Holly Compton. Research sites were designated by codenames such as *Chicago Metallurgical Laboratory* for the University of Chicago location, *Site Y* for the Los Alamos facility, and *K-25* for the gaseous diffusion research center at Oak Ridge, Tennessee. The weapons eventually produced as a result of the Manhattan Project were also codenamed: *Thin Man* for the uranium bomb dropped on Hiroshima and *Fat Man* for the plutonium bomb dropped on Nagasaki.

Typical of the use of code within the project was the message telephoned from the squash court at the University of Chicago when the first successful controlled fission reaction was carried out on 2 December 1942. Compton called James B. Conant, then president of Harvard University, to say that "the Italian navigator has just landed in the new world." The jargon was understood by Conant to

mean that the world's first atomic "pile" (reactor) had worked successfully. Conant responded by asking "Were the natives friendly?" or, in other words, were any serious problems encountered? Compton's response assured Conant of the project's complete success: "Yes," he said. "Everyone landed safe and happy."

For further reading: Leslie R. Groves, *Now It Can Be Told: The Story of the Manhattan Project*, New York: Harper & Brothers, 1962; Robert Jungk, *Brighter than a Thousand Suns*, New York: Harcourt, Brace, & World, 1958.

MANUAL FOR THE SOLUTION OF MILITARY CIPHERS

A famous book by Parker Hitt published in 1916. The book summarized nearly everything that was then known on cryptanalysis. Its special value was the practical approach taken by Hitt. He included a number of actual military crytpograms, including some in Spanish, in his examples. The book is now available in reprint from Aegean Park Press, Laguna Hills, California.

See also: Hitt, Parker.

MAPPING

A process by which one or more character sets is substituted for one or more other character sets. In a one-to-one mapping, each element in the first character set is replaced by one and only one element in the second character set. Thus, in a particular cryptosystem, plaintext letter *A* might be represented by ciphertext letter *w,* or *A* is mapped into *w.* A one-to-one mapping is characteristic of a monoalphabetic substitution system.

Other forms of mapping are possible. For example, a one-many mapping system is one in which a given plaintext letter can be replaced by more than one ciphertext letter. The equivalent ciphertext letters for any given plaintext letter are known as homophones. Similarly, many-one mappings can also occur: two or more plaintext letters can be enciphered by the same ciphertext letter. As an example, the numbers 9, 17, 25, 33, 41, and 49 can all be mapped into the same digit (1) in modulo 8 because every number in the set is a multiple of 8 with a remainder of 1.

A mapping is also called a transformation.

See also: homophones; modulo arithmetic; monoalphabetic substitution.

For further reading: Brian Beckett, *Introduction to Cryptology,* Oxford: Blackwell Scientific Publications, 1988, pp. 3–5; Henry Beker and Fred Piper, *Cipher Systems: The Protection of Communications,* New York: John Wiley & Sons, 1982, p. 126; Carl H. Meyer and Stephen M. Matyas, *Cryptography: A New Dimension in Computer Data Security,* New York: John Wiley & Sons, 1982, pp. 16–18.

MARKOV PROCESS

The name given to a particular type of event involving random variables in which the future state of the system can be predicted by knowing certain information about the present state of the system. Markov processes (Markov chains) are named after the Russian mathematician Andrei Andreevich Markov (1856–1922) who discovered their existence about 1900.

To understand a Markov process, consider a container filled with gas molecules. The molecules move about randomly, and it is impossible to say what the state of molecule A, B, or C will be at any point in the future. In Markov's time, that proposition was considered so self-evident that no one raised the possibility that it might not be true.

During his studies of probability theory, Markov discovered that some conditions exist under which the "obvious" condition described above does not hold. Certain conditions obtain—conditions known as *Markov sources*—that provide sufficient information to make accurate predictions about the future state of an otherwise random event. The series of probabilistic events that make up the event is known as a *Markov chain*.

When Markov made his discovery, he believed it had little or no practical application. At the time, the sciences were thought to be deterministic; that is, that given causes could always be associated with given effects. The revolutions that were to occur in physics during the first two decades of the twentieth century would prove this assumption wrong, however. Today, Markov processes are a fundamental part of many fields of science, including atomic and nuclear physics, genetics, and many areas of technology.

Interestingly enough, the only application Markov saw for his discovery was in the field of language, where the alteration of letters appears to be random. He tested his theory by tabulating the alteration of vowels and consonants in Pushkin's *Eugeny Onegin.* His insight turned out to be prophetic because Markov processes now play an important role in cryptanalysis. After all, the encipherment of a letter according to many cryptosystems today is intended to produce results as close to random as possible. The principle is to leave no transition from plaintext to ciphertext letter that has any identifiable design.

But mathematical techniques are now available for tracing back from a given ciphertext letter, through its seemingly random predecessors, to a likely plaintext letter, using Markov chains. For this reason, Markov's supposedly useless discovery of the early 1900s has become an essential element in modern cryptanalysis.

See also: entropy; information theory; probability.

For further reading: David Freedman, *Markov Chains,* New York: Springer-Verlag, 1983; Carl H. Meyer and Stephen M. Matyas, *Cryptography: A New Dimension in Computer Data Security,* New York: John Wiley & Sons, 1982, app. F.

MARY STUART, QUEEN OF SCOTS

See Babington plot.

MASTER KEY
See key.

"A MATHEMATICAL THEORY OF COMMUNICATION"
A paper written by Claude Shannon and published in *Bell System Technical Journal* in July 1948. The paper is arguably the single most important contribution to the early development of the field now known as information theory.

See also: Shannon, Claude.
For further reading: Claude Shannon, "A Mathematical Theory of Communication," *Bell System Technical Journal* (July 1948): 479–523.

MATRIX
A two-dimensional collection of letters, numbers, or symbols. An example of a matrix is the collection of letters in the Polybius square shown below:

	1	2	3	4	5
1	a	b	c	d	e
2	f	g	h	ij	k
3	l	m	n	o	p
4	q	r	s	t	u
5	v	w	x	y	z

The vertical and horizontal arrangements of symbols in a matrix are known as columns and rows, respectively. A matrix is defined by these two parameters so that a matrix with seven rows and five columns is a 7 x 5 matrix.

See also: Polybius.
For further reading: Brian Beckett, *Introduction to Cryptology*, Oxford: Blackwell Scientific Publications, 1988, ch. 12.

MAUBORGNE, JOSEPH
Army officer and cryptologist. Mauborgne was born in New York City on 26 February 1881. Mauborgne's name is important in cryptology both for his accomplishments in the field itself and for his efforts to improve the role of cryptology in the U.S. military establishment. With regard to the former, Mauborgne was the first person known to have solved a Playfair cipher, a cryptosystem then in use by the British as their field cipher and generally regarded as unsolvable. He announced his accomplishment in a small pamphlet, *An Advanced Problem in Cryptography and Its Solution*, published in 1914 by Leavenworth Press in Fort Leavenworth, Kansas. The pamphlet was the first cryptologic document published by the U.S. government.

Mauborgne's second accomplishment was the design of an unbreakable key. This achievement came about during the testing of a new system of automated cryptography suggested by AT&T engineer Gilbert Vernam. Vernam's cryptosystem involved the encipherment of plaintext punched out on a paper tape by a teletypewriter machine. The encipherment was accomplished by sending a second, or *key*, paper tape through a reading machine at the same time the plaintext tape was being read. Each plaintext symbol (represented by a hole or no-hole in the tape) was enciphered by being matched with a comparable position (hole or no-hole) on the key tape. According to Vernam's system, each combination of like symbols (hole + hole or no-hole + no-hole) was to be read as a no-hole, while each combination of unlike symbols (hole + no-hole or no-hole + hole) was to be read as a hole. In the language of binary mathematics:

$$0 + 0 = 0$$
$$0 + 1 = 0$$
$$1 + 1 = 1$$
$$1 + 0 = 1$$

The main defect with Vernam's system was that the paper tape containing the key was a loop. Vernam designed the tape to be of sufficient length that 999,000 combinations would be read before a repeat could occur. While that seems like a large number, it is not so large as to make cryptanalysis impossible. Mauborgne recognized this potential weakness in Vernam's system and set out to overcome it.

Mauborgne's solution was to use an endless key tape. That is, every plaintext paper tape containing letters enciphered in the Baudot code was passed through the reader along with a key paper tape of equal length. Every plaintext letter was enciphered by a keyletter on the matching paper tape that was entirely different.

The system was unbreakable because anyone who could solve any given section of ciphertext and thereby obtain the key for that section could make no use of it: the key used for that given section would never be repeated. Conversely, anyone who happened to be able to read a given section of the key tape might be able to read a given ciphertext and obtain the comparable plaintext. But that information would be of no value in the future since, again, the same key sequence would never reappear.

Of course, the phrase "never reappear" is not precisely true because, by chance alone, any given sequence has some probability of being repeated at some time in the future. However, since the occasion on which such reappearance will occur is virtually impossible to know, the Mauborgne system is, for all practical considerations, unsolvable.

As with all unbreakable codes, the difficulty with the Mauborgne solution is a practical one. The effort required to generate the endless key paper tape needed to encipher messages is enormous. In addition, ensuring that prospective decipherers also have exactly the same key tape when it is needed is an overwhelming practical problem. Nonetheless, in theory and in practice for at least some situations, the Mauborgne cryptosystem provides an absolutely secure method for transmitting correspondence by teletypewriter and related methods.

Mauborgne also deserves recognition for his accomplishments in improving the overall quality of cryptologic work carried out by the U.S. military in the years after he became chief signal officer in 1937. He argued aggressively for increased funding for cryptanalytic work within the Signal Intelligence Service, expanded training opportunities for officers interested in the subject, and improved the equipment and workstations available for cryptanalytic work. In many respects, the remarkable accomplishments of U.S. cryptanalysts during World War II can be credited to his foresight. Mauborgne died in Little Silver, New Jersey, on 5 June 1971.

See also: Playfair cipher; Signal Intelligence Service; Vernam, Gilbert.
For further reading: David Kahn, *The Codebreakers: The Story of Secret Writing*, New York: Macmillan, 1967, ch. 13; Joseph O. Mauborgne, *An Advanced Problem in Cryptography and Its Solution*, Fort Leavenworth, KS: Leavenworth Press, 1914; *Who Was Who in America*, Chicago: A. N. Marquis, 1973, vol. 5, p. 466.

MAYAN HIEROGLYPHICS

Written records left by the Mayan civilization. Like Egyptian hieroglyphics and obscure languages of other cultures, Mayan hieroglyphics are not technically codes or ciphers. They are "lost" languages in the sense that they are no longer used and have not been for very long periods of time. In most cases, no keys are available with which scholars can translate texts directly, as German can be translated to Spanish and vice versa.

Such languages are often included in discussions of cryptology because the techniques used by cryptanalysts to uncover plaintext from ciphertext are similar to those used by scholars attempting to find the meaning of ancient languages.

Mayan hieroglyphics present a particular challenge for scholars partly because they were the only written language developed in the pre-Columbian New World, and hence the only permanent record existing from peoples of the time. They have been a challenge also because the written records needed to decipher Mayan hieroglyphics very nearly disappeared forever. When the Spanish conquerors destroyed the Mayan civilization during the early 1500s, they burned virtually all documents written in the Mayan language. Their passion for holy conquest demanded that they eliminate all vestiges of this pagan New World civilization.

Fortunately, a few fragments of the hieroglyphics survived. Perhaps the most famous of these is a 74-page manuscript known as the Dresden Codex. Ignored as unreadable for more than three centuries, the codex became the target of an intensive attack by linguists in the second half of the nineteenth century. Mayan pictorial writings were so obscure, however, that they defeated nearly every challenge until the mid-1950s. Then, primarily through the efforts of the great Russian philologist Yuri Valentinovich Knorosov, the hieroglyphs yielded to translation. Today, Mayan scholars are able to read not only the Dresden Codex and the few other remaining manuscripts but also the voluminous carvings on Mayan temples and excavated structures in Guatemala, Mexico, Belize, and Honduras.

For further reading: Michael D. Coe, *Breaking the Maya Code*, New York: Thames & Hudson, 1992; Ernst Förstemann, *Commentary on the Dresden Codes*, Laguna Hills, CA: Aegean Park Press, n.d.; David H. Kelley, *Deciphering the Mayan Script*, Austin: University of Texas Press, 1976; Sylvanus G. Morley, "The Foremost Intellectual Achievement of Ancient America: The Hieroglyphic Inscriptions on the Monuments in the Ruined Cities of Mexico, Guatemala, and Honduras Are Yielding the Secrets of the Maya Civilization," *National Geographic* (February 1922): 109–130; Morley, "An Introduction to the Study of the Maya Hieroglyphs," Bulletin 57, Smithsonian Institution, 1915; Linda Schele and David Freidel, *A Forest of Kings*, New York: William Morrow, 1990.

Detail from a Mayan stele. Scholars used cryptanalytic techniques to learn the story of the carved stone.

MECANO-CRYPTOGRAPHER MODEL A 1

See Damm, Arvid.

MEMORANDUM OF UNDERSTANDING (MOU)

An agreement reached between the director of the National Institute of Standards and Technology and the director of the National Security Agency with regard to the relative roles of each agency in the implementation of Public Law 100-235 (Computer Security Act of 1987).

See also: Computer Security Act of 1987.
For further reading: The memorandum is reprinted in full in U.S. Congress, Office of Technology Assessment, *Information Security and Privacy in Network Environments*, OTA-TCT-606, Washington, DC: GPO, September 1994, app. B (*see also* pp. 164–171).

MERCURY, OR THE SECRET AND SWIFT MESSENGER

Reputed to be the first book on cryptology written in English. The author was John Wilkins, who introduced the terms *cryptographia* (secret writing) and *cryptologia* (secret speech) in the book.

MERKLE, RALPH C.

One of the originators of public-key cryptography, digital signature systems, and methods for authentication. Merkle's most famous paper is probably one he wrote in 1975, "Secure Communications over Insecure Channels." In a famous review paper, "The First Ten Years of Public-Key Cryptography," Whitfield Diffie explains that Merkle first developed his ideas about public-key cryptography in a course on computer security at the University of California at Berkeley (UCB) in 1974. The professor of the course was unable to understand the ideas, however, and Merkle dropped the course. He continued to work on his ideas, however, and corresponded with Diffie and others working at the cutting edge of public-key cryptography.

Ralph Merkle was born 2 February 1952 in Berkeley, California. He earned his master of science degree in computer science from UCB in 1977 and his Ph.D. in electrical engineering from Stanford University in 1979. His doctoral dissertation dealt with the use of one-way trap-door functions in public-key cryptography.

Merkle is currently employed by the Xerox Corporation in Palo Alto, California. His current research interests are in the area of nanotechnology, that is, the design, modeling, and manufacturing of systems that can be produced on an atomic dimension.

Merkle holds seven patents in the field of cryptology and is the author of more than two dozen articles on cryptology and nanotechnology.

See also: knapsack problem; one-way function; public-key cryptography.
For further reading: http://www.merkle.com/.

MESSAGE

Any collection of information sent from one person to another person or from one entity to another entity. In cryptology, the term *messages* suggests the concept of an encoded or enciphered transmission.

See also: ciphertext; cleartext; plaintext.

MESSAGE AUTHENTICATION

See authentication.

MESSAGE AUTHENTICATION CODE

A set of data provided by the sender of a message that will allow the receiver to confirm that the message has not been altered during the process of transmission. A message authentication code is added to the message itself and is generated by applying some key supposedly known only to sender and receiver to an algorithm also known to both. If the message authentication code calculated by the receiver matches that transmitted with the message, the receiver can assume that the message was not altered during transmission.

See also: authentication.
For further reading: D. W. Davies and W. L. Price, *Security for Computer Networks: An Introduction to Data Security in Teleprocessing and Electronic Funds Transfer,* Chichester: John Wiley & Sons, 1984, pp. 132–134; Carl H. Meyer and Stephen M. Matyas, *Cryptography: A New Dimension in Computer Data Security,* New York: John Wiley & Sons, 1982, p. 100, chs. 10, 11.

MESSAGE DIGEST

A condensed version of a message created by the application of a hashing algorithm to an original message by the sender. The purpose of generating a message digest is that the sender can thereby attach his or her private key to authenticate the message. The receiver of this kind of message has the ability to separate the electronically signed message digest from the message itself, verify that the sender is the person he or she claims to be, and then decrypt the message itself.

See also: hashing algorithm; public-key cryptography.
For further reading: Charlie Kaufman, Radia Perlman, and Mike Speciner, *Network Security: Private Communication in a Public World,* Englewood Cliffs, NJ: Prentice-Hall, 1995, ch. 4; U.S. Congress, Office of Technology Assessment, *Information Security and Privacy in Network Environments,* OTA-TCT-606, Washington, DC: GPO, September 1994, pp. 124–125.

MESSAGE INTEGRITY

Evidence that a message has been transmitted without alteration. Message integrity is of great interest in the modern world because of the risk that some third party might not only intercept and read a message, but also make changes in it. For example, suppose that Bank A makes an electronic transfer of funds in the amount of $1 million to Bank B on behalf of client C. And suppose that client C has the means to intercept that message and alter the amount of the transfer by adding an extra zero ($10 million). Bank B must have some mechanism by which it can determine that the message it receives from Bank A is correct and that some form of interference has not occurred during the process of transmission.

For further reading: Charlie Kaufman, Radia Perlman, and Mike Speciner, *Network Security: Private Communication in a Public World,* Englewood Cliffs, NJ: Prentice-Hall, 1995, pp. 341–342; U.S. Congress, Office of Technology Assessment, *Information Security and Privacy in Network Environments,* OTA-TCT-606, Washington, DC: GPO, September 1994, ch. 2.

MI8

A division of the U.S. War Department's Military Intelligence Division, established in 1917 largely because of the work of Herbert O. Yardley, who was also appointed its first head. Although widely known by the acronym MI8, the official title of the division was the Cipher Bureau.

The division consisted of five subdivisions, whose functions were as follows:

- Shorthand Bureau: Organized originally to help censors distinguish between authentic shorthand systems and ciphers.
- Secret Ink Bureau: Tested suspicious letters for the presence of invisible inks.
- Code Instruction Bureau: Provided instruction for military attachés, officers, and clerical personnel in the reading and writing of codes and ciphers.
- Code Compilation Bureau: Developed Military Intelligence Code No. 5 and other codes and ciphers.
- Communication Bureau: Served as the nerve center for a worldwide communication service. During its period of peak activity, this bureau operated 24 hours a day and was able to receive and decode messages from anywhere in the world within 20 minutes.
- At the conclusion of the war, all sections of MI8 were officially closed down except the Communication Bureau. Unbeknownst to almost everyone, however, the functions of the division were carried on by the American Black Chamber.
- MI8 was also used by the British War Office during World War II to designate its cryptanalytic division.

See also: American Black Chamber; invisible writing; Military Intelligence Division; Yardley, Herbert O.
For further reading: Harold C. Relyea, *Evolution and Organization of Intelligence Activities in the United States,* Laguna Hills, CA: Aegean Park Press, n.d., pt. 2, ch. 1; Herbert O. Yardley, *The American Black Chamber,* Indianapolis: Bobbs-Merrill, 1931.

MICRODOT

A microscopic copy of a document. During the 1930s, German cryptographers developed the technology needed to reduce the image of a written message to very small dimensions. This technology involved photographing a document and reducing it in a series of steps to dimensions no larger than 0.05 inch in diameter, or less than the size of the period at the end of this sentence. These reductions were accomplished by photographing the document through a reversed microscope. After the microdot was produced, it was removed from the photographic emulsion by means of a hypodermic needle and attached to some object, such as an otherwise innocent letter, where the microdot might be inserted as the dot over the letter "i," or as the period at the end of a sentence. The dot was so small that it would normally escape detection very easily; only the person meant to receive the object containing the microdot would think to look for it. The microdot could be read by placing it in a special device, similar to a microscope, that magnified the message and made it legible.

Originally, the microdot carried messages written in clear, since cryptographers could be relatively certain that the message would not be found by anyone for whom it was not intended. When American cryptanalysts became aware of microdot technology, however, the messages they contained were often written in ciphertext or codetext.

Microdots were successfully used by German agents just prior to the beginning of World War II and again by Soviet agents during the Cold War in the 1950s. One of the best-known Soviet agents, Rudolph Abel, prepared his own microdots, using spectroscopic film with a resolving power of 1,000 lines per millimeter. He inserted the microdots into copies of American magazines such as *Better Homes & Gardens* and sent them to contacts in Paris.

See also: Abel, Rudolph Ivanovich.

MIDWAY, BATTLE OF

An important naval battle that took place in June 1942 between the Japanese and U.S. navies off the shores of Midway Island in the central Pacific Ocean. Prior to the battle, the Japanese navy had established itself as master of much of the Pacific waters, but a battle in the Coral Sea off the coast of Australia in May 1942 had seemingly brought a temporary halt to Japanese progress. The threat to the American navy of losing all control of the Pacific was still very real a month later when American intelligence decrypted messages indicating Japanese plans to strike at Midway. Messages enciphered in the Japanese navy's JN25 code indicated that those plans included an attempt to draw American naval forces north to the Aleutian Islands by faking an attack there. As American ships left the central Pacific, then, the Japanese navy would focus all its forces on Midway.

By June 1942, however, the U.S. Combat Intelligence Unit in Pearl Harbor had broken the JN25 code and was reading supposedly secret dispatches regularly. It required only the identification of the codeword AF as Midway Island for the unit to be able to notify Adm. Chester Nimitz of the impending attack. Nimitz was able to gather his ships in time to meet the Japanese attack, with remarkable success. In the ensuing battle, the Japanese lost four aircraft carriers (to one for the United States), 322 aircraft (compared to 147 American planes), and over 2,500 personnel (compared to 347 American lives). The battle is now recognized as the single most important event in turning the tide of the war in the Pacific. While American cryptanalysts cannot take full credit for the victory, their contribution was certainly essential.

See also: Combat Intelligence Unit; Coral Sea, Battle of; J ciphers.

For further reading: David Kahn, *The Codebreakers: The Story of Secret Writing*, New York: Macmillan, 1967, ch. 17; Edwin T. Layton, with Roger Pineau and John Costello, *"And I Was There": Pearl Harbor and Midway—Breaking the Secrets*, New York: William Morrow, 1985; Ronald H. Spector, *Listening to the Enemy*, Wilmington, DE: Scholarly Resources, 1988; Peter Way, *Codes and Ciphers*, n.p.: Crescent Books, 1977, pp. 76–79.

An oil tank blazes as the World War II Battle of Midway rages in the Pacific Ocean. The U.S. Navy thwarted Japanese plans to invade and occupy the Midway Islands after the Japanese fleet's code was broken.

MILITARY INTELLIGENCE DIVISION (MID)

For the first three-quarters of this century, the section of the General Staff responsible for collecting and assessing information of use to U.S. military forces. When first created in 1903, it was the second section of the General Staff structure and was known, therefore, as G-2. Throughout the two world wars, MID was in charge of most of the cryptographic and cryptanalytic work done by and for the armed forces. It was woefully unprepared to carry out these operations, however, at the onset of both wars.

See also: MI8; Yardley, Herbert O.
For further reading: James L. Gilbert and John P. Finnegan, *U.S. Army Signals Intelligence in World War II: A Documentary History,* Washington, DC: Center of Military History, 1993.

MIND READING

The purported ability of one person to know what is in a second person's mind without being told. In general, mind reading involves trickery by the alleged mind reader and his or her associates. Information is passed from an associate to the mind reader by means of certain codes, such as physical or verbal clues. The associate might indicate that the subject whose mind is being read is a male, for example, by using a word that begins with *m*, such as by saying "Maestro, tell me the gender of the person I'm standing next to." The use of certain codewords or codenumbers can be used in this way to pass information to the blindfolded mind reader, who is apparently able to see into the subject's mind.

MINIMUM DISCLOSURE PROOF ━━━

A protocol by which user A is able to convince user B that he or she has certain information without actually revealing that information to user B. As an example, a person may have discovered a new proof for a theorem on which mathematicians have been working for many years. In order to receive priority for making the discovery, that person might like to announce the discovery to the mathematical world without actually publishing the proof. A minimum disclosure proof would provide enough of the results to convince others in the field that the discovery had actually been made.

See also: authentication; integrity.
For further reading: Gilles Brassard, *Modern Cryptology: A Tutorial*, New York: Springer-Verlag, 1988, ch. 5.

MIRABEAU CIPHER ━━━

A cryptosystem suggested by French statesman Honoré Gabriel Victor Riqueti, Comte de Mirabeau, in the late eighteenth century. According to this system, the letters of the alphabet are divided into five groups of five letters each. This necessitates combining two letters, either i and j, or u and v. The following is one way of dividing the letters:

plaintext
A B C D E F G H I K L M N O P Q R S T U V W X Y Z
ciphertext
1 2 3 4 5 1 2 3 4 5 1 2 3 4 5 1 2 3 4 5 1 2 3 4 5
group
1 2 3 4 5

To encipher a message, two numbers are selected for each letter of plaintext, the first number being that of the group, and the second, the ciphertext number for the letter. In the plaintext message ADVANCE, for example, the letter A is enciphered as 1 (for the group number) and 1 (for the cipherword for A), or 11. The plaintext word ADVANCE, then, would be enciphered as 11 14 51 11 33 13 15.

See also: monoalphabetic substitution.

MIRROR WRITING ━━━

A technique for disguising a message by writing it backward, as if it were seen in a mirror. The system is not very efficient as a way of hiding messages once a person has determined the technique. All that need be done to read the message is to hold it in front of a mirror. Probably the most famous example of mirror writing was that of Leonardo da Vinci, who for reasons not entirely understood recorded some of his work in this system.

For further reading: Robert Kingman, "Mirror Writing: The Modern Survival of Primitive Functions," *Welfare Magazine* (April 1928): 496–505; "Leonardo da Vinci," in *Dictionary of Scientific Biography*, ed. by Charles Coulson Gillispie, New York: Scribner's, 1975, vol. 8, pp. 192–245.

MIXED ALPHABET ━━━

See alphabet.

MNEMONIC KEY ━━━

An easily remembered key. The word *mnemonic* means "an aid to memory." Most students are familiar with the practice of inventing some aid to help them remember important lists of terms. For example, many science students recognize the name "ROY G. BIV" as a mnemonic aid to remembering the colors of the spectrum: **r**ed, **o**range, **y**ellow, **g**reen, **b**lue, **i**ndigo, and **v**iolet. Many of the keys developed for cryptosystems make use of mnemonic devices because they can be remembered without writing them down. An example might be the first line of the Bible: "In the beginning. . . ."

See also: Beaufort, Adm. Sir Francis.

MODES OF OPERATION ━━━

Methods for enciphering messages using block encryption when the messages are more than 64 bits long. Cryptosystems such as the Data Encryption Standard (DES), whose algorithm makes use of 64-

bit blocks, must have some technique for enciphering messages longer than the basic 64-bit unit (as are the vast majority). In general, four systems have been developed for dealing with this problem: **cipher block chaining, cipher feedback, electronic code book,** and **output feedback.**

MODULO ARITHMETIC

Also modulus arithmetic; a form of arithmetic in which a number is replaced by its remainder after being divided by some fixed number, called the modulo. For example, in the system modulo 6 (where 6 is the fixed number by which any other number is divided), the number 13 has the value of 1, its remainder when 13 is divided by 6:

$13 \div 6 = 2$ with a remainder of 1.

Modular arithmetic is an important tool in the mathematical analysis of ciphers and codes. For example, in a Caesarean cipher each letter of plaintext can be represented by a number as:

A = 1
B = 2
C = 3
D = 4
and so on.

In this form, the cipher alphabet for the Caesarean code can be represented as the plaintext alphabet + 3. That is, the cipher alphabet for the first four letters is:

a = 4
b = 5
c = 6
d = 7
and so on.

The numerical value of the cipher letters is, of course, the same as its literal meaning, in that 4 = d; 5 = e; 6 = f; and 7 = g. The problem with converting the literal alphabet to numbers, however, occurs at the end of the alphabet, when X = 24 and x = 27, Y = 25 and y = 28, and Z = 26 and z = 29, because the English alphabet has

no letters beyond number 26. If modular arithmetic is employed, however, with 26 as the modulo, the cipher equivalent for X (24) can be expressed as $27 \div 26 = 1$ with a remainder of 1. In other words, the numerical value of X is 1, and its literal value is *a*, as would be predicted from the Caesarean cipher.

Because modern computers use binary mathematics in their operation, calculations with modulo 2 are especially important in many cryptographic calculations today. The addition rules for this system are as follows. Note that the symbol ⊕ stands for *modulo 2 addition*, also known as the *exclusive OR operation*.

If A = 0 and B = 0 then A ⊕ B = 0
If A = 0 and B = 1 then A ⊕ B = 1
If A = 1 and B = 0 then A ⊕ B = 1
If A = 1 and B = 1 then A ⊕ B = 0

See also: exclusive OR operation.
For further reading: Brian Beckett, *Introduction to Cryptology,* Oxford: Blackwell Scientific Publications, 1988, ch. 5; Henry Beker and Fred Piper, *Cipher Systems: The Protection of Communications,* New York: John Wiley & Sons, 1982, pp. 180–181; D. W. Davies and W. L. Price, *Security for Computer Networks: An Introduction to Data Security in Teleprocessing and Electronic Funds Transfer,* Chichester: John Wiley & Sons, 1984, pp. 257–258; Charlie Kaufman, Radia Perlman, and Mike Speciner, *Network Security: Private Communication in a Public World,* Englewood Cliffs, NJ: Prentice-Hall, 1995, pp. 130–134; Carl H. Meyer and Stephen M. Matyas, *Cryptography: A New Dimension in Computer Data Security,* New York: John Wiley & Sons, 1982, pp. 25–26.

MONOALPHABETIC SUBSTITUTION

A form of cryptography in which a single cipher is used to replace each of the letters in a plaintext message. The example below shows that each letter in plaintext is replaced by one and only one letter of ciphertext.

A	B	C	D	E	F	G	H	I	J	K	L	M
N	O	P	Q	R	S	T	U	V	W	X	Y	Z
z	p	x	o	c	i	v	u	b	y	n	t	m
r	l	e	k	w	j	q	h	a	g	s	f	d

The ciphertext could as easily consist of numbers or any other type of symbol, as shown below.

A	B	C	D	E	F	G	H	I	J	K	L	M
13	2	45	9	31	3	61	4	22	38	11	1	8

N	O	P	Q	R	S	T	U	V	W	X	Y	Z
99	81	5	7	51	22	16	4	86	38	40	78	49

Monoalphabetic ciphertext is among the easiest forms of cryptography to decipher. Once a cryptanalyst knows that the letter *a* is represented in a code by *z*, for example, then he or she knows that *a* is *always* represented by *z* in that code. This kind of clue is not available in a polyalphabetic substitution because any one letter may be represented by any one of two or more letters at various parts in the ciphertext.

A monoalphabetic substitution in which one letter of plaintext is replaced by a single letter of ciphertext is known as a *monographic* system. The systems described above are all monographic systems. In some forms of monoalphabetic substitution, a single letter of ciphertext may be replaced by two or more letters, systems known as *digraphic* or *polygraphic* substitution. One of the best-known examples of a digraphic system is the Playfair system.

A well-known example of a monoalphabetic cipher is the one developed by Julius Caesar, known today as the Caesarean substitution cipher.

See also: Caesar, Gaius Julius; polyalphabetic substitution; substitution.
For further reading: Henry Beker and Fred Piper, *Cipher Systems: The Protection of Communications*, New York: John Wiley & Sons, 1982, ch. 1; Abraham Sinkov, *Elementary Cryptanalysis: A Mathematical Approach*, New York: Random House, 1968, ch. 1, 2; http://metronet.com/~konl/ctut01.html.

MONOGRAPHIC SUBSTITUTION

See substitution.

MONROE, JAMES

Fifth president of the United States. Much of the correspondence among Monroe (1758–1831), Thomas Jefferson, and James Madison during the revolutionary period was apparently conducted in code and cipher.

See also: Jefferson, Thomas; Madison, James.

MORRISON, PHILIP

American physicist and author of a seminal paper on the subject of extraterrestrial intelligence. In 1961, Morrison (1915–) and Giuseppe Cocconi published a paper in the journal *Nature*, discussing the possibility of communication between civilizations separated from each other by great distances in the universe. Morrison and Cocconi demonstrated that such communications were physically and technically possible. They argued that our own sun might seem a reasonable location for the development of intelligent life to other civilizations, which might therefore attempt to contact us. This paper is generally regarded as the point at which the search for intelligent life in the universe (SETI) became intellectually respectable. Shortly thereafter, the federal government considered funding SETI projects with public monies. One of them was named Project Ozma, after the mythical Princess Ozma in Frank Baum's book *Ozma of Oz*. SETI projects involve the use of codes as mechanisms for sending messages to civilizations that would be unable to understand English or any other Earth-based language.

See also: Drake, Frank D.
For further reading: Guiseppe Cocconi and Philip Morrison, "Searching for Interstellar Communications," *Nature* (19 September 1959): 844–846; Charles Moritz, et al., *Current Biography Yearbook, 1981*, New York: The H. W. Wilson Company, 1982, pp. 308–311.

MORSE CODE

A system of dots and dashes by which coded messages can be sent by means of the telegraph. When Samuel F. B. Morse invented the electromagnetic telegraph in

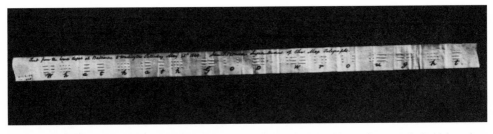

History was made on 24 May 1844 when American inventor Samuel B. Morse used his newly invented telegraph machine to send the message "What hath God wrought?," pictured here.

the 1830s, he recognized that he would also have to develop a system by which messages could first be encoded and then transmitted through the telegraph by means of tapping on the telegraph key. One of the methods he developed consisted of dots (short taps on the key) and dashes (longer taps lasting about three times as long as a dot). For example, he chose to have a single dot (·) represent the letter *e* because it is the most common letter to occur in the English alphabet and the dot is the easiest keystroke for an operator to make. Similarly, a single dash (-) is used to represent the letter *t* because it is the next most common letter and the next simplest keystroke. Other common letters are represented by other simple keystrokes: · —

for *a*, — · for *n*, and · · for *i*, for example. Uncommon letters such as *q* and *z* are represented by more complex keystrokes, — · — and — · ·, respectively.

Over time, telegraph companies and operators in various companies developed slightly different versions of Morse's original code. Then, in 1851, international agreement was reached on a single code that could be used throughout the world. Unfortunately, not all countries adopted the international code, and even today more than one version of the Morse code exists. The table below shows differences between the International and American Morse codes now in use.

On 31 March 1995, the U.S. Coast Guard announced that it would discontinue use

International and American Morse Code Symbols

Symbol	International Code	American Code	Symbol	International Code	American Code
A	· —	· —	W	· — —	· — —
B	— · ·	— · ·	X	— · · —	· — · ·
C	— · — ·	· · ·	Y	— · — —	· · · ·
D	— · ·	— · ·	Z	— — · ·	· · · ·
E	·	·	1	· — — — —	· — — ·
F	· · — ·	· — ·	2	· · — — —	· · — · ·
G	— — ·	— — ·	3	· · · — —	· · · — ·
H	· · · ·	· · · ·	4	· · · · —	· · · · —
I	· ·	· ·	5	· · · · ·	— — —
J	· — — —	— · — ·	6	— · · · ·	· · · · · ·
K	— · —	— · —	7	— — · · ·	— — · ·
L	· — · ·	— — —	8	— — — · ·	— · · · ·
M	— —	— —	9	— — — — ·	— · · —
N	— ·	— ·	10	— — — — —	— — — — ·
O	— — —	· ·	period	· — · — · —	· · · — · ·
P	· — — ·	· · · · ·	comma	— — · · — —	· — · —
Q	— — · —	· · — ·	question mark	· · — — · ·	— · · — ·
R	· — ·	· · ·	colon	— — — · · ·	— · — · ·
S	· · ·	· · ·	semicolon	— · — · — ·	· · · · · ·
T	—	—	hyphen	— · · · · —	· · · · · · · ·
U	· · —	· · —	slash	— · · — ·	· · — —
V	· · · —	· · · —	quotation mark	· — · · — ·	· · — · — ·

of the Morse code at all of its communication stations.

See also: fist; optical telegraph; telegraph.

MULTIFID

A type of cryptosystem in which each letter or number of plaintext is represented by two or more other letters, numbers, or symbols. A Polybius square, the so-called trinumeral alphabet of Trithemius, and the cipher system developed by Francis Bacon are examples of multifid ciphers.

See also: Bacon, Francis; bifid; Polybius; trifid; Trithemius, Johannes.

MULTIPLE ANAGRAMMING

A method for solving transposition ciphers first described by Edward S. Holden in the late 1870s, although not given this specific name by him. Multiple anagramming can be used to decipher messages that have two characteristics. First, the messages must contain exactly the same number of words. Second, the same key must be used to encipher both messages.

To give an abbreviated example, suppose that the enciphering key used by the correspondents has the form 5, 1, 4, 3, 2, meaning that the words are to be transposed by taking the fifth word first, the first word next, the fourth word next, and so on. The plaintext message SEND SUPPLIES TO FRIDAY HARBOR would be enciphered as HARBOR SEND FRIDAY TO SUPPLIES. To further disguise this message, codewords for certain common words or phrases (such as Friday Harbor) might be used instead of the plaintext words.

Multiple anagramming can be used to decrypt this message if at least one other message of the same length also enciphered by the 5,1,4,3,2 key is available. Holden suggested that the way to solve such messages was to arrange one of them in an order that appears to make some sense and then to arrange the second message in the same sequence as the first. There will be, he pointed out, "one order—and only one—in which the two messages will simultaneously make sense. This [order] is the key."

See also: anagram.
For further reading: Helen Fouché Gaines, *Cryptanalysis: A Study of Ciphers and Their Solution,* New York: Dover Publications, 1956, pp. 56–68; David Kahn, *The Codebreakers: The Story of Secret Writing,* New York: Macmillan, 1967, pp. 225–226.

MULTIPLE ENCRYPTION

A form of encipherment in which an algorithm is repeated more than once. The purpose of multiple encryption is to increase the security of the algorithm. Perhaps the most prominent example of multiple encryption is the triple encryption algorithm used with the Data Encryption Standard. According to this algorithm, the original plaintext is encrypted with an initial 56-bit key, decrypted with a different 56-bit key, then reencrypted with yet a third 56-bit key. The multiple encryption process using 56-bit keys provides a level of security much greater than a single encryption using a key of much larger size, such as a 112-bit key. The 112-bit key might be more secure in a single pass, but it would be much more time- and dollar-intensive than is the 56-bit key.

See also: Data Encryption Standard.
For further reading: D. W. Davies and W. L. Price, *Security for Computer Networks: An Introduction to Data Security in Teleprocessing and Electronic Funds Transfer,* Chichester: John Wiley & Sons, 1984, p. 75; R. C. Merkle and M. E. Hellman, "On the Security of Multiple Encryption," *Communications of the ACM* 24 (1981): 465–467; Carl H. Meyer and Stephen M. Matyas, *Cryptography: A New Dimension in Computer Data Security,* New York: John Wiley & Sons, 1982, app. D; William Stallings, *Network and Internetwork Security: Principles and Practices,* Englewood Cliffs, NJ: Prentice-Hall, 1995, ch. 1; U.S. Congress, Office of Technology Assessment, *Information Security and Privacy in Network Environments,* OTA-TCT-

606, Washington, DC: GPO, September 1994, pp. 121–123; Peter Wayner, "Picking the Crypto Locks: Differential Cryptanalysis," *Byte* (October 1995): 77+.

MULTIPLEXING

The practice of sending more than one signal across a communication channel at the same time. Multiplexing is a technique for encrypting messages by making them more difficult for an enemy observer to intercept and decrypt. In some cases, multiple messages are sent in the same direction across a channel, but they may also be sent in opposite directions at the same time.

Multiplexing would appear to be a valuable method for scrambling both electrical and voice transmissions. However, such transmissions can be separated electrically or electronically rather easily with only modestly sophisticated equipment.

For further reading: Henry Beker and Fred Piper, *Cipher Systems: The Protection of Communications*, New York: John Wiley & Sons, 1982, pp. 240–245.

MULTIPLICATIVE INVERSE

The number by which some given number must be multiplied in order to obtain a product of 1. For example, given the number n, the multiplicative inverse of n is $1/n$ because $n \times 1/n = 1$. As a specific illustration, the multiplicative inverse of 36 is $1/36$ because $36 \times 1/36 = 1$.

Multiplicative inverses are an important feature of public-key cryptographic systems because of their special character in modular arithmetic. For example, the product of two prime numbers such as 433 and 617 in some modulo system, such as modulo 359, can be found rather easily by multiplying the numbers and finding the value of the product:

$$
\begin{array}{rcl}
433 \times 617 &=& 267{,}161 \\
267{,}161 \div 359 &=& 267{,}096 + 65 \\
267{,}096 + 65 &=& 65 \text{ modulo } 359
\end{array}
$$

But reversing that process can be very difficult. Suppose one would like to find some number, m, such that $m \times 65 = 1$ mod 359. This operation is much more difficult than its inverse, shown above. (The actual steps by which this operation can be performed are not described here. The interested reader should refer to the reading references listed at the end of the term.)

The inverse operations defined here are important in a variety of public-key cryptographic systems, for example, the RSA algorithm.

See also: Euclidean algorithm; modulo arithmetic; public-key cryptography; RSA algorithm.

For further reading: Brian Beckett, *Introduction to Cryptology*, Oxford: Blackwell Scientific Publications, 1988, pp. 92–107; Charlie Kaufman, Radia Perlman, and Mike Speciner, *Network Security: Private Communication in a Public World*, Englewood Cliffs, NJ: Prentice-Hall, 1995, pp. 131–133, 167–168; Carl H. Meyer and Stephen M. Matyas, *Cryptography: A New Dimension in Computer Data Security*, New York: John Wiley & Sons, 1982, pp. 38–41.

MUSICAL CRYPTOGRAPHY

The use of musical notes to encrypt a message. This technique depends on the assignment of each alphabetic letter to some equivalent note in the scale. Figure 13 reproduces a hand-drawn sketch of a musical cipher, in which each of 24 musical notes has been assigned a letter.

A message can be encrypted by writing out a musical composition using a sequence of notes corresponding to the letters in the cryptogram. It is not necessary, of course, that the notes be used in a simple substitution cryptogram. Sender and recipient might agree to use every fifth note, every tenth note, or some other key to interpret the musical message. Also, the message could be transmitted not only by means of a written score but, at least in theory, by playing the message on an instrument. Probably the most

Figure 13

serious disadvantage of a musical cryptogram is the difficulty of arranging the notes in the cryptogram in such a way that they make musical sense rather than a random set of sounds.

MUSLIM CRYPTOLOGY

The construction and solution of codes and ciphers by Arabic scholars, expecially during the dominance of Islamic civilization in the Mediterranean region from 850 until 1600. The modern science of cryptology was born, according to David Kahn, in the Muslim civilization that grew up after the death of the prophet Muhammad in A.D. 632. The word *cipher* itself derives from the Arabic *sifr,* for "empty." One of the earliest works to contain information on cryptology was the *Kitab shauq al-mustaham fi ma'rifat rumuz al-aqlam* (Book

of the Frenzied Devotee's Desire To Learn about the Riddles of Ancient Scripts) written by Abu Bakr Ahmad ben 'Ali ben Washiyya an-Nabati in A.D. 855.

The most complete description of cryptology to appear during the early Muslim years was the 14-volume encyclopedia *Subh al-a 'sha,* written in 1412 by Shihab al-Din abu 'l-'Abbas Ahmad ben 'Ali ben Ahmad 'Abd Allah al Qalqashandi. Among the entries are descriptions of seven different encipherment systems. One of these is a simple substitution system; a second, a system of transposition in which the letters of a word are written in reverse order; and a third, a system in which numbers are substituted for letters in a word. The encyclopedia's special fame rests on the fact that it provides, for the first time in history, a discussion of the methods of cryptanalysis.

For further reading: Ibrahim A. Al-Kadi, "Origins of Cryptology: The Arab Contributions," *Cryptologia* (April 1992): 97–125; David Kahn, *The Codebreakers: The Story of Secret Writing*, New York: Macmillan, 1967, pp. 93–99.

MUTILATION TABLE

A code table in which all codewords are constructed with some common characteristic. As an example, the codewords that made up one codebook used by the U.S. Army during World War I were of three different forms:

1. vowel-consonant-vowel-vowel-consonant
2. consonant-vowel-vowel-consonant-vowel
3. consonant-vowel-consonant-vowel-vowel

Examples of the three forms would be:

1. AKEIN
2. BAELO
3. QEWIO

Many other forms could also be used. For example, a mutilation table might contain codewords in which all letters are different from one another by no more than two letters, such as FEGIH and VWYAC. The value of a mutilation table is that the decipherer can recognize immediately if a codeword has been garbled in transmission, as by an operator error during encoding. If a codeword appears in a message supposedly encoded with system (1) above, for example, *without* a double vowel somewhere in the word, a transmission error has occurred. Mutilation codes are also known as permutation codes.

See also: code; codebook.
For further reading: Wayne G. Barker, ed., *The History of Codes and Ciphers in the United States during World War I*, Laguna Hills, CA: Aegean Park Press, 1979, ch. 2.

MYER, ALBERT

Surgeon, cryptographer, and the first Chief Signal Officer of the U.S. Army. Fort Myer in Virginia is named in his honor. Myer (1829–1880) received his undergraduate education at Hobart College and Buffalo Medical College, from which he received his M.D. degree in 1851. To earn his way through college, Myer worked as a telegraph officer, developing an interest in codes and ciphers that would last throughout his life.

In 1854, Myer joined the army as an assistant surgeon, but two years later wrote to the War Department asking if it had any interest in developing a signaling system. The department responded affirmatively, and Myer became the nucleus of the fledgling U.S. Signal Corps.

In the ensuing years, strife developed between Myer's Signal Corps and the newly created U.S. Military Telegraph, a quasi-military organization established to operate existing commercial telegraph lines for military purposes. Conflict became so intense that Myer was relieved of his post as Chief Signal Officer at the end of the Civil War, although he won reinstatement in 1866.

Myer is perhaps best known today for the flag telegraphy (wigwag) system he invented in 1856. The system made use of flags, metal disks, or torches held in various positions in relationship to the body. The system existed in two formats, the simpler of which used only two motions, to the left and to the right; it is the one described here.

To initiate a message, the signaler would raise the flag (or disk or torch) directly overhead, drop it to his right or to his left, and immediately return it to its original overhead position. The code invented by Myer assigned the number 1 to the first of these movements (the flag dropped to the left and then raised) and the number 2 to the second of these movements (the flag dropped to the right and then raised). The meaning of these two movements was later reversed for some unknown reason, with the leftward movement being reassigned as a 2 and the rightward movement as a 1. A down-and-up movement of the flag in front of the signaler represented the number 3, used as indicated below, and in Myer's trinomial code.

The Morse code–like system developed by Myer for use with the above signals was as follows:

a	=	22	n	=	11
b	=	2112	o	=	21
c	=	121	p	=	1212
d	=	222	q	=	1211
e	=	12	r	=	211
f	=	2221	s	=	212
g	=	2211	t	=	2
h	=	122	u	=	112
i	=	1	v	=	1222
j	=	1122	w	=	1121
k	=	2121	x	=	2122
l	=	221	y	=	111
m	=	1221	z	=	2222

In addition, other signals were used to represent the end of a word (= 3), the end of a sentence (= 33), the end of a message (= 333), and other common expressions (such as "repeat": 121.121.121).

Myer also invented a variety of cipher disks that could be used along the lines of his wigwag system. The simplest of these consisted of two concentric disks with different diameters. A mixed alphabet was displayed around the circumference of the smaller disk, and codenumbers like those above around the diameter of the larger disk. Once a setting was decided upon (e.g., a = 1211), a message could be encoded simply by noting the codenumber on the larger disk adjacent to each letter in the message on the smaller disk.

More advanced disks contained a similar inner disk and an outer disk containing both letter and numerical code cipher symbols or an outer disk containing a mixed alphabet with multiple (up to four) inner disks containing mixed alphabets and the two-part code shown above or a three-part code developed later.

See also: cipher disk; Civil War cryptology; telegraph; U.S. Army Signal Corps; U.S. Military Telegraph.

For further reading: Wayne G. Barker, ed., *The History of Codes and Ciphers in the United States prior to World War I*, Laguna Hills, CA: Aegean Park Press, 1978, ch. 3; Albert J. Myer, *A Manual of Signals*, New York: D. Van Nostrand, 1868; Harold C. Relyea, *Evolution and Organization of Intelligence Activities in the United States*, pt. 1, Laguna Hills, CA: Aegean Park Press, n.d., ch. 5; Paul J. Scheips, ed., *Military Signal Communications*, 2 vols., New York: Arno Press, 1980; Fred B. Wrixon, *Codes and Ciphers*, New York: Prentice-Hall, 1992, pp. 136–138.

NATIONAL BUREAU OF STANDARDS (NBS)

Created in 1901 as a part of the U.S. Department of Commerce for the purpose of developing a unified system of measurement for the United States. The enabling legislation laid out the following primary purposes and functions of NBS:

- The custody, maintenance, and development of national standards of measurement with provisions for making measurements consistent with those standards
- The determination of physical constants and properties of materials of importance to scientific and manufacturing interests
- The development of methods for testing materials, mechanisms, and structures
- Cooperation with other government agencies and private organizations in establishing standard practices of measurement
- Providing advice to government agencies on scientific and technical problems
- Inventing and developing devices to serve special needs of the government

NBS was renamed by the Omnibus Trade and Competitiveness Act of 1988 the **National Institute of Standards and Technology (NIST),** q.v.

For further reading: "National Bureau of Standards," Washington, DC: GPO, Publication #397, 1974.

NATIONAL CRYPTOLOGIC MUSEUM

A division of the National Security Agency's Center for Cryptologic History, located at Fort George G. Meade, Maryland, between Washington, D.C., and Baltimore. Opened to the general public in 1993, the museum contains more than 7,000 items related to the history of cryptology. Important rare books are included in the collection, such as Johannes Trithemius's *Polygraphia,* Girolamo Cardano's *Subtilitas de Subtilitate Rerum* (The Subtlety of Matter), Jacopo Silvestri's *Opus Novum,* and Giovanni Battista Porta's *De Furtivis Literarum Notis.* The museum also owns a number of important cipher machines, such as the 1930s-vintage Hebern machine and the German Enigma machine. In addition to its constantly changing exhibits, the museum provides a research library for visiting scholars and researchers.

The museum can be contacted at DIRNSA, Attn: E32 (Museum), Ft. George G. Meade, MD, 20755-6000; telephone: (301) 688-5849. It is open weekdays (except holidays) from 9 A.M. to 3 P.M., and admission is free.

See also: Center for Cryptologic History.
For further reading: Louis Kruh, "A Pictorial Tour of the National Cryptologic Museum," *Cryptologia* (October 1994): 381–389.

NATIONAL INSTITUTE OF STANDARDS AND TECHNOLOGY (NIST)

Originally called the National Bureau of Standards, NIST has the responsibility of assisting industry in developing technology to improve product quality, modernizing manufacturing processes, ensuring product reliability, and facilitating rapid commercialization of products based on new scientific discoveries. Under the terms of the Computer Security Act of 1987, NIST was given primary responsibility for the development of security standards and programs for unclassified but sensitive information generated, collected, stored, and distributed by federal agencies. The act very carefully spelled out a two-prong approach to the protection of government information: one is NIST, which is responsible for security of nondefense, unclassified information; the other is the National Security Agency, which is responsible for the security of unclassified defense and all classified information.

See also: Computer Security Act of 1987.
For further reading: U.S. Congress, Office of Technology Assessment, *Information Security and Privacy in Network Environments*, OTA-TCT-606, Washington, DC: GPO, September 1994, passim (*see* index); U.S. Congress, Office of Technology Assessment, *Issue Update on Information Security and Privacy in Network Environments*, OTA-BP-ITC-147, Washington, DC: GPO, June 1995, passim (*see* index); for additional information about NIST, contact the Office of Information Services, National Institute of Standards and Technology, Department of Commerce, Gaithersburg, MD 20899, tel: (301) 975-3058.

NATIONAL SECURITY AGENCY (NSA)/CENTRAL SECURITY SERVICE (CSS)

Established by presidential directive in 1952 as a separately organized agency within the Department of Defense to be in charge of signals intelligence and communications security of the federal government. In 1984 another presidential directive charged the agency with responsibility for computer security, and a third directive in 1988 assigned the agency the responsibility of training employees in operations security.

In 1972 a presidential memorandum created the Central Security Service as the central agency for cryptology within the Department of Defense. The director of the National Security Agency was also appointed chief of the Central Security Service.

The three primary missions of NSA/CSS are information systems security, operations security training, and foreign intelligence information. Among the specific activities of the agency are the prescribing of certain security principles and procedures for the U.S. government; organizing, operating, and managing activities and facilities for the production of foreign intelligence information; organizing and coordinating research and engineering activities needed to support the agency's functions; and operating the National Computer Security Center for the protection of telecommunications and automated information systems.

A long-standing issue that concerns NSA/CSS is the extent to which the agency should, can, and will extend its responsibilities for security management beyond the areas of defense and foreign intelligence and into the civilian arena. Some precedent appears to exist for just such actions. During the 1970s, for example, the NSA copied, read, and otherwise monitored a large volume of correspondence having nothing to do with national security but rather with supposedly domestic issues. At one point, former president Richard Nixon admitted to a Senate intelligence committee that he had used the NSA to eavesdrop on civilian nonvoice communications in order to find leaks coming from the Joint Chiefs of Staff and the National Security Council.

See also: Computer Security Act of 1987.
For further reading: George A. Brownell, *The Origin and Development of the National Security Agency*, Laguna Hills, CA: Aegean Park Press, n.d.; David Kahn, *Kahn on Codes: Secrets of the New Cryptology*, New York: Macmillan, 1983, pp. 173–185; Harold C. Relyea, *Evolution and Organization of Intelligence Activities in the United States*, Laguna

Two unidentified Navajo Indians transmit messages in their native language. Navajo code talkers, who were members of the U.S. Marine Corps, played a key role in military intelligence during World War II.

Hills, CA: Aegean Park Press, n.d., pp. 244–253; U.S. Congress, Office of Technology Assessment, *Information Security and Privacy in Network Environments*, OTA-TCT-606, Washington, DC: GPO, September 1994, passim (*see* index); U.S. Congress, Office of Technology Assessment, *Issue Update on Information Security and Privacy in Network Environments*, OTA-BP-ITC-147, Washington, DC: GPO, June 1995, passim (*see* index).

NAVAJO CODE TALKERS

Members of the Navajo tribe who served as cryptologists during World War II in the U.S. Marine Corps. The idea of using Native American languages as codes extended back to World War I when eight members of the Choctaw tribe were enlisted to send and receive radiotelephone messages in their native language. Because Native American languages are generally unfamiliar to anyone outside a given tribe, there was little chance that an enemy might intercept and decode such messages.

At the beginning of World War II, 29 Navajo marines were brought to San Diego to write a codebook based on their language. The book consisted of three parts: a Navajo word, its translation, and its military meaning. The chart below illustrates what the codebook looked like.

Navajo Word	Translation	Military Meaning
cha	beaver	mine sweeper
ca-lo	shark	destroyed
dineh-nay-ye-hi	man carrier	transport
lo-tso-yazzie	small whale	cruiser
lanh	agree	affirmative
ha-ih-des-ee	watchful	alert

Using the codebook, Navajo speakers could send messages to one another anywhere on open telephone or radio circuits.

The contingent of 29 Navajo code talkers eventually grew to more than 400 at the war's conclusion. The codebook also

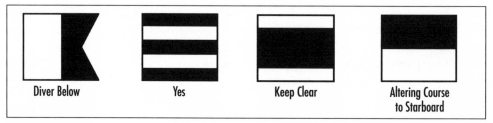

| Diver Below | Yes | Keep Clear | Altering Course to Starboard |

Figure 14

increased in size, from 274 words in its original form to 508 words at the end of the war.

For further reading: Lynn Escue, "Coded Contributions: Navajo Talkers and the Pacific War," *History Today* (July 1991): 13–20; Kawano Kenji, *Warriors: Navajo Code Talkers,* Flagstaff, AZ: Northland Publishing, 1990; Bruce Watson, "Jaysho, Moasi, Dibeh, Ayeshi, Hasclishnih, Beshlo, Shush, Gini: Navajo Code Talkers in the Pacific during WW II," *Smithsonian* (August 1993): 34–40+.

NAVAL SIGNALS

Devices used to send messages from one ship to another at sea or between land and a ship at sea. Systems for transmitting such signals probably go back to the very first water-going vessels invented by humans. The primary purposes of such signaling systems are to announce emergency conditions in which a ship requires assistance or to communicate messages from one ship to another during a military action. In either case, the purpose of such signals is normally to provide information, and not to hide or disguise it.

The categories of naval signals can generally be divided into those transmitted by sight, sound, or electrical means. Among the earliest forms of signaling was the use of torches, in which the number and position of torches represented the words or letters in a message.

Computers, linked together by a network, line a busy newsroom. Networks allow several people to access and share information, increasing the importance of encryption.

Probably the most long-standing method of transmitting naval signals is the use of flags. In some cases, a pennant of given shape and color can be used to designate a given word, as shown in Figure 14. In other cases, pennants are used to represent the letters of the alphabet and the numbers 1 through 9; messages can be sent from one ship to another by means of generally-agreed-on code systems.

See also: Myer, Albert; semaphore.
For further reading: Paul J. Scheips, ed., *Military Signal Communications,* 2 vols., New York: Arno Press, 1980; David L. Woods, ed., *Signaling and Communicating at Sea,* 2 vols., New York: Arno Press, 1980.

NETWORK

In general, any system by which a number of individual units are connected with one another to allow some kind of exchange among them all. The term is often used to describe a collection of computers and other electronic devices through which information can flow among a large number of individuals, companies, government agencies, and other entities. Examples of a computer network are the Internet and the World Wide Web.

Computer networks have become a critical feature of modern American society. They provide the mechanism by which information is transmitted worldwide about U.S. defense, products available for sale, advances in medical technology, athletic events, airline and lodging reservations, and an almost unlimited list of other topics. Networks are convenient because they are often equally and easily available to private citizens, large corporations, and government agencies.

However, this ready availability of so much information has also created serious problems and questions about privacy and the security of certain information. For example, Consumer A can readily book reservations on a flight from New York to Madrid; with additional effort, he may also be able to find out who else is booked on the same flight. The ease with which information can be accessed on computer networks has vastly expanded the role of cryptography in the everyday lives of citizens throughout the world.

Networks vary widely in the elements of which they consist, the manner in which those elements are connected, the security provided for data that flow across the network, and many other factors. For a number of years, some experts have been trying to standardize the way networks are thought of and talked about. An important influence in this area is the International Standards Organization, which has developed a model for network organization known as the OSI (Open Systems Interconnection) Reference Model.

The OSI Reference Model is an idealization of what some people think networks should do or look like. The model consists of seven layers, each of which makes use of the services of the layer(s) below it in the hierarchy shown. Actual networks may or may not (and usually do not) correspond to the OSI Reference Model, but the model provides a standard by which real networks can be discussed and analyzed. The seven layers in the OSI Model are as follows (the first layer listed is actually the lowest layer in the model and the last layer, the highest):

- *Physical layer:* Responsible for providing for the movement of unstructured bits of data across some type of link
- *Data link layer:* Responsible for organizing bits of data into coherent packages and determining where those packages should be sent
- *Network layer:* Determines pathways within the complete set of links that make up the network and transfers packages of information from source(s) to destination(s)
- *Transport layer:* Dispatcher for the network, arranging the sequence in

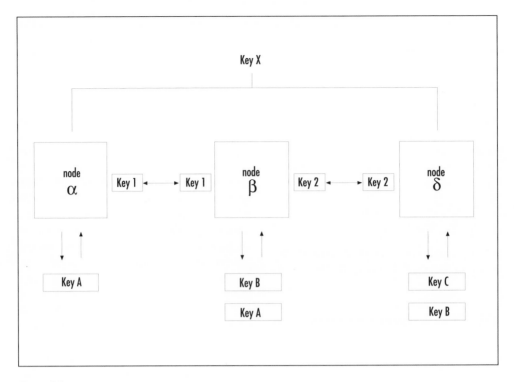

Figure 15

which data packages are to be delivered, holding packages in readiness for delivery, and retransmitting lost packages
- *Session layer:* Improves reliability of transmissions to that available from the transport layer
- *Presentation layer:* Formats data to be used in application layer
- *Application layer:* Responsible for actual use of the network for data transmission, such as electronic mail and electronic funds transfer

See also: computer; Computer Security Act of 1987; Internet; network encryption modes; privacy; security.

For further reading: D. W. Davies and W. L. Price, *Security for Computer Networks: An Introduction to Data Security in Teleprocessing and Electronic Funds Transfer*, Chichester: John Wiley & Sons, 1984, pp. 109–115; Charlie Kaufman, Radia Perlman, and Mike Speciner, *Network Security: Private Communication in a Public World*, Englewood Cliffs, NJ: Prentice-Hall, 1995, ch. 1; William Stallings, *Network and*

Internetwork Security: Principles and Practices, Englewood Cliffs, NJ: Prentice-Hall, 1995, ch. 9.

NETWORK ENCRYPTION MODES

Methods of enciphering data that pass through the various nodes in a network. The three general systems used for encrypting such data are called link, node, and end-to-end systems, and are illustrated in Figure 15.

In link encryption (also called line-level encryption), data are encrypted as they leave one node of the network and decrypted as they enter a second node. In the diagram, the data are in clear while stored within nodes α, β, γ, and so on. However, while in transit between α and β or between β and γ, data exist only in the form of ciphertext.

Node encryption (also referred to as node-by-node encryption) differs from link encryption in that data passing through an intermediary node between two more remote nodes are never in clear but always encrypted in one key or another. In the illustration here, data transmitted from node α to node β have been enciphered in key A. Within node β, the data are deciphered and then reenciphered using key B for transmission to node γ.

End-to-end encipherment depends on every user within the network having many keys, one for each node that makes use of encrypted data. Data always pass through the network in an enciphered form and are deciphered only at their final destination.

See also: network; node.
For further reading: D. W. Davies and W. L. Price, *Security for Computer Networks: An Introduction to Data Security in Teleprocessing and Electronic Funds Transfer,* Chichester: John Wiley & Sons, 1984, pp. 109–116; Carl H. Meyer and Stephen M. Matyas, *Cryptography: A New Dimension in Computer Data Security,* New York: John Wiley & Sons, 1982, pp. 195–222.

NETWORK KEY

See key.

NEWBOLD, WILLIAM ROMAINE

Former professor of philosophy and dean of the graduate school of the University of Pennsylvania. Newbold (1865–1928) was very interested in a number of topics relating to the occult and, in pursuing this interest, attempted to translate the Voynich manuscript. In 1921, he announced that he achieved some success in deciphering the text. He claimed that it suggested that a number of the sketches in the manuscript were the result of research by Roger Bacon using a microscope and telescope, representing nebulae and spermatozoa. Shortly after Newbold's death, a friend reexamined Newbold's papers and discovered that his decipherment was essentially worthless; he demonstrated that the decipherment system used by Newbold could be used to produce almost any plaintext from any given sample of ciphertext.

See also: Voynich manuscript.

For further reading: Roland G. Kent, ed., *Newbold Memorial Meeting,* Baltimore: Waverly Press, 1927; John Matthews Manly, "Roger Bacon and the Voynich Manuscript," *Speculum* (July 1931): 345–391; William Romaine Newbold, *The Cipher of Roger Bacon,* Philadelphia: University of Pennsylvania Press, 1928.

NIHILIST CIPHER

A cryptosystem developed and used by the nineteenth-century Nihilist Party in Russia. The Nihilists were a group of anarchists who advocated revolution and the violent overthrow of the Russian government. Assassination, sabotage, and other forms of terrorism were a standard part of their political philosophy and practice. As a result of vigorous prosecution by official Russian law enforcement agencies such as the *Okhrana* (Russian secret police), many Nihilists were arrested and spent extensive periods of time in prison. The Nihilist cipher, in all its various forms, was used for communication among party members in prison as well as for sending secret messages among those still free and active.

Among prisoners, the Nihilist cipher consisted of a series of knocks, similar to the Morse code, by which individuals who could not see one another could still communicate. The basis for this system was a square or rectangular box similar to that developed by Polybius nearly 2,000 years earlier. The Nihilist cipher differed slightly from Polybius's because of differences between the Greek and Russian languages. For comparison, however, the Nihilist cipher using the English language would look like this:

	1	2	3	4	5
1	a	b	c	d	e
2	f	g	h	ij	k
3	l	m	n	o	p
4	q	r	s	t	u
5	v	w	x	y	z

A message sent from one prisoner to another would use the knock cipher, in which, for example, one short knock followed by two short knocks would represent the number 12 or the letter *b* in the above table. The word *go*, then, could be represented by the numbers 22 34, or by two short knocks and two short knocks, a pause, and three short knocks and four short knocks.

This system could also be used in any form of communication in which numbers could be indicated. The handwritten message shown below is an example of how the Nihilist cipher could be hidden within an apparently harmless personal letter.

Ei leen dea rest, H ow
24 33 13 24 44 15 44 23 15 13 42 34 52 14
Incite the crowd.

Notice that the way in which letters are written differs slightly within various parts of words and at the end of some words. In the first word, for example, there is a short break between the second and third letters, the kind of break that a writer might normally make in lifting pen from paper. In this case, however, the separation of the first two letters is meant to represent the numeral 2.

The next set of letters ends with a downstroke at the end of the word *Eileen*, which indicates the end of a count. (An upstroke would mean that the letter count should continue.) The fragment indicated, *-leen*, represents the number 4, and the first numeral in the code is 24. This number represents the letter *i* or *j* (depending on the context of the message). A continuation of this analysis shows the sequence of numbers as 24 33 13 24 44 15 44 23 15 13 42 34 52 14, which corresponds to the message: I N C I T E T H E C R O W D.

The Nihilists sometimes added a second layer of encipherment on the system of numerical substitution described here. The second encipherment made use of a keyword that was converted to its numerical value and repeated over and over. Suppose that the key to be used was the word REVOLT. Using the numerical

equivalent for REVOLT of 42 15 51 34 31 44, the encipherment would be:

```
PLAIN:  I  N  C  I  T  E  T  H  E  C  R  O  W  D
        24 33 13 24 44 15 44 23 15 13 42 34 52 14
KEY:    42 15 51 34 31 44 42 15 51 34 31 44 42 15
CIPHER: 66 48 64 58 75 56 66 48 66 47 73 78 94 29
```

A decipherer could recover the plaintext, then, simply by subtracting the numerical values of the key from the ciphertext and reading the message from the Polybius square.

In an interesting turn of events, long after the Nihilist threat had been destroyed, its cryptosystem remained. The Soviet government formed after the Russian Revolution of 1917 adopted this cryptosystem for its own use and employed it for many years.

See also: knock cipher; Morse code; Polybius; superencipherment.
For further reading: Peter Way, *Codes and Ciphers*, n.p.: Crescent Books, 1977, pp. 104–107.

NODE

A component of a network; a station. Suppose that a large law firm has 35 offices around the world that are constantly in communication with one another. The set of 35 offices constitutes a network, and the 35 offices are the nodes of that network.

See also: network; network encryption modes.

NOISE
See ciphony.

NOMENCLATOR

A form of cryptography that originated among trading states in southern Europe in the late fourteenth century. It eventually became the most important single form of cryptography in Western Europe for the next 500 years. The need for increased secrecy in communications arose because of the high-stakes trading among

Venice, Naples, Mantua, Florence, and other city-states, along with the political intrigue and plotting that developed as a consequence of this economic interchange. David Kahn reports that, by the end of the sixteenth century, cryptology had become important enough for most Italian city states to employ full-time cipher secretaries. These officials were responsible for developing new nomenclators, enciphering plaintexts, deciphering incoming messages, and breaking captured cryptograms.

A nomenclator is actually a hybrid of code and cipher systems. In its earliest form, it consisted of a relatively short list of names alluded to in secret documents, along with codewords representing the names. In one nomenclator, for example, "Naples" was represented by the word *nobile* (noble), while "Florence" was represented by the word *terra* (land).

Before long, a simple monosubstitution cipher alphabet was added to the list of names. The nomenclator mentioned above, for example, used the symbol g for the letter C and the symbol T for the letter O. Over time, both the codenames and cipher alphabets used in nomenclators became more extensive and complex. Rather than a few dozen codewords, they often contained a few thousand. In place of a monosubstitution alphabet, these nomenclators employed multiple substitutes, or homophones. Nomenclators also commonly included symbols for nulls, or *nihil importantes* (nothing important), to confuse prospective cryptanalysts.

An example of a message encrypted by means of a nomenclator (using modern symbols and language) might look like the following:

PLAINTEXT: S E N D   M O N E Y   T O   S M I T H
nomenclator: x t v i k j c v e a b p c   t u l i p

See also: cipher; code; homophones; monoalphabetic substitution; null.
For further reading: David Kahn, *The Codebreakers: The Story of Secret Writing*, New York: Macmillan, 1967, ch. 3.

NONCE

A number used in a cryptographic protocol to indicate the unique character of a message. Nonces are essential when the same protocol is used many times with the same set of participants. Theoretically, it would be simple for a third party to alter any particular transmission using the protocol if no change were made in its use each time. A number of different devices can be used as nonces, including large random numbers and time-stamps.

See also: random number; time-stamp.
For further reading: Charlie Kaufman, Radia Perlman, and Mike Speciner, *Network Security: Private Communication in a Public World*, Englewood Cliffs, NJ: Prentice-Hall, 1995, pp. 244, 254–256.

NONREPUDIATION

Proof that a particular person or organization has made some type of agreement with one or more other people or organizations. Nonrepudiation means that a person or organization cannot say at some time in the future that he, she, or it never really agreed to some arrangement with another party.

Nonrepudiation is a normal and common feature of agreements in everyday life. For example, when someone wants to borrow money from a bank, he or she signs an agreement indicating that the money really was borrowed and that it will be paid back. The person cannot later say that the money was never really obtained and/or that there was never any intent to pay the money back.

Nonrepudiation is normal in business transactions also. Alice may sign an agreement with Bob to buy 10,000 shares of stock in the ABC Company for $1 million. Her signature on the agreement is accepted as proof that she made the agreement in the first place.

For many everyday transactions, a personal signature is sufficient evidence for later nonrepudiation of an agreement. In many cases, the signature may need to be witnessed by a trusted third party, such as an official of the court or a notary public.

Unlike face-to-face transactions, electronic transactions do not have the ability to record personal signatures. However, other forms of authentication, such as digital signatures, can be used to establish nonrepudiation for the transaction. A form of the notary public is also possible, provided the existence of a trusted third party to whom the digital signature of one or both individuals can be sent.

For example, suppose that Alice and Bob wish to confirm their stock transaction electronically. Alice might send her digital signature to a trusted intermediary who could then encipher Alice's signature with its own key. The enciphered signature could then be sent to Bob as evidence that Alice had truly agreed to the transaction.

See also: authentication; digital signature.
For further reading: Charlie Kaufman, Radia Perlman, and Mike Speciner, *Network Security: Private Communication in a Public World*, Englewood Cliffs, NJ: Prentice-Hall, 1995, pp. 52, 342–344; U.S. Congress, Office of Technology Assessment, *Information Security and Privacy in Network Environments*, OTA-TCT-606, Washington, DC: GPO, September 1994, pp. 20, 28, 76.

NONSECRET CODE

A code used to transmit messages with no attempt at disguising the information contained therein. Many kinds of nonsecret codes have been developed for a variety of purposes. For example, most naval codes were developed to permit ships to relay information back and forth without concern about interception by enemy vessels. Such codes might be used to indicate that a ship is in distress or needs assistance from nearby ships.

Commercial codes may be the most common and familiar of all nonsecret codes. They were developed not to keep business information secret but to reduce the cost of sending messages over telegraphic wires.

See also: naval signals; optical telegraph; semaphore; telegraph.

NORDIC CRYPTOGRAPHY

Secret writing that occurs in a number of written records, most carved on stones, by Nordic scribes in the sixth through fourteenth centuries A.D. The sticklike writing employed by the scribes is called *rune*, and was apparently used primarily for religious purposes. Runes have been uncovered in regions explored and inhabited by Nordic tribes in the sixth through ninth centuries and in a half dozen locations in the United States visited by the Nordics in the eleventh through fourteenth centuries. Two of the most famous examples of runes are the Kingigtorssuaq rune in northern Greenland and the Kensington rune found by a farmer in Minnesota in the summer of 1898.

The cryptographic techniques used by rune masters were similar to those used by cryptographers in other cultures. These methods included the substitutions of synonyms for words within the cryptogram that otherwise make no sense, deliberate misspellings of words, adding or subtracting letters to a word, combining two or more runic letters to produce a new figure, and even polyalphabetic substitution. The presence of these irregularities long mystified modern students of runology, who could make no sense of their presence in messages. For many years the most common explanation was that they represented some form of magical incantation.

Scholars have now broken the cryptograms inscribed in a number of Nordic rune stones. Some appear to be related to a perennial calendar by which the Nords dated runic messages and other important events in their history. The inscription on the Kensington stone, for example, appears to tell the story of a group of Swedes and Norwegians who arrived in what is now Minnesota in the year 1362. The nine lines on the stone read approximately as follows:

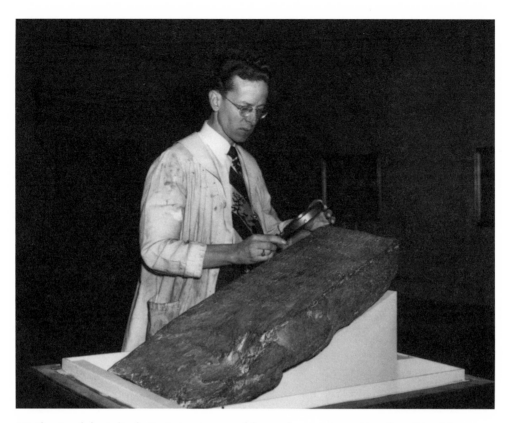

A Smithsonian scholar studies the Kensington stone, one of the most famous cryptographic artifacts. Although its authenticity has been questioned, the stone was helpful in cracking the runic code used by Nordic explorers.

[We are] 8 Goths (Swedes) and 22 Norwegians on [an] exploration-journey from Vinland through (or across the West)

We had a camp by [a lake with] 2 skerries one days-journey north from this stone

We were [out] and fished one day

After we came home [we] found 10 [of our] men red with blood and dead Av[e] M[aria]

Save [us] from evil

[We] have 10 of (our party) by the sea to look after our ships (or ship) 14 days-journey from this island [in the] year [of our Lord] 1362

For further reading: Hjalmar R. Holand, *Westward from Vinland*, New York: Duell, Sloan & Pearce, 1940; O. G. Landsverk, *Ancient Norse Messages on American Stones*, Glendale, CA: Norseman Press, 1969; Alf Monge and O. G. Landsverk, *Norse Medieval Cryptography in Runic Carvings*, Glendale, CA: Norseman Press, 1967.

NORMAL ALPHABET

See alphabet.

NP CLASS PROBLEM

See class P problem.

NULL

Without meaning. Nulls have traditionally been used in writing cryptograms as a way of confusing prospective cryptanalysts. Suppose that a cipher alphabet has been prepared in which numbers are chosen to represent letters, as, for example: a = 15; b = 23; c = 9; d = 42; e = 99; etc. Some numbers might be chosen as nulls, to represent no letter at all. The word CAB, then, might be encrypted as 9 15 67 23 with the 67 inserted as a null in the message. An enemy trying to read this message would be misled because of the assumption that the sequence of numbers represents a four-letter word. Nulls are used in other ways in cryptology, as in the construction of geometric transpositions in which additional letters are needed to complete a square, rectangle, or some other figure.

See also: columnar transposition; geometrical transposition; transposition.

NULL CIPHER

A form of concealment cipher in which only some subset of all the words or letters in the message is actually intended to be read as part of the secret message. For example, if only the second word in each sentence of the following message is read, a quite different meaning is given than might first be expected.

NO RETREAT IS POSSIBLE. ATTACK IMMEDIATELY.

NUMERICAL ALPHABET

See alphabet.

O

OBSERVATION PANEL CODES ■■■■■

Systems of communication developed during the early 1900s for transmitting messages from the ground to aircraft. At that time, such systems were necessary because the technology of radio communication was not developed sufficiently for ground-to-air use with airplanes. Observation panel codes made use of long strips of (usually white) cloth laid out in certain characteristic shapes with meanings known to aviators. For example, two parallel strips might mean "I am not receiving your signals," and two strips laid out in the form of a V might stand for "Observe for fire effect." With the development of radio communications, the need for and use of observation panel codes disappeared.

See also: nonsecret code.
For further reading: Fred B. Wrixon, *Codes and Ciphers,* New York: Prentice-Hall, 1992, pp. 147–148.

OCTAL NOTATION ■■■■■■■■■■■

A numerical system that uses the number 8 as its base. The octal digits are 0, 1, 2, 3, 4, 5, 6, and 7. Just as in the decimal system, where each position in a number represents a power of 10, in the octal system each position represents some power of 8, as shown below.

position: A B C D E F
8^5 8^4 8^3 8^2 8^1 8^0

The digit 5 in position C, therefore, represents the value 5×8^3, or $5 \times 8 \times 8 \times 8$, or 2,560.

To represent any number in octal notation, the first step is to find the largest factor of 8 contained in the number and decide how many times that factor is taken in the number. In the case of the decimal number 159, for example, the highest factor of 8 is 8^2, or 64. In the number 159, 64 occurs two times ($2 \times 64 = 128$), leaving a remainder of 31. The next largest factor of 8 is 8^1, or 8. 8 occurs in the number 31 three times ($3 \times 8 = 24$), with a remainder of 7. The next largest factor of 8 is 8^0, or 1. In the number 7, 1 occurs seven times. The octal representation of the decimal number 159, then, is 237, or

$$159 = 2 \times 8^2 + 3 \times 8^1 + 7 \times 8^0$$
$$= 128 + 24 + 7$$
$$= 159$$

See also: ASCII; binary number system.

OFFICE OF STRATEGIC SERVICES (OSS)

The primary information-gathering agency of the U.S. military during World War II. Created on 13 June 1942, the OSS was directed to "collect and analyze such strategic information as may be required by the United States Joint Chiefs of Staff." Under William J. "Wild Bill" Donovan, the OSS engaged in a whole range of intelligence activities, including spying and cryptanalysis. The OSS was abolished on 1 October 1945.

For further reading: Harold C. Relyea, *Evolution and Organization of Intelligence Activities in the United States,* pt. 3, Laguna Hills, CA: Aegean Park Press, n.d., ch. 3.

OFF-LINE ENCIPHERMENT

A term referring to the process by which plaintext is enciphered before being transmitted by some electrical or electronic means. For comparison, see on-line **encipherment.**

OGHAM

A form of writing used among the Celts during the sixth and seventh centuries, sometimes thought to be the precursor of the modern Irish language. The language consisted of 20 letters, vowels being represented by notches and consonants by lines. Existing knowledge about ogham comes primarily from inscriptions along the edges of old tombstones.

A collection of historical and genealogical information from the fifteenth century, the *Book of Ballymote,* records the existence of a variety of methods by which messages can be encrypted using ogham. The names of the methods hold an unusual and typically Irish charm. "Point against the eye," for example, makes use of a reversed alphabet for encryption. "Serpent through the heather" encrypts by means of a wavy line above and between characters. "Vexation of a poet's heart" makes use of lines that are shorter than normal in ogham.

David Kahn suspects that the systems described in the *Book of Ballymote* were never actually used for encryption, but were probably "dreamed up for fun." Historian R. A. Stewart Macalister suggests that the encryption systems may have been used as some form of sign language in which the extension and position of a person's fingers were used to encrypt letters for the expression of a secret message.

For further reading: R. A. Stewart Macalister, *The Secret Languages of Ireland,* Cambridge: Cambridge University Press, 1937; William R. McGlone, *Ancient Celtic America,* Fresno, CA: Panorama Books, 1986.

OMB CIRCULAR A-130

A set of instructions, "Management of Federal Information Resources," published by the Office of Management and Budget (OMB) in 1985 under the authority of the Privacy Act of 1974, the Brooks Act of 1965, and other legislation that directed OMB to develop procedures for providing an efficient system of collecting, maintaining, and distributing information for federal departments and agencies.

One of the important functions assigned to OMB was to establish mechanisms to ensure the privacy and security of information under the control of the federal government. That function is carried out primarily in Appendix III of the circular "Security of Federal Automated Information Systems." The purpose of this appendix is to "establish a minimal set of controls to be included in federal information systems security programs, assign responsibilities for the security of agency information systems, and clarify the relationship between these agency controls and security programs and the requirements of OMB Circular A-123" (Internal Control Systems).

Some of the specific provisions listed in Appendix III are:

1. Developing and issuing standards and guidelines for assuring the security of federal information systems
2. Establishing standards for systems used to process unclassified but sensitive information, "the loss of which could adversely affect the national security interest"
3. providing technical support to agencies in implementing standards and guidelines for security developed by the Commerce Department.

For further reading: A proposed revision of app. 3 of Circular A-130 was issued in 1995 and is available via the World Wide Web at http://csrc.ncsl.nist.gov/secplcy as "a130app3.txt."

ONE-PART CODE

A code in which plaintext words and their codeword or codenumber counterparts are listed in parallel sequential order. The following section from a codebook used by George Washington illustrates a one-part code:

1	a	17	adjourn
2	an	18	afford
3	all	19	affront
4	at	20	affair
5	and	21	again
6	art	22	april
7	arms	23	agent
8	about	24	alter
9	above	25	ally
10	absent	26	any
11	absurd	27	appear
12	adorn	28	appoint
13	adopt	29	august
14	adore	30	approve
15	advise	31	arrest
16	adjust	32	arraign

A code of this kind is easy to use since both the encoder and decoder can simply read down the list of codewords and codenumbers to write or read a message. However, the one-part code is not very secure because it provides valuable clues to a cryptanalyst. If someone trying to break a code discovers that the codenumber 00485 stands for ARTILLERY and the codenumber 01854 stands for BARRACKS, then it is obvious that a codenumber of 00995 must stand for some plaintext word between ARTILLERY and BARRACKS. A more secure type of code is the two-part code.

One-part codes are satisfactory, however, when economy—and not secrecy—is the issue. Suppose that a merchant is interested in saving money by sending a telegram in code, using a series of codenumbers to represent long phrases such as BUY ALL YOU CAN, TEN THOUSAND BARRELS, and CONFIRM AT YOUR EARLIEST OPPORTUNITY. In such a case, the merchant may not care whether someone else can figure out what the codenumbers in the message mean, because saving money is the object.

See also: two-part code.

For further reading: William F. Friedman, *Elementary Military Cryptography*, Laguna Hills, CA: Aegean Park Press, 1976, ch. 8; Laurence Dwight Smith, *Cryptography: The Science of Secret Writing*, New York: W. W. Norton, 1943, ch. 5.

ONE-TIME SYSTEM

Any cryptosystem in which the key is used once and only once. Two historically interesting forms of one-time systems are one-time pads and one-time tapes. In the simplest form of a one-time pad, a person writes down the key to be used for enciphering a message on two sheets of paper. The encipherer receives one copy of the key and the decipherer receives the second copy. When a given message has been enciphered and deciphered using that key, the two sheets of paper are thrown away, and the key is never used again.

To construct a complete cryptosystem using this approach, someone would produce not a single key with two copies but dozens or hundreds of keys, each consisting of two copies. The collection of different keys, bound together, constitutes a one-time pad. When an encipherer wishes to use a key from the pad, he or she simply notifies the receiver of the specific key used in enciphering the message. When the decipherer receives the message, he or she knows which key to use in deciphering the message. Again, when the encipherment and decipherment have been completed, the key is thrown away and never used again.

A one-time system of this design is unbreakable. Should an enemy discover the key for any given message, only the one message enciphered with that key, but no other, can be decrypted. Later messages will be sent with an entirely different key having no relationship to the intercepted message.

A second form of one-time system was developed by Joseph Mauborgne, a major in the U.S. Army, in 1918. Mauborgne's invention was a modification of an on-line enciphering machine invented by Gilbert Vernam a year earlier. In Mauborgne's system, an enciphering machine read two paper tapes at once, then converted them to a third tape carrying an enciphered message. One of the tapes read by the machine consisted of the plaintext message punched into the paper tape. The second tape carried the key, a random series of numbers also punched into paper tape. The machine matched punches in the two tapes and converted plaintext into enciphered text. The enciphered text was then punched into a third paper tape.

The Mauborgne system was a one-time system because the paper tape carrying the key was used only once. After the enciphered message was punched into the third paper tape and transmitted, the key tape was discarded and never used again. As long as the recipient of the message had a copy of the original key tape, the enciphered message could be deciphered, after which that copy of the key tape was also discarded.

Although one-time systems are unbreakable both in theory and in practice, their use has always been very limited. The problem is that one-time pads and one-time tapes must be produced and then distributed to those who will need to use them. If a military or business organization were to send only a handful of enciphered messages each week, such a system might be practical. But most organizations send out thousands of enciphered messages to thousands of different locations every week. Producing and distributing one-time pads or one-time tapes are so great a task that their use has never become widespread.

Electronic one-time pads *are* used, however, because they do not present the production and distribution problems of pads and tapes. An electronic one-time pad consists of a long string of numbers (usually binary numbers) known only to the sender and the receiver of an enciphered message. *If* a plaintext message such as 1001010010100101 is enciphered with a random string of digits such as 0001000111101011, and *if* the second string of digits is truly random, and *if* no one other than the sender and receiver know what this string of digits is, and *if* the string of digits is never used again, the enciphered message is truly unbreakable.

See also: Mauborgne, Joseph; Vernam, Gilbert.

For further reading: Henry Beker and Fred Piper, *Cipher Systems: The Protection of Communications,* New York: John Wiley & Sons, 1982, pp. 148–150 et seq.; Albrecht Beutelspacher, *Cryptology: An Introduction to the Art and Science of Enciphering, Encrypting, Concealing, Hiding and Safeguarding Described without Any Arcane Skullduggery but Not without Cunning Waggery for the Delectation and Instruction of the General Public,* Washington, DC: Mathematical Association of America, 1994, pp. 52–55; Martin Gardner, "A New Kind of Cipher That Would Take Millions of Years To Break," *Scientific American* (August 1977): 120–124; Peter Way, *Codes and Ciphers,* n.p.: Crescent Books, 1977, pp. 132–137; Fred B. Wrixon, *Codes and Ciphers,* New York: Prentice-Hall, 1992, pp. 150–152; http://rschp2.anu.edu.au:8080/OTP.html.

ONE-WAY FUNCTION

A mathematical function that can be calculated in one direction much more easily than in the reverse direction. In general, this concept means that it might be possible to calculate the value of y from the equation $y = x + 6$ for any x, but that given the value of y, the value of any x could not then be calculated. At first glance, the concept of a one-way function might seem absurd and impossible; indeed, there is as yet no mathematical proof for its existence. Yet, the concept of a one-way function is not all that unusual in everyday life. As an example, a person can easily squeeze the toothpaste out of a tube, but almost certainly cannot push it back in.

Some relatively simple examples of one-way functions in mathematics also exist. One illustration is the calculation of the product and factors of prime numbers. (Recall that a prime number is one that is divisible only by itself and 1.) It takes a bit of calculation but is still fairly easy, for example, to find the product of 853 and 607. With a handheld calculator, the answer to this problem—517,771—can be reached in a second or two. But finding the factors of a number of this size is quite a bit more difficult. See how long it takes to find the two prime factors of the number 447,553. (They are 487 and 919.)

The value of a one-way function in cryptology should be obvious. It makes it possible to convert plaintext into ciphertext relatively easily, but prevents the reverse operation (ciphertext to plaintext) by an unauthorized person. On the other hand, it does not prevent a legitimate recipient of a message from doing the necessary decipherment as long as he or she knows the key (such as the specific manner in which the product of primes was originally calculated).

One of the common applications of one-way functions is in authentication tests. In storing passwords in a central computer, for example, the passwords themselves may actually be enciphered using a one-way function. The computer is then able to test the password inputted by a customer to ensure it is authentic, but someone improperly accessing the computer would never be able to reconstruct the passwords from their enciphered form.

See also: authentication; knapsack problem; password; prime number.
For further reading: Dominic Welsh, *Codes and Cryptography*, Oxford: Clarendon Press, 1988, passim.

ON-LINE ENCIPHERMENT

The process by which a message is enciphered simultaneously with electrical or electronic transmission. The concept of on-line encipherment originated with the work of Gilbert S. Vernam in 1917. Vernam designed a cipher machine that could simultaneously read both plaintext and a cipher key punched into two separate paper tapes. The machine then enciphered the plaintext by reading the presence of holes or no-holes in both tapes, producing ciphertext in the form of a third punched paper tape. The third tape passed through a reading machine, converting the enciphered message into electrical pulses that could be transmitted along telephone wires.

See also: Vernam, Gilbert.
For further reading: Henry Beker and Fred Piper, *Cipher Systems: The Protection of Communi-*

cations, New York: John Wiley & Sons, 1982, pp. 314–315.

OP-20-G

An acronym designating the cryptologic section of the U.S. Navy's intelligence service during World War II. The acronym comes from the fact that the section was the "G" or Communications Security Section of the twentieth division of the Office of the Chief of Naval Operations (OPNAV). OP-20-G was subdivided into three subsections: OP-20-GX, responsible for interception of messages and direction finding; OP-20-GY, the cryptanalytic section; and OP-20-GZ, the translation and dissemination subsection. OP-20-GY was instrumental in breaking the Japanese JN codes and was in the process of delivering a decrypted warning of the forthcoming attack on Pearl Harbor just hours before the attack took place on 7 December 1941. The duties formerly assigned to OP-20-G have since been incorporated into the navy's Naval Security Group Command.

See also: Signal Intelligence Service.

OPEN CODE

Or open cipher; a type of concealment cipher in which the secret message is hidden within an otherwise innocent passage. In a famous series of dispatches between Tokyo and Washington just prior to the 1941 attack on Pearl Harbor, for example, codewords such as *north wind, south wind, east wind,* and *west wind*—representing the nations involved (Japan, the United States, Great Britain, and Russia)—were inserted into otherwise innocuous conversations. An open code is sometimes known as an open letter code.

See also: concealment cipher.

OPTICAL TELEGRAPH

A device to send messages over long distances by using visual signals mounted on towers. The optical telegraph was a

A Chappe optical telegraph in France transmits messages via signaling devices, located on the tops of large arms that rotate, changing positions to denote a word, phrase, or letter.

late-eighteenth-century invention that followed in the steps of signal communication systems such as the practice of lighting fires on the tops of hills, sending smoke signals, and transmitting messages by means of drumbeats.

The most sophisticated optical telegraphs were those developed by the French inventor Claude Chappe and his brothers in the early 1790s. These telegraphs consisted of tall towers with some form of signaling device attached to their peaks. The signaling device was composed of a single crossbar that could be rotated at various angles to the horizontal. At each end of the crossbar was a movable vertical bar with a metal sphere at one end to indicate an up or down position.

The most advanced forms of the Chappe telegraphs used three signaling arms that could be oriented in 98 distinct patterns. Each pattern represented a word or phrase, as in American Sign Language, although the patterns could also be used to represent letters if necessary. A codebook of 92 pages with 92 entries per page was used to transmit and interpret messages. Relay stations were placed eight to ten kilometers apart on high points such as hills, mountains, church belfries, or specially constructed towers.

Originally developed for the purpose of sending diplomatic and military messages, the optical telegraph also found some application in commercial uses. Able to compete economically with the primitive electromagnetic telegraph, it fell into disuse once the latter reached a higher level of development.

See also: nonsecret code; telegraph.
For further reading: Alexander J. Field, "French Optical Telegraphy, 1793–1855: Hardware, Software, Administration," *Technology and Culture* (April 1994): 315–347.

ORANGE BOOK

One in a series of the so-called Rainbow Books published by the U.S. government dealing with the security of computers and networks. The official title of the Orange Book is *DOD Trusted Computer System Evaluation Criteria (TCSEC)*.

One feature of the Orange Book is a rating system that specifies the level of security to be found in various computer systems. The system ranges from the least secure (Level D) to the most secure (Level A1). Five additional levels of security are indicated between these two extremes as C1, C2, B1, B2, and B3.

To compare just two of these levels, C1 (Discretionary Security Protection) and C2 (Controlled Access Protection) both describe, in general, a typical time-sharing system with a relatively low level of security. At the C1 level, only the most fundamental forms of security are expected, such as requiring users to have individual passwords and protecting data by requiring certain user access codes. At the C2 level, however, individual users may institute more rigorous access controls, and some method must be in place for detecting unauthorized intrusions.

See also: access control; password.
For further reading: *DOD Trusted Computer System Evaluation Criteria (TCSEC)*, DOD 5200.28-STD, Washington, DC: GPO, December 1985; Charlie Kaufman, Radia Perlman, and Mike Speciner, *Network Security: Private Communication in a Public World*, Englewood Cliffs, NJ: Prentice-Hall, 1995, pp. 30–33.

OUTPUT FEEDBACK MODE (OFB)

A method of enciphering messages by block encryption, in which the messages are larger than can be handled within a single 64-bit block. The method makes use of a pseudorandom number generator that operates in the following manner.

A block of some size, say 64 bits, is generated and then enciphered by means of some secret key k. The ciphertext thus created is then enciphered a second time. The product of the second encipherment is enciphered a third time, and so on. The ultimate product of this sequence is a stream of ciphers that qualifies as a pseudorandom stream.

A plaintext message is then enciphered in a process similar to that used in a Vernam one-time system. The plaintext is added by modulo 2 arithmetic to the pseudorandom stream to produce a ciphertext message.

See also: block encryption; cipher block chaining; cipher feedback.
For further reading: Gilles Brassard, *Modern Cryptology: A Tutorial,* New York: Springer-Verlag, 1988, pp. 17–19; D. W. Davies and W. L. Price, *Security for Computer Networks: An Introduction to Data Security in Teleprocessing and Electronic Funds Transfer,* Chichester: John Wiley & Sons, 1984, ch. 4; Charlie Kaufman, Radia Perlman, and Mike Speciner, *Network Security: Private Communication in a Public World*, Englewood Cliffs, NJ: Prentice-Hall, 1995, ch. 3.

OZMA

See Project Ozma.

P

PADDING

The process of adding characters to an enciphered message. The most common purpose in adding such characters is to fill out a cipher block. For example, if a message (or part of a message) contains only 58 bits and the cipher block to be filled is a 64-bit block, eight additional "padding" characters can be added to complete the block. The padding characters are typically enciphered like the message bits.

Padding is an important function to prevent cryptanalysts from detecting the end of a message. If only 58 bits were transmitted in a 64-bit block, decryption of the message might be made easier.

The addition of padding must be indicated in the message itself. This can be accomplished by adding a pad count character, which indicates the number of characters that have been added as padding. This information allows the legal recipient of the message to know whether padding has occurred and, if so, the nature of that padding.

See also: block encryption.
For further reading: Henry Beker and Fred Piper, *Cipher Systems: The Protection of Communications,* New York: John Wiley & Sons, 1982, pp. 311–314; D. W. Davies and W. L. Price, *Security for Computer Networks: An Introduction to Data Security in Teleprocessing and Electronic Funds Transfer,* Chichester: John Wiley & Sons, 1984, pp. 93–95; Carl H. Meyer and Stephen M. Matyas, *Cryptography: A New Dimension in Computer Data Security,* New York: John Wiley & Sons, 1982, pp. 73, 98.

PAINVIN, GEORGES JEAN

A famous French cryptologist, Painvain (1886–1980) is probably best known for his solution of the **ADFGVX cipher.**

PANIZZARDI TELEGRAM

A telegram sent on 2 November 1894 from the Italian military attaché Col. Alessandro Panizzardi to his superior in Rome regarding the arrest of Capt. Alfred Dreyfus of the French army general staff. Dreyfus had been arrested on 15 October 1894 for supposedly offering secret military information to France's perennial enemy, Germany. Dreyfus was charged with forwarding the information either directly to Germany or by way of the Italian military services.

Two weeks after Dreyfus's arrest, Panizzardi thought it appropriate for the Italian general staff to make some official public announcement with regard to its role (if any) in the Dreyfus affair. Accordingly, Panizzardi telegraphed Rome that he knew nothing of any involvement by Dreyfus, but that Rome should comment on the case. He sent the message in a superenciphered version of a rather simple code, the Baravelli commercial code, then in wide use.

The enciphered message was intercepted by French intelligence and turned over to the Ministry of Posts and Telegraphs' Bureau du Chiffre, headed by Charles-Marie Darmet. Within a week, the bureau's cryptanalysts decrypted the message, which read: "If Captain Dreyfus has not had relations with you, it would be wise to have the ambassador deny it officially, to avoid press comment."

In retrospect, the Panizzardi telegram could have been used in Dreyfus's defense. In fact, sentiment against Dreyfus was so strong that those fighting for his conviction managed to insert a false telegram from Panizzardi claiming to know of Dreyfus's guilt! The false telegram was eventually uncovered and the original telegram entered into evidence. But even this was not sufficient to save Dreyfus from a guilty verdict, and not until seven years later was his innocence proved and he was released from imprisonment on Devil's Island.

See also: superencipherment.
For further reading: David Kahn, *The Codebreakers: The Story of Secret Writing*, New York: Macmillan, 1967, pp. 254–262.

PAPAL CRYPTOLOGY

Cryptosystems employed by the Vatican hierarchy. Cryptography and cryptanalysts might not seem necessary within a religious organization such as the Roman Catholic Church. However, the Vatican has traditionally had a powerful political role in addition to its religious functions, particularly prior to the twentieth century.

Some of the earliest uses of cryptology can be traced to Vatican documents. David Kahn cites the use of simple substitutions in documents dating to 1326 or 1327. In these documents, the single letter *o* is used as a substitute for the title *official*, the codeword EGYPTIANS for the pro-papal league known as the Guelphs, and the codephrase CHILDREN OF ISRAEL for those supporting the Holy Roman Emperor, the Ghibellines.

Kahn claims that the first modern code can be found in early Vatican documents. In this code, single letters represent the names of individuals and places, such as *A* for king, *D* for pope, and *S* for Marcellus.

Over the next 300 years, Vatican cryptologists were among the most skillful of their breed in Western Europe. Among the most famous of this line of scholars was the Argenti family, who made the Vatican black chamber one of the finest cryptanalytic offices on the continent in the sixteenth century.

See also: Argenti family; black chamber; nomenclator.
For further reading: David Kahn, *The Codebreakers: The Story of Secret Writing*, New York: Macmillan, 1967, ch. 3.

PAPERWORK REDUCTION ACT OF 1980

A broad-ranging act (Public Law 96-511) designed to streamline and increase the efficiency of the federal government's information-gathering, maintenance, and distribution functions. The act was revised and readopted in 1995. One of its important provisions was assigning responsibility to the Office of Management and Budget (OMB) for carrying out many of its "efficiency" functions. It was under this authority that OMB published in 1985 an important circular, OMB Circular A-130, that outlines detailed instructions for maintaining the security of federal information systems.

See also: OMB Circular A-130.
For further reading: U.S. Congress, House of Representatives, *Paperwork Reduction Act of 1995—Conference Report To Accompany S. 244*, House Report 104-99, 104th Congress, First Session, 3 April 1995; U.S. Congress, Office of Technology Assessment, *Information Security and Privacy in Network Environments*, OTA-TCT-606, Washington, DC: GPO, September 1994, pp. 137–138; U.S. Congress, Office of Technology Assessment, *Issue Update on Information Security and Privacy in Network Environments*, OTA-BP-ITC-147, Washington, DC: GPO, June 1995, pp. 28–29.

PASSWORD

A mechanism by which an individual supplies authentication to a machine, allowing that person to have access to information stored in the machine. On the simplest possible level, the machine could simply store all the passwords chosen by or assigned to individual users of the system. Then, the machine simply compares the password entered by a user to the master list of passwords stored in the machine's memory. In fact, this system is much too simple and naive, because anyone breaking into the machine would be able to read all the passwords and imitate any one of the legitimate users of the system to obtain information to which he or she is not entitled. In actual situations, the master list of passwords is enciphered before being stored in the machine, reducing the risk of theft by an unqualified user.

In its 1994 report on network security, the Office of Technology Assessment lists eight criteria to be considered in maintaining "strong" passwords, that is, passwords that are not easily obtained by other individuals. They are:

1. Treat your password like your toothbrush; use it every day, change it often, and never share it.
2. Never write your password on anything near your computer. If you do write it down, do not identify it as a password, and hide it well. Never place an unencrypted password in the text of an electronic message or store it unencrypted in a file on the network.
3. Never use the default password (provided by the manufacturer).
4. Avoid proper names, nicknames, or full words for passwords, even spelled backward. Do not repeat a password that you have used before.
5. Do use long, unpronounceable acronyms, such as the first letters of an unfamiliar song or phrase, or an obscure word with vowels omitted.
6. Do use passwords with numbers or special characters inserted.
7. Do use nonsensical but pronounceable words; for example, SKRODRA8.
8. Do consider using an electronic token, a challenge-and-response system, a biometric device, or other technique that better identifies the user. (from OTA 1994, p. 33)

See also: authentication; challenge-and-response protocol; one-way function; password sniffing.

For further reading: Albrecht Beutelspacher, *Cryptology: An Introduction to the Art and Science of Enciphering, Encrypting, Concealing, Hiding and Safeguarding Described without Any Arcane Skullduggery but Not without Cunning Waggery for the Delectation and Instruction of the General Public*, Washington, DC: Mathematical Association of America, 1994, ch. 4; D. W. Davies and W. L. Price, *Security for Computer Networks: An Introduction to Data Security in Teleprocessing and Electronic Funds Transfer*, Chichester: John Wiley & Sons, 1984, pp. 180–187; Charlie Kaufman, Radia Perlman, and Mike Speciner, *Network Security: Private Communication in a Public World*, Englewood Cliffs, NJ: Prentice-Hall, 1995, pp. 177–181, passim; R. Morris and K. Thompson, "Password Security: A Case History," *Communications of the ACM* (November 1979): 594–597; Gene Steinberg, "False Security: Software Password Protection," *Macworld* (November 1995): 118–121; U.S. Congress, Office of Technology Assessment, *Information Security and Privacy in Network Environments*, OTA-TCT-606, Washington, DC: GPO, September 1994, pp. 32–33.

PASSWORD SNIFFING

A term used to describe the process by which a person attempts to capture and use a password belonging to some other person.

See also: spoofing.

PATTERN WORDS

Words having some characteristic feature that can be used during cryptanalysis. For example, pattern words of seven letters with a repeated consonant would include RUNNING, BARRIER, and DOLLARS. Pattern words of five letters with two vowels separated by a consonant would include VOCAL, ABIDE, and STOLE.

Pattern words are helpful in solving cryptograms because patterns of ciphertext letters may begin to show up early in a solution before much other information is available. If a consistent vowel pattern can be detected, a list of pattern words may aid the cryptanalyst in identifying important words and recognizing probable words.

See also: probable word.

For further reading: Sheila A. Carlisle, *Pattern Words—Nine Letters in Length,* Laguna Hills, CA: Aegean Park Press, n.d.; Carlisle, *Pattern Words—Three Letters to Eight Letters in Length,* Laguna Hills, CA: Aegean Park Press, n.d.; Robert W. Wallace, *Pattern Words—Ten Letters and Eleven Letters in Length,* Laguna Hills, CA: Aegean Park Press, n.d.; Wallace, *Pattern Words—Twelve Letters and Greater in Length,* Laguna Hills, CA: Aegean Park Press, n.d.

PEARL HARBOR

Site of an important U.S. naval base in the Hawaiian Islands and target of an attack by Japanese military forces that precipitated World War II in the Pacific theater of action. The name of Pearl Harbor will have a lasting place in the history of cryptology because of the controversy over how much U.S. government officials knew about the impending attack and when they knew it.

The debate arises because U.S. cryptanalysts had solved Japanese diplomatic and naval codes many months before and were reading sensitive transmissions on a fairly regular basis. News of the imminent attack on Pearl Harbor was being decrypted by cryptanalysts at the Navy's OP-20-GY at virtually the same moment the Japanese ambassador in Washington was reading the same messages.

The battleship USS *Arizona* explodes during the Japanese attack on Pearl Harbor. Rumors had circulated that the U.S. government had intercepted encrypted plans detailing this attack.

The issue is whether U.S. officials had sufficient foreknowledge of the attack, in the days before 7 December 1941, to have warded off the resulting slaughter. A number of congressional hearings were held on the subject, and the official conclusion was that officials had acted responsibly in the time available with the information they had. The story of the attack on Japanese codes and ciphers in the months before Pearl Harbor, however, continues to be one of the most intriguing and fascinating in the annals of cryptology.

See also: OP-20-G.
For further reading: *Investigation of the Pearl Harbor Attack,* Report of the Joint Committee, Congress of the United States, Pursuant to Senate Concurrent Resolution 27, 79th Congress, Laguna Hills, CA: Aegean Park Press, n.d.; David Kahn, *The Codebreakers: The Story of Secret Writing,* New York: Macmillan, 1967, ch. 1; Kahn, "Pearl Harbor and the Inadequacy of Cryptanalysis," *Cryptologia* 15:4 (1991): 273–294.

PEPYS, SAMUEL

English writer and civil servant. For the better part of the 1660s, Pepys (1633–1703) kept a diary in which early entries were written in a form of shorthand known as tachygraphy, developed by Thomas Shelton. Tachygraphy was so complex and cumbersome, however, that Pepys soon developed a shorthand system of his own, with which he completed the diary. Pepys's diary entries began on 1 January 1660, and he made his last entry on 31 May 1669. He ended his work, he said, because he was "not able to do it [to write] any longer, having done now so long as to undo my eyes almost every time that I take a pen in my hand."

Pepys never explicitly revealed the reason for keeping his diary in shorthand, but certainly it allowed him to record events, thoughts, and feelings much more frankly than had he written in English. Publicly, Pepys had the reputation of being an upstanding citizen committed to moral purity. Selections from the diary,

however, show that he was a lecher who lived a less pure life. The secrecy accorded Pepys by the use of tachygraphy allowed him to write with an openness that is charming and fascinating to readers even three centuries later. The original text was so shocking, however, that the publisher of the first edition deleted large chunks of Pepys's material.

After his death in 1703, Pepys's diary remained unread in the library at Magdalene College for over a century. Tachygraphy fell into disuse soon after Pepys's death, and no one troubled to decipher the diary. In 1819, however, book collector Thomas Grenville rediscovered the diary and deciphered the first dozen pages of the book rather easily. Grenville gave the task of deciphering the rest of the work to John Smith, an undergraduate in St. John's College. Smith spent nearly three years completing the task. The final product was a 56-volume work filling 9,325 pages and including 1.3 million words. The book is still reprinted regularly today and read in many English literature classes.

See also: tachygraphy.
For further reading: W. Matthews, "Samuel Pepys, Tachygraphist," *Modern Language Review* (October 1934): 397–404; Leslie Stephen and Sidney Lee, eds., *Dictionary of National Biography,* London: Oxford University Press, 1947, vol. 15, pp. 805–811.

PERFECT SECRECY (OR SECURITY)

An encrypted message that contains no information whatsoever, except possibly length, about the plaintext from which it was created. Any such message would constitute an unbreakable cipher, but perfect secrecy is not a practical reality for a number of reasons. For example, Claude Shannon has shown that such a message would require a key of roughly the same length as the message itself and that the key could not be used a second time. Nonetheless, in the most highly secret situations, perfect secrecy can be approximated or attained. The Red Telephone that connects Washington and Moscow employs such a system.

See also: one-time system; unbreakable cipher.

For further reading: Albrecht Beutelspacher, *Cryptology: An Introduction to the Art and Science of Enciphering, Encrypting, Concealing, Hiding and Safeguarding Described without Any Arcane Skullduggery but Not without Cunning Waggery for the Delectation and Instruction of the General Public,* Washington, DC: Mathematical Association of America, 1994, pp. 48–55.

PERMUTATION

A change in the order of items; in mathematics, a change in the order of digits that make up a number. As an example, the permutations of the digits 1, 2, and 3 are as follows: 123, 132, 213, 231, 312, 321. The number of permutations, P, of any set of n objects can be expressed mathematically as:

$$P_n = n(n-1)(n-2)\ldots \times 3 \times 2 \times 1$$

As an example, the number of permutations of the 26 letters of the English alphabet is:

$$P_n = 26 \times 25 \times 24 \times 23 \times 22 \times 21 \times 20 \times 19 \times 18 \times 17 \times 16 \times 15 \times 14 \times 13 \\ \times 12 \times 11 \times 10 \times 9 \times 8 \times 7 \times 6 \times 5 \times 4 \times 3 \times 2 \times 1$$

Permutations are extensively used in cryptography in the process of transposition. For example, one way of enciphering the binary number 00110011 is to transpose its digits as, for example, to 11001100. The number of possible ways in which this kind of transposition can be accomplished can be determined by using the formula above. With the binary number given above, the total number of permutations would be:

$$P_8 = 8 \times 7 \times 6 \times 5 \times 4 \times 3 \times 2 \times 1 = 40,320$$

For one application of this principle, see **data encryption standard.**

PERMUTATION TABLE

See mutilation table.

PERSONAL AUTHENTICATION CODE (PAC)

A function that can be used to recognize and authenticate an individual who wishes to engage in some transaction with a financial institution, such as making a withdrawal at an automatic teller machine. A personal authentication code involves the use of nonsecret information by which the individual can be recognized (such as the person's name), secret information provided by the individual to the financial institution (such as the maiden name of the person's mother), and secret information provided by the financial institution to the individual (such as the person's personal identification number). The information involved in the use of the PAC must be entirely secret and known only to the financial institution and the individual wishing to make the transaction.

See also: authentication; electronic funds transfer; message authentication code; personal identification number.

For further reading: D. W. Davies and W. L. Price, *Security for Computer Networks: An Introduction to Data Security in Teleprocessing and Electronic Funds Transfer,* Chichester: John Wiley & Sons, 1984, ch. 7; Carl H. Meyer and Stephen M. Matyas, *Cryptography: A New Dimension in Computer Data Security,* New York: John Wiley & Sons, 1982, ch. 11.

For further reading: Brian Beckett, *Introduction to Cryptology,* Oxford: Blackwell Scientific Publications, 1988, ch. 2; D. W. Davies and W. L. Price, *Security for Computer Networks: An Introduction to Data Security in Teleprocessing and Electronic Funds Transfer,* Chichester: John Wiley & Sons, 1984, pp. 54–61; Charlie Kaufman, Radia Perlman, and Mike Speciner, *Network Security: Private Communication in a Public World,* Englewood Cliffs, NJ: Prentice-Hall, 1995, pp. 58–59.

PERSONAL IDENTIFICATION NUMBER (PIN)

A number, usually consisting of four to six digits, assigned to or chosen by a customer of a financial institution to be used with a cash debit card in making transactions through the institution's automatic teller machine. The PIN acts as a secondary key when used with the customer's debit card to confirm that he or she is, in fact, the owner of the card. The restriction of a PIN to a relatively short number (four to six digits) reflects one of the common trade-offs encountered in commercial security systems. A longer number would provide greater security by decreasing the likelihood that an unauthorized person would be able to figure out the PIN that goes with a stolen or found card. On the other hand, a longer number would be more difficult for a customer to remember and increase the chances that he or she would write down the number of the debit card, greatly increasing the likelihood of its illegal use.

> See also: authentication; electronic funds transfer; personal authentication code; personal key.
> For further reading: D. W. Davies and W. L. Price, *Security for Computer Networks: An Introduction to Data Security in Teleprocessing and Electronic Funds Transfer*, Chichester: John Wiley & Sons, 1984, ch. 7, pp. 306–321; Carl H. Meyer and Stephen M. Matyas, *Cryptography: A New Dimension in Computer Data Security*, New York: John Wiley & Sons, 1982, ch. 11.

PERSONAL KEY

A means of identifying the user of a computer system (such as in an electronic funds transfer system) when the security offered by a personal identification number (PIN) alone is insufficient. One disadvantage of using only a PIN as a means of identifying a user is that such numbers usually consist of four to six digits. A person who really wants to find someone's PIN can probably do so by testing all possible permutations of a four- or six-digit number. Additional security can be provided by issuing a personal key as well as a PIN.

Like a PIN, a personal key is a number or code that an individual can easily remember. When the individual wishes to use a network, he or she enters both a PIN and a personal key. The computing device at the point of entry (such as an automatic teller machine) accumulates these data and sends them to the central processing unit at the financial institution. The PIN and personal key, along with the user's personal identification, are computed according to some given algorithm. The result of this computation is compared with a similar result obtained from data stored for that individual in the financial institution's central storage banks. If the calculations match, the user is verified and a transaction is permitted. If the calculations do not match, the user is not verified and no transaction is permitted.

> See also: authentication; electronic funds transfer; personal authentication code; personal identification number.
> For further reading: Carl H. Meyer and Stephen M. Matyas, *Cryptography: A New Dimension in Computer Data Security*, New York: John Wiley & Sons, 1982, ch. 11.

PERS Z

The Z section of the Personnel and Administrative Division of the German foreign office, created in 1936. Pers Z was responsible for both cryptographic and cryptanalytic activities of the Foreign Ministry throughout World War II.

> For further reading: David Kahn, *The Codebreakers: The Story of Secret Writing*, New York: Macmillan, 1967, ch. 14.

PHELIPPES, THOMAS

See Babington plot.

PIG LATIN

A form of secret speech in which words are modified by removing the first letter of the word to the end and adding the suffix *-ay*. Thus, *pig Latin* becomes *igpay atinlay*. Pig Latin is a common form of communication among children who wish to keep secrets from the uninitiated. The system has severe limitations, however, since the rules are easily learned and the uninitiated are soon able to join the ranks of the cognoscenti.

See also: jargon code.

PIGPEN CIPHER

See Freemasons' cipher.

PLACODE

An abbreviation for plain code, which is used during the process of superencipherment. As an example, suppose that the codenumber for the phrase SELL ONE THOUSAND SHARES is 33551. This codenumber can be further enciphered in a variety of ways, such as transposing its digits to give 15533. The codenumber that has been transposed is known as the plain code, or the placode.

See also: encicode, superencipherment.

PLAINTEXT

The message from which a code or cipher is written, or the message revealed when a code or cipher is deciphered. Suppose, for example, that the message RETREAT AT DAWN is to be enciphered by means of a simple monoalphabetic substitution cipher in which each cipher letter is obtained by moving two places to the right from the plaintext letter. Then R becomes t, E becomes g, T becomes v, and so on. The ciphertext for this message would then read tgvtg cvcvf cyp. The original message from which this ciphertext was obtained, or the message obtained by deciphering the ciphertext, is the plaintext.

PLAINTEXT ALPHABET

The letters from which a plaintext message are constructed; normally, the letters that make up the alphabet of the language in question.

See also: cipher alphabet.

PLAINTEXT LETTER

Any letter, number, or symbol that constitutes part of a plaintext message.

PLAYFAIR CIPHER

A cryptosystem originally developed by English physicist Sir Charles Wheatstone, but made famous by Wheatstone's friend, Lyon Playfair, the first Baron Playfair of St. Andrews. Playfair first described Wheatstone's cipher at a dinner party given by the president of the governing council in January 1854. The cipher rapidly grew in popularity and became known by Playfair's name rather than its inventor's.

The Playfair cipher is the first literal digraphic cipher in history. The basis for the cipher is a 5 x 5 square containing the letters of the English alphabet (*i* and *j* being taken together) arranged according to some keyword. Assume the keyword is AMNESTY. The square would be constructed with the keyword in the first seven positions, followed by the rest of the alphabet, as shown below:

```
A M N E S
T Y B C D
F G H IJ K
L O P Q R
U V W X Z
```

The first step in enciphering a letter using the Playfair cipher is to divide the plaintext into groups of two letters. Suppose that the plaintext to be enciphered is the following:

SEND AS MANY MEN AND WEAPONS AS POSSIBLE.

Next, separate the message into two-letter groups, as follows:

SE ND AS MA NY ME NA ND WE AP ON SA SP OS SI BL EX

Notice that with an odd number of letters, an extra letter is added at the end to complete the last group. Also, if a pair of like letters appear next to each other, an X or Z is inserted between them. The pair AA would be treated as if it were AXA.

Locate the position of each letter pair in the Playfair square. If both letters of the pair occur in the same row, replace each by the letter immediately to its right. The first digraph, SE, would be enciphered as *as*. Note that each row is considered continuous, with the last letter of the row being followed by the first letter of the same row.

If both letters of the pair occur in the same column, they are replaced by the letters immediately below them. The digraph EX, then, would be enciphered as *ce*.

Finally, if the two letters of a pair lie in different rows and different columns, the encipherment rule is as follows: determine the row in which the first letter occurs in the Playfair square. Move along that row until you get to the column in which the second letter of the digraph appears. Consider the digraph ND as an example. The first letter of the digraph, N, lies in the first row. Read across the first row until you come to the column in which D appears (the last column). Read the letter that lies at the intersection of this row and column. The letter is *s*.

Now locate the second letter of the digraph, D in this case. Read across the row in which this letter appears until you come to the column that contains the first letter, N. The intersection of this row and column is the letter *b*, which becomes the second letter of the enciphered digraph. The enciphered digraph corresponding to ND, then, is *sb*.

The decipherment of any cryptogram written with the Playfair cipher is a simple matter as long as the decipherer knows the keyword and, therefore, what the square looks like.

See also: bigram; Wheatstone, Charles.

For further reading: Brian Beckett, *Introduction to Cryptology*, Oxford: Blackwell Scientific Publications, 1988, pp. 169–172; Donald D. Millikin, *Elementary Cryptography and Cryptanalysis*, Laguna Hills, CA: Aegean Park Press, n.d., ch. 15; Peter Way, *Codes and Ciphers*, n.p.: Crescent Books, 1977, pp. 32–34; http://rschp2.anu.edu.au:8080/playfair.html.

POE, EDGAR ALLAN

American poet and short-story writer. Poe (1809–1849) was not only one of America's greatest writers but also one of its greatest devotees to the use of cryptology in his stories. His earliest use of cryptology appears to be in *The Narrative of Arthur Gordon Pym*. The story is allegedly told to Poe by a traveler, Pym, who was shipwrecked at sea and cast upon a strange island called Tsalal. In exploring the island, Pym and his companion discover a cave in which strange markings on the wall appear to give some sort of directions. In a note appended to the story itself, Poe suggests that the figures come from the Ethiopian, Arabic, and Egyptian languages.

In December 1839, Poe published an article in Philadelphia's *Alexander Weekly Messenger* entitled "Enigmatical and Conundrum-ical," outlining some simple principles of monoalphabetic substitution and inviting readers to send in their own cryptograms for Poe's solution. The response was overwhelming. Readers from all over the United States sent in their challenges to Poe's offer. He was able to solve many of them, and eventually developed a reputation as a master of cryptanalysis. However, Poe was not quite the master he claimed to be, or at least allowed others to believe that he was. He was unable to decrypt many of these challenges, although he continued to remind readers of his earlier successes.

Nonetheless, Poe continued to write extensively on cryptology. In July 1841, he published his longest essay on cryptography, "A Few Words on Secret Writing," in Philadelphia's *Graham's Magazine*.

Fascinated with the macabre, American author Edgar Allan Poe was bewitched by cryptography as well.

Poe had become editor of *Graham's* a year earlier, and in the April issue repeated his challenge to readers to send in their "riddles" for him to solve. He pledged to solve them even if the keyphrases were in "French, Italian, Spanish, German, Latin, or Greek (or in any of the dialects of these languages)."

In 1843, Poe wrote the short story for which he is most famous among cryptologists, "The Gold Bug." He submitted the story to the *Dollar Newspaper* and won a $100 prize for it. Two years later, the story was reprinted in a collection of his works.

Poe died of alcoholism on 7 October 1849 and was buried in Baltimore's Westminster Presbyterian Cemetery.

See also: "The Gold Bug."
For further reading: Clarence S. Brigham, "Edgar Allan Poe's Contribution to *Alexander's Weekly Messenger*," *Proceedings of the American Antiquarian Society* (April 1942): 45–125; *The Complete Tales and Poems of Edgar Allan Poe*, New York: Vintage Books, 1975; William F. Friedman, "Edgar Allan Poe, Cryptographer," *American Literature* (November 1936): 266–280; Edgar Allan Poe, "A Few Words on Secret Writing," *Graham's Magazine* (July 1841): 33–38; Shawn Rosenheim, "'The King of "Secret Readers,"': Edgar Poe, Cryptography, and the Origins of the Detective Story," *ELH* (Summer 1989): 375–400; W. K. Wimsatt, Jr., "What Poe Knew about Cryptography," *Publications of the Modern Language Association* (September 1943): 754–779.

POLYALPHABETIC SUBSTITUTION

A form of cryptography in which more than one cipher alphabet is used. For example, one could encipher the message BUY SOUTHERN RAILWAY TODAY by using the three different cipher alphabets shown below in sequence.

PLAIN:
A B C D E F G H I J K L M N O P Q R S T U V W X Y Z
cipher 1:
y h n u j m i k o l p q a z w s x e d c r f v t g b
cipher 2:
w s x e d c r f v t g b y h n u j m i l k o p z a q
cipher 3:
m n o p q r s t u v w x y z a b c d e f g h i j k l

In making this encipherment, the cryptographer might use cipher alphabet 1 for the first letter, cipher alphabet 2 for the second letter, cipher alphabet 3 for the third letter, and so on until the complete plaintext is enciphered. Using this system, the plaintext and ciphertext would read as follows:

```
B U Y     S O U T H E R     N
R A I L W A Y     T O D A Y
h k k     d n g c f q e     h
d y v x v w k     c n p y a
```

The ciphertext would usually be rearranged in five-letter groups to disguise word lengths that might be helpful to the cryptanalyst.

hkkdn gcfqe hdyvx vwkcn pyarz

Note that two nulls are added at the end of the message to complete the last set of letters.

Ciphers written in polyalphabetic substitution systems are considerably more difficult for the cryptanalyst to decipher than those written in a monoalphabetic system. It might be determined, for example, that B = h in the first cipher alphabet, but that would provide no information at all as to the encipherment of B in the second or third cipher alphabet.

Simpler examples of polyalphabetic substitution may contain some relationship between cipher alphabets. For example, cipher alphabet 2 might involve a shift of all letters three spaces to the right from cipher alphabet 1, and cipher alphabet 3 might involve a shift of all letters six spaces to the right from cipher alphabet 2. Such a system makes it easier to decipher for the person who receives the message, but it also makes it easier for an enemy. For this reason, a truly sophisticated polyalphabetic system involves only random relationships among the various cipher alphabets employed.

See also: monoalphabetic substitution; Vigenère square.
For further reading: William F. Friedman, *Elementary Military Cryptography*, Laguna Hills, CA: Aegean Park Press, 1976, ch. 5; Helen Fouché Gaines, *Cryptanalysis: A Study of Ciphers and Their Solution*, New York: Dover Publications, 1956, ch. 12–20; Donald D. Millikin, *Elementary Cryptography and Cryptanalysis*, Laguna Hills, CA: Aegean Park Press, n.d., ch. 13; Abraham Sinkov, *Elementary Cryptanalysis: A Mathematical Approach*, New York: Random House, 1968, ch. 3.

POLYBIUS

A Greek historian (ca. 203–120 B.C.) who invented a system for sending secret messages by means of handheld torches. The first step in Polybius's system consists of a substitution cipher in which each letter is represented by a pair of numbers, as indicated in the following square.

	1	2	3	4	5
1	a	b	c	d	e
2	f	g	h	ij	k
3	l	m	n	o	p
4	q	r	s	t	u
5	v	w	x	y	z

Polybius suggested that each letter in the alphabet could then be represented, using this table, by holding up a certain number of torches in each hand. If a person held up three torches in the left hand and one torch in the right hand, the combination would represent the letter *l*. If a person held two torches in the left hand and two in the right, the letter indicated was *g*.

The system described by Polybius would certainly be regarded as cumbersome by modern standards, but it would have worked very satisfactorily for his era. No evidence exists, however, to show that the system was ever put into use. The historical importance of Polybius's ideas is not the system of torches but the concept of representing letters of the alphabet by means of various combinations of numbers. This concept was later used in a number of other cryptosystems such as fractionating ciphers and knock ciphers.

See also: ADFGVX cipher; bifid; Chase, Pliny Earle; checkerboard; cipher; fractionating cipher; signal communications.
For further reading: F. W. Walbank, *Polybius*, Berkeley: University of California Press, 1972.

POLYGRAM

A set of two or more letters. The term is usually applied to sets containing four or more letters since two-letter sets are more commonly called *bigrams* (or *digraphs*) and three-letter sets are known as *trigrams* (or *trigraphs*). Development of substitution cryptosystems based on the use of polygrams is possible, but such systems are usually too cumbersome to be practical.

See also: bigram; trigram.
For further reading: Brian Beckett, *Introduction to Cryptology*, Oxford: Blackwell Scientific Publications, 1988, pp. 43–65.

POLYGRAPHIA LIBRI SEX

Six Books on Polygraphy; an important book on cryptology written by Johannes Trithemius, first published in 1518.

See also: Trithemius, Johannes.

POLYGRAPHIC SUBSTITUTION ━━━

See substitution.

POLYNOMIAL TIME ALGORITHM ━━━

See algorithm.

POLYPHONE ━━━━━━━━━━━━

A cipher symbol that may have more than one plaintext equivalent. For example, one might invent a cryptosystem in which the number 31 sometimes represents the letter *e*, sometimes the letter *r*, and sometimes the letter *y*. In order to work, the encipherer must make it clear which letter is suggested by the use of the polyphone.

The use of polyphones differs from that of polyalphabetic substitution. Under normal circumstances, the latter system allows the use of virtually any cipher letter to stand for a given plaintext letter, while in the case of polyphones, only a relatively small number of cipher letters is used to represent a single plaintext letter.

PORTA, GIOVANNI ━━━━━━━

An Italian scientist and the author of an important book on cryptology, Porta (1535–1615) was born in Vico Equense, near Naples, Italy, in 1535. He came from a well-educated family and soon displayed an active curiosity in a wide variety of subjects. Probably his best-known work is *Magia naturalis*, published when he was age 22. The work is a detailed analysis of magic and the ways in which it might be used to control the environment. He made other, more valuable, contributions in the field of physics, with his experiments on the camera obscura and on the relationship between light and heat. Porta's major work, the *Magia naturalis*, eventually grew to fill 20 volumes.

One of Porta's best-known contributions to cryptology is his development of the first digraphic cipher, a system in which two letters of plaintext are represented by a single symbol. The table below shows what a portion of Porta's digraphic cipher might look like (although the symbols are different from those used by Porta himself).

	A	B	C	D	E	F
A	0	1	2	3	4	5
B	6	7	8	9	a	b
C	c	d	e	f	g	h
D	i	j	k	l	m	n
E	o	p	q	r	s	t
F	u	v	w	x	y	z

To illustrate how this cipher system is used, suppose that the word to be written is DEFACE. The first two letters in the plaintext are DE. Read across the top of the table until you come to D and then read down the "D" column until you come to E. The symbol at the intersection of this column and row is r. Repeat this process for the next two letters of the plaintext, FA. The symbol for this pair of letters is 5. Finally, locate the symbol for the last two letters, CE. This symbol is q. Therefore, the ciphertext for the word DEFACE using the Porta cipher is r5q.

Porta's digraphic cipher appeared in his book *De Furitivis Literaum Notis*, which David Kahn, the greatest of all historians of cryptology, calls an extraordinary book. "Even today, four centuries later," Kahn says, "it retains its freshness and charm and—remarkably—its ability to instruct." In this book, Porta classified and critiqued then-known cryptographic methods and introduced an important cryptanalytic technique known as the probable word. Porta also constructed a number of cipher disks of the design originated by Alberti more than a century earlier.

See also: bigram; cipher disk.
For further reading: David Kahn, *The Code-breakers: The Story of Secret Writing*, New York: Macmillan, 1967, pp. 137–143; Thomas (Penn) Leary, "Cryptology in the 15th and 16th Century," *Cryptologia* (July 1996): 223–241; Charles Jastrow Mendelsohn, "The Earliest Solution of a Multiple Alphabet Cipher Written with the Use of a Key,"

The Signal Corps Bulletin (October–December 1939): 33–47; Derek J. de Solla Price, *John Baptista Porta's Natural Magick*, New York: Basic Books, 1957; George Sarton, *Six Wings: Men of Science in the Renaissance*, Bloomington: Indiana University Press, 1957.

POTOMAC CODE

See Code Compilation Section.

PRACTICAL CRYPTANALYSIS

A term used by David Kahn to describe the theft of codes, keys, and other cipher material in place of traditional cryptanalytical practices. Traitors and paid informers certainly make the breaking of another nation's codes and ciphers easier, but the risk is much greater than with more conventional methods of cryptanalysis.

For further reading: David Kahn, *The Codebreakers: The Story of Secret Writing*, New York: Macmillan, 1967, pp. 636–638, 685–687.

PRETTY GOOD PRIVACY (PGP)

A data encryption system developed by Philip Zimmerman in 1991. The system can be used for encrypting files and protecting electronic mail transmissions by algorithms similar to those used in the Data Encryption Standard, RSA cryptography, and Privacy Enhanced Mail (PEM).

Zimmerman's philosophy on public-key cryptography is somewhat libertarian and iconoclastic. His original intent was to make PGP generally available without charge to anyone who wanted to use it. He made the system available on the Internet and suggested that everyone give away copies to all their friends. He has been quoted as saying that "If privacy is outlawed, only outlaws will have privacy."

Unfortunately (or fortunately, depending on one's viewpoint), Zimmerman was prevented from carrying out this philosophy by two major organizations: the U.S. government, which has banned the export of cryptographic algorithms,

and RSA Data Security, Inc. (RSADSI), which controls the licensing of most patented public-key cryptographic software. In one case, PGP was regarded as a potential threat to national security, and in the other, an infringement of one or more patent rights.

The actions by the federal government and RSADSI did not necessarily put an end to the public distribution of PGP. Copies could still be obtained via the Internet from foreign sources because the importation of cryptographic software from other countries is not necessarily illegal. In May 1996, however, Zimmerman announced that he was establishing a company known as PGP Inc. to market the system commercially; he created a second company, PGP Phone, for the purpose of developing modifications of PGP to encrypt telephone conversations.

See also: Data Encryption Standard; electronic mail; export controls; Internet; Privacy Enhanced Mail; RSA algorithm.

For further reading: Ronald Bailey, "Code Blues: National Security Agency Cracks Down on Illegal Export of P. Zimmerman's Pretty Good Privacy Program," *Reason* (May 1994): 36–37; Simson Garfinkle, *PGP: Pretty Good Privacy*, Sebastopol, CA: O'Reilly & Associates, 1995; Charlie Kaufman, Radia Perlman, and Mike Speciner, *Network Security: Private Communication in a Public World*, Englewood Cliffs, NJ: Prentice-Hall, 1995, ch. 14; Dan Lehrer, "Clipper Chips and Cypherpunks," *The Nation* (10 October 1994): 376–380; Steven Levy, "Battle of the Clipper Chip," *New York Times Magazine* (12 June 1994): 44–51+; William Stallings, *Network and Internetwork Security: Principles and Practices*, Englewood Cliffs, NJ: Prentice-Hall, 1995, ch. 8; http://rschp2.anu.edu.au:8080/howpgp.html#basic; http://thegate.gamers.org/~tony/pgp.html.

PRICE TAG

A tag attached to items for sale in retail stores listing the price at which the item is to be sold and, in many cases, its wholesale price. The wholesale price is listed as a code that will not be readily apparent to a shopper. For example, a simple mononumeric substitution system might be used, such as the following:

1 = A	6 = Y
2 = Z	7 = F
3 = Q	8 = H
4 = M	9 = P
5 = C	0 = O

The price tag on an item whose whole-sale price is $215, then, would read ZAC. Listing the wholesale price on the price tag helps a salesperson make necessary price adjustments in order to make a sale.

In today's world, many prices are encrypted by means of bar code technology, which is not easily accessible to either buyer or salesperson.

PRIMARY ALPHABET

The mixed alphabet used for encipherment in a Vigenère-type cryptosystem. For example, with the keyword AIRPLANE, the primary alphabet would look like this:

PLAIN:
A I R P L N E B C D F G H J K M O Q S T U V W X Y Z
cipher:
t c k d e x o a g y h l j l z m n f p b q s u v w r

The encipherer can see from this pattern that the letter A is to be enciphered as *t*, the letter I as *c*, the letter R as *k*, and so on.

The cryptanalyst has no such direction to follow, of course, and will arrange the decrypted plaintext alphabet in alphabetical order, as shown below:

PLAIN:
A B C D E F G H I J K L M N O P Q R S T U V W X Y Z
cipher:
t a g y o h l j c l z e m x n d f k p b q s u v w r

Written in this form, the alphabet is known as the secondary alphabet.

See also: alphabet; Vigenère square.

PRIME NUMBER

Any number divisible only by itself and 1. The first ten prime numbers are 2, 3, 5, 7, 11, 13, 17, 19, 23, and 29. Because all even numbers can be divided by 2, all prime numbers *other than 2* are odd numbers.

Prime numbers have long been of considerable theoretical interest to mathematicians. For example, one of the challenges to which number theorists have addressed themselves is to identify the largest prime number that can be found. Prime numbers are also the subject of a number of important mathematical propositions and problems.

Prime numbers have taken on considerable interest in the field of cryptography as a result of the development of public-key cryptographic systems. The basis for this interest is that finding the product of two or more prime numbers is a relatively simple mathematical operation. For example, it is easy to find the product of 47 x 59 x 89. That product is 246,797. Any number that is the product of two or more prime numbers is known as a composite number.

But finding the prime factors of any given composite number is often quite difficult. For example, what are the prime factors of the composite number 220,631? The answer can certainly be obtained with a little perseverance. The approach is to try various prime factors systematically one at a time. First, divide 220,631 by 3 (since 2 is obviously not a factor), then by 5, then by 7, then by 11, and so on. The process would be quite lengthy, however, since the first prime factor to be determined is 37 (the others are 67 and 89). With modern computers, however, factoring a number with six digits is still a very simple process.

The challenge becomes more difficult as the sizes of the prime factors and composite number get larger. With a composite number of 300 digits, for example, and a computer performing a million operations per second, it would take about 4.9 x 10^{15} years to check all possible factors of the number. While the *actual* time taken to factor such a number might be less, the task is still quite daunting. One of the recent accomplishments in this field was reported in June 1994 by researchers at Oregon State University. They successfully factored a 162-digit number as the product of two prime numbers of 44 and 119 digits. Their result was as follows:

```
1653723785156468892426140704164885399065774 3
x 4971786780032337881877633990059600164874 76
5983495392115697470057591532282419111670432 0
0927016884285731030248831349126419
= 221962052865970195266012074307610042739092
435707339655167703393733532074305023580242 73
032756332005408066894606696792219545093967 12
7330845624462896060302682123 17
```

This result was obtained using 30 computer workstations for eight weeks, plus a few additional hours on the most powerful supercomputer currently available—a Cray supercomputer located in Amsterdam.

In late 1996, the largest prime number ever reported was found by researchers working on a Cray computer in Chippewa Falls, Wisconsin. The number has 378,632 digits and would fill 12 newspaper pages of standard type. The number is equivalent to the expression $2^{1,257,787} - 1$.

The calculation of a composite number from its primes and the reverse operation are an example of a one-way or trap-door function, essential in the development of most public-key cryptographic systems.

See also: one-way function; public-key cryptography; strong prime; trap-door function.

For further reading: Brian Beckett, *Introduction to Cryptology*, Oxford: Blackwell Scientific Publications, 1988, pp. 130–134; Dr. Crypton, "Prime Numbers and National Security," *Science Digest* (October 1985): 86–88; Charlie Kaufman, Radia Perlman, and Mike Speciner, *Network Security: Private Communication in a Public World*, Englewood Cliffs, NJ: Prentice-Hall, 1995, pp. 138–139, 152, 156; Carl H. Meyer and Stephen M. Matyas, *Cryptography: A New Dimension in Computer Data Security*, New York: John Wiley & Sons, 1982, pp. 33–43; P. Ribenbolm, *The Book of Prime Number Records*, Berlin: Springer-Verlag, 1988.

PRIMING KEY

An invention made by Blaise de Vigenère in the late 1500s. The priming key consists of a single letter, known to both encipherer and decipherer, of a message that gives the latter a clue to deciphering the message. In the example below, *j* is the priming key.

```
KEY:    j g o o d n e w s w i l l f o l l
PLAIN:  G O O D N E W S W I L F O L L O W
CIPHER: p u c r q r a o o e t q z q z z h
```

The decipherer recognizes that *j* is the priming key and knows that the first alphabet used is the *j* alphabet. In the *j* alphabet, the cipher letter *p* corresponds to the plaintext letter *g*, which means that the next letter of the key must also be *g*. The decipherer can then turn to the *g* alphabet in the Vigenère alphabets and find that the plaintext letter *o* corresponds to the cipher letter *u*, and so on.

See also: autokey; Vigenère, Blaise de.

PRINTING TELEGRAPH

See Vernam, Gilbert.

PRIVACY

Freedom from another's intrusion into a person's condition or affairs. Most Americans place a high regard on the right to withhold information about themselves for which society has no need. The right to a secret ballot reflects one aspect of the right to privacy of a person's political convictions. In any society, however, the right to privacy is unlikely to be absolute. To function properly, society may need to obtain personal information that an individual might prefer not to disclose. In the United States, all citizens are required and expected to answer personal questions during a decennial census that might be considered an imposition on personal privacy (age, sex, and ethnicity, for example) except that the federal government has decided that obtaining this information has social value worth violating personal privacy.

The spread of computers and other devices for the storage and exchange of information has raised privacy issues to a new level in the past half century. Today, it is probably more difficult to maintain personal privacy than ever before. Even when a person's privacy is violated for an otherwise legitimate reason—medical care, for example—personal information may be passed on to individuals or entities that do *not* have a legitimate reason to collect that information. Cryptology offers an important mechanism by which personal privacy can be expressed and, if properly employed, offers a reasonable balance between personal privacy and social needs.

The Canadian government has taken some significant steps to ensure the privacy of its citizens from unauthorized electronic snooping, and a number of bills have been introduced into the U.S. Congress to achieve similar results. In 1995, Representative Cardiss Collins introduced H.R. 184, the Individual Privacy Protection Act, which would create, among other things, a Privacy Protection Commission. So far, no bill as comprehensive as Canadian laws has yet been passed in the United States.

See also: Privacy Act of 1974.
For further reading: W. Diffie and M. E. Hellman, "Privacy and Authentication: An Introduction to Cryptography," *Proceedings of the IEEE* 67 (1979): 397–427; H. Feistel, "Cryptography and Computer Privacy," *Scientific American* (May 1973): 15–23; Industry Canada, *Privacy and the Canadian Information Highway*, Ottawa: Minister of Supply and Services Canada, 1994 (also available on http://debra.dgbt.doc.ca/isc/isc.html); Charlie Kaufman, Radia Perlman, and Mike Speciner, *Network Security: Private Communication in a Public World*, Englewood Cliffs, NJ: Prentice-Hall, 1995, pp. 336–338; Carl H. Meyer and Stephen M. Matyas, *Cryptography: A New Dimension in Computer Data Security*, New York: John Wiley & Sons, 1982, pp. 397–427; U.S. Congress, Office of Technology Assessment, *Information Security and Privacy in Network Environments*, OTA-TCT-606, Washington, DC: GPO, September 1994,

passim (*see* index); http://www.itd.nrl. navy.mil/ITD/5540/ieee/cipher/cipher-archive.html.

PRIVACY ACT OF 1974 ━━━━

A federal law (Public Law 93-579) that describes principles to ensure that an individual's personal privacy will be respected during the collection, processing, storage, and distribution of data by federal agencies.

For further reading: U.S. Congress, Office of Technology Assessment, *Information Security and Privacy in Network Environments*, OTA-TCT-606, Washington, DC: GPO, September 1994, pp. 80–85.

PRIVACY ENHANCED MAIL (PEM) ━━━

A proposed set of standards to provide security for electronic mail messages sent across the Internet. PEM provides three kinds of security. The first is designated as MIC-CLEAR and provides an integrity check to the message, but transmits the message itself in clear. This level of security does no more than authenticate the person who has sent the message.

A second level of security is designated as MIC-ONLY and provides both authentication and encoding of the message. The encoded message cannot be read by humans, but is decoded at its destination by an appropriate machine program.

The highest level of security is designated as ENCRYPTED. At this level, the integrity check is provided, the message is encoded, and the whole transmission is encrypted using a secret key known only to the sender and the receiver. In this case, the recipient must know the secret key used for encipherment in order to decipher the message and confirm the integrity of the message and authenticate the sender.

The use of PEM depends on the establishment of certification authorities that can issue certificates at various levels of security, such as "high security," "medium security," and "low or no security."

See also: authentication; certification authority; electronic mail; integrity; Internet; security.
For further reading: Charlie Kaufman, Radia Perlman, and Mike Speciner, *Network Security: Private Communication in a Public World,* Englewood Cliffs, NJ: Prentice-Hall, 1995, ch. 13; Stephen T. Kent, "Internet Privacy Enhanced Mail," *Communications of the ACM* (August 1993): 48–59; Reuven M. Lerner, "Protecting E-mail: Public-Key Cryptography; Work of Ronald L. Rivest," *Technology Review* (August/September 1992): 11; William Stallings, *Network and Internetwork Security: Principles and Practices,* Englewood Cliffs, NJ: Prentice-Hall, 1995, ch. 8.

PRIVATE-KEY CRYPTOGRAPHY ▬▬▬

A cryptosystem that uses symmetric encryption. The form of cryptography with which most people are familiar is private-key cryptography. Two or more persons who wish to send secret messages back and forth among themselves agree on an algorithm in which messages will be enciphered and a key used with that algorithm. The encipherer uses the algorithm and the mutually-agreed-on key to write the secret message, and the decipherer uses the same key and algorithm to read the secret message.

The fundamental problem with private-key cryptography is key management: the system works only when everyone who needs the key—but no one else—has it in his or her possession. Centuries ago, that might have meant sending the key from one person to another under secure guard.

Key management became a much more difficult problem with the increasing use of cryptography made possible by the telegraph. Keys had to be shared not just between two people or among a handful of people but among hundreds or thousands of individuals, such as soldiers at the front. As more and more people needed or had access to private keys, the risk of losing a key or having it stolen increased dramatically, and symmetric cryptography became increasingly less secure.

In 1976, Whitfield Diffie and Martin Hellman proposed a different way of encrypting and decrypting messages using asymmetric cryptography based on the concept of a public key. This approach has spread widely throughout institutions in which secure communications are essential or important.

See also: asymmetric cryptography; public-key cryptography.

PROBABILITY ▬▬▬▬▬▬▬▬▬▬▬

The likelihood that some event will occur. For example, if a "fair" coin (one that has not been tampered with) is tossed a large number of times, the coin would be expected to turn up heads about half the time and tails about half the time. The probability of tossing heads in this experiment is 0.50 and the probability of tossing tails is 0.50. Probabilities are generally expressed as a decimal fraction between 0 and 1, with a value of 0 representing no probability at all and a value of 1 representing certainty.

The theory of probability was first studied by the great French mathematicians Pierre de Fermat (1601–1665) and Blaise Pascal (1623–1662). It has since grown to a large field of mathematics with applications in both the theoretical sciences and the everyday world. For example, scientists now believe that the most accurate way of describing very small particles (such as the electron) is by determining the probability of certain types of behavior for the particles. In the everyday world, large gambling operations survive and make a profit by adjusting the games they control to produce probabilistic results that will be favorable to them while still allowing their customers to experience some success with the games.

By its very nature, probability is a topic of fundamental concern to cryptologists. As a simple illustration, the probability of encountering various letters in any language is not the same; in English, for example, the probability of encountering the letter *e* is significantly greater than the probability of encountering any other letter.

This information can be used in decrypting ciphertext. If a cryptanalyst finds that the letter *w* occurs more frequently than any other letter in a cryptogram known to have been enciphered by means of monoalphabetic substitution, then the probability that ciphertext letter *w* represents plaintext letter *e* is very good.

See also: frequency distribution.

For further reading: Andrew M. Gleason, *Elementary Course in Probability for the Cryptanalyst*, Laguna Hills, CA: Aegean Park Press, n.d.; G. R. Grimmett and D. J. A. Welsh, *Probability: An Introduction*, Oxford: Oxford University Press, 1986; Solomon Kullback, *Statistical Methods in Cryptanalysis*, Laguna Hills, CA: Aegean Park Press, 1976.

PROBABLE WORD

A guess made by a cryptanalyst about the plaintext interpretation of an unknown word in ciphertext, based on the presence of certain letters and the context of the message being analyzed. Use of the probable word is an important technique in deciphering a message. Suppose that a cryptanalyst is working on a message intercepted from an enemy transmitter during wartime. The passage shown below might represent as much of the message as the cryptanalyst has been able to determine thus far:

ciphertext:	x e i n p	i f o g e	c l k k c	x z i j d
plaintext:	B	T L	U E S	D

Since this is a military message, it would not be unreasonable to assume that the first three letters of the plaintext thus far deciphered might be part of the word BATTLE. Should that be the case, the missing relationships in this part of the cipher might be guessed to be: n = A; p = T; and o = E. Similarly, the next portion of the deciphered text might be a part of the word TUESDAY. If so, it would be reasonable to guess that l = T; z = A; and i = Y in this part of the message.

The probable word method does not automatically provide the correct decipherment, of course. The first word above might also be BOTTLE, less likely in a military dispatch but still not impossible. Or it might be portions of two separate words, such as BOATL[EFT]. Nevertheless, the probable word gives the cryptanalyst a suggestion for the next effort in deciphering the rest of the message.

PROGRESSIVE KEY

A key in which all available cipher alphabets are used before any one such alphabet is used a second time. The earliest example of a progressive key was developed by Johannes Trithemius. In the Trithemius cryptosystem, a 24 x 24 matrix (lacking the letters *j* and *v*) was used for encipherment. The first word of plaintext was enciphered by the first cipher alphabet (beginning a b c d e f g . . .), the second word of plaintext by the second cipher alphabet (beginning b c d e f g h . . .), the third word of plaintext by the third cipher alphabet (beginning c d e f g h i . . .), and so forth until the twenty-fourth letter of plaintext was enciphered by the twenty-fourth cipher alphabet.

See also: Trithemius, Johannes.

PROHIBITION ERA

See Friedman, Elizabeth Smith.

PROJECT OZMA

A scientific project begun in May 1960 to search for extraterrestrial intelligence. The project was given this name by its director, Frank D. Drake, in honor of the queen in Frank L. Baum's book *Ozma of Oz*. Ozma was, according to Drake, "the queen of the imaginary land of Oz, a place very far away, difficult to reach, and populated by exotic beings." Drake obviously felt that his search for extraterrestrial intelligence might result in the discovery of something similar to the life on Oz described by Baum.

Drake's project was conducted with an 85-foot radio telescope located at the National Radio Astronomy Observatory in Green Bank, West Virginia. He aimed the telescope at two stars in particular, Tau Ceti and Epsilon Eridani, which appeared to have the possibility of possessing planets that might contain intelligent life. During the three months of the project's existence, Drake detected no signals that could be interpreted as having originated from intelligent beings.

The lack of positive results from Project Ozma did not discourage Drake and others interested in the search for extraterrestrial intelligence (SETI). Russian astronomers tuned a radio telescope to 21- and 30-centimeter wavelengths in the direction of 12 stars similar to our own sun. This project, and others like it, have yet to produce plausible indications for the existence of extraterrestrial intelligence.

See also: Drake, Frank D.
For further reading: Ronald Bracewell, *Intelligent Life in Outer Space*, San Francisco: W. H. Freeman, 1975; Carl Sagan, *The Cosmic Connection: An Extraterrestrial Perspective*, New York: Dell, 1973.

PROOF OF DATA ORIGIN
See authentication.

PROPRIETARY RIGHTS
See intellectual property.

PROTOCOL
An agreement that governs the procedures used to exchange information between two users. Among the issues included in a protocol are the amount of information to be transmitted, frequency of transmission, recovery of transmission errors, and parties legitimately involved in the transmission.

PROTOCRYPTOGRAPHY
A term for the earliest stages of cryptography. David Kahn describes the use of special words and symbols in the Bible as an example of protocryptography. The key element lacking in protocryptography but found in true cryptography is secrecy. Protocryptographic texts are usually designed to show off the writer's special literary skills or perform some function other than keeping a message secret.

PSEUDORANDOM NUMBERS
See random number.

PUBLIC-KEY CRYPTOGRAPHY
A cryptosystem in which messages are encrypted and decrypted by using a combination of keys, one of which is available to the general public and one of which is private. The concept of a public key for enciphering and deciphering messages is relatively new, and has developed because of dramatic changes in the nature of cryptology. Throughout most of history, the problem of enciphering, deciphering, and decrypting messages was interesting to a relatively small number of individuals. Those individuals who wanted to communicate in cipher could do so simply by exchanging algorithms and keys with each other.

Today, with the general availability of computer communication, hundreds or thousands of individuals send and receive enciphered messages, and a much greater number of individuals have the potential for intercepting and decrypting those messages.

One method for solving the problem of sending secure messages over insecure channels of communication was proposed in 1976 by two researchers at Stanford University, Whitfield Diffie and Martin Hellman. The fundamental principle behind the Diffie-Hellman system is that a person should be able to encipher a message to someone without

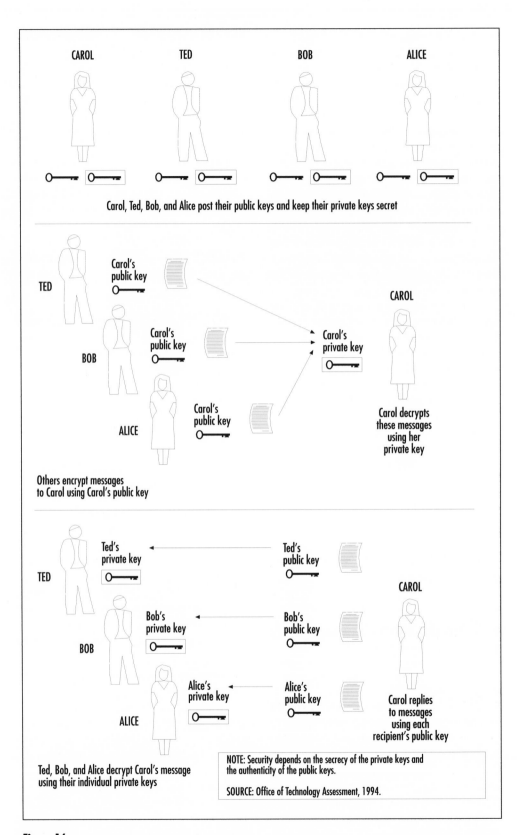

Carol, Ted, Bob, and Alice post their public keys and keep their private keys secret

Others encrypt messages to Carol using Carol's public key

Carol decrypts these messages using her private key

Ted, Bob, and Alice decrypt Carol's message using their individual private keys

Carol replies to messages using each recipient's public key

NOTE: Security depends on the secrecy of the private keys and the authenticity of the public keys.

SOURCE: Office of Technology Assessment, 1994.

Figure 16

necessarily being able to decipher it himself or herself.

In order to use the Diffie-Hellman system, the "user" would choose two separate algorithms. One, known as the public enciphering algorithm and telling how to encipher a message, can be made generally available to anyone who wants it. The second algorithm is retained by the user and tells how to decipher the message. The Diffie-Hellman system works if, and only if, no way exists for someone to figure out a person's deciphering algorithm by knowing the enciphering algorithm. In fact, this problem can be solved by developing mathematical algorithms that have just this property.

Today, many individuals and organizations have pairs of algorithms that meet these requirements, one part of which is published in a directory available for purchase by the general public. The other algorithm is retained by the individual or organization to decipher messages enciphered by means of the public key. Figure 16 illustrates the use of public-key cryptography to encrypt and decrypt a message.

Development of the principles and methods of application of public-key cryptography can also be credited to R. C. Merkle and to R. L. Rivest, A. Shamir, and L. M. Adleman. Merkle and the Rivest, Shamir, and Adleman group both announced their results in 1978.

See also: Diffie-Hellman key exchange; RSA algorithm.

For further reading: Henry Beker and Fred Piper, *Cipher Systems: The Protection of Communications*, New York: John Wiley & Sons, 1982, ch. 10; Albrecht Beutelspacher, *Cryptology: An Introduction to the Art and Science of Enciphering, Encrypting, Concealing, Hiding and Safeguarding Described without Any Arcane Skullduggery but Not without Cunning Waggery for the Delectation and Instruction of the General Public*, Washington, DC: Mathematical Association of America, 1994, ch. 5; D. W. Davies and W. L. Price, *Security for Computer Networks: An Introduction to Data Security in Teleprocessing and Electronic Funds Transfer*, Chichester: John Wiley & Sons, 1984, ch. 8; W. Diffie, "The First Ten Years of Public-Key Cryptography," *Proceedings of the IEEE* (May 1988): 560–577; Martin Gardner, "A New Kind of Cipher That Would Take Millions of Years To Break," *Scientific American* (August 1977): 120–124; M. E. Hellman, "The Mathematics of Public-Key Cryptography," *Scientific American* (August 1979): 146–157; Hellman, "An Overview of Public-Key Cryptography," *IEEE Transactions on Communications* (November 1978): 24–32; Charlie Kaufman, Radia Perlman, and Mike Speciner, *Network Security: Private Communication in a Public World*, Englewood Cliffs, NJ: Prentice-Hall, 1995, ch. 5; William Stallings, *Network and Internetwork Security: Principles and Practices*, Englewood Cliffs, NJ: Prentice-Hall, 1995, ch. 3; U.S. Congress, Office of Technology Assessment, *Information Security and Privacy in Network Environments*, OTA-TCT-606, Washington, DC: GPO, September 1994, passim; http://www.ozemail.com.au/~firstpr/crypto/.

PUBLIC-KEY CRYPTOGRAPHY STANDARD (PKCS)

A set of nine standards developed by RSA Data Security, Inc., for the enciphering of data and messages. The standards deal with a number of practical problems that may develop when people use public-key cryptography for the protection of stored or transmitted data. As an example, a sender may try to encipher a message that can be decrypted rather easily by an eavesdropper. If this were to happen, the security of the algorithm might be compromised. The PKCS standards are designed to reduce the likelihood of such problems developing.

For further reading: Charlie Kaufman, Radia Perlman, and Mike Speciner, *Network Security: Private Communication in a Public World*, Englewood Cliffs, NJ: Prentice-Hall, 1995, pp. 145–147.

PULSE CODE MODULATION

A form of speech scrambling in which sounds are converted into pulses separated by moments of silence, or "nonpulses." The system is similar to other systems in which pieces of information are converted into one of two alternate forms: dot or dash, pulse or no-pulse, hole or no-hole, on or off, or 1 or 0 (in the binary number system). In pulse code modulation, the number of pulses produced per second is proportional to the frequency of the sound. A high-pitched sound is expressed as a relatively larger number of pulses than a low-pitched sound.

Pulse code modulation is useful because messages that are converted into bits (0s and 1s) can be manipulated in a host of ways. The sequence of bits can be transposed, for example, according to some system (the key) with which both the sender and receiver of a message are familiar.

For further reading: Henry Beker and Fred Piper, *Cipher Systems: The Protection of Communications*, New York: John Wiley & Sons, 1982, pp. 358–361; K. W. Cattermole, *Principles of Pulse Code Modulations*, London: Iliffe, 1969.

PUNCTURE CIPHER

A form of steganography in which small pinpricks are used to indicate specific words in a written passage that make up a secret message. The procedure was first suggested by the Greek writer Aeneas and has been used on numerous occasions. The system is rather easy to detect, however, and has never been a particularly successful method for transmitting important messages.

To illustrate a puncture cipher, suppose that the dot above each word in the following passage indicates a word to be included in the message. Then the actual message being transmitted is quite different from the one suggested by the plaintext itself.

ALL MEN ARE TO AVOID LEAVING STOP CANCEL MENS PLANS TO GO ANYWHERE

The story is told that puncture ciphers were used in eighteenth-century En-gland, where the cost of mailing newspapers was much less than the cost of sending postcards or letters. A writer would mail a friend a newspaper (at lower cost) and indicate the message he or she wanted to send with pinpricks in the news stories.

See also: concealment cipher; steganography.

PURPLE

Spelled as both PURPLE and Purple; the codename given by American cryptanalysts to the Japanese cipher machine officially known as 97-shiki obun injiki, or Alphabetical Typewriter '97. The designation '97 indicated the year, according to the Japanese calendar (2597), in which the machine was invented (1937).

PURPLE was a very sophisticated enciphering machine in which a plaintext message could be typed in at one keyboard, pass through a complex internal circuitry, and be printed out at a second keyboard. As the first step in this process, the cipher clerk attached the wire connections from the cipher machine to the first typewriter according to specific instructions given in a master codebook. The settings were prescribed in the book for any given day and changed daily. The clerk next set the daily code by turning four disks on the machine to a setting also prescribed for the day by the codebook. When a message was typed into this keyboard, it passed through a maze of 26 wires that converted each plaintext letter into its ciphertext equivalent. The permutations and combinations made possible by various keys and switching mechanisms within the machine produced millions of possible encipherments.

The Japanese government was supremely confident of the security of the Alphabetical Typewriter '97, and installed it in foreign capitals such as Washington, London, and Berlin for the purpose of handling communiqués of the highest secrecy. Yet U.S. cryptanalysts had begun breaking PURPLE cryptograms as early as August 1940. One Japanese mistake that made U.S. success easier was that Japanese clerks sometimes transmitted messages using both the Alphabetical Typewriter and an earlier version of the machine, known by the codename RED. Since RED communiqués had been easier to decrypt and were read on a routine basis by U.S. cryptanalysts, the duplication of PURPLE messages made their task much easier. Eventually, U.S. cryptanalysts were able to build a working model of the Alphabetical Typewriter with which they could automate the decryption of Japanese messages.

American success in breaking PURPLE very nearly changed the course of events on 7 December 1941 when Japanese air and naval forces attacked Pearl Harbor. The final message from Tokyo to Washington alerting the Japanese staff of an imminent attack was intercepted and cryptanalyzed by workers at the Navy's OP-20-GY in Washington almost in time to alert the president and cabinet members. A variety of factors having nothing to do with cryptology prevented that from happening.

American cryptanalysts experienced many more successes in the coming four years of warfare. The Japanese government, as unable to accept the fact that their Alphabetical Typewriter might have been broken as the German government was to accept the decryption of its Enigma machine, continued to use PURPLE long after its messages had become an open book to American cryptanalysts. As a consequence, U.S. and other Allied forces were able to intercept Japanese forces over and over again, giving them a tactical advantage that meant the difference between victory and defeat.

See also: cipher machine; Combat Intelligence Unit.

For further reading: David Kahn, *The Codebreakers: The Story of Secret Writing,* New York: Macmillan, 1967, ch. 1; Peter Way, *Codes and Ciphers,* n.p.: Crescent Books, 1977, ch. 4.

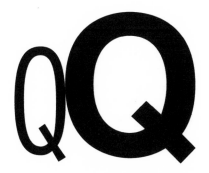

Q CODE

A nonsecret code designed for use in various systems of communication around the world. The development of instruments such as the telegraph and radio made long-distance communications possible in the nineteenth century. Commensurate with the development of such inventions, businesses and nations found it necessary to create systems by which operators and receivers using such devices could get in touch with, identify and recognize, and communicate with one another. One of the first conferences on this subject was the Berlin International Radiotelegraph Conference of 1906.

One of the codes developed as a result of such meetings was the Q code, a system in which codewords beginning with the letter Q were used to transmit information such as weather conditions; location of airports, radio stations, and other important facilities; movement of aircraft; and potentially dangerous conditions in a region. Some typical abbreviations used in the Q code were:

QAA   At what time do you expect to arrive at [location]? OR I expect to arrive at [location] at. . . .

QFB   Are fresh meteorological observations required? OR Fresh meteorological observations are required.

QFS(b)   Please place your radiobeacon at . . . in operation OR The radiobeacon at . . . will be in operation in . . . minutes.

Notice that each codeword can be understood as either a question or new information.

QUADRATIC CODE

A code developed by Gen. Leslie Groves, director of the Manhattan Project, which led to the construction of the world's first nuclear weapon. Groves developed this rather simple but highly effective code as a medium for communicating with other important figures in the project. Groves retained a different code for each individual, and apparently he was the only person to have access to all of them. One of Groves's codes, as reprinted in David Kahn's *The Codebreakers,* is shown below.

	1	2	3	4	5	6	7	8	9	0
1	I_8	P	I		O	U	O		P	N
2	W	E	U	T	E	K_6		L	O	
3	E	U	G	N	B_4	T	N		S	T
4	T	A	Z_2	M	D		I	O	E	
5	S_9	V	T	J		E		Y		H
6	N_7	A	O	L	N	S	U	G	O	E
7		C	B	A	F	R	S_5		I	R
8	I	C	W	Y_3	R	U	A	M		№
9	M	V	T		H_0	P	D	I	X	Q
0	L	S	R_1	E	T	D	E	A	H	E

The code shown here was written out on a square about three and one-half by four inches. Groves used it for correspondence with the Chief of Security at the Los Alamos Laboratory, Lt. Col. Peer da Silva. Using this system, the word MANHATTAN could be enciphered as 88 08 10 50 62 93 24 42 65. The system was not particularly sophisticated, but it more than satisfied Groves's needs for communicating with his subordinates.

See also: Manhattan Project.

QUANTUM CRYPTOGRAPHY ▬▬▬▶

A technique for enciphering and transmitting messages using subatomic-size particles, such as photons. Photons can be polarized in discrete orientations, such as up, down, or diagonal at certain angles to the vertical. In principle, messages can be enciphered using these photons in a manner similar to that by which a magnetic core can be magnetized as on or off (1 or 0). Thus, messages can be enciphered by using the orientations of photons. One important advantage of enciphering messages in this way is the ease with which an intruder can be detected. At the photon level, the laws of quantum physics apply, one of which says that any observation made on a particle will disturb the properties (position, speed, orientation) of that particle. It would thus be an easy matter for a sender and/or a receiver to know if a quantum message had been intercepted by an unwanted third party. The practical problem of dealing with polarized photons for the encipherment of messages is still substantial, however.

For further reading: Charles H. Bennett, "Quantum Cryptography: Uncertainty in the Service of Privacy," *Science* (7 August 1992): 752–753; Bennett, "Quantum Information and Computation," *Physics Today* (October 1995): 24–30; Gilles Brassard, *Modern Cryptology: A Tutorial*, New York: Springer-Verlag, 1988, ch. 6; Graham P. Collins, "Quantum Cryptography Defies Eavesdropping," *Physics Today* (November 1992): 21–23; Ivars Peterson, "Bits of Uncertainty: Blazing a Quantum Trail to Absolute Secrecy," *Science News* (10 February 1996): 90–92; Simon J. D. Phoenix, "Quantum Cryptography: How To Beat the Code Breakers Using Quantum Mechanics," *Contemporary Physics* (May/June 1995): 165–195; Carl Zimmer, "Perfect Gibberish," *Discover* (September 1992): 92–99; http://www.ecst.csuchico.edu/~altman/Crypto/quantum/quantum-index.html.

R

RADIO SERIALS

Ongoing radio broadcasts designed for young listeners that were widely popular in the 1930s and 1940s. Programs such as *The Green Hornet; Jack Armstrong, the All-American Boy; Orphan Annie; Dick Tracy; Captain Midnight;* and *The Shadow* all focused on ongoing dramatic situations that were seldom completely resolved. Each episode ended with the hero, heroine, or another character in a desperate situation that would not be settled until the next broadcast.

A common theme of these programs was their producers' efforts to develop a sense of camaraderie among listeners. Opportunities were offered to obtain decoder rings, badges, and other simple cipher devices that could be used for the transmission of messages from broadcast hero or heroine to listeners or between listeners. In many cases, these devices were earned by sending in box tops from cereal or other food products. Advertisers thus benefited financially from a program's efforts to keep its listeners tuned in from week to week.

Most of the messages transmitted in cipher from radio programs to listeners were clues to coming broadcasts or other "inside" information unavailable to those who did not possess the cipher device. Listeners were made to feel that they belonged to a secret club consisting of other fans of a particular program. Only Jack Armstrong club members would know, for example, that four short whistles meant "we are being watched."

For further reading: Jim Harmon, *Radio Mystery and Adventure and Its Appearances in Film, Television, and Other Media,* Jefferson, NC: McFarland, 1992.

RAIL FENCE CIPHER

A form of route transposition in which ciphertext is created from plaintext by following a geometric pattern that resembles the top of a rail fence. The term is also used to describe a variety of other geometrical transpositions.

In the simplest form of the rail fence cipher, the plaintext is written in a zigzag pattern on two lines, as shown below.

PLAINTEXT:
NOTIFY THE COMMANDER IMMEDIATELY

MATRIX:
```
N T F T E O M N E I M D A E Y
 O I Y H C M A D R M E I T L
```

The ciphertext is taken off by reading across the top line of the text from left to right, and then across the bottom line in the same way:

CIPHERTEXT:
ntfte omnei mdaey oiyhc madrm eitlz

The matrix used to write ciphertext can be more complicated and consist of three or more rows rather than two. The same message could be written as follows:

PLAINTEXT:
NOTIFY THE COMMANDER IMMEDIATELY

MATRIX:
```
N I T C M D I E A L
 O F H O A E M D T Y
  T Y E M N R M I E Q
```

235

The ciphertext in this case would read:

CIPHERTEXT:
nitcm dieal ofhoa emdty tyemn rmieq

To decipher a rail fence cipher, the decipherer only needs to know the number of rows and the pattern used in enciphering the message.

> See also: geometrical transposition; route transposition.
> For further reading: Martin Gardner, *Codes, Ciphers and Secret Writing*, New York: Dover, 1972, pp. 12–14; JOT, "The Railfence Cipher," *The Cryptogram* (July–August 1994): 6-7.

RAINBOW SERIES BOOKS

See Orange Book.

RANDOM ALPHABET

A cipher alphabet in which letters have no consistent relationship to the plaintext alphabet. An example of a random alphabet is the following:

PLAIN: A B C D E F G H I J K L M N O P Q R S T U V W X Y Z
cipher: b h u n j i m k o p l y g v t f c x z a s d r e w q

> See also: alphabet.

RANDOM CIPHER

A concept developed by Claude Shannon as a means of mathematically analyzing the properties of various types of cipher systems. For detailed discussions of the mathematical basis of the random cipher, *see* Henry Beker and Fred Piper, *Cipher Systems: The Protection of Communications*, New York: John Wiley & Sons, 1982, ch. 3, and Carl H. Meyer and Stephen M. Matyas, *Cryptography: A New Dimension in Computer Data Security*, New York: John Wiley & Sons, 1982, ch. 12.

RANDOM NUMBER

Any number that has an equal chance of being chosen along with all other numbers in any given situation. People at-tempt to make random selections commonly in everyday life. The magician, for example, may instruct his or her subject to "Pick a card, any card." The implication is that all 52 cards in the deck have an equal chance of being selected, so the chosen card is picked completely by chance, or at random. In order to ensure randomness, the magician usually shuffles the cards carefully before giving instructions to the subject.

Randomness, or lack of it, is a central issue in cryptology. The primary goal in writing a cryptogram is to convert the nonrandomness characteristic of any plaintext message into a totally random ciphertext. Cryptanalysts depend on the failure of cryptologists to accomplish this goal. For example, the use of frequency tables and probable words in deciphering a message depends on the fact that letters and words in a message do not really occur at random. Some letters and some words are more likely to occur than others. The essence of effective cryptography, then, is to write a cipher message such that the arrangement of letters is so close to random that a cryptanalyst cannot detect patterns that could be used in decipherment.

Mathematicians have learned that generating random numbers is much more difficult than it may seem. A person asked to recite a list of letters or numbers "at random" will produce a set of symbols for which nonrandomness can be detected. Today, cryptographers and others who need to use random numbers rely on computer-generated programs that spin out long lists of totally random numbers for use in the construction of cipher systems or for other works requiring secrecy.

In fact, the "random numbers" generated by many computer programs are themselves not truly random, and are referred to as pseudorandom numbers. The term comes from the fact that they are generated by a program beginning with a number sequence that is truly random (the seed), which then generates a much longer list according to instructions provided to the computer. Because the instructions themselves provide a pattern for the generation of the numbers, the final list is not truly random, but has very much the appearance of one.

See also: frequency distribution; one-time system; probable word; Vernam, Gilbert.
For further reading: Brian Beckett, *Introduction to Cryptology*, Oxford: Blackwell Scientific Publications, 1988, pp. 243–255; Henry Beker and Fred Piper, *Cipher Systems: The Protection of Communications*, New York: John Wiley & Sons, 1982, pp. 169–174, 195–198; L. Blum, M. Blum, and M. Shub, " A Simple Unpredictable Pseudo-Random Number Generator," *SIAM Journal of Computing* 15:2 (1986): 364–383; D. W. Davies and W. L. Price, *Security for Computer Networks: An Introduction to Data Security in Teleprocessing and Electronic Funds Transfer*, Chichester: John Wiley & Sons, 1984, pp. 145–148; Carl H. Meyer and Stephen M. Matyas, *Cryptography: A New Dimension in Computer Data Security*, New York: John Wiley & Sons, 1982, pp. 315–316; William Stallings, *Network and Internetwork Security: Principles and Practices*, Englewood Cliffs, NJ: Prentice-Hall, 1995, ch. 2.

REBUS

A representation of a word or phrase by means of a picture or group of pictures that suggests the word or phrase. For example, a picture of a dog sitting next to an automobile tire might suggest the phrase "dog-tired." Some of the earliest forms of secret writing were Egyptian hieroglyphics, in which scribes represented a word, name, or phrase by means of a suggestive symbol.

RED

A term used for both U.S. and Japanese cryptosystems. Like other "color codes" used by the U.S. diplomatic corps, the U.S. RED code was given its name because of the red binding in which it was published. The code was used by the State Department and the Navy Department until about 1913. The U.S. RED code was so simple that, according to

David Kahn, it made the United States "the laughingstock of every cryptanalyst in the world."

The Japanese RED code was first put into use about 1920. U.S. intelligence agents discovered RED codebooks in New York City shortly after it was put into operation and were soon capable of reading virtually any message transmitted in RED.

A decade later, the Japanese developed a new cipher machine to which U.S. cryptanalysts gave the codename RED. The machine was among the most sophisticated of its kind then available, but U.S. cryptanalysts Solomon Kullback and Frank Rowlett successfully analyzed its operations by 1936. After that time, Japanese messages enciphered in RED were also read on a routine basis by U.S. agents.

See also: PURPLE.
For further reading: Fred B. Wrixon, *Codes and Ciphers*, New York: Prentice-Hall, 1992, pp. 173–174.

REDUNDANCY

The repetition of information. For example, a check contains the amount of money to be paid out in two places, once written as a number and once written out in words. Both items provide the same information, so redundancy is provided in the check. This redundancy serves a useful function in that it allows the payer of the check to compare the two numbers to make sure they are the same.

Claude Shannon focused on the principle of redundancy in his early theories on the mathematical basis of communication. He argued that a high degree of redundancy is a common feature of all languages. His calculations showed, for example, that about three-quarters of everything written in the English language is redundant.

Probably the most obvious example of this redundancy in English is the letter *q*. No word in English begins with *q* that is *not* followed by the letter *u*. In other words, the letter u is redundant in such instances because q never occurs without it.

Shannon was able to calculate redundancy in language by taking a prose selection and asking human subjects to read the selection with greater or lesser numbers of letters included. His research was not very different in concept from the popular television quiz show *Wheel of Fortune*. Contestants in this game are challenged to identify a person's name, a place, or a familiar phrase by seeing as few letters in the item as possible displayed on a board.

For example, how many people could recognize a familiar phrase such as the following with the few letters shown?

```
T___ M_ __T T_ TH_ __LL__M_
```

The answer is, not many.

But as the number of letters increases, the likelihood of identification increases.

```
T_K_ ME O_T T_ TH_ B_LL__M_
```

Eventually, the message becomes obvious *even when some letters remain unidentified:*

```
TAK_ ME OUT T_ TH_ B_LLGAM_
```

The principle of redundancy, Shannon pointed out, is what makes cryptanalysis possible. If an eavesdropper obtains a section of ciphertext to decrypt, he or she knows that natural characteristics of the language make it easier to determine the plaintext equivalent for the ciphertext. For example, if a cryptanalyst is able to determine that ciphertext W replaces plaintext q in some cryptosystem, it follows that the next ciphertext letter after W will be equivalent to plaintext u.

Of course, this straightforward analysis applies only in the case of monoalphabetic substitution ciphers. But the principle is the same for more complex systems, because any clue of this kind provides a wedge into the cryptanalysis of the message.

Shannon also pointed out that redundancy becomes a more and more useful tool as the amount of ciphertext available increases in length. At one point he wrote that

> The key gives a certain amount of freedom to the cryptogram but, as more and more letters are intercepted, the consistency conditions use of the freedom allowed by the key. Eventually, there is only one [combination of] message and key which satisfies all the conditions and we have a unique solution.

One of the most useful conclusions that Shannon was able to draw from his study of redundancy in language was the *unicity distance* of a cipher. Unicity distance is the name he gave to the number of characters within a ciphertext for which one and only one solution exists. That is, suppose that the unicity distance for a ciphertext can be calculated as 38.5 characters. That information means that a sample of the ciphertext with less than 38.5 characters will have more than one possible solution. A sample with 38.5 characters or more will have only one possible solution.

See also: entropy; information theory; Shannon, Claude.

For further reading: Henry Beker and Fred Piper, *Cipher Systems: The Protection of Communications,* New York: John Wiley & Sons, 1982, ch. 3; David Kahn, *The Codebreakers: The Story of Secret Writing,* New York: Macmillan, 1967, pp. 744–751; Carl H. Meyer and Stephen M. Matyas, *Cryptography: A New Dimension in Computer Data Security,* New York: John Wiley & Sons, 1982, ch. 12; Claude Shannon, "Communication Theory of Secrecy Systems," *Bell Systems Technical Journal* (October 1949): 656–715; Shannon, "A Mathematical Theory of Communications," *Bell Systems Technical Journal* (July and October 1948): 479–523 and 623–656.

RELATIVE PRIMES

Two integers whose greatest common divisor is 1. Relatively prime numbers are not necessarily themselves prime. For example, the numbers 8 and 15 are both composite numbers. In the one case,

8 = 2 x 4 and in the other, 15 = 3 x 5. Still, 8 and 15 are relatively prime because the only number that divides into both of them evenly is 1. Relatively prime numbers are very important in cryptology because they provide a mechanism for factoring very large prime numbers such as those used in various public-key cryptography systems.

See also: Euclidean algorithm; greatest common divisor; public-key cryptography; RSA algorithm.
For further reading: Brian Beckett, *Introduction to Cryptology*, Oxford: Blackwell Scientific Publications, 1988, pp. 101–102; Charlie Kaufman, Radia Perlman, and Mike Speciner, *Network Security: Private Communication in a Public World*, Englewood Cliffs, NJ: Prentice-Hall, 1995, pp. 132, 165.

REPUDIATION
See nonrepudiation.

RESTRICTED USE CRYPTOSYSTEM
See cryptosystem.

REVERSE STANDARD ALPHABET
A monosubstitution alphabet in which the cipher alphabet consists of letters offset to the left or right of the standard plaintext alphabet *as written in reverse*. The following is an example of a reverse standard alphabet in which the cipher alphabet has been offset by three places from the reversed plaintext alphabet.

```
Z Y X W V U T S R Q P O N M L K J I H G F E D C B A
x y z a b c d e f g h i j k l m n o p q r s t u v w
```

Up until World War I, the U.S. Army employed a form of the reverse standard alphabet as its official encipherment system. The device used, the Signal Corps Cipher Disk, consisted of a plastic disk with the standard plaintext alphabet written around the outer edge of the disk and the reversed cipher alphabet around the inside. To encipher a message, a clerk simply looked up the appropriate plaintext alphabet letter on the disk, found the cipher alphabet letter corresponding to it,

and wrote down that letter. The Signal Corps Cipher Disk was constructed along the lines of a similar device invented by Porta 300 years earlier, although it lacked the sophistication of the earlier model.

See also: cipher disk; direct standard alphabet; monoalphabetic substitution; Porta, Giovanni.

REVOLVING GRILLE
See grille.

RIVERBANK
See Fabyan, George.

RIVERBANK PUBLICATIONS
See Friedman, William.

"RIVER SERIES" OF CODES
See Code Compilation Section.

RIVEST, RONALD L.
One of the creators, along with Leonard Adleman and Adi Shamir, of arguably the most powerful public-key cryptographic system yet developed. In 1978, Rivest, Adleman, and Shamir published a classic paper in the history of cryptology, "A Method for Obtaining Digital Signatures and Public-Key Cryptosystems." The paper described methods by which individuals can communicate with one another secretly even when they are using public systems.

Ronald Rivest received his B.A. degree in mathematics from Yale University in 1969 and his Ph.D. degree in computer science from Stanford University in 1974. Rivest is currently professor of computer science at the Massachusetts Institute of Technology (MIT), associate director of MIT's Laboratory for Computer Science, and head of its Theoretical Computer Science Group. He is also one of the founders of RSA Data Security, Inc., a company created to develop and market public-key algorithms.

See also: RSA algorithm.

ROOM 40 ━━━━━━━━━━━━━━

The name given to the British Admiralty's cryptanalysis section, which operated during and immediately following World War I. The section was formed shortly after the outbreak of the war in the fall of 1914. At first the staff worked out of the offices of Sir Alfred Ewing, the director of Naval Education and, according to David Kahn, the "only man at the Admiralty to take any interest in cryptology" at the war's outset. The section's activities expanded rapidly, and it soon moved to a new location, Room 40 of the Old Buildings of the Admiralty. That location gave the section its unofficial name, one it retained even after receiving its formal name of I.D. 25 (section 25 of the Intelligence Division) and moved to larger quarters.

Room 40 was confronted with a daunting challenge almost from the moment of its creation. As one of its first acts of war, the British navy cut the trans-Atlantic cables on which Germany depended for most of its long-distance communications. The Germans were forced to switch to radio and telegraph as their primary means of correspondence with other nations and with their own overseas representatives and military commanders. The steady flow of wire and wireless communications, therefore, gave the British an extraordinary opportunity to eavesdrop on German plans.

The major problem, however, was that the German code and cipher system was entirely secure at the beginning of the war, and the British had no clue as to how German communications could be broken. In one of the great and fortunate accidents of the war, however, the British got the break they so badly needed. Shortly after the German light cruiser *Magdeburg* was sunk in September 1914, the body of one of its drowned officers floated to the surface, was recovered, and was discovered to be clutching the ship's codebooks. The British were ecstatic. They had the clues they needed to begin decrypting German communications.

In fact, success came slowly until Charles J. E. Rotter, a member of Room 40, discovered that German messages were being superenciphered, with each codeword converted by means of a simple monoalphabetic substitution. With this breakthrough, the staff of Room 40 began to break German messages with a satisfying regularity. Between its creation in October 1914 and its closing in February 1919, Room 40 intercepted and cryptanalyzed an estimated 15,000 German communications.

Probably Room 40's most important single accomplishment was the decryption of the Zimmermann telegram, which David Kahn called "the single most far-reaching and most important solution in history" (when Kahn wrote that statement he was not aware of the solution of the Enigma cryptosystem by Alan Turing).

Shortly after the war ended, Room 40 was merged with the British army's intelligence section M.I.1b to create the Government Code & Cypher School, the government's new cryptographic and cryptanalytical service.

See also: Enigma; Government Code & Cypher School; Zimmermann telegram.

For further reading: Patrick Beesly, *Room 40: British Naval Intelligence 1914–1918*, London: Hamish Hamilton, 1982; Francis H. Hinsley, *British Intelligence in the Second World War*, New York: Cambridge University Press, 1993; Hugh Cleland Hoy, *40 O.B.; or How the War Was Won*, London: Hutchinson, 1932; William James, *The Codebreakers of Room 40*, New York: St. Martin's, 1956; David Kahn, *The Codebreakers: The Story of Secret Writing*, New York: Macmillan, 1967, ch. 9; Peter Way, *Codes and Ciphers*, n.p.: Crescent Books, 1977, pp. 50–51.

ROSETTA STONE ━━━━━━━━━━

A piece of stone found in 1799 by an Egyptian worker named Dhautpoul near the town of Rashid, along the banks of the Nile River. A message was written on the stone in three different languages:

Dating as far back as 196 B.C., the Rosetta stone was the key to deciphering Egyptian hieroglyphics.

Greek, demotic, and hieroglyphics. Translation of the Greek indicated that the text involved a decree of Ptolemy V issued in 196 B.C.

The stone was of enormous linguistic significance because neither the demotic nor the hieroglyphic texts were then deci-

pherable. A number of scholars labored for more than two decades to translate the unknown languages. In 1822, a French linguist, Jean Françoise Champollion, announced that he had solved the riddle of the stone. Only 12 years of age when the stone was discovered, he made it his goal in life to decipher the demotic and hieroglyphic versions of the text.

Champollion's colleagues were not entirely convinced by his decipherment, and debate about the validity of his work continued for another three decades, until the discovery of the Decree of Canopus confirmed his work. Meanwhile, Champollion died of a stroke at the age of 42 without achieving the international recognition that was his due.

For further reading: Carol Andrews, *The British Museum Book of the Rosetta Stone,* New York: Dorset, 1991; James Giblin, *The Riddle of the Rosetta Stone,* New York: Crowell, 1990.

ROSICRUCIANS' CIPHER

A cryptosystem used by members of the secret society known as the Rosicrucians, which flourished in the seventeenth and eighteenth centuries. The society was apparently named for the fifteenth-century mystic Christian Rosenkreuz. It chose as its symbol a rose inscribed on a cross in recognition of the founder's name (*rosen-* = "rose"; *-kreuz* = "cross"). Rosicrucians were devoted to esoteric wisdom, with emphasis on psychic and spiritual enlightenment.

Like many other fraternal organizations, the Rosicrucians developed an array of signs and symbols by which they could communicate with one another in secrecy. Included among their secrets was a cryptosystem that baffled nonadherents for many years. The system was remarkably similar to that of another fraternal group, the Freemasons.

See also: Freemasons' cipher.
For further reading: H. Spencer Lewis, *Rosicrucian Questions and Answers,* San Jose, CA: Rosicrucian Press, 1932.

ROSSIGNOL, ANTOINE

France's first full-time cryptologist. Rossignol (1600–1682) was, according to David Kahn, the first person to have had a biography written about him solely as a result of his work in cryptology. One of Rossignol's important contributions was the development of the concept of a two-part nomenclator, one containing the plaintext in alphabetical (and/or numerical) order and the codewords in random order, and the other containing the codewords in alphabetical (or numerical) order and the plaintext terms in random order.

See also: nomenclator.
For further reading: David Kahn, *The Codebreakers: The Story of Secret Writing,* New York: Macmillan, 1967, pp. 158–162; Peter Way, *Codes and Ciphers,* n.p.: Crescent Books, 1977, pp. 28–30.

ROTATING GRILLE

See grille.

ROTOR

A ciphering wheel. A rotor is a disk-shaped piece of nonconducting material such as rubber or Bakelite, about three inches in diameter and on-half inch thick, with the shape and appearance of a hockey puck. It contains 26 contact points, usually made of brass, on the disk's flat sides. Each contact point represents one letter of the alphabet: *a, b, c,* and so on. Wires connect each point on one side of the disk with another point on the opposite side of the disk.

The contact points are also connected to exterior appliances—a typewriter on one side and a printer or set of lightbulbs on the other. When a letter is pressed on the typewriter keyboard, current flows through a wire connecting that key to one of the 26 contact points on one side of the rotor. The current then flows through the wire buried inside the rotor, emerging at another contact point on the opposite side of the disk. The current flows out of that contact point through a wire connected to the printer or other form of display. The current causes a letter to print out, a lamp to light up, or some other signal to be activated.

The rotor provides a simple but exquisite technique for enciphering a message. As an operator types the plaintext messages into a typewriter, the rotor automatically enciphers the message and prints out or displays the ciphertext of the message.

As described thus far, the rotor is suitable for producing only monoalphabetic substitution ciphers. That is, every time the w key on the keyboard is struck, the rotor translates it into the corresponding ciphertext letter, say i. But then, the same relationship $w \rightarrow i$ obtains in every encipherment.

The rotor contains an additional feature, however, that improves the secrecy of its products. Each time a key is struck on the typewriter keyboard, the rotor advances one position. Thus, when the operator presses a w for the second time, the path taken by the electrical circuit is different because the rotor has moved since the first w was pressed. The current from the w key to the rotor following the second touch now flows to the contact on the rotor *adjacent to but one position beyond* the contact made following the first touch. Therefore, the ciphertext letter produced when the w key is pushed the second time is different from the letter produced in the first instance. In this form, the rotor is able to produce a polyalphabetic substitution cipher.

This system provides some level of security, but has the disadvantage of having a period of 26. That is, after the letter w has been pushed for the twenty-seventh time, the rotor will have returned to its original position, and the same cipher alphabet will be in use as with the first pressing of the letter.

A period of 26 may seem like a large number of cipher alphabets to pass through, but it does not present an insurmountable problem for the cryptanalyst. After all, many of the best-known systems of polyalphabetic substitution (such as the Vigenère cipher) yield to aggressive cryptanalysis.

A simple improvement in the rotor can change the complexity of the system immensely. If a second rotor were added to the first, the number of possible permu-

tations would increase vastly. For example, suppose that the letter w is pressed on the typewriter keyboard and then enciphered as the letter i by the first rotor. But then suppose that the contact point representing the output letter i is connected not to a printer or display system but to a second rotor. The second rotor would look just like the first except that its internal wiring would be completely different.

Electrical current flowing out of the i contact point on the back of the first rotor would travel to some contact point on the upper face of the second rotor, a contact point that might be labeled, say, as d. Current enters that contact point, passes through the internal wiring of the second rotor, and emerges at a contact point on the reverse of the second rotor. That contact point might be labeled as q. The internal encipherment that has occurred, then, would be $w \rightarrow i \rightarrow d \rightarrow q$.

The period of this system is now 26 x 26, or 676. That is, the encipherment $w \rightarrow i \rightarrow d \rightarrow q$ would not occur again until the 677th pressing of the letter w on the typewriter keyboard. Similarly, the addition of a third, fourth, and fifth rotor would increase the period even more, the relevant values being 17,576, 456,976, and 11,881,376, respectively.

The concept of the rotor was invented almost simultaneously by three men in three parts of the world in the years following World War I: Arvid Damm in Sweden, Edward Hebern in the United States, and Arthur Scherbius in Germany. All three built cipher machines containing rotors, but the most famous was probably Scherbius's Enigma machine. At one point, the Enigma was made even more effective by adding a plugboard, a kind of reflecting mirror, to the system. Electrical impulses originating in a typewriter keyboard key passed through four or more rotors, reflected off the plugboard, and passed back through the rotors a second time. In the military form of the Enigma used during World War II, seven pairs of letters were connected through the plugboard. With this arrangement, a total of 1,305,093,289,500 permutations for any one inputted letter was possible. No wonder that Scherbius, the German military, and many cryptanalysts believed that the Enigma was unsolvable!

The introduction of rotors in cipher machines raised the level of cryptographic security by several orders. Machines such as Scherbius's Enigma and Hebern's Electric Code Machine brought about a revolution in cryptography and, as a consequence, in cryptanalysis. The revolution would be somewhat short-lived, however. Once the computer was invented, faster ways of achieving the same kinds of encipherment became possible, and the relatively sluggish operation of electrical systems such as the rotor became outmoded.

See also: Damm, Arvid; Electric Code Machine; Enigma; Hebern, Edward H.; Scherbius, Arthur; Turing, Alan.
For further reading: Cipher A. Deavours and James Reeds, "The Enigma; Part 1: Historical Perspectives," *Cryptologia* (October 1977): 381–391 (Part 2 was never published); Andrew Hodges, *Alan Turing: The Enigma,* New York: Simon & Schuster, 1983, ch. 4; David Kahn, *The Codebreakers: The Story of Secret Writing,* New York: Macmillan, 1967, pp. 411–415.

ROUTE TRANSPOSITION

A form of transposition in which plaintext is transcribed into ciphertext by arranging the former in some geometric pattern and then taking off words one at a time in some pattern (route) predetermined by both encipherer and decipherer. For example, the plaintext message in Figure 17 has been written in normal sequence from left to right, top row to bottom row. (The last three words in the matrix are added as nulls.) One of many possible routes by which the message can be encrypted is shown by means of the arrows drawn on the message.

The enciphered message can be made more difficult to decrypt by adding codewords, such as BLACK for venture, WEST for home, and BUGGY for commander.

See also: geometrical transposition; rail fence cipher.
For further reading: Wayne G. Barker, ed., *The History of Codes and Ciphers in the United States prior to World War I,* Laguna Hills, CA: Aegean Park Press, 1978, pp. 49–75; Donald D. Millikin, *Elementary Cryptography and Cryptanalysis,* Laguna Hills, CA: Aegean Park Press, n.d., ch. 7; Laurence Dwight Smith, *Cryptography: The Science of Secret Writing,* New York: W. W. Norton, 1943, pp. 40–47.

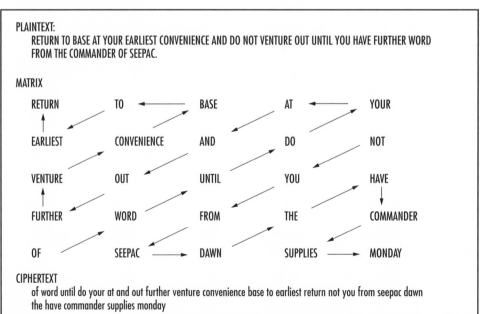

PLAINTEXT:
RETURN TO BASE AT YOUR EARLIEST CONVENIENCE AND DO NOT VENTURE OUT UNTIL YOU HAVE FURTHER WORD FROM THE COMMANDER OF SEEPAC.

MATRIX

RETURN	TO	BASE	AT	YOUR
EARLIEST	CONVENIENCE	AND	DO	NOT
VENTURE	OUT	UNTIL	YOU	HAVE
FURTHER	WORD	FROM	THE	COMMANDER
OF	SEEPAC	DAWN	SUPPLIES	MONDAY

CIPHERTEXT
of word until do your at and out further venture convenience base to earliest return not you from seepac dawn the have commander supplies monday

Figure 17

ROWLETT, FRANK ━━━━━━━━━━●

U.S. cryptologist. Rowlett (1908–) was one of the first three assistants hired in 1930 by William F. Friedman of the Signal Intelligence Service (SIS). Hired at the same time were Solomon Kullback and Abraham Sinkov.

Rowlett made contributions to both cryptography and cryptanalysis during his tenure with the SIS. In the former case, he collaborated with Friedman to modify Edward Hebern's Electric Code Machine so that it was sufficiently secure to serve as the U.S. military's primary cipher machine during World War II. One observer has remarked that "the course of military cryptography in the United States was changed by Frank B. Rowlett's idea. . . . What would the scenario of World War II have been if the enemy had been able to read the secret communications of the U.S., just as the U.S. was able to read German and Japanese secret communications?"

In the field of cryptanalysis, Rowlett also made important contributions to the MAGIC project, which resulted in the breaking of the Japanese RED and PURPLE cipher machines. He was appointed chief of the General Cryptanalytic Branch of the Signal Security Agency in 1943, a post he held until the end of the war. In May 1946, he retired from active duty. From 1953 to 1958, he served with the Central Intelligence Agency and then was appointed special assistant to the director of the National Security Agency. Among the many honors awarded Rowlett in recognition of his cryptologic works are the Distinguished Intelligence Medal, the National Security Medal, and a $100,000 cash grant from the U.S. Congress for his contributions to the development of the M-134-C cipher machine.

See also: Electric Code Machine; Friedman, William; SIGABA.

For further reading: Wayne G. Barker, ed., *The History of Codes and Ciphers in the United States during the Period between the World Wars, Part II: 1930–1939,* Laguna Hills, CA: Aegean Park Press, 1978, passim.

RSA ALGORITHM ━━━━━━━━━●

A public-key cipher developed at the Massachusetts Institute of Technology in 1977 by Ronald Rivest, Adi Shamir, and Leonard Adelman (hence the name RSA). The RSA algorithm is currently regarded as the only completely secure public-key system—at least until some means is found to break it.

The system is based on the use of prime numbers and a simple mathematical concept: it is relatively simple to multiply two prime numbers, p and q, to obtain some product, r. But it is relatively difficult to extract from some given composite number, r, its prime factors, p and q.

As an example, it is fairly easy to multiply 37 by 89 (both prime numbers) and obtain the product, 3,293. Any person with a handheld calculator can perform this operation instantly. However, it is somewhat more difficult to present someone with the composite number 6,499 and ask that person to find the two prime factors of the number. (They are 67 and 97.) This computation is very difficult using a handheld calculator, although it is quite simple and fast with a high-speed computer.

The problem becomes even more difficult when a very large prime number is selected (those having at least 50 digits). The product of two large prime numbers of this size is a composite number of about 100 digits. Factoring such a number into its prime factors is quite difficult even with a high-speed computer.

The RSA algorithm expands on this concept and introduces additional mathematical concepts that increase the security of the system. The following presentation excludes the mathematical details of the algorithm, which can be found in any of the references listed at the end of this entry.

To begin, a user selects any two prime numbers, p and q, usually consisting of about 256 bits. These two numbers are designated as secret and retained by the user. The user calculates the product of these two numbers, r, which is regarded as a nonsecret (or public) number. The assumption here is the one described above, namely that one can safely publish the composite number r without much fear that anyone will be able to determine from it the values of p and q.

As an example (using numbers of manageable size), if $p = 29$ and $q = 53$, then $r = 1,537$.

The next value to be determined is some function of r, $\phi(r) = (p-1)(q-1)$. That is, 1 is subtracted from each of the original primes. In our example, $p - 1 = 28$ and $q - 1 = 52$. In this case, the value of $\phi(r)$ is $28 \times 52 = 1,456$. This number is also secret because it is based on the original two secret primes.

In the next step, the user selects a private key that is relatively prime to $\phi(r)$. Two numbers are relatively prime to each other if the largest number by which they can be divided evenly is 1. In the example used here, the user might select the number 541 since there is no number other than 1 that can be divided evenly into both 1,456 and 541. This number, k, can be defined as either the public key or the secret key.

Finally, a mathematical operation is performed on the chosen number (541 in this case) to obtain the multiplicative inverse. (The mathematical procedure is beyond the scope of this presentation.) The product of this operation is the key other than that chosen above. That is, if 541 is selected as the private key, k_s, then the product of the last operation is the public key, k_p. Conversely, if 541 is selected as the public key, k_p, then the product of the final operation would be the private key, k_s.

After this preparation is concluded, the user can publish his or her public key, which consists of r and k_p. Anyone anywhere in the world can use this key to encipher a message by applying the key to a plaintext message m. Lacking the user's private key, however, no one anywhere in the world can decrypt the same message once it is enciphered.

On the other hand, the user has information in his or her own private key that allows himself or herself—and no one else—to reverse the mathematical operations by which the message was first enciphered.

The security of the RSA algorithm (as with any cryptosystem) is the subject of considerable debate. While regarded as "essentially secure" by many experts, some breaks in the system have been reported. In 1994, Arjen Lensta of the Bellcore Corporation in Redbank, New Jersey, and his colleagues reported that they had factored a 129-digit number into its two primes. The number, widely known as RSA-129, was shown to be the product of a 64-digit and a 65-digit number.

This breakthrough must be viewed in light of the effort it required. More than 600 volunteers working together on the Internet and by means of electronic mail obtained the solution in eight months. Their work showed that the RSA algorithm is not invincible, although it remains daunting.

See also: binary number system; prime number; public-key cryptography.

For further reading: Brian Beckett, *Introduction to Cryptology*, Oxford: Blackwell Scientific Publications, 1988, pp. 134–145; Henry Beker and Fred Piper, *Cipher Systems: The Protection of Communications*, New York: John Wiley & Sons, 1982, pp. 380–387; Albrecht Beutelspacher, *Cryptology: An Introduction to the Art and Science of Enciphering, Encrypting, Concealing, Hiding and Safeguarding Described without Any Arcane Skullduggery but Not without Cunning Waggery for the Delectation and Instruction of the General Public*, Washington, DC: Mathematical Association of America, 1994, pp. 120–124; Gilles Brassard, *Modern Cryptology: A Tutorial*, New York: Springer-Verlag, 1988, pp. 28–32; D. W. Davies and W. L. Price, *Security for Computer Networks: An Introduction to Data Security in Teleprocessing and Electronic Funds Transfer*, Chichester: John Wiley & Sons, 1984, pp. 237–245; Whitfield Diffie, "The First Ten Years of Public-Key Cryptography," *Proceedings of the IEEE* (May 1988): 560–574; Martin Gardner, "A New Kind of Cipher That Would Take Millions of Years To Break," *Scientific American* (August 1977): 120–124; Charlie Kaufman, Radia Perlman, and Mike Speciner, *Network Security: Private Communication in a Public World*, Englewood Cliffs, NJ: Prentice-Hall, 1995, pp. 134–145; Steven Levy, "Battle of the Clipper Chip," *New York Times Magazine* (12 June 1994): 44–51+; Carl H. Meyer and Stephen M. Matyas, *Cryptography: A New Dimension in Computer Data Security*, New York: John Wiley & Sons, 1982, pp. 33–48; R. L. Rivest, A. Shamir, and L. Adleman, "A Method for Obtaining Digital Signatures and Public-Key Cryptosystems," *Communications of the ACM* (February 1978): 120–126; William Stallings, *Network and Internetwork Security: Principles and Practices*, Englewood Cliffs, NJ: Prentice-Hall, 1995, ch. 3; Gary Taubes, "Small Army of Code-Breakers Conquers a 129-Digit Giant," *Science* (6 May 1994): 776–777; http://rschp2.anu.edu.au:8080/howpgp.html#basic.

RSA DATA SECURITY, INC. (RSADSI)
A company formed in 1982 by Ronald Rivest, Adi Shamir, and Leonard Adleman, creators of the RSA digital signature algorithm, for the purpose of controlling and marketing commercial use of that algorithm. The company obtained the patent rights for the algorithm from the Massachusetts Institute of Technology, to whom those rights had been originally assigned. RSADSI has also developed a number of other public-key cryptographic systems, including a series known as the MD (message digest) algorithms.

See also: RSA algorithm.

RUMRUNNERS
See Friedman, Elizebeth Smith.

RUNE
See Nordic cryptography.

RUNNING KEY
A key that consists of a very long, nonrepetitive text. The text of the Declaration of Independence, for example, might serve as the key in a cryptosystem, provided that all relevant senders and receivers are familiar with the text. The main element in the running key is that letters and words do not repeat themselves in an identifiable pattern. Of course, in the case of the Declaration of Independence, a cryptanalyst might recognize a portion of the text in the key and thereby reconstruct the whole key. For this reason, a less familiar text, such as a specific page in an obscure book known to senders and receivers, might be more useful.

For further reading: William F. Friedman, *Methods for the Solution of Running-Key Ciphers*, Geneva, IL: Riverbank, 1918.

S

SACCO, LUIGI

Italian army officer, cryptologist, and specialist in radio communications. Sacco became interested in cryptology as an engineer in the Italian army during World War I. He taught himself the fundamentals of cryptography and cryptanalysis, and eventually achieved at least partial decryption of many German cryptograms even though he spoke no German. Sacco's work was sufficiently impressive to earn him a promotion to chief of the Reparto Crittografico (Cryptographic Unit) of the Supreme Command's intelligence service.

Sacco remained in the army following World War I and rose to the rank of lieutenant general, the first man in one of the technical divisions of the services to do so. He abandoned his work in cryptology in 1923, but earned worldwide fame for his textbook on cryptology, *Manuale di crittografia*. The first edition of this work was published privately in 1925 under the title *Nozioni di crittografia* and republished under its better-known title of *Manuale di crittografia, 2ª edizione, riveduta e aumenta*. A third edition was published in 1947 and is available from Aegean Park Press.

For further reading: Gen. Luigi Sacco, *Manual of Cryptography*, Laguna Hills, CA: Aegean Park Press, n.d.

SAINT-CYR SLIDE

A simple cipher machine named after the French national military academy in which it was taught. The slide consists of a long, rectangular piece of cardboard or other flexible material called the stator. Printed on the stator are the 26 evenly spaced letters of the alphabet. Two short slits are cut into the stator close to its two long ends and slightly below the alphabet itself. The slits permit the insertion of a long, narrow sheet of cardboard into the stator, as shown below.

> ABCDEFGHIJKLMNOPQRSTUVWXYZ
> fghijklmnopqrstuvwxyzabcdef

The narrow sheet is itself the slide. The slide contains two complete alphabets, either standard or reversed, written in succession. The slide alphabets then become the cipher alphabet for the plaintext alphabet contained on the stator.

In the arrangement shown above, plaintext letter A is enciphered by ciphertext letter *g*, plaintext letter B is enciphered by ciphertext letter *h*, and so on.

As customarily used, the first keyletter of the key is placed beneath the first letter of the plaintext alphabet by moving the slide back and forth as necessary. Suppose that the keyword to be used in enciphering a message is GOLD. The first step in using the St.-Cyr slide would be to move the slide so that the first keyletter of the key, *g*, is beneath the A on the stator. With this setting, the encipherment of the first letter in the plaintext can be made.

Suppose the plaintext message is MOVE YOUR TROOPS. Then the first

249

letter in the cipher is u. To encipher the next letter, the slide must be moved so that the next keyletter in the keyword (O) is beneath the first letter in the stator. The next plaintext letter (also an O) can be enciphered by finding the cipher letter corresponding to it on the slide.

It is obvious, therefore, that the St.-Cyr slide is a simplified method for using a Vigenère tableau. Moving the slide back and forth underneath the plaintext alphabet is equivalent to moving a finger up and down the Vigenère tableau to find the correct ciphering alphabet for a given keyword. The St.-Cyr slide can also be compared to a cipher disk in which one of the circular disks is rotated to provide an enciphering alphabet according to some predetermined keyword.

See also: cipher disk; Porta, Giovanni; Vigenère square.
For further reading: Helen Fouché Gaines, *Cryptanalysis: A Study of Ciphers and Their Solution*, New York: Dover Publications, 1956, pp. 110–111.

S-BOX

A stage in the Data Encryption Standard algorithm during which substitution takes place. Each S-box is a matrix consisting of 4 rows and 16 columns of bits.

See also: Data Encryption Standard.
For further reading: D. W. Davies and W. L. Price, *Security for Computer Networks: An Introduction to Data Security in Teleprocessing and Electronic Funds Transfer*, Chichester: John Wiley & Sons, 1984, pp. 52–58; Charlie Kaufman, Radia Perlman, and Mike Speciner, *Network Security: Private Communication in a Public World*, Englewood Cliffs, NJ: Prentice-Hall, 1995, pp. 69–72; Carl H. Meyer and Stephen M. Matyas, *Cryptography: A New Dimension in Computer Data Security*, New York: John Wiley & Sons, 1982, pp. 156–159.

SCHERBIUS, ARTHUR

German electrical engineer and inventor of the Enigma cipher machine. Scherbius was born in Frankfurt am Main on 20 October 1878 and earned a doctorate in electrical engineering from the Technical College at Hanover at the age of 25. After working for various German and Swiss electrical firms, he founded the firm of Scherbius & Ritter with another electrical engineer, E. Richard Ritter. The creation of the firm allowed Scherbius to devote a large amount of time to research, publishing, and invention.

The latter activity appeared to be his special passion, and he soon turned his attention to the development of a cipher machine that could be sold commercially. One of the first devices he produced was a machine for enciphering commercial, nonsecret codes. The machine was one of the first to use electrical connections to convert codenumbers into cipher. Scherbius offered it to both the navy and the foreign office, but neither was interested.

Scherbius was not discouraged, however, and returned to the drafting board. He created a variation of the first machine, one that converted plaintext letters into ciphertext letters by passing an electric current through a maze of wires buried within a rubber disk. The device was to become known as a rotor, and for the invention of this revolutionary device Scherbius shares credit with Arvid Damm in Sweden and Edward Hebern in the United States.

Scherbius again offered the cipher machine to the navy and the foreign office, and was again turned down. He decided to focus instead on the commercial market, and in 1923 sold the machine's patent rights to the firm of Gewerkschaft Securitas. The company marketed the cipher machine aggressively but, despite favorable reviews from experts, in the field of cryptology, found few buyers for its product.

In 1925, however, a dramatic change occurred. The German navy discovered that British intelligence had been reading its code and cipher messages for many years. Changing from one cryptosystem to another had little or no effect on the efficiency with which the British decrypted their messages, so the navy decided that it should reconsider the offer Scherbius made seven years earlier. Naval cryptologists restudied the cipher machine, now vastly improved from the earlier model, and decided it would meet their needs. They placed a substantial order with the manufacturers and, by 1926, had taken delivery of the first machines. The Scherbius machine, given the name Enigma, would become one of the most famous cipher machines in history.

Scherbius himself realized little financial gain from his invention. In the spring of 1929, he was injured in a horse-and-wagon accident, and he died 13 May at the age of 50.

See also: cipher machine; Enigma; rotor; ULTRA.

SCHMIDT, HANS-THILO

A cipher clerk in the Cipher Center, or Chiffrierstelle, of the German Signal Corps, and the man David Kahn called "the spy who most affected World War II." Schmidt was born in Berlin on 13 May 1888 and, although unable to find work during the depressed years of the 1920s and 1930s, was given a job in the Chiffrierstelle through the influence of his brother, an officer of the unit. Schmidt's fate was largely determined by his love of luxury and his desire to live a life of "wine, women, and song"—without the financial resources to afford such a lifestyle.

To attain what he wanted out of life, Schmidt decided to betray government secrets to the enemy, specifically to the French. Over a period of years, he handed over codes of the Abwehr (the German counterespionage agency) and the armed forces espionage agency, cipher manuals and monthly keys for the German army, ciphers used for correspondence within both military and civilian agencies, field manuals for the German interception service, and quarterly reports on German successes in breaking codes of other nations. Schmidt was also known by his codename of ASCHE (in French, pronounced ahsh-ay), a corruption of his agent designation HE.

His most important betrayal by far was information about the German Enigma ciphering machine. At the time, the Enigma represented the most advanced kind of cipher machine available anywhere. Efforts by cryptanalysts from other nations to figure out how it worked had been completely unsuccessful. As a result of information given by Schmidt to the French, and later passed on to Polish cryptanalysts, the secret of the Enigma was eventually broken.

Schmidt paid for his treachery with his life. He was denounced by a captured French spy in 1942, arrested by the Gestapo, tried, found guilty, and executed in July 1943.

See also: Enigma; Turing, Alan.
For further reading: C. A. Deavours, "Enigma before Ultra," *Cryptologia* (July 1987): 142–155; David Kahn, *Kahn on Codes: Secrets of the New Cryptology,* New York: Macmillan, 1983, pp. 76–88.

SCRAMBLER, VOICE

See ciphony.

SCYTALE

Pronounced SIT-a-lee, from the Greek *skytale;* stands for both an object and a system of encipherment. The object is a cylindrical rod carried by government officials and military officers. As far back as the fourth century B.C., the scytale was apparently used to transmit coded messages. A long, thin strip of parchment was wrapped in a spiral around the rod, and a message written vertically down the parchment, one letter per turn above and below each other.

The message ATTACK AT NOON ON THE WEST BEACH would appear as shown in Figure 18. When unwrapped from the rod, the message would appear to be nonsense: ANH . . . TOE . . . ANW . . . KOS . . . etc. A person receiving the parchment and possessing an identical

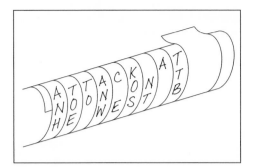

Figure 18

rod could read the message simply by rewrapping the parchment on that rod.

The scytale has been adopted as the official symbol of the American Cryptogram Association. The message carried on this symbol is *Intellegere est praevalere*, or "To understand is to succeed."

See also: steganography.

SECONDARY ALPHABET

See primary alphabet.

SECRECY

In cryptology, the protection of cryptanalysis available in any given ciphertext. Secrecy is generally described as either theoretical (or perfect) or practical. Theoretical secrecy refers to the fact that it should be possible to devise a system such that an enemy would be able to capture only a given amount of ciphertext, with no plaintext corresponding to that ciphertext. Furthermore, the amount of ciphertext captured should be insufficient to permit the enemy to determine the key in which the ciphertext was enciphered. Therefore, it would be safe to say that the ciphertext transmitted was unbreakable.

The concept of perfect secrecy is useful in discussing the theory of cryptography, but it has little value in everyday life. Such large volumes of information are transmitted today that it is virtually impossible to assume that an enemy will be unable to capture or otherwise obtain some portion of plaintext corresponding

to a given ciphertext. Analysts agree, therefore, that perfect secrecy is unattainable in the real world. In fact, the only example of perfect secrecy known today is the one-time system.

Practical secrecy focuses on developing cryptosystems that require so great an effort on the part of a cryptanalyst to break that they are, for all practical purposes, secure. The amount of work needed to break such systems is known as the *work factor,* which is a measure of the computer time and costs needed to obtain plaintext from any given sample of ciphertext. The goal of practical secrecy efforts is to make the work factor so large that any potential cryptanalyst is discouraged from attempting to break the cryptosystem involved.

See also: one-time system; security.
For further reading: Henry Beker and Fred Piper, *Cipher Systems: The Protection of Communications,* New York: John Wiley & Sons, 1982, ch. 3, 4; Carl H. Meyer and Stephen M. Matyas, *Cryptography: A New Dimension in Computer Data Security,* New York: John Wiley & Sons, 1982, ch. 12.

SECRET-KEY SYSTEM

Any cryptosystem in which both the enciphering and deciphering algorithms are kept secret.

See also: key; symmetric encipherment.

SECRET SOCIETY

An organization established for social, political, or other reasons whose membership is limited to certain individuals. Secret societies traditionally employ a variety of devices to keep their customs and activities secret from the uninitiated. These devices may include secret handshakes, secret initiation ceremonies, and secret codes and ciphers by which members communicate with one another. As an example, see **Freemasons' cipher.**

For further reading: Caxton C. Foster, "Secret Musical Codewords," *Cryptologia* (April 1995): 216.

SECURE HASH STANDARD (SHS) ▬▬

An algorithm developed in 1993 by mathematicians at the National Security Agency and promulgated for use with the Data Encryption Standard (DES) as FIPS Publication 180. SHS was written to provide a standard means for hashing encrypted messages produced by the DES. A short time after the standard was released, a "minor flaw" was discovered, and a "technical correction" was released in 1994.

> See also: Data Encryption Standard; Federal Information Processing Standard; hashing algorithm.
> For further reading: Charlie Kaufman, Radia Perlman, and Mike Speciner, *Network Security: Private Communication in a Public World*, Englewood Cliffs, NJ: Prentice-Hall, 1995, pp. 101, 123–125; William Stallings, *Network and Internetwork Security: Principles and Practices*, Englewood Cliffs, NJ: Prentice-Hall, 1995, ch. 6; U.S. Congress, Office of Technology Assessment, *Information Security and Privacy in Network Environments*, OTA-TCT-606, Washington, DC: GPO, September 1994, passim.

SECURITY ▬▬▬▬▬▬▬▬

Protection against any form of unwelcome intrusion. Protecting data files and communications against unwelcome intrusion by enemies and/or eavesdroppers is a crucial issue in cryptology today. Computers now store and exchange huge volumes of data about individuals, corporations, government agencies, and other entities that must be protected from unwanted break-ins. Examples of such break-ins include the potential theft of private or patented information, domestic and international espionage activities against the government, and the destruction or damage of information for political or commercial reasons.

> See also: secrecy; signal security.
> For further reading: Albrecht Beutelspacher, *Cryptology: An Introduction to the Art and Science of Enciphering, Encrypting, Concealing, Hiding and Safeguarding Described without Any Arcane Skullduggery but Not without Cunning Waggery for the Delectation and Instruction of the General Public*, Washington, DC: Mathematical Association of America, 1994, pp. 48–52; D. W. Davies and W. L. Price, *Security for Computer Networks: An Introduction to Data Security in Teleprocessing and Electronic Funds Transfer*, Chichester: John Wiley & Sons, 1984, ch. 1; Charlie Kaufman, Radia Perlman, and Mike Speciner, *Network Security: Private Communication in a Public World*, Englewood Cliffs, NJ: Prentice-Hall, 1995, pp. 26–33, passim; R. C. Merkel, *Secrecy, Authentication, and Public Key Systems*, Epping: Bowker, 1979; Merkel, "Secure Communications over Insecure Channels," *Communications of the ACM* 21:4 (1978): 294–299; Bruce Schneier, "Data Guardians, *Macworld* (February 1993): 144–151; http://www.itd.nrl. navy.mil/ITD/5540/ieee/cipher/cipher-archive.html.

SECURITY POLICY BOARD (SPB) ▬▬

An entity created by President Bill Clinton in Presidential Decision Directive 29 (PDD-29) on 16 September 1994. The action brought together from different parts of government a number of groups and committees that had been responsible for various aspects of security in the federal government. Members of the SPB include the director of the Central Intelligence Agency, deputy secretary of defense, vice-chairman of the Joint Chiefs of Staff, deputy secretary of state, undersecretary of energy, deputy secretary of commerce, deputy attorney general, and one other deputy secretary from a nondefense-related agency.

According to a fact sheet produced by the SPB, its duties are to:

> consider security policy issues raised by its members or others, develop security policy initiatives and obtain comments for the SPB from departments and agencies, evaluate the effectiveness of security policies, monitor and guide the implementation of security policies to ensure coherence and consistency, and oversee application of security policies to ensure they are equitable and consistent with national goals.

The controversy surrounding the establishment of the SPB well illustrates the rapid growth, confusion, instability, and conflict that was characteristic of security issues during the 1990s. In some of its earliest announcements, the SPB appeared to promote the concept of a "new order" in security systems, in which the needs of sensitive but unclassified systems would be linked with those of classified systems. It argued that techniques and programs that had worked well for the defense and intelligence communities might also be applied to civilian needs.

This vision generated serious concern within the business community and among nondefense- and nonintelligence-related government agencies. Administrators in the National Institute of Standards and Technology and the Department of Commerce expressed the concern that SPB's early pronouncements might be "viewed by many as an attempt to impose new restrictions on access to government information." Furthermore, the writers pointed out, the expertise of defense and intelligence agencies "in protecting national security systems is not readily transferable to civil agency requirements." The debate continues as to the most appropriate way in which security issues in a variety of government and nongovernment settings can best be resolved.

For further reading: U.S. Congress, Office of Technology Assessment, *Issue Update on Information Security and Privacy in Network Environments*, OTA-BP-ITC-147, Washington, DC: GPO, June 1995, ch. 4; the presidential directive on which the Security Policy Board is based is Presidential Decision Directive 29 (PDD-29), which is unclassified but has not been released, and therefore is not available to the general public.

SEED
See initializing vector.

SELECTED PLAINTEXT ATTACK
See attack.

SELF-SYNCHRONIZATION
An encryption process that, after one or a small number of errors has occurred, begins once again to encrypt properly. A self-synchronizing algorithm is of considerable value because it guarantees that the vast majority of an enciphered message can be successfully deciphered even if some small portion of it contains errors that make decipherment impossible. Self-synchronization is especially useful in cipher block chaining because an error that occurs within one block will not be propagated in later blocks.

See also: cipher block chaining.
For further reading: Brian Beckett, *Introduction to Cryptology*, Oxford: Blackwell Scientific Publications, 1988, p. 167; Henry Beker and Fred Piper, *Cipher Systems: The Protection of Communications*, New York: John Wiley & Sons, 1982, ch. 7; Charlie Kaufman, Radia Perlman, and Mike Speciner, *Network Security: Private Communication in a Public World*, Englewood Cliffs, NJ: Prentice-Hall, 1995, p. 97; Carl H. Meyer and Stephen M. Matyas, *Cryptography: A New Dimension in Computer Data Security*, New York: John Wiley & Sons, 1982, pp. 71–72.

SEMAGRAM
A term coined by David Kahn to describe any type of steganogram that uses symbols other than letters or numbers. The opportunities available in the use of semagrams are virtually limitless, because two people can agree on modifications of almost any common visual object that will have some significance to both of them. A deck of cards could be sent through the mail arranged in such a way that the sequence of individual cards has meaning. An original piece of artwork might be constructed so that various elements represent some previously-agreed-on code. The number of leaves on each branch of a tree, for example, might represent the numerical value of a commonly understood code.

See also: steganography.
For further reading: Fred B. Wrixon, *Codes and Ciphers*, New York: Prentice-Hall, 1992, pp. 189–190.

SEMAPHORE

A device or system in which messages can be sent by a visual signal. The word is derived from two Greek words, *sema-*, for "sign" or "signal," and *-phore*, for "a means of carrying." One of the earliest forms of semaphore was the optical telegraph invented and used by Claude Chappe in the 1790s.

Probably the best-known semaphore is the two-flag signal system developed in the 1880s. According to this system, the position of two flags held by the signaler represent each of the letters of the alphabet, numbers, and other symbols. The semaphore system used by the U.S. Navy is shown in Figure 19.

Prior to the invention of the telegraph, semaphore was a very popular method of transmitting messages at sea. As long as two ships were within sight of each other, the wigwagging of flags permitted communication. In bad weather or at night, systems similar to semaphore but using some form of light, such as lanterns, were used instead of semaphore flags.

Figure 19

See also: naval signals.

For further reading: Clinton B. De Soto, "Visual Signalling: How To Read International Flag and Semaphore Codes," *QST* (June 1942): 42–45+; H. P. Mead, "The Story of the Semaphore," *Mariner's Mirror* (January 1934) (reprinted in David L. Woods, ed., *Signaling and Communicating at Sea*, 2 vols., New York: Arno Press, 1980, pp. 93–105); *Military Signalling*, Washington, DC: U.S. Infantry Association, 1920; Gordon A. J. Petersen and Marshall McClintock, *A Guide to Codes and Signals*, Racine, WI: Whitman Publishing, 1942; George Henry Preble, *Origin and History of the American Flag . . .* , Philadelphia: Nicholas L. Brown, 1917, vol. 2, pt. 7; Paul J. Scheips, ed., *Military Signal Communications*, 2 vols., New York: Arno Press, 1980.

SESSION KEY
See Diffie-Hellman key exchange; key.

SHAKESPEARE CIPHERS
Texts traditionally credited to William Shakespeare (1564–1616), but thought by some critics to have been written by someone else. The most common candidate as the "true" author of the Shakespearean texts is Sir Francis Bacon.

The debate over the true authorship of the Shakespearean texts is perhaps the most vigorously and widely contested popular issue in the history of cryptology. The first person to raise the question appears to have been Ignatius Donnelly, once lieutenant governor of Minnesota and a three-term representative to the House of Representatives. In 1878, Donnelly became convinced that William Shakespeare may not have been the author of most or all of the works generally credited to him. He set out to reread those works, looking for proof that Bacon, and not Shakespeare, was the true author.

A decade later, Donnelly published the results of his research in his most famous work, *The Great Cryptogram*. In that book, Donnelly described in exhaustive detail the process by which he had decrypted Francis Bacon's ciphers, which told of his authorship of the disputed texts. He followed up *The Great Cryptogram* with a second publication, *The Cipher in the Plays and on the Tombstone*, adding further confirmation to his contention that Bacon was the author of Shakespeare's works.

Donnelly's discoveries, however, were complete nonsense. As David Kahn points out, ". . . nothing like it has appeared in cryptology before or since. And with good reason, for the system is no system at all; there is neither rhyme nor reason to the choice of numbers ['discovered' by Donnelly as the keys to the cipher] that lead to the result."

With Donnelly's research thoroughly refuted, the question of authorship of Shakespeare's work might have receded from public attention. Instead, others took up the search for hidden messages in Shakespeare's works that could be used to prove that Bacon (or someone else) was the true author. Perhaps the greatest effort in this direction was launched by a wealthy textile manufacturer, George Fabyan, who devoted a large section of his 500-acre estate, Riverbank, at Geneva, Illinois, to the search for proof that Shakespeare was not the author of the works attributed to him.

Among the experts hired by Fabyan for this project were cryptologists William Friedman and Elizabeth Smith, later Mrs. William Friedman. For the better part of three years, the Friedmans unsuccessfully searched for evidence that would support Fabyan's theories. At the end of their research, they were completely convinced that no codes or ciphers exist in Shakespeare's writings that could be construed as clues of authorship by anyone else. In 1957, they published a book, *The Shakespearean Ciphers Examined*, in which they review the various theories and research of others on the question of authorship. They point out that the question is one that can be answered in a straightforward method by applying the principles of cryptanalysis. When this type of attack is launched, the supposed decryptions of the Shakespearean texts fall, and no evidence remains to support claims that some other author exists.

The Friedmans' book never completely resolved the debate over authorship of the Shakespearean works. Committed Baconians continue to write about the possibility that Sir Francis, and not Shakespeare, created these great works. Joseph Galland's monumental *Bibliography of the Literature of Cryptology*, for example, probably lists more articles and books on this subject than on any other popular subject in cryptology.

The long debate over the Shakespearean texts has not been without its beneficial by-products, however. During William Friedman's employment at Riverbank, he wrote some of the most important fundamental publications in the fields of cryptography and cryptanalysis in the history of cryptology.

See also: Fabyan, George; Friedman, Elizebeth Smith; Friedman, William.
For further reading: Walter C. Arensberg, *The Cryptography of Shakespeare: Evidence that William Shakespeare Is the Pseudonym of Francis Bacon*, Los Angeles: Howard Brown, 1922; Ignatius Donnelly, *The Great Cryptogram: Francis Bacon's Cipher in the So-Called Shakespeare Plays*, Chicago: R. S. Peale, 1888; William F. Friedman and Elizebeth Friedman, *The Shakespearean Ciphers Examined: An Analysis of Cryptographic Systems Used as Evidence That Some Author Other than William Shakespeare Wrote the Plays Commonly Attributed to Him*, Cambridge: Cambridge University Press, 1957; Elizabeth Wells Gallup, *The Bi-lateral Cypher of Sir Francis Bacon Discovered in His Works and Deciphered by Mrs. Elizabeth Wells Gallup*, Detroit: Howard, 1899; David Kahn, *The Codebreakers: The Story of Secret Writing*, New York: Macmillan, 1967, pp. 873–889.

SHAMIR, ADI

One of the inventors of the RSA public-key algorithm. For a time, the RSA algorithm was regarded as essentially unbreakable, and it has been extensively used for encrypting and decrypting data as well as providing authentication by means of digital signatures. Shamir was born in Tel Aviv on 6 July 1952. He received his B.Sc. from Tel Aviv University in 1972 and his M.S. and Ph.D. in computer science from the Weizmann Institute in 1975 and 1977, respectively. After serving as a research assistant at the University of Warwick for one year, he was appointed assistant professor of computer science at the Massachusetts Institute of Technology (MIT). He now divides his time between MIT and the Weizmann Institute in Israel.

See also: digital signature; public-key cryptography; RSA algorithm.

SHANNON, CLAUDE

American mathematician. Shannon (1916–) is widely regarded as the father of information theory. Between 1936 and 1940, at the Massachusetts Institute of Technology (MIT), Shannon developed the fundamental concepts by which mathematical operations can be used to describe systems of communications. His basic theories are laid out in two papers, "The Mathematical Theory of Communication," published in *Bell System Technical Journal* (July and October 1948) and "Communication Theory of Secrecy Systems," published in the same journal in October 1949.

Shannon received his B.S. degree from the University of Michigan in 1936 and his master's degree and doctorate in electrical engineering and mathematics from MIT, the latter in 1940. He was a National Research Fellow at the Institute for Advanced Study for one year and then accepted a position as a research mathematician at Bell Telephone Laboratories. He has remained at Bell Labs throughout his life and continues to do research on information theory.

See also: information theory.
For further reading: Emily J. McMurray, ed., *Notable Twentieth-Century Scientists*, vol. 4, pp. 1814–1816; Claude E. Shannon and Warren Weaver, *The Mathematical Theory of Communication*, Urbana: University of Illinois Press, 1962.

SHIFT CIPHER ████████████

A form of substitution encipherment in which the whole ciphertext alphabet is moved in one direction or another from the plaintext by a certain number of positions. In the example below, the ciphertext alphabet has been shifted one position to the right of the plaintext alphabet.

    ABCDEFGHIJKLMNOPQRSTUVWXYZ
    zabcdefghijklmnopqrstuvwxy

See also: Caesar, Gaius Julius.
For further reading: Brian Beckett, *Introduction to Cryptology,* Oxford: Blackwell Scientific Publications, 1988, ch. 6; Henry Beker and Fred Piper, *Cipher Systems: The Protection of Communications,* New York: John Wiley & Sons, 1982, pp. 48–50.

SHIFT REGISTER ████████████

A method for generating pseudorandom binary bit strings for use as keys. Figure 20 illustrates how a shift register generates such strings. A single binary digit is entered into each memory cell or register on the cipher machine. Some operation is then used to generate a binary bit to add to the pseudorandom string.

For example, suppose that a memory cell contains the binary digits 0 0 1, as shown in the figure. Then suppose the algorithm to be followed is that the digit in the rightmost cell is moved out of the cell to join the string at the same time that the digits in the second and third cells are added to each other. The sum of this ad-

dition (0 + 1) results in the formation of a new digit, 1, which is then moved into the first cell of the register.

The placement of the digit 1 in the first cell of the register moves each digit in the register one position to the right. The 0 originally found in the first cell moves to the second cell, and the 0 in the second cell moves to the third cell. In the next step, the process is repeated. The digit in the third (rightmost) cell moves out into the stream, while the digits in the second and third cells (0 + 0) are added to each other (to give a 0). The new digit thus created moves into the first memory cell, and the process is repeated.

At each repetition of the operation, a new binary digit is added to the stream, which for this illustration results in a product of 10010.

This process does not generate random numbers because eventually it repeats itself. For many practical purposes, however, the stream is sufficiently random to provide security for an enciphered message.

For further reading: Wayne G. Barker, *Cryptanalysis of the Shift-Register Generated Stream Cipher Systems,* Laguna Hills, CA: Aegean Park Press, n.d.; Brian Beckett, *Introduction to Cryptology,* Oxford: Blackwell Scientific Publications, 1988, pp. 251–253; Henry Beker and Fred Piper, *Cipher Systems: The Protection of Communications,* New York: John Wiley & Sons, 1982, ch. 5; Albrecht Beutelspacher, *Cryptology: An Introduction to the Art and Science of Enciphering, Encrypting, Concealing, Hiding and Safeguarding Described without Any Arcane Skullduggery but Not without Cunning Waggery for the Delectation and Instruction of the General Public,* Washington, DC: Mathematical Association of America, 1994, pp. 55–63; Solomon W. Golomb, *Shift Register Sequences,* rev. ed., Laguna Hills, CA: Aegean Park Press, n.d.

SHORTHAND ████████████

A system of speed writing sometimes used for the purpose of enciphering messages. Shorthand systems have existed almost as long as writing itself. Some his-

Figure 20

0	0	1
1	0	0
0	1	0
1	0	1
1	1	0

torians trace the earliest shorthand system to the Greek scholar Xenophon, who transcribed the memoirs of Socrates. Similar systems were developed by the Romans, the most notable being that of Tiro, who compiled what may have been the first dictionary of shorthand.

By the late sixteenth century, shorthand systems were widely popular in Great Britain. Some authorities argue that the British physician Timothy Bright should be given credit as the father of modern shorthand because of his book *The Arte of Shorte, Swifte and Secrete Writing,* published in 1588. Other experts point out that Bright's system was "utterly impracticable" and that the real founder of modern shorthand is John Willis. Willis's book, *The Art of Stenographie,* first appeared in 1602, and was reprinted again and again for at least six decades.

Shorthand systems are of three major types. The first category makes use of symbols to represent sounds of vowels, consonants, and various letter groups. The second uses symbols to stand for letters and groups of letters. In the third category, abbreviations are devised for letters and groups of letters, as in modern systems known as speed writing.

The most common use of shorthand in the modern world is for taking notes quickly and efficiently. One of the skills traditionally required of secretaries is the ability to take dictation, that is, to take down and transcribe messages given to them by others. In this respect, shorthand is not a form of cryptography at all but merely an efficient method for recording communications.

On the other hand, shorthand is a form of cryptography among those who are not trained in the skill. A message could easily be sent from one stenographer to another in Gregg shorthand, for example, with some degree of confidence that most people would not be able to read the message contained therein. The cryptogram would not be very secure, however, since a third stenographer could easily be found to decipher the message.

This class at the Haskell Institute circa 1910 studies techniques of shorthand, a speed-writing technique believed to have been used by the ancient Greeks and Romans.

Still, throughout history shorthand has been used from time to time specifically for the purpose of hiding messages. Perhaps the most famous example is the work of Samuel Pepys, who kept a diary of his thoughts and activities during the period 1660 to 1669.

See also: Pepys, Samuel; tachygraphy; Tironian shorthand.
For further reading: Thomas Anderson, *History of Shorthand,* London: W. H. Allen, 1882; Hans Glatte, *Shorthand Systems of the World: A Concise History and Technical Review,* New York: Philosophical Library, 1959; John Robert Gregg, *The Story of Shorthand,* New York: Gregg Publishing, 1941; E. T. Williams and Helen M. Palmer, *Dictionary of National Biography,* Oxford: Oxford University Press, 1971, vol. 62, p. 18 (on John Willis); Fred B. Wrixon, *Codes and Ciphers,* New York: Prentice-Hall, 1992, pp. 191–193.

SIDE INFORMATION

Information about a cryptogram that comes from a source other than the ciphertext or codetext itself. Side information is also known as *collateral information*. In a military transmission, for example, a cryptanalyst might know the location from which a message was sent and look for some allusion to that place within the ciphertext as a clue to decrypting the message.

SIGABA

Short name given to the U.S. Army's cipher machine whose full name was the Converter M-134-C. The history behind SIGABA's development and eventual adoption by the U.S. military provides an interesting commentary not only on the development of cipher machines in the United States but also on the cryptologic relationship of the U.S. Army and the U.S. Navy.

Prior to World War II, each branch of the service had its own cryptologic organizations, which were, for the most part, unable to correspond or share information with one another. By the early 1930s, the navy was exploring the use of relatively sophisticated cipher machines of the type invented by Edward Hebern. Despite the failure of Hebern's company, the navy pushed forward with research on the rotor-based devices he had created and developed. As the earliest indications of World War II were appearing, the first of these navy cipher machines, the Electric Cipher Machine (ECM), was just completing its testing. The navy accepted delivery on the first of these devices in 1939.

At the same time, the U.S. Army was working on its own rotor-based machine, the first example of which was the M-134-T1. The first M-134-T1, completed and tested in January 1933, consisted of a single rotor and required the input of a key by means of paper tape. About a year later, an improved version of the M-134-T1, called the M-134-T2, was introduced. The M-134-T2 contained five rotors and was connected directly to an electric typewriter. Plaintext typed into the device was printed out on the typewriter at a rate of about 40 words per minute.

In 1937–1938, the M-134-T2 (now called the M-134-A) was subjected to severe testing by William Friedman and his colleagues. They were satisfied that the machine was secure, and units were shipped to army bases in Panama, San Francisco, and Honolulu. Just as it appeared that the army had committed itself to a cipher machine, however, Friedman was informed of the existence of the ECM. After witnessing a demonstration of its operation, he was convinced that the ECM, not the M-134-A, was the cipher machine for the U.S. military.

The attack on Pearl Harbor in December 1941 brought about some major changes in the debate over cipher machines. In the first place, petty rivalries among the branches of the U.S. military could no longer be tolerated; success in the war demanded cooperation. Second, the superiority of the ECM over the M-134-A had been so clearly demonstrated that the army and navy agreed to adopt the former machine and share its operation. Although still called the ECM by the navy, the army gave it the name Convertor M-134-C (or SIGABA).

See also: Hebern, Edward H.; Friedman, William; rotor.

For further reading: Wayne G. Barker, ed., *The History of Codes and Ciphers in the United States during the Period between the World Wars, Part II: 1930–1939*, Laguna Hills, CA: Aegean Park Press, 1978, ch. 2.

SIGNAL COMMUNICATIONS

Messages sent across a distance by means of signs, impulses, electromagnetic waves, or some other process. Signal communications are perhaps as old as human society itself. The Greek historian Polybius, for example, described communication systems based on fire signals. Two well-known systems are the smoke signals used by Native Americans and drumming by African tribes. In both of these examples, a word or letter could be represented by some combination of short and long impulses: a brief puff of smoke or a short tap on a drum compared to a longer puff of smoke or a longer tap on a drum.

As the need for communication across great distances increased, so did the sophistication of signal systems. The difficulty of communication between two ships at sea and between land stations and ships led to the development of flag systems, or semaphores, which are still in use today. In the late eighteenth century, a popular system was the use of the optical telegraph. However, it was used only briefly because of the development of the telegraph in the 1830s.

The invention of the radio, or "wireless telegraph," in 1895 by Guglielmo Marconi extended the possibilities of signal communications even further. Today, the vast majority of the messages sent around the world—enciphered or not—travel by some form of signal communication.

The widespread use of signal communications in the mid-nineteenth century (in contrast to written correspondence) brought about a revolution in cryptology. The earlier practice by which messages were written out in longhand, carried from one place to another by courier, and then deciphered by the receiver rapidly became obsolete. As a consequence, many of the cryptosystems that had served humans reasonably well for centuries were no longer satisfactory, and entirely new approaches to the encryption, decryption, and cryptanalysis of messages became necessary.

See also: signal security.

An Allied soldier demonstrates a heliograph, just one of many methods of signal communication.

SIGNAL INTELLIGENCE
See SIGNIT.

SIGNAL INTELLIGENCE SCHOOL
A program for the training of (primarily) military personnel in cryptography and cryptanalysis. The school was created in an effort to educate army officers in basic fundamentals of these two subjects, but never involved more than a handful of students until World War II. In its first year (1929), for example, 11 men were enrolled, a number that grew to 16 the next year and fell to 0 in 1931, when no funds were available. In 1932 and 1933, the number of students rose to 5 in each year.

At first, William F. Friedman, chief of the Signal Intelligence Service, taught all of the courses at Camp Vail, New Jersey. He was later joined by a number of other instructors, including Abraham Sinkov, Solomon Kullback, and Mark Rhoads, who offered courses in subjects such as permutation tables, statistical methods in cryptanalysis, and transposition ciphers.

One of the somewhat unexpected benefits of establishing the school was the publications that resulted from it. The army published seven textbooks that Friedman wrote, based on lectures given at the school. These included *Elements of Cryptanalysis* (1924), *Elementary Military Cryptography* (1935, 1943), *Advanced Military Cryptography* (1935, 1943), and *Military Cryptanalysis, Parts I, II, III, and IV* (1938 and 1942; 1938, 1941, and 1943; 1939; and 1941). These volumes have since been republished by Aegean Park Press of Laguna Hills, California.

For further reading: Wayne G. Barker, ed., *The History of Codes and Ciphers in the United States during the Period between the World Wars, Part II: 1930–1939,* Laguna Hills, CA: Aegean Park Press, 1978, pp. 57–65.

SIGNAL INTELLIGENCE SERVICE (SIS) ▬

A division of the U.S. Army Signal Corps formed in 1929 and merged with other cryptologic departments in 1945 to form the Army Security Agency. During its relatively brief lifetime, the SIS was fortunate to have among its directors two of the most powerful figures in the history of American cryptology: William F. Friedman and Joseph O. Mauborgne.

At its inception, SIS was organized into four sections: Code and Cipher Compilation, Code and Cipher Solution, Intercept and Goniometry (direction finding), and Secret Ink. For much of its first decade, however, SIS was extremely limited with respect to the amount of work it could actually accomplish. In the first place, the world was still at peace, with no major military crises calling for cryptographic and cryptanalytic efforts. In the second place, a national and worldwide depression made financial resources very limited, and SIS employed far fewer workers than it might otherwise have wished. Between 1930 and 1937, the service's activities were carried out entirely by a staff of seven on a budget of no more than $17,400 per year.

As war clouds began to build over Europe, the government allocated more resources to SIS, and it grew from 11 employees in 1938 to 14 in 1939. Then, under the direction of Mauborgne and increasing demands for military intelligence, SIS mushroomed in size. By 7 December 1941, it had a staff of 331, and near the end of the war it peaked in size with 10,609 employees.

The contributions made by SIS to the war effort can hardly be overemphasized. One project alone, codenamed MAGIC, led to the breaking of every important Japanese code, including the military's most complex and most secret PURPLE code. Although that accomplishment did not save the United States from the disaster of Pearl Harbor, it led directly to a number of other U.S. victories that contributed directly to the winning of World War II, the Battle of Midway being one of the best known.

At the conclusion of World War II, SIS (by then renamed the Secret Security Agency) was merged with a number of other cryptologic sections within the army to form the Army Security Agency. That agency, in turn, was later merged with intelligence branches in other branches of the armed forces to form the National Security Agency.

For further reading: Wayne G. Barker, ed., *The History of Codes and Ciphers in the United States during the Period between the World Wars, Part II: 1930–1939,* Laguna Hills, CA: Aegean Park Press, 1978, ch. 1; James L. I. Gilbert and John P. Finnegan, *U.S. Army Signals Intelligence in World War II: A Documentary History,* Washington, DC: Center of Military History, 1993.

SIGNAL SECURITY ▬▬▬▬▬▬▬

Any attempt to prevent an enemy from breaking into and reading a private communication. Cryptography is a very old example of signal security because it attempts to transform a written message into a form that cannot be read by anyone for whom the message is not intended. Other forms of signal security are now common, however, such as scrambling of voice transmissions and shifting of frequencies in the transmission of radio messages.

See also: signal communications.

SIGNIT ▬▬▬▬▬▬▬▬

Any effort to obtain information from an enemy transmission. Cryptanalysis is an example of signal intelligence in which a person attempts to break into what is otherwise intended to be a private communication to find out what is contained in it. Signal intelligence includes far more than cryptanalysis, however, since it also involves processes such as electronic reconnaissance of enemy radio, telephone, and radar transmissions and traffic analysis studies aimed at discovering the location and character of messages sent by the enemy.

See also: COMINT; ELINT; signal communications; signal security.

For further reading: Christopher Andrew, *Codebreaking and Signals Intelligence*, Totawa, NJ: Frank Cass, 1986; Mario de Arcangelis, *Electronic Warfare: From the Battle of Tsushima to the Falklands and Lebanon Conflicts*, Poole, Dorset: Blandford Press, 1985; David Kahn, *Kahn on Codes: Secrets of the New Cryptology*, New York: Macmillan, 1983, pp. 292–296; Wesley K. Wark, "Cryptographic Innocence: The Origins of Signals Intelligence in Canada in the Second World War," *Journal of Contemporary History* (October 1987): 639–665.

SIGN LANGUAGE

A type of nonsecret code by which two people communicate using their hands rather than their voices. The earliest forms of sign language were probably developed in Spain during the sixteenth century by Juan Pablo Bonet. Bonet used a manual alphabet, with each letter of the alphabet represented by positioning the hand in a certain way.

Manual alphabets are still used by the hearing-impaired and those who wish to communicate with them. These alphabets involve the use of one or two hands to form or indicate letters. In an older form of manual alphabet, for example, the letter *i* is indicated by pointing at the eye. The most commonly used form of manual alphabet today employs only one hand, which is used to form various shapes representing the letters. The letter *c*, for example, is indicated by forming a half circle with the thumb and index finger. The use of manual alphabets is also referred to as finger spelling.

The most common form of sign language used in the United States is known as American Sign Language (ASL), also

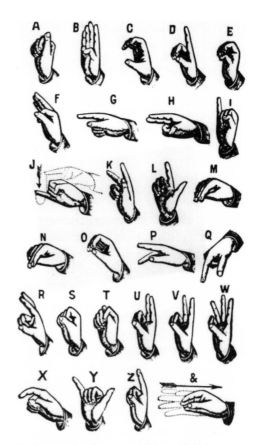

The American Sign Language alphabet is likely the evolution of a manual code developed over 400 years ago in Spain.

called Amesian. ASL is a conceptual language because various ideas are represented by the position of movement of the hands. The word *soil*, for example, is represented by rubbing one's thumbs across the fingers.

The fundamental purpose of sign language, of course, is to provide a means of communicating with people who are deaf or hearing-impaired. However, it can also be used to carry out secret communication between two or more people who are conversant with the language in the presence of those who are not.

For further reading: Louis Fant, Jr., *Amesian, An Introduction to American Sign Language*, Silver Springs, MD: National Association for the Deaf, 1973; Laura Greene and Eva Barash Dicker, *Sign Language*, New York: Franklin Watts, 1981; Lt. Gen. Charles R. Myer, "Viet Cong SIGNIT and U.S. Army

COMSEC in Vietnam," *Cryptologia* (April 1989): 143–150; Paul J. Scheips, ed., *Military Signal Communications*, 2 vols., New York: Arno Press, 1980; Donald J. Sexton, Jr., comp., *Signals Intelligence in World War II: A Research Guide*, Westport, CT: Greenwood Press, 1996; William Tomkins, *Universal Indian Sign Language of the Plains Indians of North America . . .*, 6th ed., San Diego: W. Tomkins, 1936.

SINKOV, ABRAHAM

U.S. Army officer and cryptologist. Sinkov (1907–) was one of three men (the others being Solomon Kullback and Frank Rowlett) who were appointed to assist William Friedman in the Signal Intelligence Service (SIS) in April 1930. The four cryptologists are credited with revolutionizing American cryptologic services in the years just prior to and during World War II. Along with his colleagues, Sinkov was instrumental in constructing the PURPLE cipher machine analog used to solve the most secret ciphers transmitted by the Japanese navy and diplomatic service.

Born in Pennsylvania, Sinkov taught mathematics in New York City public high schools (along with Kullback) before joining the SIS. He was assigned to head a signals intercept station in Panama in 1936 and was then posted to Australia, where he served as commanding officer of the Central Bureau, a joint U.S.-Australian communications intelligence operation located in Brisbane. At the conclusion of World War II, Sinkov was appointed chief of the Security Division of the Army Security Agency. He later held a similar post in the newly created National Security Agency (NSA). He retired from NSA in 1962 and moved to Phoenix, where he taught courses in computer science and cryptography at Arizona State University for a number of years.

See also: Friedman, William; Kullback, Solomon; PURPLE; Rowlett, Frank; Signal Intelligence Service.

For further reading: Wayne G. Barker, ed., *The History of Codes and Ciphers in the United States during the Period between the World Wars, Part II: 1930–1939*, Laguna Hills, CA: Aegean Park Press, 1978, passim.

SKIPJACK

Spelled both SKIPJACK and Skipjack; a symmetric encryption algorithm developed by the National Security Agency in the 1980s. It is classified; that is, it has not been published publicly nor is it available for examination to anyone without appropriate government clearance.

An early application of the Skipjack algorithm was in a program known as Clipper, but it is far better known today as the encryption algorithm for the Clinton administration's Escrowed Encryption Standard widely used for government telephonic communications.

The secret key for Skipjack is 80 bits long and is constructed so as to allow legally approved electronic surveillance by law enforcement agencies.

Skipjack is designed to be installed only in tamper-resistant hardware systems. This feature preserves the algorithm's secrecy and allows its installation with or without the electronic surveillance function.

During review of the Escrowed Encryption Standard, an outside panel of cryptographic experts was allowed to examine Skipjack. The panel concluded that there was no danger that Skipjack would be broken within the next three or four decades, that no shortcut method of attack would break the algorithm, and that the algorithm was secure not because of, but despite, its remaining classified information.

See also: Escrowed Encryption Standard; Law Enforcement Access Field.
For further reading: E. Brickell, "SKIPJACK Review Interim Report—The SKIPJACK Algorithm," Albuquerque, NM, Sandia National Laboratories, 28 July 1993; William Stallings, *Network and Internetwork Security: Principles and Practices*, Englewood Cliffs, NJ: Prentice-Hall, 1995, ch. 6; U.S.

Congress, Office of Technology Assessment, *Information Security and Privacy in Network Environments*, OTA-TCT-606, Washington, DC: GPO, September 1994, pp. 117–119, passim; U.S. Congress, Office of Technology Assessment, *Issue Update on Information Security and Privacy in Network Environments*, OTA-BP-ITC-147, Washington, DC: GPO, June 1995, pp. 54–57, passim; http://cpsr.org/cpsr/privacy/crypto/clipper/skipjack_interim_review.txt.

SLIDE, CRYPTOGRAPHIC

See Saint-Cyr slide.

SMART CARD

A plastic card that looks like a credit card and functions in somewhat similar ways. Smart cards are also known as active cards. A variety of smart card designs have been suggested, perhaps the simplest of which is simply a memory card, on which certain information is stored for later retrieval and use. The information cannot be accessed until and unless the correct PIN (personal identification number) is entered on the card.

More complex smart cards have central processing units (CPUs) in addition to a memory function, which expands their use far beyond that of a credit card. A credit card is essentially a passive tool that provides the user access to an account of some kind. A smart card with a CPU allows interactive transactions between the cardholder and a central computer at a financial or retail institution.

Sophisticated smart cards contain an input/output element, a CPU, and three types of memory. Two of these are familiar: a RAM (random-access memory) and ROM (read-only memory). The third memory function consists of three regions or "zones." The "open zone" consists of items readily available to any machine or to any person. These items would include the holder's name, address, and telephone number. The "secret zone" holds data to which no one, including the cardholder, has access. This zone might include such information as the holder's password, the card's serial number, and financial information input by the bank or agency issuing the card.

Finally, the "working zone" is used by the CPU when the card has been legitimately activated, as when placed into a sales terminal. This zone allows the smart card to carry out a wide variety of operations.

One form of the smart card contains a cryptographic key with which information can be encrypted and decrypted, provided a correct PIN has been entered. When the card is inserted into a terminal, a central computer at a bank or other institution can challenge the card to encrypt or decrypt a certain message. If the card responds properly, the central computer can be certain that the card and the PIN have been legitimately entered, and that business can be transacted.

In this regard, the smart card is somewhat similar to a credit card, which can also be challenged by a central computer but in a less sophisticated way. Smart cards tend to be much more difficult to duplicate than credit cards, whose information is stored on magnetic strips.

See also: personal identification number.
For further reading: Albrecht Beutelspacher, *Cryptology: An Introduction to the Art and Science of Enciphering, Encrypting, Concealing, Hiding and Safeguarding Described without Any Arcane Skullduggery but Not without Cunning Waggery for the Delectation and Instruction of the General Public*, Washington, DC: Mathematical Association of America, 1994, pp. 85–91; D. W. Davies and W. L. Price, *Security for Computer Networks: An Introduction to Data Security in Teleprocessing and Electronic Funds Transfer*, Chichester: John Wiley & Sons, 1984, pp. 192–194, 327–331; Charlie Kaufman, Radia Perlman, and Mike Speciner, *Network Security: Private Communication in a Public World*, Englewood Cliffs, NJ: Prentice-Hall, 1995, pp. 219–220; Robert McIvor, "Smart Cards," *Scientific American* (November 1985): 152–159.

SMOOTH NUMBER

A composite number that is the product of two reasonably small prime numbers. This definition is of limited value per se because there is no generally accepted definition of "reasonably small." The term is used in the discussion of attacks on public-key cryptosystems such as the RSA algorithm in which an enemy attempts to factor some large composite number into its prime factors. If the "large composite number" is a smooth number, this kind of attack has some chance of success. In general, however, the "large composite number" is made so large intentionally that a smooth number attack is impossible.

See also: RSA algorithm.
For further reading: Y. Desmedt and A. M. Odlyzko, "A Chosen Text Attack on the RSA Cryptosystem and Some Discrete Logarithm Schemes," in *Advances in Cryptology—CRYPTO '85 Proceedings,* Berlin: Springer-Verlag, 1986, pp. 516–521; Charlie Kaufman, Radia Perlman, and Mike Speciner, *Network Security: Private Communication in a Public World,* Englewood Cliffs, NJ: Prentice-Hall, 1995, pp. 143–144.

SORO, GIOVANNI

A Venetian cryptologist whom David Kahn calls "perhaps the West's first great cryptanalyst." Soro was appointed cipher secretary to the Council of Ten in 1506 and, over the next three decades, earned the reputation of being able to solve any cryptogram that came to him. Soro later wrote an important book on cryptology, but it has never been found and is known only from references to it made by his successors.

SPANISH-AMERICAN WAR CODES AND CIPHERS

Codes and ciphers used during the Spanish-American War of 1898. Relatively little is known about the use of cryptology during this war, although indications are that the codes and ciphers

employed were fairly simple. One officer later described the system with which he was most familiar as one in which the number 1898 was added to every code-number before it was transmitted. One historian has called such a system "very insecure . . . indeed."

For further reading: Wayne G. Barker, ed., *The History of Codes and Ciphers in the United States prior to World War I,* Laguna Hills, CA: Aegean Park Press, 1978, pp. 115–118.

SPOOFING

A term used to describe the creation of fake origination addresses so that a message can appear to have been sent from a legitimate address, such as a World Wide Web site on the Internet.

See also: password sniffing.
For further reading: D. W. Davies and W. L. Price, *Security for Computer Networks: An Introduction to Data Security in Teleprocessing and Electronic Funds Transfer,* Chichester: John Wiley & Sons, 1984, pp. 152–153; Michael Neubarth, et al., "Internet Security," *Internet World* (February 1995): 31–72; William Stallings, *Network and Internetwork Security: Principles and Practice,* Englewood Cliffs, NJ: Prentice-Hall, 1995, ch. 6.

SQUARE TABLE

An arrangement of cipher alphabets consisting of the same number of letters and/or numbers in each direction of the table. Credit for the invention of the first square table is normally given to Johannes Trithemius (1462–1516), who showed how it could be used to carry out encipherment with polyalphabetic substitution. Trithemius called his table a *tabula recta.* A square table is also referred to as a tableau.

Each row in a square table consists of a complete set of letters arranged in a sequence different from any other row in the table. If the plaintext alphabet is written across the top of the table, any one of the cipher alphabets can be used in any sequence for enciphering any one of the plaintext letters. In the simple example below, the word COME can be enciphered by using each of the first four cipher alphabets in sequence as *cpoh* (C = *c*, O = *p*, M = *o*, E = *h*).

PLAIN:

A B C D E F G H I J K L M N O P Q R S T U V W X Y Z

cipher1:

a b c d e f g h I j k l m n o p q r s t u v w x y z

cipher2:

b c d e f g h I j k l m n o p q r s t u v w x y z a

cipher3:

c d e f g h I j k l m n o p q r s t u v w x y z a b

cipher4:

d e f g h I j k l m n o p q r s t u v w x y z a b c

(and so on)

See also: polyalphabetic substitution; Trithemius, Johannes.

STAFF CODE (WORLD WAR I)

See Code Compilation Section.

STAGER, ANSON

Telegrapher and cryptographer. Stager began his career as a telegraph operator, then rose rapidly to become the first general superintendent of the Western Union Company. In 1861, he was asked by Governor Dennison of Ohio to develop a cipher by which he and the governors of Indiana and Illinois could communicate with one another. Word of Stager's success later reached Gen. George McClellan, who invited Stager to join his forces and create a new cipher by which the general could communicate with his forces in the field. Stager later was placed in charge of the U.S. Military Telegraph, which controlled essentially all telegraphic communications during the Civil War.

Stager is probably best known today for the cipher he invented for McClellan. Because of the availability of the recently invented telegraph, the Stager cipher is given credit for being the first widely used military cipher in history. The Stager cipher used a form of route trans-

position in which the plaintext message was written out in a normal, horizontal fashion from left to right and then copied off according to some prearranged route, such as down one column and up the next. Codewords were introduced, as needed, for names of important individuals and places.

Stager's career with the U.S. Military Telegraph was enlivened by an ongoing confrontation with Albert J. Myer, first Chief Signal Officer of the U.S. Army, over priority for cryptographic and telegraphic responsibilities during the Civil War. Stager was successful in discrediting Myer, causing the Chief Signal Officer to lose his appointment, at least temporarily. By the conclusion of the war, however, Myer was reinstated to his military post, and Stager returned to his position with Western Union.

See also: Civil War cryptology; Myer, Albert; route transposition; telegraph; U.S. Military Telegraph.
For further reading: Wayne G. Barker, ed., *The History of Codes and Ciphers in the United States prior to World War I*, Laguna Hills, CA: Aegean Park Press, 1978, ch. 3; Dumas Malone, ed., *Dictionary of American Biography*, New York: Charles Scribner's Sons, 1935, vol. 17, pp. 492–493; *The National Cyclopedia of American Biography*, Clifton, NJ: James T. White, 1893, vol. 4, pp. 454–455; Harold C. Relyea, *Evolution and Organization of Intelligence Activities in the United States*, Laguna Hills, CA: Aegean Park Press, n.d., ch. 5.

STANDARD ALPHABET

See alphabet.

STATISTICS

A branch of mathematics dealing with the collection, analysis, and interpretation of any large set of data. For example, the mission of the U.S. Census Bureau is to collect any number of individual facts about every citizen and/or resident of the United States. Those individual facts are combined to produce large masses of data that can be analyzed in various ways. For example, the average age of all Americans, the percentage of Americans in various age groups, the number of Americans over a certain age, and so on can be determined.

The association between statistics and cryptology, especially cryptanalysis, would appear to be self-evident. The cryptanalyst is confronted with the task of examining large collections of symbols (letters, numbers, and other kinds of symbols) and discovering distinctive patterns within those collections. As a simple example, the most common letter in the English letter is *e*. In any given ciphertext generated by using monoalphabetic substitution, then, the cipher letter that occurs most frequently is probably equivalent to *e* in plaintext.

As cryptology has become more and more mathematical in recent decades, the applications of statistics have become more important.

See also: frequency distribution; probability.
For further reading: Henry Beker and Fred Piper, *Cipher Systems: The Protection of Communications*, New York: John Wiley & Sons, 1982, pp. 25–32, 50–58, 75–124; Lawrence C. Hamilton, *Modern Data Analysis: A First Course in Applied Statistics*, Pacific Grove, CA: Brooks/Cole, 1990; Solomon Kullback, *Statistical Methods in Cryptanalysis*, Laguna Hills, CA: Aegean Park Press, n.d.

STATOR

The stationary portion of a device that also has a movable portion. For example, in a St.-Cyr slide, a long, narrow piece of cardboard is made to slide back and forth within slits cut into a larger rectangle of cardboard. The larger piece of cardboard is said to be the stator of the slide.

See also: Saint-Cyr slide.

STEGANOGRAM

A message whose meaning is hidden by means of some steganographic technique.

See also: steganography.

STEGANOGRAPHIA

The title of a class work that includes extensive discussions of cryptology written by Johannes Trithemius and published in 1606.

See also: Trithemius, Johannes.
For further reading: Joseph S. Galland, *Bibliography of the Literature of Cryptology*, Laguna Hills, CA: Aegean Park Press, n.d., pp. 181–183.

STEGANOGRAPHY

Any method by which a message is transmitted secretly. The message itself may be written in plaintext, ciphertext, or codetext. The word *steganography* comes from the Greek word for "covered writing." Although not itself a form of cryptography, steganography has long been used to disguise and transmit messages.

One of the earliest reports about the use of steganography can be found in the *Histories* written by the Greek historian Herodotus in the sixth century B.C. Herodotus writes that Histiaeus, a resident of the Persian court, is involved in a plot to incite a revolt against the Persian king. He decides to write to his son-in-law, Aristagoras of Miletus, to gain his support. To send his message, Histiaeus shaves the head of one of his servants, tatoos the message on the slave's bald head, and then waits for his hair to grow back before sending him to Miletus. Upon the slave's arrival in Miletus, Aristagoras has the slave's head shaved once more and reads the secret message. The ending of the story is a happy one, at least for Histiaeus and Aristagoras, as the revolt is successful and the king is overthrown.

Other examples of the use of steganography from ancient sources include the following:

- A message is inscribed on the belly of a hare and the hair on the animal is allowed to grow back. The hare is then killed and sent with a hunter to its intended recipient.
- A message is inscribed on a piece of wood and then covered with wax.

- A message is written on tree leaves, which are then used to cover the sores of a leper, who is made to deliver the message.
- A message is tattooed onto the skin of a leprous beggar.
- A message is engraved on a thin piece of lead and attached to the thigh of a swimmer.

Many forms of steganographic communication have been developed over the centuries. The story is told, for example, that Sir John Trevanion was imprisoned in Colcester Castle during the Protectorate of Oliver Cromwell in the 1650s, awaiting his death by execution. On the eve of that event, however, he receives a letter from a friend that reads as follows:

> Worthie Sir John:—Hope, that is ye beste comfort of ye afflicted, cannot much, I fear me, help you now. That I would saye to you, is this only: if ever I may be able to requite that I do owe you, stand not upon asking me. 'Tis not much that I can do: but what I can do, bee ye verie sure I wille. I knowe that, if dethe comes, if ordinary men fear it, it frights not you, accounting it for a high honor, to have such a rewarde of your loyalty. Pray yet that you may be spared this soe bitter, cup. I fear not that you will grudge any sufferings; only if bie submission you can turn them away, 'tis the part of a wise man. Tell me, an if you can, to do for you anythinge that you wolde have done. The general goes back on Wednesday. Restinge your sevant to command. —R.T.

Sir John was able to decipher the code hidden in the letter by reading the third letter after every punctuation mark. The message read: PANEL AT EAST END OF CHAPEL SLIDES.

There appears to be no end to the imagination of cipherers in finding other ways of hiding messages, such as concealing them inside objects, like the head of a cane or the bottom of a box, or using new technologies, such as microdots that can be pasted on letters, magazines, and other forms of communication. One of the most extensively used forms of steganography is invisible inks.

See also: grille; jargon code; null cipher; open code; semagram.

For further reading: D. W. Davies and W. L. Price, *Security for Computer Networks: An Introduction to Data Security in Teleprocessing and Electronic Funds Transfer*, Chichester: John Wiley & Sons, 1984, pp. 14–16; J. W. Thompson and S. K. Padover, *Secret Diplomacy: A Record of Espionage and Double-Dealing: 1500–1815*, London: Jarrolds, 1937, intro.; Peter Wayner, "Strong Theoretical Steganography," *Crytologia* (July 1995): 285–299.

STRADDLING CHECKERBOARD ━━━

A variation of the checkerboard cipher first devised by the Argentis in the sixteenth century, but employed most recently by Communists during the Spanish civil war. An example of a straddling checkerboard is shown below.

	0	9	8	7	6	5	4	3	2	1
	f	r	a	n	c	o				
1	b	d	e	g	h	ij	k	l	m	p
2	q	r	s	t	u	v	w	x	y	z

The keyword here is FRANCO, written in the first line of the checkerboard. The remaining plaintext letters are then written in the two rows below, labeled 1 and 2.

Letters in plaintext can now be enciphered as either single or double numbers. Assume that the message to be enciphered is ATTACK MADRID. This message will be enciphered with the above checkerboard as 8 27 27 8 6 14 12 8 19 29 15 19. The message can then be run together as 82727861412819291519.

The decipherer will have no problem understanding the message. He or she knows that every ciphernumber must be a two-digit number beginning with 1 (if the plaintext letter is in row 1) or 2 (if the plaintext letter is in row 2) or a one-digit number between 3 and 0. For example, the decipherer knows that the first digit in the ciphertext 82727861412819291519 (8) must stand for the plaintext letter *a* since no two-digit number can begin with 8. The next digit in the ciphertext, 2, must be the first digit of a two-digit number because no plaintext letter corresponds to the single digit 2. The number to be deciphered, then, is 27, which the decipherer knows to be the ciphernumber for plaintext letter *r*.

The cipher is called a *straddling* checkerboard because a decrypter has no way of knowing how to group the numbers in the ciphertext. He or she ends up combining pairs of numbers that should not be pairs or, conversely, treating the components of a pair as single numbers when they should be treated as pairs.

See also: checkerboard.

STREAM ENCIPHERMENT

A form of encipherment in which a stream of binary digits is generated and then combined with plaintext to produce ciphertext. Gilbert Vernam was the first person to suggest the use of encipherment by this technique. In the cipher machine that he invented, a plaintext was converted to binary digits and then punched into a paper tape, which was passed through a tape reader. At the same time, a second punched tape carrying a random sequence of binary digits was also passed through the machine. The machine combined the information on the two tapes using modulo 2 arithmetic to produce a new punched tape carrying the ciphertext.

Block and stream encipherment are the two most common forms of generating ciphertext with modern cipher machines. The primary difference between the two systems is that block encipherment takes single blocks of data at a time, while stream encipherment is accomplished bit-by-bit and requires no minimum size unit on which to operate. Another important difference between the two systems is that the encipherment of each bit of plaintext with block encipherment involves a complex mathematical function, while encipherment with stream encipherment involves the simple modular 2 arithmetic addition of the key to each plaintext bit.

See also: bit-stream generator; block encryption; one-time system; Vernam, Gilbert.
For further reading: Brian Beckett, *Introduction to Cryptology*, Oxford: Blackwell Scientific Publications, 1988, pp. 166-168, ch. 15; Henry Beker and Fred Piper, *Cipher Systems: The Protection of Communications*, New York: John Wiley & Sons, 1982, ch. 5; D. W. Davies and W. L. Price, *Security for Computer Networks: An Introduction to Data Security in Teleprocessing and Electronic Funds Transfer*, Chichester: John Wiley & Sons, 1984, pp. 38–40; Carl H. Meyer and Stephen M. Matyas, *Cryptography: A New Dimension in Computer Data Security*, New York: John Wiley & Sons, 1982, ch. 2.

STRIP CIPHER

See M-138.

STRONG ALGORITHM

An algorithm that is, for all practical purposes, unbreakable. In order for an algorithm to be called *strong*, it must meet two general criteria. First, it must be sufficiently complex mathematically to defeat its solution by standard analytical techniques. Second, it must be sufficiently difficult to solve that the computer resources needed for solution are so great as to discourage an enemy from attacking the system.

For example, an algorithm might require that a computer try each of 2^n possible solutions in order to find the correct key or plaintext. If n is reasonably small (say, no more than about 20), a modern high-speed computer can process this many guesses (2^{20}) in a reasonable period of time, say a few days or weeks. An algorithm of this type cannot be said to be strong. If n is much larger (say, 60), the number of choices to be made is so large that the time and cost involved in running the computer search is too great to attempt. In this case, the algorithm can be said to be strong.

The conditions established for a strong algorithm are not modest. In the first place, the reference to a "computer" does not mean just any computer, nor does it refer to the fast, most modern machines currently available. It includes the fastest and most sophisticated computer of which experts can currently conceive. In the second place, mention of "reasonable time" does not mean a few months, a few years, or a few decades. Instead, it generally suggests very long periods of time, such as thousands of years.

See also: algorithm; computational complexity. For further reading: "Cryptography," in *McGraw-Hill Encyclopedia of Science & Technology*, 7th ed., New York: McGraw-Hill, 1987, vol. 3, p. 565; Carl H. Meyer and Stephen M. Matyas, *Cryptography: A New Dimension in Computer Data Security*, New York: John Wiley & Sons, 1982, p. 22.

STRONG PRIME

A prime number with particularly useful properties in public-key cryptographic systems. A prime number P is said to be a *strong* prime provided that the following condition is met:

$$P = \frac{p-1}{2}$$

where p is any other prime number.

Thus, if the number 733 is prime (and it is), then $733 - 1 \div 2 = 366$ is a strong prime. The mathematical significance of strong primes is beyond the scope of this book.

For further reading: Charlie Kaufman, Radia Perlman, and Mike Speciner, *Network Security: Private Communication in a Public World*, Englewood Cliffs, NJ: Prentice-Hall, 1995, p. 152; M. R. Schroeder, *Number Theory in Science and Communication*, Berlin: Springer-Verlag, 1984, pp. 199–201.

SUBSTITUTION

One of the two primary methods by which a message can be encrypted, the other being transposition. Substitution

can be accomplished by using a single cipher alphabet in which one and only one letter is used to replace each letter of plaintext. A system of this kind is called *monographic*. In other substitution systems, two or more letters at a time are used to replace any single letter of plaintext. Such systems are called, in general, *polygraphic* or *digraphic* if two letters at a time are used, *trigraphic* if three are used, and so on. Probably the best-known example of a digraphic system is the Playfair cipher. Any substitution system in which more than one alphabet is used to encipher plaintext is known as a polyalphabetic system.

See also: monoalphabetic substitution; polyalphabetic substitution.
For further reading: Karl Andreassen, *Computer Cryptology: Beyond Decoder Rings*, Englewood Cliffs, NJ: Prentice-Hall, 1988, ch. 7; Wayne G. Barker, *Cryptanalysis of the Simple Substitution Cipher with Word Divisions*, Laguna Hills, CA: Aegean Park Press, n.d.; Brian Beckett, *Introduction to Cryptology*, Oxford: Blackwell Scientific Publications, 1988, ch. 11; Henry Beker and Fred Piper, *Cipher Systems: The Protection of Communications*, New York: John Wiley & Sons, 1982, ch. 1; D. W. Davies and W. L. Price, *Security for Computer Networks: An Introduction to Data Security in Teleprocessing and Electronic Funds Transfer*, Chichester: John Wiley & Sons, 1984, ch. 1; Helen Fouché Gaines, *Cryptanalysis: A Study of Ciphers and Their Solution*, New York: Dover Publications, 1956, ch. 21; Abraham Sinkov, *Elementary Cryptanalysis: A Mathematical Approach*, New York: Random House, 1968, ch. 4.

SUPERENCIPHERMENT

The process by which a code or cipher is enciphered a second time. In theory, any code or cipher can be manipulated to produce a new cipher. For example, consider the message shown below. In the first step, the plaintext is enciphered by means of a simple monoalphabetic substitution. The enciphered text is then subjected to a transposition in which its letters are simply reversed.

PLAINTEXT:
S E L L T H R E E T H O U S A N D S H A R E S
FIRST CIPHERTEXT:
z p f f t o y p p t o g k z q e s z o q y p z
SECOND CIPHERTEXT:
z p y q o z s e q z k g o t p p y o t f f p z

Historically, the superencipherment of codes, rather than ciphers, was probably more commonly used. The reason was that codebooks often expressed code-words in terms of codenumbers, which were then easily manipulated by either substitution or transposition. For example, suppose that the codenumber for SELL in the above message is 84351. A first step in the superencipherment of this codenumber might be to add some constant value to this number (and all other codenumbers in the message). Suppose that the constant value chosen for this purpose is 18439. Then the enciphered codenumber would be 84351 + 18439, or 02790, the initial 1 being disregarded.

The next stage of superencipherment in this example might be to transpose the digits in this number in some previously-agreed-on fashion, resulting in a final codenumber of, say, 29070. This number is known as the encicode, an abbreviation for enciphered code.

See also: additive; code; encicode; mono-alphabetic substitution; transposition.
For further reading: Henry Beker and Fred Piper, *Cipher Systems: The Protection of Communications*, New York: John Wiley & Sons, 1982, pp. 133–135; William F. Friedman, *Advanced Military Cryptography*, Laguna Hills, CA: Aegean Park Press, 1976, ch. 16; Friedman, *Elementary Military Cryptography*, La-guna Hills, CA: Aegean Park Press, 1976, ch. 9.

SYMMETRIC ENCIPHERMENT

A form of encipherment in which the same key is used to both encipher and decipher a message. Until the invention of public-key cryptography in 1976, all cryptography made use of symmetric encipherment, or private-key cryptography. In this form of cryptography, both the sender and recipient of an enciphered message must know the key used to encipher the message. The person who receives the message uses that key to decipher the message by the inverse of the process by which it was enciphered.

Throughout history, symmetric encipherment has been troubled by one overwhelming issue: how to transmit securely the secret key among all persons who need to have that key. Should that secret key become available to an enemy or eavesdropper, the key is no longer of any value, and secure messages can no longer be sent using it.

See also: public-key cryptography.
For further reading: Charlie Kaufman, Radia Perlman, and Mike Speciner, *Network Security: Private Communication in a Public World*, Englewood Cliffs, NJ: Prentice-Hall, 1995, ch. 3; G. J. Simmons, "Symmetric and Asymmetric Encryption," *ACM Computing Surveys*, vol. 11, no. 4: 305–330; U.S. Congress, Office of Technology Assessment, *Issue Update on Information Security and Privacy in Network Environments*, OTA-BP-ITC-147, Washington, DC: GPO, June 1995, pp. 46–50.

T

TABLEAU

See square table.

TABULA RECTA

See square table.

TACHYGRAPHY

An early form of shorthand invented by Englishman Thomas Shelton. The word derives from the Greek words for "rapid" (*tachys-*) and "writing" (*-graphein*). Many of the shorthand letters were similar to those of their longhand counterparts, but in some cases vowels were replaced by one or more dots or by the consonant following them. Perhaps the most famous surviving example of the use of tachygraphy are the diaries written by Samuel Pepys in the 1660s.

See also: Pepys, Samuel; shorthand; Tironian shorthand.
For further reading: Thomas Shelton, *A Tutor to Tachygraphy, or Short-Writing (1642) and Tachygraphy (1647)*, Los Angeles: Augustan Reprint Society, 1970.

TAMPERER

A cryptanalyst who not only intercepts and reads a message but who also attempts to alter it. A tamperer is sometimes called an active cryptanalyst, in contrast to a passive cryptanalyst, who merely attempts to decrypt a message.

See also: eavesdropper; enemy.

TANNENBERG, BATTLE OF

A battle between Russian and German troops on 25–30 August 1914. This engagement is a classic example of the role that cryptology can and cannot play in war. The Russians were on the offensive, planning to sweep across Germany's eastern borders in East Prussia. Russian troops were woefully ill-equipped, however, to carry out the long-distance communications that were necessary across such a broad battlefront. They had insufficient wire for the laying of telegraph lines and too few radios for the many levels of commands to which orders had to go.

The Russian cryptologic capability was so inadequate, in fact, that the vast majority of communications were sent in clear. German observers had no trouble whatsoever in listening to and receiving the same messages that were being sent from Russian commanders to their troops at the front.

When the battle was actually joined on 26 August, Russian forces were simply overwhelmed. German troops knew exactly what the enemy plans were and where their weak points would be. They feinted a drawback and then enveloped the attacking Russian army from both sides. When the battle ended four days later, about 30,000 Russian troops had been killed and another 100,000 had been captured. The once fearsome Second Army had been completely destroyed. One historian called the battle "one of the greatest victories in history."

For further reading: Barbara Tuchman, *The Guns of August*, New York: Macmillan, 1962.

TEAPOT DOME SCANDAL ━━━━━

An instance of official corruption involving the sale of oil well leases during the
administration of President Warren G.
Harding in the 1920s. The scandal involved Secretary of the Interior Albert B.
Fall, Edward C. Doheny of the Pan American Petroleum Company, and Edward
B. McLean, president of the *Washington
Post* newspaper. Fall granted a lucrative
lease for oil developments on the Teapot
Dome naval reserve region in Wyoming
to Doheny and Harry F. Sinclair. The deal
was consummated in secrecy, however,
because of "national security concerns"
expressed by Fall.

As is often the case in matters of political intrigue, the Teapot Dome story is
very complex. Essentially it involved
questions as to whether a $100,000 pay-
ment made by McLean to Fall had anything to do with the secretary's decision
to award oil rights to Doheny and
Sinclair. McLean claimed that he did not
even know Sinclair, and that he had no
interest in the Teapot Dome affair at all.

During congressional investigations
about Fall's leasing decision, coded messages among McLean, Fall, and Doheny
were uncovered. The messages were not
much of a cryptanalytic challenge since
they were all encoded in generally available private and public codes. The task
of decoding and verifying the messages

An early telegraph. Samuel F. B. Morse produced the first
working electric telegraph in 1835.

was given to William Friedman, then of
the U.S. Army Signal Corps. Friedman
confirmed that McLean did indeed know
Sinclair and had communicated with him
in code. The payment he made to Fall was
in fact a payoff from Doheny, presumably
in exchange for receiving drilling rights
at Teapot Dome.

Doheny and Sinclair were acquitted of
all charges brought against them, but Fall
was convicted of accepting a bribe and
spent a year and a day in jail. Although
cryptology played a relatively minor, albeit interesting, role in this whole event,
the story of Teapot Dome continues to
stand as one of the moral tragedies of
modern American politics.

For further reading: Burl Noggle, *Teapot Dome:
Oil and Politics in the 1920s,* Baton Rouge:
Louisiana State University Press, 1962.

TELEGRAPH ━━━━━

A device by which messages can be sent
along electrical wires. The concept was
investigated by inventors in France, Germany, and England during the early
nineteenth century, but the American
inventor and artist Samuel F. B. Morse
brought it to fruition. Morse obtained his
first patent for a telegraph in 1840; three
years later, the U.S. Congress appropri-
ated funds for the construction of a telegraph line between Washington, D.C.,
and Baltimore. On this line in 1844,
Morse sent the first telegraphic message:
"What hath God wrought?"

The telegraph completely revolutionized the field of cryptography. Enciphered messages that once had to be
written out and delivered in person could
now be sent almost instantaneously
across hundreds or thousands of miles.
In addition, the same message could be
relayed to dozens of individuals at once
rather than to one or two at a time. The
first use of telegraphic communications
for military purposes occurred during the
Crimean War, but it was not until the Civil
War that the telegraph became an important military communications element.

See also: Civil War cryptology; Morse code.
For further reading: *From Semaphore to Satellite*, Geneva: International Telecommunications Union, 1965; William R. Plum, *The Military Telegraph during the Civil War in the United States*, Chicago: Jansen, McClurg, 1882 (republished by the University of Nebraska Press, 1996).

TELETYPEWRITER

See Vernam, Gilbert.

TICKET

An encrypted message prepared by a Key Distribution Center (KDC) that allows two nodes in a network to communicate with each other for a given period of time. The ticket is prepared on behalf of one entity (say, Alice) who wishes to initiate a correspondence with a second entity in the same network (say, Bob). It consists of the session key prepared by the KDC for the given communication (say, K_{AB}) and is forwarded by the KDC to Alice, who in turn sends it on to Bob. The ticket cannot be read by Alice because it includes a session key encrypted with Bob's master key (as well as with Alice's master key), but can be read by Bob. The ticket confirms to Bob that it is indeed Alice who wishes to communicate with him. The ticket generally includes, in addition to the session key itself, other pertinent information needed for the communication. This information might include the names of one or both of the entities involved and the expiration time for the ticket.

See also: key; Key Distribution Center; trusted intermediary.
For further reading: Charlie Kaufman, Radia Perlman, and Mike Speciner, *Network Security: Private Communication in a Public World*, Englewood Cliffs, NJ: Prentice-Hall, 1995, pp. 189, 243–249, 266–267.

TIME CODE

A code based on the location of the numbers on the face of a clock. As shown in

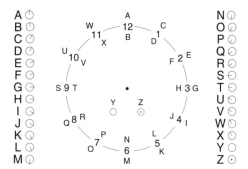

Figure 21

Figure 21, the 12 numbers on a clock face can be used to locate 24 of the 26 letters in the English alphabet. Any two of the less frequently used letters (such as *q* and *z*) can be omitted or represented by some other symbol. Each plaintext letter in a code can then be represented, as shown, by drawing a circle for the clock and indicating the position of the hour hand. Since each number represents two different letters (12 = A and B, for example), the letter indicated can be shown by the position of the hour hand inside or outside the clock circle.

TIME-DIVISION SCRAMBLE

See ciphony.

TIME-STAMP

A mechanism to certify the time at which some transaction took place. Time-stamps are common in everyday life; for example, a secretary stamps the date and time on a communication sent from or received at an office. In some cases, precise records of time are very important, as in the case of a bid on a contract.

Time-stamps are especially important for electronic communications because messages are sent essentially instantaneously. This situation is very different than for normal mail (U.S. Postal Service) or even one-day services such as Federal Express or United Parcel Service (UPS).

With these slower forms of service, a matter of a few hours, minutes, or seconds is inconsequential. With instantaneous electronic mail or communication via the Internet, such limitations no longer apply.

One method of indicating the time at which a message is sent or received is for the sender or recipient to mark the message with the time indicated on his or her own clock. This system is generally unsatisfactory, however, given that two clocks may differ from each other and/or the sender or recipient may falsify the time in question.

For these reasons, time-stamping may be mediated by a trusted third party, such as a certification authority or Key Distribution Center. Such entities can validate the times at which transactions take place just as they can authenticate individuals and agencies involved in the transactions. The trusted third party is likely to use a universal time-recording system such as the UNIX protocol, based on time zero = 00:00:00 GMT (Greenwich Mean Time) 1 January 1970.

> See also: certification authority; digital signature; electronic mail; Key Distribution Center; trusted intermediary.
> For further reading: D. W. Davies and W. L. Price, *Security for Computer Networks: An Introduction to Data Security in Teleprocessing and Electronic Funds Transfer,* Chichester: John Wiley & Sons, 1984, pp. 154–155; Charlie Kaufman, Radia Perlman, and Mike Speciner, *Network Security: Private Communication in a Public World,* Englewood Cliffs, NJ: Prentice-Hall, 1995, pp. 255, 280; Carl H. Meyer and Stephen M. Matyas, *Cryptography: A New Dimension in Computer Data Security,* New York: John Wiley & Sons, 1982, p. 524; U.S. Congress, Office of Technology Assessment, *Information Security and Privacy in Network Environments,* OTA-TCT-606, Washington, DC: GPO, September 1994, pp. 76–78.

TIRONIAN SHORTHAND

An early form of tachygraphy apparently invented by the Roman scribe Tiron in the seventh century A.D. At first, the symbols used by Tiron were alphabetic, differing little from their longhand counterparts. Eventually they evolved into forms more similar to Chinese ideographs. In Tironian shorthand, vowels were typically represented by one or more dots or by the consonant following them in the alphabet. Often, the conversion involved replacing the letter *i* by one dot, the letter *a* by two, the letter *e* by three, the letter *o* by four, and the letter *u* by five dots. Thus, the word *propinqua* might be represented either as pr×××××p×nq××××× ×× or as prppknqwb (*i* and *j* being equivalent, and *v* and *w* also being equivalent). Although devised primarily as a method of speed writing, Tironian shorthand could also be used for writing cryptograms of limited security.

TOMOGRAPHIC CIPHER

A synonym for **fractionating cipher,** q.v.

TRAFFIC ANALYSIS

The study of intercepted messages as an aid in decrypting them, determining their relative significance, and providing other useful information. Unquestionably, knowing that a message was sent from point A to point B by an enemy transmitter can be useful information. However, it might be even more useful to know that point A is the general headquarters of the enemy staff and point B is an advance sector of the enemy army, or that the message from A to B is the tenth such message in the past week, or that point B has been moving from north to south toward Island X during that time, and so on.

David Kahn lists some of the valuable information that can be obtained from traffic analysis: "the length of the message, its originator, the time of day at which it was sent, the circuit used, the addressees, and stereotypes in the text of the cryptogram itself, plus an intuitive 'feel' based on day-in, day-out listening-in to . . . communications." Such information was probably first critical in military operations during the Battle of the Pacific in World War II.

See also: fist; side information.

For further reading: Lambros D. Callimahos, *Traffic Analysis and the Zendian Problem*, Laguna Hills, CA: Aegean Park Press, n.d.; David Kahn, *The Codebreakers: The Story of Secret Writing*, New York: Macmillan, 1967, ch. 11, 17.

TRANSPOSITION

One of the two primary mechanisms of enciphering a message (the other being substitution). In transposition, the letters of the plaintext message are retained, but their order is changed. For example, reversing the sequence of letters in the word REMINDER gives the cipher word rednimer. This form of transposition is easy to use, but it is also much too easy to decipher and is therefore of no value in enciphering a message.

A great variety of transposition systems have been devised. Many can be classified as geometrical systems, columnar transposition, or route transposition. Whatever their specific form, all systems of transposition require that both sender and receiver of a ciphertext know the pattern, or key, to be used in enciphering the plaintext.

See also: columnar transposition; geometrical transposition; route transposition.

For further reading: Karl Andreassen, *Computer Cryptology: Beyond Decoder Rings*, Englewood Cliffs, NJ: Prentice-Hall, 1988, ch. 6; Brian Beckett, *Introduction to Cryptology*, Oxford: Blackwell Scientific Publications, 1988, ch. 2; *A Course in Cryptanalysis*, Laguna Hills, CA: Aegean Park Press, n.d., sec. 2; D. W. Davies and W. L. Price, *Security for Computer Networks: An Introduction to Data Security in Teleprocessing and Electronic Funds Transfer*, Chichester: John Wiley & Sons, 1984, ch. 2; William F. Friedman, *Advanced Military Cryptography*, Laguna Hills, CA: Aegean Park Press, 1976, pt. A; Friedman, *Elementary Military Cryptography*, Laguna Hills, CA: Aegean Park Press, 1976, ch. 4; Helen Fouché Gaines,

Cryptanalysis: A Study of Ciphers and Their Solution, New York: Dover Publications, 1956, ch. 3–7; Donald D. Millikin, *Elementary Cryptography and Cryptanalysis*, Laguna Hills, CA: Aegean Park Press, n.d., ch. 7; Abraham Sinkov, *Elementary Cryptanalysis: A Mathematical Approach*, New York: Random House, 1968, ch. 5.

TRAP-DOOR FUNCTION

A one-way function that gets its name from the analogy of a real-life trapdoor. That is, it's easy enough to go in one direction in a trapdoor; you simply fall through the door. But it's very difficult to go the other direction, to crawl back out the door to the space above.

In cryptology, the idea of a trap-door function is to devise a mathematical scheme that is comparatively simple for a person to use for encrypting a message (going through the trapdoor in one direction) and that will be relatively easy for the intended recipient to decrypt. At the same time, however, the scheme has to be difficult for an unintended recipient to "climb back out of."

As a simple example, imagine that Alice and Bob have agreed to exchange secret messages with each other according to the following scheme. The message will consist of two parts, one of which has the form of x^a and the other part of the form y^b. These two parts are then multiplied to get a product of the form x^a x y^b.

With this scheme, it is easy for the sender to encrypt a message simply by performing this multiplication. It is also easy for the recipient to decipher the message if he or she knows one of the two factors. But a person for whom the message is not intended will have a very difficult task. The number produced by multiplying x^a x y^b is conceivably very large, and it will take considerable skill to deduce the values of $x, a, y,$ and b knowing only the final product itself.

See also: authentication; one-way function.

For further reading: Brian Beckett, *Introduction to Cryptology*, Oxford: Blackwell Scientific

Publications, 1988, pp. 130–134; D. W. Davies and W. L. Price, *Security for Computer Networks: An Introduction to Data Security in Teleprocessing and Electronic Funds Transfer*, Chichester: John Wiley & Sons, 1984, pp. 246–250; Carl H. Meyer and Stephen M. Matyas, *Cryptography: A New Dimension in Computer Data Security*, New York: John Wiley & Sons, 1982, pp. 48–53; M. R. Schroeder, *Number Theory in Science and Communication*, Berlin: Springer-Verlag, 1984, ch. 9; A. C. Yao, "Theory and Applications of Trapdoor Functions," *IEEE FOCS* 23 (1982): 80–91.

TRENCH CODE

A code used by soldiers fighting on the front lines during military action. The earliest trench codes were produced by the French army in early 1916 when it became apparent that messages transmitted in clear over the telephone were too risky. The first such codes were relatively modest one-part codes, consisting of two-letter groups representing about 50 expressions normally expected in a military conversation. The codes were printed in small books that soldiers could easily carry in their breast pockets.

Later trench codes became more sophisticated, using two-part codes of three-letter groups and a larger number of codegroups, which were subdivided into various categories according to their potential use (such as for artillery or the infantry) or the types of phrases included (numbers, common words, place-names, names of individuals, and so on). The categorized trench codes were also known as *caption codes*.

As World War I progressed, the concept of trench codes spread to other armies with, as to be expected, the Germans developing some of the most complex of the genre. By the war's end, some trench codes were partially enciphered to increase the difficulty of decryption.

See also: field cipher.
For further reading: Wayne G. Barker, ed., *The History of Codes and Ciphers in the United States during World War I*, Laguna Hills, CA: Aegean Park Press, 1979, pp. 128–136; William F. Friedman, *American Army Field Codes in the American Expeditionary Forces during the First World War*, Washington, DC: GPO, 1942.

TRIFID

A cryptosystem in which a letter or number is represented by some combination of three other letters, numbers, or symbols. The trinumeral alphabet attributed to Johannes Trithemius has a trifid form in which:

a = 111	e = 122	i = 133
b = 112	f = 123	j = 211
c = 113	g = 131	k = 212
d = 121	h = 132	l = 213, and so on.

See also: bifid; multifid; Trithemius, Johannes.
For further reading: William M. Bowers, *Practical Cryptanalysis: The Trifid Cipher*, American Cryptogram Association, 1961.

TRIGRAM

Also trigraph; a series of three letters occurring within a ciphertext. The presence of trigrams can provide clues to the analysis of a ciphertext because some three-letter combinations, in English or any other language, are more likely to occur than are other three-letter combinations. THE, AND, THA, ENT, and ION are, in descending order, the most common three-letter combinations found in English. The presence of the trigram gms in a ciphertext more commonly than any other trigram might, for example, suggest that it represents the plaintext THE, or in other words: g = T, m = H, and s = E.

See also: bigram.
For further reading: William F. Friedman, *Elements of Cryptanalysis*, Laguna Hills, CA: Aegean Park Press, 1976, sec. 6; Donald D. Millikin, *Elementary Cryptography and Cryptanalysis*, Laguna Hills, CA: Aegean Park Press, n.d., ch. 3.

TRINOME

A set of three numbers. For example, 548 is a trinome.

TRIPLE DES

See multiple encryption.

TRITHEMIUS, JOHANNES

German abbot, writer, and cryptologist, born as Johannes of Heidenberg, son of a vintner by the same name. He attended the University of Heidelberg on a scholarship for the poor, awarded because of the impression he made on the chancellor of the university. While attending Heidelberg, he took on the name *Trithemius*, by which he has been known ever since.

Soon after leaving Heidelberg, Trithemius (1462–1516) entered the Benedictine order and, at the age of 22, was elected abbot at the abbey of Saint Martin at Spanheim. Over the next decade, Trithemius wrote prolifically on a wide range of theological, historical, and biographical subjects. In 1494 he published the book for which he is probably best known, *Liber de scriptoribus ecclesiasticis*, a list of 7,000 theological works by 963 authors arranged chronologically. The book earned him the title of father of bibliography not because it was the first bibliography produced, but because it was the first scholarly work in the field.

In 1499, Trithemius began work on a second major project, a work that eventually included eight volumes: the *Steganographia* (Covered Writing). The work claimed to report on a discussion the abbot had with a spirit in a dream. It included discussions of magical, mysterious, occult, astrological, alchemical, and telepathic subjects. Religious friends to whom he showed the book were horrified at its subject matter. The work remained unpublished until 1606; three years later, it was placed on the Catholic Church's Index of Prohibited

Books, where it remained for more than two centuries.

Meanwhile, Trithemius turned his attention to the subject of cryptology in his book *Polygraphia* (Many Forms of Writing). The greatest portion of this 540-page text contains a code system in which each letter of the alphabet is represented by one or more Latin words. For example, the first page of the book contains the terms *Deus* and *clemens* as codewords for the letter *a*, and the terms *Creator* and *clementissimus* for the letter *b*. This system allowed the writing of an apparently innocuous message or prayer that encoded a secret message.

Book Five of the *Polygraphia* contains Trithemius's ideas on polyalphabetic substitution. He designed a 26 x 26 alphabetic matrix in which each row shifts one place to the left from the row above. The first few rows of the table, which Trithemius called a *tabula recta* (square table), looked like this (using English rather than Latin):

```
abcdefghijklmnopqrstuvwxyz
bcdefghijklmnopqrstuvwxyza
cdefghijklmnopqrstuvwxyzab
defghijklmnopqrstuvwxyzabc
efghijklmnopqrstuvwxyzabcd
```

To use this table, Trithemius suggested enciphering the first letter of the message with the first row of the table, the second letter of the message with the second row, the third letter of the message with the third row, and so on. Thus, to encipher the message DEPART AT FOUR, the first letter of the message (D) would be enciphered as *d*, the second letter (E) as *f*, the third letter (P) as *r*, the fourth letter (A) as *d*, and the fifth letter (R) as *v*, for a cipher word of dfrdv.

In this system, all 26 cipher alphabets are used before returning to the first alphabet, the first example in history of a progressive key.

See also: code; polyalphabetic substitution; progressive key.
For further reading: Noel L. Brann, *The Abbot Trithemius (1462–1516): The Renaissance of*

Monastic Humanism, Leiden: E. J. Brill, 1981; David Kahn, *The Codebreakers: The Story of Secret Writing,* New York: Macmillan, 1967, pp. 130–137; Peter Way, *Codes and Ciphers,* n.p.: Crescent Books, 1977, pp. 14–16.

TROJAN HORSE
See malicious software.

TRUSTED INTERMEDIARY
An entity through which two parties can communicate with each other securely without first generating a special key between themselves. Two common examples of trusted intermediaries are Key Distribution Centers and certification authorities.

See also: certification authority; fair cryptography; Key Distribution Center.
For further reading: Charlie Kaufman, Radia Perlman, and Mike Speciner, *Network Security: Private Communication in a Public World,* Englewood Cliffs, NJ: Prentice-Hall, 1995, pp. 188–196; U.S. Congress, Office of Technology Assessment, *Information Security and Privacy in Network Environments,* OTA-TCT-606, Washington, DC: GPO, September 1994, pp. 55–56, 77–78, 91–92.

TRUTH TABLE
A technique for determining the output of an operation given various possible

Input			Output
x_1	x_2	x_3	y
0	0	0	1
0	0	1	1
0	1	0	0
0	1	1	1
1	0	0	0
1	0	1	0
1	1	0	1
1	1	1	0

Figure 22

inputs. As an example, suppose that three inputs to a particular algorithm may have either one of two values, 0 or 1. The truth table providing the possible outputs for such a system is depicted in Figure 22.

See also: exclusive OR operation; modulo arithmetic.
For further reading: Henry Beker and Fred Piper, *Cipher Systems: The Protection of Communications,* New York: John Wiley & Sons, 1982, pp. 226–233.

TURING, ALAN
British mathematician and cryptanalyst. Turing (1912–1954) was born in London on 23 June 1912. He attended Sherborne School and King's College, Cambridge University, and was awarded his Ph.D. in mathematics by Princeton University in 1938. During World War II, Turing worked for the British Government Code & Cypher School at Bletchley Park on the German Enigma code system. He was in charge of a research team headquartered in Hut 8, responsible for breaking the naval version of the Enigma by which messages were transmitted to German surface and underwater vessels.

In 1940, Turing discovered that certain approaches to encryption were logically impossible within a particular ciphertext. Any time one of these logical contradictions occurred within a message, a large number of possible coding systems could be excluded. The application of this discovery reduced the possible number of encryption systems from hundreds of thousands to a few hundred.

Turing invented a machine called the bombe that would sort through thousands of possible coding systems every hour, looking for these logical inconsistencies. The bombe made it possible to speed up enormously the analysis and eventual deciphering of coded messages.

Turing's work led to the supply of up-to-date information on the location of and plans for German naval movements to the British navy and air force, allowing them to provide better protection for Allied shipping on the Atlantic. Experts generally agree that Turing's work on the naval Enigma almost certainly shortened the war and saved countless lives.

Turing is also famous as one of the inventors of the modern computer and as a pioneer in the field of artificial intelligence. However, after an unsuccessful effort to live as an openly gay man in a hostile social environment, Turing committed suicide in Manchester on 7 June 1954.

See also: Bletchley Park; bombe; Enigma; Government Code & Cypher School; Huts at Bletchley Park; Turing machine.
For further reading: Andrew Hodges, *Alan Turing: The Enigma*, New York: Simon & Schuster, 1983; Sara Turing, *Alan M. Turing*, Cambridge: W. Heffer & Sons, 1959; Hugh Whitemore, "Breaking the Code" (a play about Turing's life), Garden City, NY: Fireside Theatre, 1987.

TURING MACHINE

A device first suggested by the English mathematician Alan Turing in the 1930s. The Turing machine is regarded as the prototype of the modern computer. It consists essentially of an infinitely long supply of paper tape on which a machine performs essentially two operations. It can move the tape forward and backward, and it can write on and erase marks from the tape.

Despite the simple design of the Turing machine, it can carry out any operation performed by the most sophisticated existing computer. Because it embodies the basic function of any computer, it is often used by mathematicians in studying properties of mathematical systems such as cryptographic systems.

See also: Turing, Alan.
For further reading: Andrew Hodges, *Alan Turing: The Enigma*, New York: Simon & Schuster, 1983, pp. 96–99; Dominic Welsh, *Codes and Cryptography*, Oxford: Clarendon Press, 1988, pp. 141–143.

Alan Turing

TURNING GRILLE

See grille.

TWO-KEY CRYPTOGRAPHY

See public-key cryptography.

TWO-PART CODE

A type of code in which codewords or codenumbers are *not* written in some sequential order in relationship to plaintext words. The example below illustrates a two-part code.

APPEAR	3710	2357	MONDAY
APPOINT	1093	2358	RETREAT
ARMY	5581	2359	SUPPLIES
ARREST	7710	2360	CANNON
ARRIVE	0386	2361	NAVY
ARTILLERY	1203	2362	SUPPORT
ASSAULT	4611	2363	CONFIRM
ATTACK	0019	2364	THREE
AWAY	2351	2365	BERLIN

The encoder uses the column at the left, reading down to find the plaintext word to be encoded and then writing down the appropriate codenumber. The same column could be used only with great difficulty by the decoder, who might have to look through hundreds of terms before finding the correct codenumber. Instead, the right-hand column allows the decoder to look at the encoded message, read down the list of codenumbers arranged in sequence, and find the correct plaintext word corresponding to each codenumber.

See also: one-part code.
For further reading: William F. Friedman, *Elementary Military Cryptography*, Laguna Hills, CA: Aegean Park Press, 1976, ch. 8; Friedman, *Elements of Cryptanalysis*, Laguna Hills, CA: Aegean Park Press, 1976, pt. 2; Laurence Dwight Smith, *Cryptography: The Science of Secret Writing*, New York: W. W. Norton, 1943, ch. 5.

TYPEX

A sophisticated cipher machine used by the British in World War II to encipher many of their communications. The fundamental design of the Typex was based on the German Enigma machine invented by Arthur Scherbius toward the end of World War I. The Enigma machine was a revolutionary development in that it made use of electrical currents to encipher messages. The machine was widely advertised and demonstrated in the decade following its invention, so its fundamental operation was well known to most cryptologists.

During the 1920s, the British government purchased copies of the Enigma, studied its construction and operation, and developed its own modification. During World War II, the British army and royal air force used the Typex to encipher many, although by no means all, of its communications. The foreign office and the admiralty continued to rely on old-fashioned hand systems for their ciphers.

Historians of cryptology suggest that overall the Typex was a more effective cipher machine during the war than its parent, the Enigma. One important reason for this superiority was that, while the structure of the Enigma was generally well known by most cryptologists, the Typex had been developed essentially in secret and provided a more difficult challenge for enemy cryptanalysts.

See also: Enigma.
For further reading: Fred B. Wrixon, *Codes and Ciphers*, New York: Prentice-Hall, 1992, pp. 215–216.

ÜBCHI

Spelled both ÜBCHI and übchi; a famous double-columnar transposition cipher used by the Germans during World War I. Here are the steps in using the cipher:

1. A keyphrase is selected and the letters in the phrase numbered in alphabetical order.

   Keyphrase: WATCHMAN
   Numbering of letters: W = 8; A = 1; T = 7; C = 3; H = 4; M = 5; A = 2; N = 6.

2. The plaintext is written in columnar form under the numerical values of the keyphrase. Suppose that the plaintext message is DIVISION TEN STRIKES AT PARIS ON MONDAY. The enciphering block would look like this:

   ```
   8 1 7 3 4 5 2 6
   d i v i s i o n
   t e n s t r i k
   e s a t p a r i
   s o n m o n d a
   y
   ```

3. The vertical columns in the above table are taken off in the sequence indicated by the keynumber and written in horizontal order, again beneath the keynumber.

   ```
   8 1 7 3 4 5 2 6
   i e s o o i r d
   i s t m s t p o
   s t p o i r a n
   n k i a v n a n
   d t e s y w
   ```

The W added in the last row is chosen because the system calls for the addition of the same number of nulls as words in the keyphrase; in this case, one.

4. The letters are taken off once more in the sequence dictated by the keynumber and arranged in five-letter groups:

estkt rpaao moaso sivyi trnwd onnst pieii snd

For further reading: David Kahn, *The Codebreakers: The Story of Secret Writing*, New York: Macmillan, 1967, pp. 301–306.

ULTRA

Spelled both ULTRA and Ultra; the codename given to efforts by British cryptanalysts to solve codes and ciphers used by the Germans during World War II. Those efforts were carried out largely at Bletchley Park by members of the British Government Code & Cypher School and were aimed at solving both traditional German manual codes and the much more difficult machine-encrypted codes, such as those produced by the Enigma and Geheimschreiber machines.

See also: Bletchley Park; Enigma; Geheimschreiber; Government Code & Cypher School; Huts at Bletchley Park; Turing, Alan.
For further reading: Ralph Bennett, *Ultra in the West: The Normandy Campaign, 1944–45*, London: Hutchinson, 1979; Jeffrey K. Bray, *Ultra in the Atlantic*, 6 vols., Laguna Hills, CA: Aegean Park Press, n.d.; Harry

Hinsley, "The Enigma of Ultra," *History Today* (September 1993): 15–20; Ronald Lewin, *Ultra Goes to War: The First Accounts of World War II's Greatest Secret Based on Official Documents*, New York: McGraw-Hill, 1978; Bradley F. Smith, *The Ultra-Magic Deals and the Most Secret Special Relationship, 1940–1946*, Novato, CA: Presidio Press, 1993; Peter Way, *Codes and Ciphers*, n.p.: Crescent Books, 1977, ch. 5; Gordon Welchman, *The Hut Six Story: Breaking the Enigma Codes*, New York: McGraw-Hill, 1982; F. W. Winterbotham, *The Ultra Secret*, New York: Harper & Row, 1974.

THE ULTRA SECRET ━━━━━━

A book published in 1974 by British author F. W. Winterbotham that first revealed major features of the British effort during World War II to break the secret of the German military codes and its Enigma cipher machine.

See also: Enigma; Schmidt, Hans-Thilo; Turing, Alan; ULTRA.

UNBREAKABLE CIPHER ━━━━━━

A cipher that cannot be solved. Throughout history, a variety of individuals have invented cryptosystems that they regarded as unsolvable. Indeed, some have been so for various periods of time.

Eventually it became clear, however, that only one type of cipher is truly unbreakable: the one-time system. In a one-time system (such as a one-time pad or one-time tape), a plaintext message is enciphered with a key that is used only once and then destroyed, never to be used again. With such a system, a given ciphertext may be broken if both the key and ciphertext are available. But this solution is of no value, because the key will never be used again, and the recovery of another ciphertext will be as enigmatic as the first.

See also: Mauborgne, Joseph; one-time system; random number; Vernam, Gilbert.
For further reading: Henry Beker and Fred Piper, *Cipher Systems: The Protection of Communications*, New York: John Wiley & Sons, 1982, pp. 148–150.

UNICITY DISTANCE ━━━━━━

The length of a ciphertext, from which a cryptanalyst can reasonably expect to obtain only one meaningful decryption of the text.

See also: redundancy.
For further reading: Brian Beckett, *Introduction to Cryptology*, Oxford: Blackwell Scientific Publications, 1988, pp. 43–44; Henry Beker and Fred Piper, *Cipher Systems: The Protection of Communications*, New York: John Wiley & Sons, 1982, pp. 150–157; C. A. Deavours, "Unicity Points in Cryptanalysis," *Cryptologia* 1 (1977): 46–68; Carl H. Meyer and Stephen M. Matyas, *Cryptography: A New Dimension in Computer Data Security*, New York: John Wiley & Sons, 1982, pp. 608, 619–624, 729–733; Dominic Welsh, *Codes and Cryptography*, Oxford: Clarendon Press, 1988, pp. 116–122.

U.S. ARMY SIGNAL CORPS ━━━━━━

A branch of the U.S. Army created in 1861 to deal with new problems of communication, cryptography, and cryptanalysis created by the first widespread use of the telegraph during the Civil War. The Signal Corps was assigned responsibility for the development of codes and ciphers and for the interception and breaking of enemy codes and ciphers. The first chief signal officer was Gen. Albert J. Myer.

During the war, which lasted from 1861 to 1865, communication and cryptology functions were divided, sometimes with considerable acrimony, between Myer's Signal Corps and the U.S. Military Telegraph, headed by Anson Stager. At the war's conclusion, the Military Telegraph was dissolved, and the Signal Corps assumed exclusive responsibility for communication and cryptology functions in the army.

A history of the corps during the Spanish-American War provides a flavor of the kinds of activities for which it was responsible at the time. The corps was assigned responsibilities such as:

. . . to establish and maintain intercommunication between the territorial components of the nation, by submarine or overland telegraph and telephone; with its armies in the field, wherever they may be located; between the subdivisions of its armies, in camp, in campaign, and in battle, by visual signals and by flying or semi-permanent telegraph and telephone lines; and the gathering of such valuable military information as its command of the channels of communication may make possible. As its duties indicate, its work embraces the construction and operation of all military telegraph and telephone lines, the manipulation of submarine cables, the operation of captive balloons, visual signaling and telegraph censorship. (Howard A. Giddings, *Exploits of the Signal Corps in the War with Spain*. Kansas City, MO: Hudson-Kimberly Publishing Company, 1900.)

Over the next two decades, the cryptologic functions of the military were dispersed in a number of directions, some handled by the Signal Corps, some by MI8, and some by the adjutant general's office. During peacetime, especially in a world in which cryptology was not yet an issue of widespread concern, such decentralization posed no serious problems. But the potential for confusion and conflict in case of war was of greater concern.

An officer in the Signal Corps, Maj. Owen S. Albright, conducted a study of the code and cipher needs of the army in 1929. Albright concluded that all cryptographic and cryptanalytic functions should be centralized within a single office in the Signal Corps. Apparently at the suggestion of the chief of the Cipher Bureau, William F. Friedman, the new agency was given the title Signal Intelligence Service.

Led by Albert J. Myer, the U.S. Army Signal Corps was created specifically to study cryptography.

During World War II, most of the cryptologic functions of the Signal Corps remained under its administrative command, but were in point of fact under the control of the War Department. Four days after the war ended, the illogic of this arrangement was remedied when the Signal Intelligence Service (by then known as the Signal Intelligence Agency) and all cryptologic activities of the Signal Corps were merged into a new body, the Army Security Agency. That body, in turn, eventually evolved during the process of military service unification into today's National Security Agency.

For further reading: Paul J. Scheips, ed., *Military Signal Communications*, 2 vols., New York: Arno Press, 1980; George Raynor Thompson, et al., *The Signal Corps: The Test*, Washington, DC: GPO, 1957; George Raynor Thompson and Dixie R. Harris, *The Signal Corps: The Outcome*, Washington, DC: GPO, 1966.

U.S. COAST GUARD ━━━━━━━━

A division of the U.S. Department of Transportation. Created by an act of Congress in 1915, the Coast Guard was originally assigned two duties: protection of human life and patrolling the nation's coastlines to intercept illegal acts. Until the Prohibition Era, cryptology had a relatively modest role in Coast Guard activities, and the service had only one intelligence officer. With the increasing attempts to bring bootleg liquor into the country, however, cryptanalysis assumed a much more important role.

A common practice of ships carrying illegal shipments of liquor was to lie just outside the 12-mile territorial waters of the United States, contact land representatives by radio to establish a rendezvous site, deliver their goods to that site, and leave as quickly as possible. Radio communications could be monitored easily by the Coast Guard, so the bootleggers commonly transmitted their messages in code or cipher.

By the spring of 1927, the Coast Guard had intercepted hundreds of messages, but was unable to read them, seriously hampering its efforts to intercept bootlegger traffic. To help solve this issue, the Coast Guard hired Elizabeth Smith Friedman, wife of William F. Friedman, one of the great cryptologists in American history. Mrs. Friedman decrypted essentially all of the captured messages within a two-month period, providing the service with the key that allowed it to become much more effective in its interdiction. Once the Prohibition Era ended, cryptanalysis lost its importance to the Coast Guard.

For further reading: David Kahn, *The Codebreakers: The Story of Secret Writing*, New York: Macmillan, 1967, ch. 22.

U.S. MILITARY TELEGRAPH ━━━━━━━━

A quasi-military organization created in 1861 for the operation of commercial telegraph lines during the Civil War. The organization was disbanded at the end of the war, but during its short career the Military Telegraph achieved significant success in the development of ciphers and the transmission of messages between military units. At the same time, however, it was involved in an ongoing controversy with the newly created U.S. Army Signal Corps.

See also: Myer, Albert; Stager, Anson; U.S. Army Signal Corps.
For further reading: Wayne G. Barker, ed., *The History of Codes and Ciphers in the United States prior to World War I*, Laguna Hills, CA: Aegean Park Press, 1978, pp. 27–34; David Homer Bates, *Lincoln in the Telegraph Office*, New York: Century, 1907 (republished by the University of Nebraska Press, 1996); Harold C. Relyea, *Evolution and Organization of Intelligence Activities in the United States*, Laguna Hills, CA: Aegean Park Press, n.d., pp. 50–57; Paul J. Scheips, ed., *Military Signal Communications*, 2 vols., New York: Arno Press, 1980.

U.S. WAR DEPARTMENT TELEGRAPH CODES ━━━━━━━━

Codes and ciphers prepared by and for the use of the former U.S. War Department. The War Department merged with the Navy Department in 1947, forming the present cabinet department known as the Department of Defense.

The earliest known War Department Telegraph Code was prepared in 1885 by Lt. Col. J. F. Gregory. It was an adaptation of an existing commercial code known as the Telegraphic Code, originally prepared by Robert Slater in 1870. The code contained about 25,000 words in a one-part arrangement that required superencipherment by the addition or subtraction of a constant additive, 5555.

Revisions of the War Department Telegraph Code took place in 1899, 1902, 1906, 1915, and 1919, the primary motivation in most cases being economy. The 1899 code, for example, is said to have had "no security whatsoever," but was prepared strictly because of the "extraordinary telegraphic expenses" arising from the use of the 1885 code.

The level of sophistication of codes and ciphers up until—and even during— World War I was very low. The code in use when the war broke out, for example, had been prepared and printed by a commercial printer in Ohio, guaranteeing that it was essentially worthless for purposes of security. In sum, one historian of the period wrote that "the Army was without adequate cryptographic systems for the preserving [of] the security of its communications, [and] it also possessed no 'cryptanalytic service,' although there were among its officers a number who had studied this phase of cryptology to some extent."

At the conclusion of World War I, the latest version of the code, the *War Department Telegraph Code 1919*, was still in use, not for secret messages but for saving money on routine transmissions.

For further reading: Wayne G. Barker, ed., *The History of Codes and Ciphers in the United States during the Period between the World Wars, Part I: 1919–1929*, Laguna Hills, CA: Aegean Park Press, 1979, ch. 1; Barker, *The History of Codes and Ciphers in the United States during the Period between the World Wars, Part II: 1930–1939*, Laguna Hills, CA: Aegean Park Press, 1978, p. 36; Barker, *The History of Codes and Ciphers in the United States during World War I*, Laguna Hills, CA: Aegean Park Press, 1979, ch. 2; Barker, *The History of Codes and Ciphers in the United States prior to World War I*, Laguna Hills, CA: Aegean Park Press, 1978, ch. 6.

UNIVERSAL PRODUCT CODE (UPC) ⬤

A nonsecret code attached to many commercial products sold in the United States and other nations. The Universal Product Code was first suggested in the 1930s, but it did not become widely used until the 1970s. During the latter decade, grocery stores in particular began to recognize the advantages of stocking and selling products that carry a UPC.

One advantage is speed of checkout. Instead of looking at each individual product for a price and then ringing that price into a cash register by hand, a clerk simply passes the product over a scanner. The scanner shines a beam of light on the product code and reads its reflection. The information contained in the code is transmitted to the cash register, where the price of the item is recorded automatically.

A second advantage of the UPC is improved inventory control. When the scanner reads the code on an item, it also transmits to a central computer the fact that the item has been sold. The computer adjusts the inventory to reflect the sale of the item.

The UPC contains 12 digits consisting of four sets. The first set is a single digit indicating the general nature of the product. The digits currently assigned to the code are as follows:

0 = all national brand products with the exception of the specific categories listed below
2 = items with variable weights, such as meats and cheeses
3 = drugs, pharmaceuticals, and other medical and health products
4 = store-specific products (items offered specifically within a given store)

5 = coupons

6 & 7 = available for assignment to products as of the first quarter of 1990

The second set of digits consists of five numbers that identify the manufacturer of the item. Each manufacturer is assigned a specific code by the Uniform Code Council, the organization created in 1972 to oversee the development and management of the Universal Product Code system.

The third set of digits in the UPC also contains five numbers and identifies the specific product. These digits are established by the item's manufacturer and describe the item's nature, weight, size, color, expiration date, and other vital information.

The final digit in the UPC is a check-digit used to detect errors that may be present in the rest of the code.

The Universal Product Code is also referred to as a "bar code" because the digits of which it is made are represented on packages not only by numbers, but also by black lines (bars) of various thicknesses, specific combinations of which represent certain digits. Bars facilitate the scanning of the code by laser beams, and the numerical code assists human clerks in checking the UPC of an item.

The UPC was first used by grocery stores, and is probably still its most common application. However, the principle of bar codes can, in theory, be applied to virtually any product on which the bar code can be printed. Today, everything from books to television sets may carry a UPC.

For further reading: Lawrence E. Hicks, *The Universal Product Code*, New York: AMACOM, 1975.

USER AUTHENTICATION ━━━━━
See authentication.

UTAH DIGITAL SIGNATURE ACT OF 1995
See digital signature.

V

VARIANT BEAUFORT ▬▬▬▬▬

A form of polyalphabetic substitution closely related to both the Vigenère and Beaufort ciphers. The relationship among these three famous cryptosystems can be illustrated using the Vigenère tableau shown below.

```
a b c d e f g h i j k l m n o p q r s t u v w x y z
b c d e f g h i j k l m n o p q r s t u v w x y z a
c d e f g h i j k l m n o p q r s t u v w x y z a b
d e f g h i j k l m n o p q r s t u v w x y z a b c
e f g h i j k l m n o p q r s t u v w x y z a b c d
f g h i j k l m n o p q r s t u v w x y z a b c d e
g h i j k l m n o p q r s t u v w x y z a b c d e f
h i j k l m n o p q r s t u v w x y z a b c d e f g
i j k l m n o p q r s t u v w x y z a b c d e f g h
j k l m n o p q r s t u v w x y z a b c d e f g h i
k l m n o p q r s t u v w x y z a b c d e f g h i j
l m n o p q r s t u v w x y z a b c d e f g h i j k
m n o p q r s t u v w x y z a b c d e f g h i j k l
n o p q r s t u v w x y z a b c d e f g h i j k l m
o p q r s t u v w x y z a b c d e f g h i j k l m n
p q r s t u v w x y z a b c d e f g h i j k l m n o
q r s t u v w x y z a b c d e f g h i j k l m n o p
r s t u v w x y z a b c d e f g h i j k l m n o p q
s t u v w x y z a b c d e f g h i j k l m n o p q r
t u v w x y z a b c d e f g h i j k l m n o p q r s
u v w x y z a b c d e f g h i j k l m n o p q r s t
v w x y z a b c d e f g h i j k l m n o p q r s t u
w x y z a b c d e f g h i j k l m n o p q r s t u v
x y z a b c d e f g h i j k l m n o p q r s t u v w
y z a b c d e f g h i j k l m n o p q r s t u v w x
z a b c d e f g h i j k l m n o p q r s t u v w x y
```

(The Beaufort table differs slightly from the Vigenère tableau by having an extra row at the bottom and an extra column at the right, but this difference does not affect the description that follows.)

Assume that the plaintext message to be enciphered begins with the words SEND TROOPS TO . . . and the key to be used is the word FIGHT. In the Vigenère system, the first row contains the letters in the keyword or keyphrase, and the first column contains the letters in the plaintext. The body of the tableau itself contains the ciphertext letters.

To encipher the above message using the Vigenère method, find the first letter of the keyword (F) in the first row, the first letter of the plaintext (S) in the first column, and then find the equivalent ciphertext letter at the intersection of the F column and the S row. That letter is *x*. Continuing by this method, the ciphertext produced by the Vigenère method is xmtkm wwuwl yw.

In the Beaufort cipher, the first column of the table contains the letters of the plaintext, and the first row contains the letters of the ciphertext. The letters that make up the body of the table are the letters in the keyword or keyphrase. To encipher the same message with the same keyword, look down the first column for the first word of the plaintext (S). Then read across the S row until the first letter of the keyword (F) is found. Finally, read up the F column to the top of the table to find the first letter of the ciphertext *(n)*. Continuing this procedure, the ciphertext produced by the Beaufort method would be netem oussb vu.

Finally, in the Variant Beaufort system, the first column of the table contains the letters of the keyword or keyphrase, the body of the table contains the plaintext letters, and the first row of the table contains the ciphertext letters. The first letter of the above message (S) would be enciphered by looking down the first column to find the first letter of the keyword (F), reading across to the S column, and looking at the top of that column for the first ciphertext letter (*n*). Continuing this procedure, the ciphertext produced by the Variant Beaufort method would be nwhwa mgiiz og.

The Vigenère and Variant Beaufort are reciprocal systems to each other because encipherment of a message in one system is equivalent to decipherment in the other system of the same message in enciphered form. In contrast, the Beaufort cipher is internally reciprocal in that encipherment and decipherment both take place by way of the key, which is buried within the body of the tableau itself.

See also: Beaufort, Adm. Sir Francis; Vigenère square.
For further reading: Helen Fouché Gaines, *Cryptanalysis: A Study of Ciphers and Their Solution*, New York: Dover Publications, 1956, pp. 121–125; Laurence Dwight Smith, *Cryptography: The Science of Secret Writing*, New York: W. W. Norton, 1943, pp. 80–81.

VERNAM, GILBERT

American cryptologist and inventor, probably best known for his invention of the first automated system of cryptography.

Vernam was born in Brooklyn in 1890. He worked for the American Telephone & Telegraph Company (AT&T) on methods to make transmissions via the teletypewriter (a printing telegraph) more secure. This led to the idea for an automated system of encipherment.

The teletypewriter is a machine in which a message can be typed directly onto a conventional typewriter keyboard and transmitted without further human assistance across telegraph lines to a receiving telegraph. The principle behind the teletypewriter is that the striking of a key by the human operator activates an electrical switch, causing one or more metal pins to punch out holes in a paper strip. The code used by the machine is

the familiar Baudot code, in which five positions on a tape may be punched out or not punched out. The total number of symbols that can be represented by the Baudot code, then, is 32 (2^5). The 32 positions represent the 26 letters of the English alphabet plus six control characters (such as "shift" or "return").

If the operator strikes the *k* key on the typewriter keyboard, for example, pins are activated within the machine to punch out holes in the first four of the five possible positions on the paper tape: hole hole hole hole no-hole. Another way to represent this configuration is by binary notation: 11110.

Once the plaintext message has been punched into the paper tape, the tape is run through a device with metal pins arranged at all possible Baudot positions above the tape and an electrical contact below the tape. When the pins drop onto the tape, they pass through holes in the tape, making an electrical contact and sending an electrical pulse through the wire. If a pin encounters a no-hole space, however, it does not penetrate the paper tape, does not make contact with the plate below, and does not initiate an electrical pulse in the circuit. The hole hole hole hole no-hole designation on the tape, therefore, is converted into a pulse pulse pulse pulse no-pulse signal in the telegraph circuit.

At the receiving end, this process is reversed. Electrical pulses arrive at the receiving set, activate tiny punches that penetrate a new paper tape, making holes. The absence of a pulse results in the formation of a no-hole condition, of course. A second machine passes pins through the newly made holes in the paper tape, forming contacts such as 11110, which it is able to read and print as the letter *k*.

As with any form of telegraphic communication, a concern of senders and receivers of messages is how secure they are. It is a relatively simple process to tap into a telegraphic communication and read off the message.

Two Russian women study the transmitted message coming over the teletype, one of Gilbert Vernam's most significant contributions to cryptography.

The wiring of the teletypewriter could be modified rather easily so that the striking of the k key (for example) might actually result in the printout of a different key, such as the q letter. But a monoalphabetic substitution of this type is also decrypted rather easily.

Vernam's great contribution was to develop a system by which the message typed into a teletypewriter could simultaneously be enciphered in a rather secure fashion. His idea was to attach a second paper tape to the machine that read holes in the paper tape and converted them to electrical signals at the sending end of the system. The second tape also used the Baudot code with holes or no-holes in each of the five possible spaces for every position on the tape. The second, or key tape, could then be enciphered in the same way as the plaintext message tape. Vernam also devised a code that indicated how various combinations of holes and no-holes would be read by the machine. He said that the

combination of two like symbols (two holes or two no-holes) would produce a no-hole, while the combination of two unlike symbols (one hole and one no-hole) would produce a hole. In binary notation:

$$0 + 0 = 0$$
$$1 + 0 = 1$$
$$1 + 1 = 0$$
$$0 + 1 = 0$$

Imagine now that one paper tape containing the plaintext message indicated by P below is passed through the reading machine. At the same time, a second paper tape containing the key indicated by K below is passed through the same machine. According to the rules previously described, the combinations of holes and no-holes will produce a ciphertext designated as C below as:

```
P  1  0  0  1  0
K  1  1  0  0  1
─────────────────
C  0  1  0  1  1
```

In this example, the plaintext sequence 10010 represents the letter *d,* while the ciphertext sequence 01011 represents the letter *g.* The encipherment of the letter (and, of course, the whole message) was accomplished simply by having the operator type in the plaintext letter.

Vernam's invention was a brilliant breakthrough in cryptography. However, it contained some aspects that made it decryptable without unreasonable effort. Changes made by Maj. Joseph Mauborgne of the U.S. Army Signal Corps made it possible to employ the Vernam system as one of the few truly unbreakable ciphers.

Vernam continued to invent cryptographic devices, receiving 65 patents for his ideas. At one time or another, he worked for International Communication Laboratories (a division of AT&T), the Postal Telegraph Cable Company, Western Union, and various branches of the U.S. armed forces. He died in Hackensack, New Jersey, on 7 February 1960.

See also: Baudot code; Mauborgne, Joseph; one-time system; unbreakable cipher.
For further reading: D. W. Davies and W. L. Price, *Security for Computer Networks: An Introduction to Data Security in Teleprocessing and Electronic Funds Transfer,* Chichester: John Wiley & Sons, 1984, pp. 38–40; "G. S. Vernam," *New York Times* (10 February 1960): 37; David Kahn, *The Codebreakers: The Story of Secret Writing,* New York: Macmillan, 1967, ch. 13; Carl H. Meyer and Stephen M. Matyas, *Cryptography: A New Dimension in Computer Data Security,* New York: John Wiley & Sons, 1982, pp. 53–61; G. S. Vernam, "Cipher Printing Telegraph Systems for Secret Wire and Radio Telegraphic Communications," *American Institute of Electrical Engineers Journal* (February 1926): 109–115.

VERNE, JULES ━━━━━━━━

French novelist perhaps best known for his science fiction works. Verne (1828–1905) introduced cryptologic themes in three of his works: *Voyage to the Center of the Earth, La*

Jangada, and *Mathias Sandorff.* In the first of these, the story opens with Professor Otto Lidenbrock discovering an old piece of parchment on which a cryptographic message is written. He converts the runic characters to Roman letters, but is still unable to decipher the message. A short time later, his nephew accidentally discovers that the message is actually written in Latin letters that have been reversed. The cryptogram carries a pregnant message: "Descend the crater of the volcano of Sneffels when the shadow of [Mount] Scartaris comes to caress it before the calends of July, audacious voyager," it says, "and you will reach the center of the earth. I have done it. [signed] Arne Saknussemm." The challenge is all that Lidenbrock and his colleagues need to set them off on the voyage that is the subject of the book.

For further reading: E. F. Bleiler, "Jules Verne and Cryptography," *Extrapolation* (Spring 1986): 5–18; W. F. Friedman, "Jules Verne as Cryptographer," *Signal Corps Bulletin* (April–June 1940): 70–107; Frederick Gass, "Solving a Jules Verne Cryptogram," *Mathematics Magazine* (February 1986): 3–11; Charles W. R. Hooker, "The Jules Verne Cipher," *The Police Journal* (January 1931): 107–119; André Lange and E.-A. Soudart, *Traité de cryptographie,* Paris: Librairie Felix Alcan, 1925, app.

VIARIS, MARQUIS G. H. L. DE ━━━━━

An early proponent of the concept of expressing cryptologic ideas in mathematical terms. In a series of articles in the scientific journal *Le Génie Civil* in 1888, de Viaris (1847–1901) suggested that the encipherment and decipherment of ciphertexts could be viewed as a mathematical equation in which any plaintext letter is represented by the letter c, any keyletter by the Greek letter γ, and any ciphertext letter by the Greek letter χ. The enciphering process using a Vigenère system, for example, could be represented by the following equation:

$$c + \gamma = \chi$$

De Viaris's suggestion represented a remarkable piece of foresight; it was one of the earliest suggestions for converting the problem of changing literal ciphers into numerical ciphers in a way that would allow them to be manipulated by standard mathematical operations. As such, it marks a turning point in the fundamental processes of cryptology, from primarily manipulating letters to the processing of numerical expressions. Unfortunately, the idea arrived before cryptologists quite knew what to do with it, and it fell into oblivion for more than half a century.

De Viaris also designed a cipher machine that would print out an enciphered message at the touch of a button. He is also famous for an ongoing controversy with another famous cryptologist of the time, Étienne Bazeries, over a cipher machine that Bazeries designed and built.

See also: Brazeries, Étienne; cipher machine; Hill, Lester; Vigenère square.

For further reading: For a list of de Viaris's writings, *see* Joseph S. Galland, *Bibliography of the Literature of Cryptology*, Laguna Hills, CA: Aegean Park Press, n.d., pp. 192–193.

VIGENÈRE, BLAISE DE ━━━━━━

A French diplomat and cryptographer. Vigenère was born in the village of Saint-Pourçain (between Paris and Marseilles) on 5 April 1523. At the age of 17, Vigenère entered diplomatic service, an occupation he followed for the next 30 years. During this time he served in the court of the Duke of Nevers and made a number of trips to Rome, where he became familiar with cryptographers working for the papal curia. He retired in 1570 and turned his attention to writing, eventually publishing more than 20 books on a variety of topics, the most famous of which was his treatise on ciphers, *Traicté des Chiffres*. The book not only attempted

to summarize current knowledge on cryptography, but also contains, according to David Kahn, "a hodgepodge of other topics," including "the first European representation of Japanese ideograms . . . the foundations of alchemy, licit and illicit magic, the secrets of the kabbalah, the mysteries of the universe, recipes for making gold, and philosophic speculations."

One of the topics *not* discussed in the book was cryptanalysis, which Vigenère regarded as "a worthless cracking of the brain." Instead, he focused on a review of and improvement on systems of polyalphabetic substitution, as proposed earlier by Johannes Trithemius, Giovanni Porta, and Girolamo Cardano. Vigenère's system consisted of a square table like the *tabula recta* of Trithemius, along with an autokey similar to that developed by Cardano. *See* **Vigenère square** for a discussion of the table.

Vigenère's autokey was an improvement on Cardano's for two reasons. First, he did not begin the key over again with each new word, as had Cardano. For example, in enciphering the message HOW MANY TROOPS ARE LEAVING, Cardano would have used the following system:

KEY:
how howm howman how howmany
PLAIN:
HOW MANY TROOPS ARE LEAVING
CIPHER:
lql jiek ticzei kom crkabcq

This system opens the possibility of certain repetitions that make cryptanalysis relatively easy. Instead, Vigenère would allow the key to continue running from word to word, as follows:

KEY:
rhowmanytroopsareleavin
PLAIN:
HOWMANYTROOPSARELEAVING
CIPHER:
yvkimnlrkfcdhsrvppevdvt

The first letter in the key, *r*, represents the second improvement made by Vigenère: the priming key. This was a single letter, known to both encipherer and decipherer, that defined the alphabet used to encipher the first letter of plaintext. With this information, the decipherer would be able to decipher the second letter of the cipher, which was used to encipher the second letter of plaintext, and so on.

In a peculiar twist of history, the important improvements made by Vigenère on the work of his predecessors were largely lost or ignored in the decades following his death, and he is remembered instead for his much simpler accomplishment, the Vigenère square. Vigenère died of throat cancer in 1596.

See also: autokey; Cardano, Girolamo; Porta, Giovanni; running key; Trithemius, Johannes; Vigenère square.
For further reading: Brian Beckett, *Introduction to Cryptology,* Oxford: Blackwell Scientific Publications, 1988, pp. 146–154; Helen Fouché Gaines, *Cryptanalysis: A Study of Ciphers and Their Solution,* New York: Dover Publications, 1956, ch. 12; David Kahn, *The Codebreakers: The Story of Secret Writing,* New York: Macmillan, 1967, pp. 145–150; Charles J. Mendelsohn, "Blaise de Vigenère, and the 'Chiffre Carré,'" *Proceedings of the American Philosophical Society* (22 March 1940): 103–129; Donald D. Millikin, *Elementary Cryptography and Cryptanalysis,* Laguna Hills, CA: Aegean Park Press, n.d., ch. 14; Fletcher Pratt, *Secret and Urgent: The Story of Codes and Ciphers,* Garden City, NY: Blue Ribbon Books, 1942, passim; Laurence Dwight Smith, *Cryptography: The Science of Secret Writing,* New York: W. W. Norton, 1943, pp. 69–82; http://rschp2. anu.edu.au:8080/vignere.html.

VIGENÈRE SQUARE

A cryptosystem ascribed to Blaise de Vigenère that consists of a 26 x 26 matrix for use in making polyalphabetic substitution ciphers. The attribution is not an entirely correct one, however, since Vigenère actually produced considerably more complex systems of encipherment that were either lost or ignored for many years after his death. Nonetheless, the Vigenère square has been described by David Kahn as "probably the most famous cipher system of all time."

A Vigenère square is shown below. Note that it consists of 26 cipher alphabets, each shifted by one letter from the one above it.

```
Plaintext: A B C D E F G H I J K L M N O P Q R S T U V W X Y Z
           a b c d e f g h i j k l m n o p q r s t u v w x y z
           b c d e f g h i j k l m n o p q r s t u v w x y z a
           c d e f g h i j k l m n o p q r s t u v w x y z a b
           d e f g h i j k l m n o p q r s t u v w x y z a b c
           e f g h i j k l m n o p q r s t u v w x y z a b c d
           f g h i j k l m n o p q r s t u v w x y z a b c d e
           g h i j k l m n o p q r s t u v w x y z a b c d e f
           h i j k l m n o p q r s t u v w x y z a b c d e f g
           i j k l m n o p q r s t u v w x y z a b c d e f g h
           j k l m n o p q r s t u v w x y z a b c d e f g h i
           k l m n o p q r s t u v w x y z a b c d e f g h i j
           l m n o p q r s t u v w x y z a b c d e f g h i j k
           m n o p q r s t u v w x y z a b c d e f g h i j k l
           n o p q r s t u v w x y z a b c d e f g h i j k l m
           o p q r s t u v w x y z a b c d e f g h i j k l m n
           p q r s t u v w x y z a b c d e f g h i j k l m n o
           q r s t u v w x y z a b c d e f g h i j k l m n o p
           r s t u v w x y z a b c d e f g h i j k l m n o p q
           s t u v w x y z a b c d e f g h i j k l m n o p q r
           t u v w x y z a b c d e f g h i j k l m n o p q r s
           u v w x y z a b c d e f g h i j k l m n o p q r s t
           v w x y z a b c d e f g h i j k l m n o p q r s t u
           w x y z a b c d e f g h i j k l m n o p q r s t u v
           x y z a b c d e f g h i j k l m n o p q r s t u v w
           y z a b c d e f g h i j k l m n o p q r s t u v w x
           z a b c d e f g h i j k l m n o p q r s t u v w x y
```

In order to use the Vigenère square, a keyword is also needed. For purposes of illustration, suppose that the keyword is CONQUEST. The keyword is written above the plaintext of the message as often as necessary, as shown below:

KEYWORD:
```
c o n q u  e s t  c o n q u e s  t c o n q u
```
PLAIN:
```
O R D E R  S I X  H U N D R E D  C O P I E S
```

To obtain the ciphertext, read down the first column at the left until you come to the keyletter *c* and read across to the column under the plainletter *O*. The cipher letter indicated at the intersection of this row and column is *q,* the first letter of the ciphertext. Repeating this process for each letter in the plaintext produces the following ciphertext:

KEYWORD:
    c o n q u   e s t   c o n q u e s   t c o n q u
PLAIN:
    O R D E R   S I X   H U N D R E D   C O P I E S
CIPHER:
    q f q u l   w a q   j i a t l i v   v q d v u m

Normally, this ciphertext would then be rewritten in five-letter blocks, as qfqul waqji atliv vqdvu mjezb, with nulls added to complete the final block.

In order to decipher a message enciphered with this system, only the keyword is needed because the Vigenère square itself is always the same.

> See also: Beaufort, Adm. Sir Francis; polyalphabetic substitution; Variant Beaufort.
>
> For further reading: Wayne G. Barker, ed., *The History of Codes and Ciphers in the United States prior to World War I*, Laguna Hills, CA: Aegean Park Press, 1978, pp. 84–97; Brian Beckett, *Introduction to Cryptology*, Oxford: Blackwell Scientific Publications, 1988, pp. 146–154; Henry Beker and Fred Piper, *Cipher Systems: The Protection of Communications*, New York: John Wiley & Sons, 1982, pp. 32–34, passim; William F. Friedman, *Elementary Military Cryptography*, Laguna Hills, CA: Aegean Park Press, 1976, pp. 54–59; Helen Fouché Gaines, *Cryptanalysis: A Study of Ciphers and Their Solution*, New York: Dover Publications, 1956, ch. 12; David Kahn, *The Codebreakers: The Story of Secret Writing*, New York: Macmillan, 1967, pp. 145–150; Donald D. Millikin, *Elementary Cryptography and Cryptanalysis*, Laguna Hills, CA: Aegean Park Press, n.d., ch. 14; Laurence Dwight Smith, *Cryptography: The Science of Secret Writing*, New York: W. W. Norton, 1943, pp. 69–82.

VIRUS ━━━━━━
See malicious software.

VOWEL CIPHER ━━━━━━
A variation of a Polybius square in which the vowels *a, e, i, o,* and *u* are used in place of numbers along the edges of the square, as shown below.

	A	E	I	O	U
A	a	b	c	d	e
E	f	g	h	ij	k
I	l	m	n	o	p
O	q	r	s	t	u
U	v	w	x	y	z

Using this system, the word HAZARD would be enciphered as

IE AA UU AA EO OA

See also: Polybius.

VOYNICH MANUSCRIPT ━━━━━━
A text of about 200 manuscript pages that has been called "the world's most mysterious manuscript." It was purchased by Rudolph II, Holy Roman Emperor, in 1586 for the considerable sum of 600 gold ducats. Rudolph believed that the manuscript had been written by the English philosopher and scientist Roger Bacon in the thirteenth century and that it contained, in ciphertext, a formula for the preparation of an elixir of life, a liquid that would provide eternal youth.

Decipherment of the manuscript proved to be more difficult than Rudolph's scholars could manage, however, and it remained untranslated when Rudolph abdicated in 1611. It passed to Rudolph's botanist, Jacobus de Tepenecz, and later to Marcus Marci, rector of the University of Prague. Eventually the manuscript disappeared from sight for two and half centuries, only to resurface in 1912 when it was brought for sale to an eminent rare-book dealer, Wilfrid Voynich. Voynich encouraged cryptanalysts to try their hand at deciphering the manuscript, and many made the effort. The text appears to be written in a relatively simple style common among late-medieval texts. But the experts to whom Voynich sent copies of the manuscript were unable to crack the code, nor has anyone been successful to this day.

This does not mean that the manuscript is still a complete mystery. Authorities have figured out the meaning of many of the hundreds of sketches of plants, animals, and astronomical objects. They know that the basic alphabet used in the book is a form of numerology, and they have determined that the manuscript was written not in the thirteenth century (and therefore not by Bacon) but in the sixteenth. Even so, the text itself remains as obscure to modern readers as it was to Rudolph and his scholars in the 1600s.

For further reading: Robert S. Brumbaugh, *The Most Mysterious Manuscript: The Voynich "Roger Bacon" Cipher Manuscript,* Carbondale and Edwardsville: Southern Illinois University Press, 1978; John Matthews Manly, "The Most Mysterious Manuscript in the World: Did Roger Bacon Write It and Has the Key Been Found?" *Harper's Magazine* (June 1921): 186–197; Manly, "Roger Bacon and the Voynich Manuscript," *Speculum* (July 1931): 345–391; Peter Way, *Codes and Ciphers,* n.p.: Crescent Books, 1977, pp. 138–141; http://www.cs.ruu.nl/wais/html/na-dir/puzzles/archive/cryptology.html.

W

WALLIS, JOHN

One of the great, if not the greatest, English mathematicians of the seventeenth century. He was responsible for the establishment of the first English black chamber. Wallis was born in Ashford, Kent, on 3 December 1616 and died at Oxford on 8 November 1703. He was ordained as a clergyman in 1640, and earned bachelor's and master's degrees at Cambridge with the goal of becoming a physician. His career was interrupted, however, by the English civil war of 1642–1649, during which he gained great fame as a cryptanalyst. He solved (in many cases with considerable ease) enciphered dispatches sent between King Charles I and his commanders in the field. Some historians claim that Wallis's cipher solutions were crucial in the case developed by the Parliament against Charles, which resulted in the king's execution.

Even though Wallis ended up on the losing side of the civil war, he was retained by Charles II, at least partly because the mathematician voted against the execution of the new king's father. Without question, Wallis's cryptanalytic skills were also a factor in Charles's decision to offer him a court post.

Wallis's talents were even more fully utilized after William and Mary assumed the throne in 1689. William's secretary of war, the earl of Nottingham, flooded Wallis with enciphered dispatches from France, Poland, Prussia, and other European states for crypt-analysis. Because of his many accomplishments in the field, Wallis is generally regarded as the father of English cryptology.

See also: black chamber.
For further reading: David Kahn, *The Codebreakers: The Story of Secret Writing*, New York: Macmillan, 1967, pp. 166–169; David E. Smith, "John Wallis as a Cryptographer," *Bulletin of the American Mathematical Society* 24 (1917): 83–96; Peter Way, *Codes and Ciphers*, n.p.: Crescent Books, 1977, pp. 26–27; E. T. Williams and Helen M. Palmer, *Dictionary of National Biography*, Oxford: Oxford University Press, 1971, vol. 59, pp. 141–145.

WEATHER MAP SYMBOLS

Letters, numbers, and symbols used to indicate weather conditions on weather maps. The symbolic representation of current weather conditions has become a highly complex system that extends far beyond the relatively familiar symbols for "high" (H), "low" (C), cold front, warm front, and the like. Today, a whole host of weather conditions are first encoded in a standard symbolic form and then converted to a numerical code for transmission between stations.

As an example, the following is the general format of a message in symbolic form:

$$\text{iii Nddff VVwwWPPPTT } N_h C_L h C_M C_H T_d T_d \text{ a pp 7 RR } R_1 \text{ s}$$

Each of these symbols represents a particular weather condition as, for example:

iii = station number for the reporting station

N = total amount of cloud cover (ranges from 0 to 8)

dd = direction from which wind is blowing; the direction is given as an angular measurement, from 0° to 360°, with the final zero omitted. Thus 230° is written as 23

ff = wind speed, in knots

VV = visibility in miles and fractions of miles

The measured values for each of these weather conditions is then encoded as a number in the same general format as shown above. An encoded message might read, for example, as follows:

405 83220 12716 24731 67292 30228 74542

In this code, the first three digits, 405, represents the station number, iii. The next digit, 8, represents cloud cover (complete). The next four digits represent the wind direction and wind speed (32 = 320°) and 20 = 20 knots. The next two digits represent visibility (12 = 12 miles), and so on.

When these weather conditions are actually plotted on a weather map, they are converted once more to a set of symbols with which any trained meteorologist is familiar. Figure 23 shows only a few of the many standard symbols used to represent weather conditions on a weather map.

For further reading: C. Donald Ahrens, *Meteorology Today*, 2d edition, St. Paul, MN: West Publishing, 1985, app. B; Joe R. Eagleman, *Meteorology: The Atmosphere in Action*, 2nd edition, Belmont, CA: Wadsworth Publishing Company, 1985.

WHEATSTONE, CHARLES

English physicist and inventor. Although lacking formal training in the sciences, Wheatstone (1802–1875) had a creative and active mind, and he produced a number of useful inventions. He constructed an electromagnetic telegraph some years before Morse, researched and wrote on acoustics and electromagnetism, and invented the concertina, an accordionlike musical instrument. He is best known today for the Wheatstone bridge, a device for measuring small electrical currents. Although Wheatstone was not the inventor of the device, he demonstrated its usefulness and his name eventually became associated with it.

Wheatstone's contribution in the field of cryptology was also not entirely original. He designed a cipher disk similar to one built by the Italian cryptologist Leon Battista Alberti and a more recent one by U.S. Army officer Decius Wadsworth. Wheatstone's cipher disk consisted of two concentric disks, one larger than the other, joined to each other at their center. The outer disk was divided into 27 sections for the 26 letters of the English alphabet plus one blank space. The inner disk was divided into 26 sections, into which were inscribed the 26 letters of the alphabet in a scrambled sequence. Attached to the disks were two hands, like the hands on a clock, the longer pointing to the outer disk and the shorter to the inner disk.

To encipher a message, the longer hand was placed on the blank space with

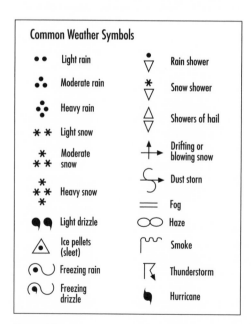

Figure 23

the shorter hand aligned immediately below. The longer hand was pivoted until it pointed to the first letter of plaintext. A gear mechanism joining the long and short hands caused the shorter hand to move to some position on the inner disk, where it pointed at the first cipher letter of the message. The longer hand was then moved sequentially to each of the following letters of the first word, with the shorter hand thereby spelling out the first cipher word. At the end of the first word, the long hand was reset on the blank space and the whole process repeated for the second, third, and successive words of the message.

Although Wheatstone cannot claim credit for originating the cipher disk, he produced another important accomplishment in cryptology: a cipher designed for use with the telegraph. Ironically, just as he received more credit than was his due for the cipher disk he invented, he received less credit for the telegraph cipher, which is now known as the Playfair cipher.

See also: Alberti, Leon Battista; cipher disk; Playfair cipher.
For further reading: Donald W. Davies, "Charles Wheatstone's Cryptograph and Pletts' Cipher Machine," *Cryptologia* (April 1985): 155–161; Roy Porter, ed., *The Biographical Dictionary of Scientists,* 2nd ed., New York: Oxford University Press, 1994, pp. 717–718.

WIGWAG CODE
See Myer, Albert.

"WINDS" CODE
An open code devised by the Japanese Foreign Office in 1941 for distribution to its agents in the United States. The code made use of certain wind and weather forecasts to indicate impending changes in the status of diplomatic relationships between the two countries. As contained in Circular 2353 sent to Washington on 19 November of that year, the code was explained as follows:

Charles Wheatstone's cipher wheel, a device similar to Leon Battista Alberti's cipher disk.

Regarding the broadcast of a special message in an emergency.

In case of emergency (danger of cutting off our diplomatic relations), and the cutting off of international communications, the following warning will be added in the middle of the daily Japanese language short-wave news broadcast:

1) In case of Japan-U.S. relations in danger: HIGASHI NO KAZE AME ("east wind rain")

2) Japan-U.S.S.R. relations: KITA NO KAZE KUMORI ("north wind cloudy")

3) Japan-British relations: NISHI NO KAZE HARE ("west wind clear")

This signal will be given in the middle and at the end as a weather forecast and each sentence will be repeated twice. When this is heard please destroy all code papers, etc. This is as yet to be a completely secret arrangement.

Forward as urgent intelligence.

Circular 2353 was originally sent from Tokyo to Washington encrypted in the Japanese code known to U.S. cryptanalysts as J-19. Naval cryptanalysts decrypted it soon after it reached the United States, and the code became part of the information possessed by the U.S. military with regard to possible Japanese plans to attack the United States. It is unclear, however, as to whether the winds code was actually used in preparation for the attack on Pearl Harbor.

See also: open code.
For further reading: David Kahn, *The Code-breakers: The Story of Secret Writing*, New York: Macmillan, 1967, ch. 1.

WORK FACTOR

A measure of the amount of effort that must be expended in order to break a cryptographic algorithm. Although there is no universally accepted mathematical definition of work factor, the term generally refers to the number of hours of computer time, the time spent by a cryptanalyst or cryptanalytic team, the number of mathematical and/or logical operations that need to be carried out, or the calendar time in days, weeks, months, or years required to break the algorithm. The bottom-line consideration in determining work factor is the financial cost needed to achieve a breakthrough.

In dealing with an algorithm, the goal of a cryptographer, obviously, is to increase the work factor to some maximum possible level. Even if the algorithm is not unbreakable in either a theoretical or practical sense, it can still be considered unbreakable if the work factor is large enough to discourage a cryptanalyst from even attempting to break the system.

See also: unbreakable cipher.
For further reading: Carl H. Meyer and Stephen M. Matyas, *Cryptography: A New Dimension in Computer Data Security*, New York: John Wiley & Sons, 1982, pp. 18–19.

WORLD WIDE WEB

An international network for the exchange of information among individuals, corporations, government agencies, and other entities. Considerable overlap now exists between the World Wide Web and the Internet, and some experts predict that the two will eventually become essentially coterminous.

See also: Internet.
For further reading: Bill Eager, *Using the World Wide Web*, Indianapolis: Que Corp., 1994.

WORM

See malicious software.

XOR (EXCLUSIVE OR) GATE ▬▬▬▬▬

A logic statement relating two quantities that have mutually exclusive values, such as yes or no. The XOR gate is used in computer operations because it reflects the two opposite conditions that may exist in the state of a computer component: on or off. Since these conditions are normally represented in binary arithmetic, the two exclusive conditions are 1 and 0.

The XOR gate is used to represent various combinations of the two conditions, as follows:

If $A = 1$ and $B = 0$, then $A \oplus B = 1$
If $A = 0$ and $B = 1$, then $A \oplus B = 1$
If $A = 1$ and $B = 1$, then $A \oplus B = 0$
If $A = 0$ and $B = 0$, then $A \oplus B = 0$

See also: binary number system; modulo arithmetic.

For further reading: Brian Beckett, *Introduction to Cryptology*, Oxford: Blackwell Scientific Publications, 1988, pp. 237–242; Henry Beker and Fred Piper, *Cipher Systems: The Protection of Communications*, New York: John Wiley & Sons, 1982, pp. 166–168, 180–188.

YARDLEY, HERBERT O. ━━━━━

American cryptologist, founder of the first U.S. code and cipher department, and author of *The American Black Chamber*. Yardley is one of the heroic figures of American cryptology, his life filled with astounding accomplishments and heartbreaking disappointments. He was born in Worthington, Indiana, on 13 April 1890, and soon demonstrated a bright, inquisitive mind. Popular with his classmates, he was elected president of the senior class, captain of the football team, and editor of the school newspaper.

Yardley's first job was as a railroad telegrapher, a skill he learned from his father, who was employed in the same field. In 1913, Yardley moved to Washington, D.C., where he was hired as a telegrapher and code clerk for the State Department. During his four years with the State Department, Yardley developed a passionate interest in cryptology, reading everything he could find on the subject at the Library of Congress (which was apparently not a great deal). He developed sufficient skill in cryptanalysis to break a number of supposedly secret State Department communiqués. Yardley claims that his superior was "shocked out of his complacency" when he learned that the department's codes and ciphers had been read by a lowly cipher clerk.

When World War I broke out, Yardley obtained a commission as first lieutenant in the U.S. Army Signal Corps. He convinced his commanding officer of his skills in the field of cryptography and cryptanalysis, and was authorized to create a new Cipher Bureau within the Military Intelligence Division. The section's official name was MI8, although it was and is also widely known by its Cipher Bureau designation.

Most of what we know about the Cipher Bureau's work during World War I is preserved in Yardley's own record, *The Achievements of the Cipher Bureau (MI-8) in the First World War,* published by the Historical Unit of the Signal Security Agency, and in *The American Black Chamber.* In both publications, Yardley describes the bureau's work in solving German diplomatic codes and ciphers, discovering and reading messages written in invisible inks, and breaking through some rather arcane German shorthand systems. Yardley reports in *Achievements,* for example, that the bureau solved a total of 578 cryptosystems and decrypted 10,735 messages over an 18-month period.

At the war's conclusion, Yardley suggested to the State Department that a code and cipher agency should be retained within the U.S. government. When he received approval for the idea, he established an office in New York City; although the organization is still known officially as the Cipher Bureau, it was more commonly referred to as the American Black Chamber.

Yardley's New York operation remained in existence for a decade, from July 1919 to June 1929. By far its most important accomplishment during that period was the solution of various diplomatic, military, and naval codes and ciphers used by the Japanese government. The accomplishment was a crucial one, perhaps the highlight of Yardley's life. At the conclusion of World War I, Japan formulated a more expansive and aggressive foreign policy aimed at creating a New Order in East Asia. The United States, Great Britain, Russia, and other nations began to monitor more closely the goals and aspirations of the new threat to their hegemony in the Pacific.

As an example, an important issue at the Washington Disarmament Conference (12 November 1921 to 6 February 1922) was the allocation of ship tonnage among the three great naval powers (the United States, Great Britain, and Japan). The ability of Yardley's Cipher Bureau to read encrypted Japanese dispatches and pass that information on to U.S. and British negotiators was critical to the final agreement reached on this topic, one not very favorable to the Japanese.

The election of Herbert Hoover as president, and Hoover's selection of Henry L. Stimson as secretary of state, marked a turning point in U.S. attitudes and policies toward cryptology. The Cipher Bureau formally closed on 31 October 1929, although the agency had in fact been out of business months earlier.

The end of Yardley's tenure at the Cipher Bureau occurred almost coterminously with the stock market crash of 1929. Yardley soon found himself financially destitute and decided to survive in the only way he knew how, by writing a history of MI8 and the American Black Chamber. The book he published carried the title of the latter agency, *The American Black Chamber.* It was a resounding financial success, but an ethical furor resulted over Yardley's decision to release details of secret U.S. government activities. In fact, while some historians praise the book highly (David Kahn calls it "the most famous book on cryptology" published until then), others express negative feelings ranging from misgivings to outrage at Yardley's actions.

Yardley died from a stroke in Orlando, Florida, on 7 August 1958. His life has since been discussed in considerable detail by those interested in the history of cryptology in the United States in general, and Yardley's role in that history in particular. Judgments on the latter point have varied widely, from David Kahn's view that he was "perhaps the most engaging, articulate, and technicolored personality in the business" to a variety of official government reports that suggest that writing *The American Black Chamber* was largely an expression of egotism that led to the inclusion of "a large number of inaccuracies . . . [making it] a very untrustworthy record of the events it pretended to describe." More important, some historians argue that writing the book at all may have been an act of treason!

See also: American Black Chamber; *The American Black Chamber;* J ciphers; MI8; Military Intelligence Division; U.S. Army Signal Corps.

For further reading: Wayne G. Barker, ed., *The History of Codes and Ciphers in the United States during the Period between the World Wars, Part I: 1919–1929,* Laguna Hills, CA: Aegean Park Press, 1979, passim; Barker, *The History of Codes and Ciphers in the United States during World War I,* Laguna Hills, CA: Aegean Park Press, 1979, passim; David Kahn, *Kahn on Codes: Secrets of the New Cryptology,* New York: Macmillan, 1983, pp. 62–71; Herbert O. Yardley, *The American Black Chamber,* Indianapolis: Bobbs-Merrill, 1931; Yardley's other publications include a series of articles in the *Saturday Evening Post* such as "Ciphers" (9 May 1931), "Codes" (18 April 1931), "Cryptograms and Their Solution" (21 November 1931), and "Secret Inks" (4 April 1931), as well as two other major books, *The Blond Countess* (New York: Longmans, Green, 1934) and *Red Sun of Nippon* (New York: Longmans, Green, 1934).

Z

0075

A German diplomatic code in which the famous Zimmermann telegram was encoded. The code was one in a long series of codes employed by the German Foreign Office during the first two decades of the twentieth century.

See also: Zimmermann telegram.

ZERO-KNOWLEDGE PROTOCOL

A system by which one person is able to convince a second person that he or she possesses some given (secret) information without actually revealing it. The name for the system comes from the fact that the second person can be convinced that the first person actually possesses the secret without ever having firsthand evidence that the secret exists.

The description below is based on a system developed in 1986 by two Israeli mathematicians, Amos Fiat and Adi Shamir. The description outlines the mathematical basis of the system and is illustrated with a very much oversimplified example. In a real situation, the values chosen for p, q, and s would be very large, of the order of 50 digits or more.

A zero-knowledge protocol is established when someone (either the user or a central authenticating agency such as a Key Distribution Center) selects two numbers, n and s. The number n is defined as the product of two large primes, p and q. The number s is a secret number known only to the user and perhaps to the central authenticating agency. In this case, n is a public key and s a private key. In the example that follows, assume that $p = 3$; $q = 5$; and $s = 9$. Then, to begin,

$$n = p \bullet q = 15$$

Either the user or the authenticating agency must then calculate a function $v = s^2 \bmod n$. In this example, the value of v would be

$$v = (9)^2 \bmod 15$$
$$v = 81 \bmod 15$$
$$v = 6 \bmod 15$$

The value of v can then become part of the public key, which can be expressed as $<n,v>$.

The user (we'll call her Alice) can now prove to an authenticating center who she is by the following procedure. Alice selects any random number r and calculates a function x such that $x = r^2 \bmod n$. For this example, assume that Alice selects $r = 4$ to calculate this function. Then,

$$x = (4)^2 \bmod 15$$
$$x = 16 \bmod 15$$
$$x = 1 \bmod 15$$

Alice next calculates two other functions, y_1 and y_2, such that

$$y_1 = r \bullet s \bmod n \text{ and } y_2 = r \bmod n$$

which, in this example, would give

$$y_1 = 4 \bullet 9 \bmod 15 \text{ and } y_2 = 4 \bmod 15$$
$$y_1 = 36 \bmod 15 \text{ and } y_2 = 4 \bmod 15$$
$$y_1 = 6 \bmod 15 \text{ and } y_2 = 4 \bmod 15$$

The values of y_1 and y_2 are then sent to the authentication center, where computers are asked to confirm two relationships:

$$y_1^2 \bmod n = x \bullet v \bmod n \text{ and } y_2^2 \bmod n = x$$

Using the numbers chosen for this example,

$y_1^2 \bmod n = x \bullet v \bmod n \text{ and } y_2^2 \bmod n = x$
$(6)^2 \bmod 15 = 1 \bmod 15 \bullet 6 \bmod 15 \text{ and } (4)^2 \bmod 15 = 1 \bmod 15$
$36 \bmod 15 = 6 \bmod 15 \text{ and } 16 \bmod 15 = 1 \bmod 15$
$6 \bmod 15 \equiv 6 \bmod 15 \text{ and } 1 \bmod 15 \equiv 1 \bmod 15$

The authenticating center confirms, therefore, that Alice is the person she claims to be without ever having received her secret number ($s = 9$) in the process.

See also: authentication.
For further reading: Albrecht Beutelspacher, *Cryptology: An Introduction to the Art and Science of Enciphering, Encrypting, Concealing, Hiding and Safeguarding Described without Any Arcane Skullduggery but Not without Cunning Waggery for the Delectation and In-*struction of the General Public, Washington, DC: Mathematical Association of America, 1994, pp. 80–85; U. Feige, A. Fiat, and A. Shamir, "Zero-Knowledge Proofs of Identity," in *Proceedings of the 19th ACM Symposium on the Theory of Computing*, New York: ACM Press, 1987, pp. 210–217; Charlie Kaufman, Radia Perlman, and Mike Speciner, *Network Security: Private Communication in a Public World*, Englewood Cliffs, NJ: Prentice-Hall, 1995, pp. 158–161; Ivars Peterson, "Computing a Bit of Security: Zero Knowledge Proofs in Data Encryption," *Science News* (16 January 1988): 38; Ian Stewart, "Proof of Purchase on the Internet: Zero-Knowledge Protocols," *Scientific American* (February 1996): 124–125; Peter Wayner, "Zero-Knowledge Proofs: Data Encryption," *Byte* (October 1987): 149–152.

German foreign secretary Arthur Zimmermann found himself embroiled in controversy when British officials intercepted his telegram proposing a German alliance with Mexico intended to distract the United States from entering World War I.

ZIMMERMANN TELEGRAM

A telegram sent from German foreign minister Arthur Zimmermann to Heinrich von Eckardt, German ambassador to Mexico in 1917. The telegram consisted of about a thousand codegroups and contained two essential messages. First, the Germans had decided to begin unrestricted submarine warfare in the Atlantic, hoping to cut off Great Britain from the supplies it needed to continue the war. Second, the telegram proposed an alliance between Germany and Mexico to distract the United States from entering the war. In return for accepting this proposal, Mexico was promised that Texas, New Mexico, and Arizona would be returned to it after the war's completion by a victorious Germany.

The telegram was twice transmitted from Berlin to Mexico City, along two different routes (once by way of Sweden and Argentina to Mexico City and once by way of the German embassy in Washington, D.C.). The telegram was intercepted along both routes by cryptanalysts at Room 40 and looked important enough to require immediate and intense examination. Largely through the efforts of two workers, William Montgomery and Nigel de Grey, the telegram was decoded.

Its contents were enormously important, both to Great Britain and the United States (as well as to Germany, as it turned out). British and French armies were suffering horrible casualties on the Western Front, and Great Britain hoped desperately that the United States would soon enter the war against the Germans. However, President Woodrow Wilson (along with a large portion of the U.S. population) was adamantly opposed to joining the conflict.

The British position was made even more difficult because release of the telegram's contents to the United States was likely to alert the Germans to the fact that Room 40 had broken its codes, causing them to shift to new and more secure codes and ciphers.

In the end, the British decided to make the United States aware of the telegram's contents. On 22 February 1917, Captain William Hall, chief of naval intelligence for the Admiralty, handed over a portion of the decrypted telegram to the American ambassador in London. The clerk who first received the transcription could hardly believe his eyes. The threat of Germany extending its submarine warfare was bad enough, but to imagine that the Germans were promising to give away large chunks of the United States to Mexico was almost incredible.

Two days later, American ambassador Walter H. Page sent the decrypted Zimmermann telegram to Washington, with a partial explanation as to how the British had obtained it (thus preserving Room 40's secret about the German codes). Nothing happened for almost a week in the nation's capital, until Secretary of State Robert Lansing returned from a trip to White Sulphur Springs. The decision was then made to release the telegram to the Associated Press, which broke the story on 1 March. Within hours, Congress began debate on arming merchant ships, and a month later it declared war on Germany. Zimmermann's telegram had initiated a profound reversal in the direction of the war, perhaps saving the Allied cause and committing the United States to a long and bloody conflict.

For further reading: William F. Friedman and Charles J. Mendelsohn, *The Zimmermann Telegram of January 16, 1917 and Its Cryptographic Background*, Washington, DC: GPO, 1938, reprinted by Aegean Park Press, Laguna Hills, CA (n.d.); David Kahn, *The Codebreakers: The Story of Secret Writing*, New York: Macmillan, 1967, ch. 10; Barbara W. Tuchman, *The Zimmermann Telegram*, New York: Viking Press, 1958; Peter Way, *Codes and Ciphers*, n.p.: Crescent Books, 1977, pp. 40–54.

ZIP CODE

A nonsecret code developed by the U.S. Postal Service for use on mail distributed in the United States. The acronym ZIP stands for Zone Improvement Plan, a program developed in the early 1960s to increase the efficiency of mail deliveries. The fundamental principle behind ZIP codes is that numerical addresses are read and sorted by electronic scanners more easily than addresses written in words. Thus, a machine may not be able to read 1064 Fairmount Street, Grand Rapids, Michigan, very easily, but it has no trouble reading 49506-3183. The ZIP code system was developed, therefore, at the point at which the Postal Service was converting much of its mail sorting to mechanized processes.

The ZIP code plan is a geographic system in which each number in the code (moving from left to right) represents a smaller region. In the ZIP code 97520, for example, the first digit, 9, represents a group of western states that includes California, Oregon, Washington, Alaska, and Hawaii. The next digit, 7, represents a specific state within that region: Oregon. The third digit represents a central post office within the state (often a city post office), from which mail is distributed. In the ZIP code 97520, the 5 indicates that mail is distributed from the Medford post office. The final two digits indicate the substation out of which mail is distributed. In the example used here, the digits 20 stand for the Ashland substation of the Medford post office. By comparison, the 30 in the ZIP code 97530 stands for the Jacksonville substation of the Medford post office.

When mail is received at a central post office, it is scanned electronically for the ZIP code and then sorted automatically according to the information contained in that code. The Postal Service provides economic incentives to companies who convert their numerical ZIP codes to a bar-code form because bar codes are easier for electronic scanners to read than handwritten or printed numbers.

In the early 1990s, the Postal Service announced a new ZIP + 4 system that included four additional digits in a ZIP code as, for example, 97520-3618. The last four digits of the ZIP + 4 code indicate the specific carrier route and the portion of that route for which the item is intended. The Postal Service claims that the new system should make it possible to designate the exact street address to which any piece of mail is to be delivered.

Appendix

Data Encryption Standard

The announcement of the Data Encryption Standard was made in Federal Information Processing Standards Publication 46 on 15 January 1977. The publication is reprinted here.

Name of Standard. Data Encryption Standard (DES).

Category of Standard. Operations, Computer Security.

Explanation. The Data Encryption Standard (DES) specifies an algorithm to be implemented in electronic hardware devices and used for the cryptographic protection of computer data. This publication provides a complete description of a mathematical algorithm for encrypting (enciphering) and decrypting (deciphering) binary coded information. Encrypting data converts it to an unintelligible form called cipher. Decrypting cipher converts the data back to their original form. The algorithm described in this standard specifies both enciphering and deciphering operations that are based on a binary number called a key. The key consists of 64 binary digits (0s or 1s), of which 56 bits are used directly by the algorithm and 8 bits are used for error detection.

Binary coded data may be cryptographically protected using the DES algorithm in conjunction with a key. Each member of a group of authorized users of encrypted computer data must have the key that was used to encipher the data in order to use it. This key, held by each member in common, is used to de- cipher the data received in cipher form from other members of the group. The encryption algorithm specified in this standard is commonly known among those using the standard. The unique key chosen for use in a particular application makes the results of encrypting data using the algorithm unique. Selection of a different key causes the cipher that is produced for any given set of inputs to be different. The cryptographic security of the data depends on the security provided for the key used to encipher and decipher the data.

Data can be recovered from cipher only by using exactly the same key used to encipher it. Unauthorized recipients of the cipher who know the algorithm but do not have the correct key cannot derive the original data algorithmically. However, anyone who has both the key and the algorithm can easily decipher the cipher and obtain the original data. A standard algorithm based on a secure key thus provides a basis for exchanging encrypted computer data by issuing the key used to encipher it to those authorized to have the data.

Applications. Data encryption (cryptography) may be utilized in various applications and in various environments. In general, cryptography is used to protect data while it is being communicated between two points or while it is stored in a medium vulnerable to physical theft. Communication security provides protection to data by enciphering it at the transmitting point and deciphering it at the receiving point. File security provides protection to data by enciphering it when it is recorded on a storage medium and deciphering it when it is read back from the storage medium. In the first case, the key must be available at the transmitter and receiver simultaneously during communications. In the second case, the key must be maintained and accessible for the duration of the storage period.

Qualifications. The cryptographic algorithm specified in this standard transforms a 64-bit binary value into a unique 64-bit binary value based on a 56-bit variable. If the complete 64-bit input is used (i.e., none of the input bits should be predeterminated from block to block) and if the 56-bit variable is randomly chosen, no technique other than trying all possible keys using known input and output for the DES will guarantee finding the chosen key. As there are over 70,000,000,000,000,000 (70 quadrillion) possible keys of 56 bits, the feasibility of deriving a particular key in this way is extremely unlikely in typical threat environments. Moreover, if the key is changed frequently, the risk of this event is greatly diminished. However, users should be aware that it is theoretically possible to derive the key in fewer trials (with a correspondingly lower probability of success depending on the number of keys tried), and are cautioned to change the key as often as practical. Users must change the key and provide it a high level of protection in order to minimize the potential risks of its unauthorized computation or acquisition.

When correctly implemented and properly used, this standard will provide a high level of cryptographic protection to computer data.

Bibliography

Until the 1970s, the number of books of wide appeal dealing with cryptology was very small. The subject is of rather arcane interest, and most works dealt with the application of cryptology to military topics. However, such books were often of interest to the layperson curious about codes and ciphers. Imagination, inquisitiveness, and a willingness to work hard were all that was really needed to master the general concepts of pre-1980 cryptology.

The invention of the computer and public-key cryptography has dramatically changed the situation. Today, cryptology is a distinct branch of mathematics with critical applications not only in military subjects but also in business, diplomacy, and other fields. Generally, the reader cannot pick up a book on cryptology today and read through it with anything but the most general understanding.

One purpose of this book is to provide enough information for readers to recognize concepts in cryptology and then to pursue those topics in as much detail as the reader's background in mathematics permits.

The bibliography below includes primarily books and articles of general interest, those dealing with the subjects of cryptography and cryptanalysis or with some broad application of the two. As a general rule, books written after 1980 deal primarily with the topic of public-key cryptography in all its many manifestations and applications. More specific references to individual topics are placed at the ends of entries concerning those topics.

Books

The Administration's Clipper Chip Key Escrow Encryption Program. Hearing before the Subcommittee on Technology and the Law of the Senate Committee on the Judiciary, 103rd Congress, Second Session, 3 May 1994. SOSC: Govt Doc Y 4.J 89/2: S.HRG. 103-1067.

Andreassen, Karl. *Computer Cryptology: Beyond Decoder Rings.* Englewood Cliffs, NJ: Prentice-Hall, 1988.

> The first few chapters of this book provide a general introduction to the topic of cryptology, written in a clear, charming style easily understood by the amateur. The main body of the book is devoted to a discussion of the use of the personal computer in the study of a number of topics in cryptography and cryptanalysis.

Applied Cryptology, Cryptographic Protocols and Computer Security Models. Providence, RI: American Mathematical Society, 1983.

> A general introduction to public-key cryptography and its applications.

Asimov, Isaac. *Asimov's Biographical Encyclopedia of Science and Technology,* 2nd rev. ed. Garden City, NY: Doubleday, 1982.

> Although Asimov writes very little about cryptology in particular, his biographical sketches of many important figures in the field are valuable for background information.

Bacard, André. *The Computer Privacy Handbook: A Practical Guide to E-mail Encryption, Data Protection and PGP Privacy Software.* Berkeley, CA: Peachpit Press, 1995.

An excellent summary of many aspects of data protection and electronic communication. The four main sections deal with the role of computers in our daily lives and the problems of privacy they create; the U.S. government's Clipper chip proposal; Pretty Good Privacy (PGP) as a means of providing security for e-mail correspondence; and a PGP user's manual.

Barker, Wayne G., ed. *The History of Codes and Ciphers in the United States prior to World War I.* Laguna Hills, CA: Aegean Park Press, 1978.

————. *The History of Codes and Ciphers in the United States during World War I.* Laguna Hills, CA: Aegean Park Press, 1979.

————. *The History of Codes and Ciphers in the United States during the Period between the World Wars, Part I: 1919–1929.* Laguna Hills, CA: Aegean Park Press, 1979.

————. *The History of Codes and Ciphers in the United States during the Period between the World Wars, Part II: 1930–1939.* Laguna Hills, CA: Aegean Park Press, 1978.

The four books listed here are edited versions of a history of codes and ciphers in the United States between 1776 and 1939 prepared by the historical section of the Army Security Agency in 1946. The books provide useful information on the growth of the intelligence and security agencies of the U.S. government, including their cryptographic and cryptanalytic activities.

Beckett, Brian. *Introduction to Cryptology.* Oxford: Blackwell Scientific Publications, 1988.

Although a number of books call themselves "introductions" to the subject of cryptology, most start from a rather advanced basis. This text is probably the most truly introductory of all such books. Using modern terminology it discusses in great detail the primary cryptologic algorithms that have been developed throughout history and then describes some of the modern issues created by extended computer and electronic communication, as well as techniques used to solve such issues.

Beker, Henry, and Fred Piper. *Cipher Systems: The Protection of Communications.* New York: John Wiley & Sons, 1982.

A text that utilizes rigorous mathematical explanations for fundamental cryptologic concepts. The introductory chapters provide interesting and well-written introductions to the historical background of cryptology as well as to the most important basic ideas of the science and art.

Beth, Thomas, M. Frisch, and G. J. Simmons, eds. *Public-Key Cryptography: State of the Art and Future Directions.* Berlin: Springer-Verlag, 1992.

A heavily mathematical approach dealing with topics such as one-way functions, knapsacks, trapdoors, hash functions, and factorization.

Beutelspacher, Albrecht. *Cryptology: An Introduction to the Art and Science of Enciphering, Encrypting, Concealing, Hiding and Safeguarding Described without Any Arcane Skullduggery but Not without Cunning Waggery for the Delectation and Instruction of the General Public.* Washington, DC: Mathematical Association of America, 1994.

The title provides a hint of the lighthearted manner in which the book is written. It is a superb introduction to basic issues in modern cryptology such as authentication, smart cards, and public-key cryptography. The mathematics is challenging, but not as intimidating as in most introductory texts on cryptology.

Brassard, Gilles. *Modern Cryptology: A Tutorial.* New York: Springer-Verlag, 1988.

Adapted from a series of lectures given at the twenty-ninth *IEEE Computer Conference* in San Francisco, this book provides "an overview of recent cryptographic achievements and techniques, and their present and potential applications."

Davies, D. W., and W. L. Price. *Security for Computer Networks: An Introduction to Data Security in Teleprocessing and Electronic Funds Transfer.* Chichester: John Wiley & Sons, 1984.

A clearly written technical presentation of the fundamental principles of cryptology with emphasis on techniques used in providing security for modern communications.

Farago, Ladislas. *The Broken Seal: "Operation Magic" and the Secret Road to Pearl Harbor.* New York: Bantam Books, 1968.

A popular history of American cryptology in the years before World War II, beginning with a description of Herbert O. Yardley's *The American Black Chamber.*

Friedman, William F. *Elements of Cryptanalysis.* Laguna Hills, CA: Aegean Park Press, 1976.

This book is a reprint of Friedman's original 1920 version, in which the term *cryptology* was originally coined. It provides an exhaustive discussion of some of the most fundamental concepts of cryptanalysis.

———. *Elementary Military Cryptography.* Laguna Hills, CA: Aegean Park Press, 1976.

———. *Advanced Military Cryptography.* Laguna Hills, CA: Aegean Park Press, 1976.

These two books were originally written in 1935 by Friedman for use with army extension courses on cryptology, listed as Special Text Numbers 165 and 166, respectively. They are still very useful as easily understood introductions to the fundamental concepts of cryptography.

Gaines, Helen Fouché. *Cryptanalysis: A Study of Ciphers and Their Solution.* New York: Dover Publications, 1956.

This book was originally published in 1939 as *Elementary Cryptanalysis,* a standard elementary and intermediate text for those interested in learning how to solve crytograms.

Galland, Joseph S. *Bibliography of the Literature of Cryptology.* Laguna Hills, CA: Aegean Park Press, n.d.

This book, a reprint of an original edition published by Northwestern University in 1945, included "the most important works that have been written, not only on the subject of crytptology, but also on its manifestations in related fields." An invaluable historical resource.

Hodges, Andrew. *Alan Turing: The Enigma.* New York: Simon & Schuster, 1983.

Although primarily a biography of Turing, this volume provides a great deal of valuable information about the role and use of cryptology during World War II. The reference to "the Enigma" in the title refers both to Turing himself and to the German cipher machine whose solution was so much the result of Turing's work.

Kahn, David. *The Codebreakers: The Story of Secret Writing.* New York: Macmillan, 1967.

Kahn is arguably the greatest popular writer on cryptology of the modern day, and this book has become the standard work on the history of cryptology. It is a stunning tour de force that provides a complete background on almost every aspect of cryptology up to the time it was published. The book was republished in a revised editon in 1997. The revision includes a new chapter summarizing important changes in cryptology since the first edition was published. Anyone interested in cryptology must begin with a study of this work.

———. *Kahn on Codes: Secrets of the New Cryptology.* New York: Macmillan, 1983.

A selection of about two dozen articles, most of them previously published in magazines and journals, on a wide variety of topics by the master chronicler of cryptology.

Kaufman, Charlie, Radia Perlman, and Mike Speciner. *Network Security: Private Communication in a Public World.* Englewood Cliffs, NJ: Prentice-Hall, 1995.

Arguably the most interestingly written and readable of all current books on the general issue of protecting data and electronic communication in today's world. The book is divided into four general sections: Cryptography (general information, secret-key cryptography, hashes and message digests, public-key algorithms, and number theory), Authentication (authentication systems, authentication of people, security handshake pitfalls, and Kerberos V4 and V5), Electronic Mail (electronic mail security, Privacy Enhanced Mail, Pretty Good Privacy, and X.400), and "Leftovers." This book can be recommended as "fun" read-

ing even if you know or care little about cryptology.

Konheim, Alan G. *Cryptography: A Primer.* New York: John Wiley & Sons, 1981.

An advanced, mathematical treatment of cryptography. Despite its title, it is not easy going for the reader without a substantial background in mathematics.

Laffin, John. *Codes and Ciphers: Secret Writing through the Ages.* London: Abelard-Schuman, 1964.

A simple but comprehensive introduction to historically important codes and ciphers. The book would be a useful first reader for someone who has little or no background in cryptology.

Meyer, Carl H., and Stephen M. Matyas. *Cryptography: A New Dimension in Computer Data Security.* New York: John Wiley & Sons, 1982.

This book is a rather remarkable accomplishment in that it presents the fundamental principles of modern cryptology in a language that is highly readable even for those unfamiliar with advanced mathematics, yet its discussion of these concepts is rigorously precise from a mathematical standpoint. For anyone interested in taking on modern cryptology from a mathematical standpoint, one could hardly do better than start with this work.

Millikin, Donald D. *Elementary Cryptography and Cryptanalysis.* Laguna Hills, CA: Aegean Park Press, n.d.

This volume is a reproduction of a text originally written for students in an introductory course in cryptology taught at New York University in 1943. It is remarkably easy to read for those with a minimal background in the subject and is highly recommended for those beginning a study of the subject.

Petersen, Gordon A. J., and Marshal McClintock. *A Guide to Codes and Signals: International Flag Code, Secret Ciphers, Weather Signals, Morse Code, Sign Language, Etc. with Flags of All Nations.* Racine, WI: Whitman Publishing, 1942.

An interesting compendium of a wide variety of symbolic means of communication.

Pomerance, Carl, ed. *Cryptology and Computational Number Theory.* Providence, RI: American Mathematical Society, 1990.

A discussion of number theory issues in cryptology, such as primarity, factorization, discrete logarithms, and knapsack problems.

Pratt, Fletcher. *Secret and Urgent: The Story of Codes and Ciphers.* Garden City, NY: Blue Ribbon Books, 1942.

This book is an early attempt to provide a readable history of cryptology, and it holds some interest as a historic piece. But Kahn's *Codebreakers* is so far superior that Pratt's book should be viewed as no more than a historical relic.

Relyea, Harold C. *Evolution and Organization of Intelligence Activities in the United States.* Laguna Hills, CA: Aegean Park Press, n.d.

Originally published in 1976 by the U.S. Senate Select Committee To Study Governmental Operations with Respect to Intelligence Activities under the mandate of Senate Resolution 21 with the title "The Evolution and Organization of the Federal Intelligence Function: A Brief Overview (1776–1975)," this work has now been republished by Aegean Park Press. The book covers the complete gamut of intelligence activities and shows how cryptologic activities have been woven into the fabric of the intelligence community.

Sears, Peter. *Secret Writing.* New York: Teachers & Writers Collaborative, 1986.

The author, a poet and teacher of writing, uses cryptology in an interesting way to teach the basic principles of grammar and good writing. The text is intriguing not only because of the excellent quality of the writing but also because of its unusual approach to cryptology.

Seberry, Jennifer, and Joseph Pieprzyk. *Cryptography: An Introduction to Computer Security.* New York: Prentice-Hall, 1989.

A short introduction to classical cryptology with primary emphasis on issues of public-key cryptography.

Shannon, Claude E., and Warren Weaver. *The Mathematical Theory of Communication.* Urbana: University of Illinois Press, 1962.

To a very large extent, modern cryptology has evolved out of ideas in information theory first proposed by Shannon and Weaver in the two papers reprinted in this book. Although they are difficult to read, they provide a very useful hint as to the way that words, concepts, and ideas can be represented by mathematics and how mathematical operations can then be used to manipulate those words, concepts, and ideas.

Simmons, Gustavus J. *Secure Communications and Asymmetric Cryptosystems.* Boulder, CO: Westview Press, 1982.

Reprints of most of the fundamental papers on public-key cryptography.

Sinkov, Abraham. *Elementary Cryptanalysis: A Mathematical Approach.* New York: Random House, 1968.

An excellent discussion of crypt-analysis from a mathematical stand-point, but presented at a level that is comparatively easy to understand. This book is a good source on the use of modular arithmetic in the solution of cryptograms.

Smith, Laurence Dwight. *Cryptography: The Science of Secret Writing*. New York: W. W. Norton, 1943.

A very basic introduction to cryptology that covers such fundamental topics as substitution and transposition ciphers, cryptanalysis, and a brief history of cryptology.

Stallings, William. *Network and Internetwork Security: Principles and Practices*. Englewood Cliffs, NJ: Prentice-Hall, 1995.

A sound text dealing with the fundamental principles and issues of network security.

Thompson, J. W., and S. K. Padover. *Secret Diplomacy: A Record of Espionage and Double-Dealing: 1500–1815*. London: Jarrolds Publishers, 1937.

The interest in this book lies not so much in any sophisticated discussion of cryptology but in fascinating stories of how European rulers of this period used cryptography in their dealings with one another.

U.S. Congress, Office of Technology Assessment. *Information Security and Privacy in Network Environments*, OTA-TCT-606. Washington, DC: GPO, September 1994.

A report prepared by the OTA in response to a request from the Senate Committee on Governmental Affairs and the Senate Committee on Telecommunications and Finance concerning the security of unclassified information stored by federal agencies and transmitted between those agencies, and between agencies and private entities. This report and the update listed below provide some of the most comprehensive, understandable, and useful information about the role of cryptography in computer and information security available today.

U.S. Congress, Office of Technology Assessment. *Issue Update on Information Security and Privacy in Network Environments*, OTA-BP-ITC-147. Washington, DC: GPO, June 1995.

This report is an update of the preceding report. It reviews major features of the earlier report and includes new information available since release of that report.

Way, Peter. *Codes and Ciphers*. n.p.: Crescent Books, 1977.

Way has written an interesting story about the development of codes and ciphers through the centuries with special emphasis on especially interesting events, such as the Zimmermann telegram, the Nihilist plot in Russia, and the PURPLE and ULTRA organizations of the two world wars. The book presents relatively little technical detail, but provides thorough and easily understood examples of some famous codes and ciphers.

Weber, Ralph E. *Masked Dispatches: Cryptograms and Cryptology in American History, 1775–1900*. Fort George G. Meade, MD: National Security Agency, 1993.

An interesting survey of the first 125 years of cryptology in the United States. The book consists of individual articles covering a broad variety of topics, from the first codes used by the Continental Congress to the State Department's BLUE Code of 1899.

———. *United States Diplomatic Codes and Ciphers, 1775–1938*. Chicago: Precedent Publishing, 1979.

Although this book includes relatively little discussion and/or analysis of the history of codes in the United States, it provides a fascinating look at the evolution of codes and ciphers used in the United States for its diplomatic transmissions of the period indicated.

Welsh, Dominic. *Codes and Cryptography.* Oxford: Clarendon Press, 1988.

One of the most mathematically rigorous of the books on cryptology available. This reference is recommended only to readers with an advanced understanding of mathematics.

Wrixon, Fred B. *Codes and Ciphers.* New York: Prentice-Hall, 1992.

An excellent general introduction to the subject of cryptology, written in encyclopedic style, with special emphasis on the biographical, historical, and human-interest aspects of the subject. One of the handful of "must-have" books for the beginning student of cryptology and an excellent resource for any serious scholar of the subject.

Yardley, Herbert O. *The American Black Chamber.* Indianapolis: Bobbs-Merrill, 1931.

One of the most famous books on cryptology ever written, this book is a personal recollection of Yardley's life and contribution to American cryptology at the end of World War I.

Articles

Dror, Asael, "Secret Codes: Encryption," *Byte* (June 1989): 267–270.

A general introduction to modern issues in the field of cryptography for computers and network systems.

Luciano, Dennis, "Cryptology: From Caesar Ciphers to Public-Key Cryptosystems," *College Mathematics Journal* (January 1987): 2–17.

A general review article on the topic of cryptology with an interesting historical background.

Electronic Sources

Information about cryptologic issues can now be found at a number of locations on the Internet. A fair amount of this information deals with specific issues surrounding government attempts to limit public access to certain types of information. The sites below are only a few of those that can be explored.

Bibliography: ftp://scss3.cl.msu.edu/pub/crypt/docs/crypto.bib

CIPHER (Newsletter of the IEEE Computer Society's Technical Committee on Security and Privacy): http://www.itd.nrl.navy.mil/ITD/5540/ieee/cipher/cipher-archive.html

Computer Professionals for Social Responsibility: http://cpsr.org/dox/home.html

Computer Security Resource Clearinghouse: http://csrc.ncsl.nist.gov/

Cryptographic Policy: http://www.epic.org/crypto/

Cryptography: http://econ-www.newcastle.edu.au/~jon/cryptology

Cryptography FAQ: http://www.cis.ohio-state.edu/hypertext/faq/usenet/cryptography-faq/top.html

International Cryptography Pages: http://www.cs.hut.fi/crypto/

RSA's Frequently Asked Questions: http://www.rsa.com/rsalabs/faq/faq-gnrl.html

Tools for Privacy: Cryptography: ftp://ftp.crl.com/users/ro/smart/TFP/briefhistory.html

Illustration Credits

Index